D1473426

DATE			

BAKER & TAYLOR

THE CAT FANCIERS' ASSOCIATION
CAT
ENCYCLOPEDIA

THE CAT FANCIERS' ASSOCIATION
CAT
ENCYCLOPEDIA

Simon & Schuster
New York • London • Toronto • Sydney • Tokyo • Singapore

Simon & Schuster
Rockefeller Center
1230 Avenue of the Americas
New York, New York 10020

Designed by Studio Cancelli, Milan
Edited for the Cat Fanciers' Association by Will Thompson
Photo Research: Ann Deborah Levy

Printed in Spain by Artes Graficas Toledo, S.A.
D.L.TO: 68 - 1995

1 3 5 7 9 10 8 6 4 2

Library of Congress Cataloging-in-Publication Data Available on Request

ISBN: 0-684-80186-8

CONTENTS

THE BREEDS — 13

Abyssinian	14
American Curl	18
American Shorthair	20
American Wirehair	24
Balinese	26
Bengal	30
Birman	32
Bombay	35
British Shorthair	37
Burmese	44
Burmilla	48
Chartreux	50
Ceylon	52
Colorpoint Shorthair	54
Cymric (The Longhaired Manx)	56
Egyptian Mau	58
European Shorthair	61
Exotic	68
Havana Brown	72
Japanese Bobtail	74
Javanese	76
Korat	78
Maine Coon	80
Manx	83
Norwegian Forest Cat	87
Ocicat	90
Oriental Shorthair	92
Persian	97
Ragdoll	113
Rex (Cornish Rex)	114
Rex (Devon Rex)	118
Rex (German Rex)	121
Russian Blue	122
Scottish Fold	126
Siamese	128
Singapura	137
Snowshoe	139
Somali	140
Sphynx	142
Tiffany	144
Tonkinese	146
Turkish Angora	148
Turkish Van	151

CAT FANCIERS' ASSOCIATION SHOW STANDARDS — 155

LIVING WITH A CAT — 195

ANATOMY	196
CHOOSING A CAT	199
FEEDING	202
AT HOME AND TRAVELING	204
GROOMING	206
REPRODUCTION	208
CAT HEALTH	209
HANDLING CATS AND ADMINISTERING MEDICINES	211
FIRST AID	213
GLOSSARY	219
CREDITS	220

PREFACE

Cats, from magnificent fluffy Persians to the plainest street cat, have accompanied man for more than five millennia, sharing our lives in ways that are different from other domesticated animals. They have a mystique that is unparalleled. They are eminently adaptable — able to live well as pampered pets in tiny big-city apartments, or to rule a tiny kingdom in the green fields of a farm as a working cat.

Their history encompasses great shifts in opinion, from the height of their popularity in Egypt, when they were revered as deities, to the depths of their persecution during the middle ages, when association with a cat was enough to brand someone as a witch. Even now, when the cat is again enjoying great popularity as a pet, outstripping dogs in numbers owned, there are vast differences in how a cat is regarded. To the person not yet converted to the love of cats, they are believed to be fickle, egotistical, solitary, aloof and incapable of affection. Those of us who understand and love cats know that on the contrary, cats are loving, wonderful companions, willing to return love and affection to the people with whom they live. They can maintain their wonderful independent spirit while sharing the minutiae of our everyday lives.

Even the most dedicated cat lover is captivated by the wildness of our gentle pets. Who among us has not been enchanted by the actions of a tiny, playful kitten — only to realize that these cute games are practice for adult hunting behavior. Cats are almost perfect predators — sleekly muscled, with incredible agility and speed, able to catch prey quickly. True, most of our pampered pets never hunt anything more vital than a catnip mouse, but to observe our feline friend in action is to watch an efficient predator. All the more wonder, then, that these little wild animals have chosen to be domesticated house cats. As one observes a cat in action, one is struck by the elegance of its bearing and the perfection of its proportions.

In breeding our pedigreed cats, we have selected for specific traits present in the gene pool of cats which appeal to us. Even though we currently have breeds as diverse as the Cornish Rex, with its short wavy coat, extremely fine bone and slender body, and the Persian, with thick fur, a compact, short dense body, and short thick legs, each breed has its own integrity of design. The preface to the book of Show Standards of the Cat Fanciers' Association ends with two paragraphs which perfectly epitomize the concept of the pedigreed cat:

The ideal cat is a perfectly proportioned animal, of pleasing appearance and superb refinement, a sophisticated version of a domesticated feline. The whole presentation is pleasant to the eye, well groomed, friendly, and manageable, ready for the competition of that day of showing when the judge goes through the mechanical, the ethical, the artistic, and the comparable selections of Bests and Best in Show.

If the various parts of a cat are harmoniously balanced and complement each other well, the whole will be greater than the sum of its parts. The total will be a beautiful cat.

The cats in this book are examples of the best that the Cat Fanciers' Association and other foreign registries have to offer — beautiful cats which conform to their standards, but which still afford the mystery and fascination which the cat has always held for man.

D. J. WILLIAMS
Immediate Past President
The Cat Fanciers' Association

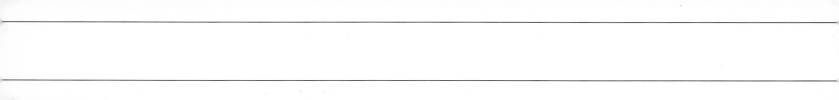

THE BREEDS

ABYSSINIAN

As its name indicates, the Abyssinian is believed by many to have originated in Abyssinia, better known today as Ethiopia. This ancient short-haired breed contends with the Egyptian Mau for the honor of being the most direct descendent of ancient Egyptian cats. In fact, some of its physical characteristics, such as its bone structure and the color of its coat, closely resemble those of the mummified remains of Egyptian cats and the cats that appear in wall paintings in tombs. The Abyssinian was introduced to Europe in 1860 by the wife of an English officer stationed in Ethiopia who had been given one as a gift, and its beauty and regal elegance immediately attracted the attention of breeders. Even so, the standards for the breed were not set until 1929. Since then, the Abyssinian has come near extinction in Europe on three occasions: during the two world wars, as a result of the lack of proper diet, and between 1960 and 1970, as the result of an epidemic of the feline leukemia virus. In recent years the breed has experienced a magnificent revival, and the Abyssinian is today among the most popular breeds.

1

2

1. Baton Rouge's Yankee... 5 month old male kitten. Although quite young, this kitten already shows typical Aby characteristics... a muscular body, the slightly rounded planes of the wedge shaped head, and the alert, large, moderately pointed ears.

2. The overall impression of the Abyssinian is a colorful cat with a distinctly tipped coat, medium in size and regal in appearance. Note the almond shaped eyes and alert, large and moderately pointed ears.

The Abyssinian is lively, curious, and tireless; it needs what might be called "an enriched environment" with plenty of room and sources of stimulation on which to focus its attention and interest. This is not, however, an overly independent or solitary cat; on the contrary, it needs constant attention from an ever-present and indulgent owner. The owner should have time to share games and adventures, give long periods of affectionate attention, be careful about daily care, and make his or her presence constantly known. Deprived of this close attention, the Abyssinian will lose its playful spirit and may become unsociable. Establishing a good relationship with an Abyssinian is not always easy. Much patience, affection, and good will are required to overcome initial distrust. However, once trust has been gained, Abyssinians quickly become closely attached to their owner and are often exclusive. The owner will then have an affectionate pet, full of life and spirit, intelligent, sometimes surprisingly so, and decidedly charming, capable of learning tricks, even amenable to being taken on walks with a leash if trained when young. The Abyssinian is never a background character: its presence can be demanding but is always highly personal.

3. The solid body, well-developed, strong and muscular, is always poised and ready to leap into action. The Aby's constant attention to surroundings, indicated by the large, alert ears and concentration in the eyes, denotes this breed's vivacity, courage, and independence. Selective breeding has retained the original qualities of robustness and strength, while improving both the harmonious conformation of the cat and the clarity (free from vestigial tabby markings) of the coat.

3

	Body	Head	Ears	Eyes	Nose	Chin	Legs and Feet	Tail	Coat	Varieties
C.F.A.	Medium long, lithe, graceful and muscular.	Modified, slightly rounded wedge.	Alert, large, and moderately pointed; broad and cupped at the base.	Almond-shaped, large, brilliant and expressive. The eye color may be gold or green.	Gentle contour with a slight rise from bridge of nose to the forehead.	Firm and well shaped.	Small, oval and compact giving the impression of standing on tiptoe.	Thick at the base; fairly long and tapering.	Soft, silky, fine in texture, dense and resilient with 2-3 bands of darker ticking.	Ruddy, red, blue, and fawn.

4

At first glance, the coat of the Abyssinian appears to be uniformly ticked. This type of coat is referred to technically as agouti, named for a rodent (the agouti) that has thick fur composed of brown hairs that are not, however, of uniform color... each single hair has a light colored section at the root and then has two or three darker-colored bands. Agouti fur has the merit of providing good camouflage and is common among many wild animals, chief among them the rabbit; in fact, at one time, the Abyssinian was called the rabbit or hare cat. Although agouti coats occur in other breeds and varieties of cats, only in the Abyssinian is it so colorful and striking.

The remarkable aspect of this is that the Abyssinian, with its splendidly uniform agouti fur, is genetically a tabby cat, but the stripes of the pattern are not visible. Until a few years ago faint traces of the tabby pattern could be seen on the head, chest, legs, and tip of the tail; the patient work of breeders has confined these markings to the head and tip of the tail. The Abyssinian should have a coat as nearly uniform as possible; at most, darker shading on the top of the head between the ears and at the tip of the tail is permitted.

4. Fellow's Hot Ferrarri, 4½ month old kitten. Although still a kitten, the eyes are alert, interested, investigative, and already displaying typical adult traits. Parental care is well-developed in Abyssinians; the kittens receive attention not only from the dam but also from the sire. Given the characteristic liveliness of Aby kittens, it is not surprising that they are highly playful and full of enough energy to exhaust even the most affectionate parent. While the mother rests, the sire minds the enthusiastic kittens and vice versa. In certain cases, particularly when the litter is large and one parent may begin to tire, he or she calls to the other, always nearby, who comes to give support.

5. This alert blue Aby shows the characteristic "old rose" color of the nose leather. The clarity of the chest color lacks and signs of vestigial tabby markings.

5

The stripes, once visible on the neck and front legs of the Abyssinian, are generally completely absent today; these were a part of the ticked tabby pattern still seen in some other breeds. Two other basic patterns, found in breeds other than the Abyssinian, exist: the mackerel tabby, or tiger, with thin, orderly stripes; and the classic or blotched tabby, with broad stripes that form a spiral pattern on the sides. Each of these three patterns is determined by a variant, or allele, of the same gene, the same unit of genetic transmission. Therefore, a "package" of genetic material exists that contains all the instructions necessary for the creation of a tabby coat; another package, similar but not identical to the first, is responsible for the classic tabby; and a third, just a little different from the first two, designated T(a), makes the 'converted' tabby of today's Abyssinian almost imperceptible. Each allele "decides" the quantity of dark pigmentation, or melanin, that will be present in the coat . . . the maximum amount in tabbies and the minimum in the Abyssinian.

If a female Abyssinian mates with a male having a well-defined tabby pattern, she will produce tabby kittens which retain merely a few, but obvious, evanescent stripes. The maternal T(a) allele thus seems to determine the characteristic of the coat more than the paternal allele but without completely canceling the influence. Geneticists point out that the first allele exercises incomplete domination over the second.

6

6. Grand Champion Shomra's Cassiopeia.

7. Baton Rouge's Pipi, international Champion 14 month old female. In Abyssinians, warm colors, such as ruddy and red, are particularly prized as they often appear to emphasize the breed's bright liveliness.

Although smaller than the male, the female is no less muscular. While the physical structure of the male suggests sturdiness and solidity, that of the female indicates agility and strength. The chest and thorax are less broad, the neck is often longer, and the characteristic rounded planes of the wedge-shaped head may be a bit sharper since the adult male usually develops jowls (stud jowls). All in all, the body of the female is generally more refined than that of the male. Both female and male move with an elegant, harmonious fluidity without recklessness but always with great composure.

7

The American Curl is a new breed, a natural mutation which was discovered in California in 1981. Joe and Grace Ruga were a happy couple who neither had nor wanted any pets. However, when they discovered a lost kitten with strange, curling ears in their garden, they couldn't resist giving it a home. They named this semi-longhaired black foundling Shulamith. In a short time, there were five cats in the Ruga household, Shulamith and her four kittens. Two of these, a male and a female, had their mother's curling ears, but the female had short hair rather than semi-long hair. News of the event attracted the attention of a cat fancier, who, in 1983, recognizing the uniqueness of the cats' curling ears and the ease with which this interesting characteristic was transmitted from generation to generation, undertook a serious program of selective breeding that eventually led to the creation and formal recognition of this new, American breed.

1, 2. The unique shape of the ears, with their curved tips, and the walnut-shaped eyes (oval on top and round on bottom) emphasize and accentuate the unique look of the cat. The overall effect is pleasing, if a little odd when seen for the first time. The physical structure is moderately muscular; the intermediate size, slender rather than massive body is a semi-foreign, rectangular shape. The tail is flexible, wide at the base, and tapering. The coat is accepted in both longhaired and shorthaired varieties.

This breed and the Scottish Fold breed share the honor of having truly special ears; the ears of the Scottish Fold, however, are relatively small and fold forward and downward forming a cap for the rounded skull. Those of the American Curl curve upward and backward in a smooth arc when viewed from the front. The shape of the ears in the two breeds is very different and is caused by two different mutant alleles. In both cases, however, the mutant allele is dominant over the corresponding genetic form found in cats with normal ears; the effects of the mutant allele cancel out those of the allele for normal ears. For this reason, the characteristic ears can be transmitted by pairing not only two American Curls but also an American Curl with a normal or straight eared cat. To maintain the unique look of the American Curl and ensure optimum health, the program of selection that is leading to the definition of the distinctive traits of the breed involves controlled pairings of American Curls with non-pedigreed long and short hair domestic cats. Fortunately, and unlike the case with some other breeds, the allele responsible for the distinctive ears of the American Curl does not cause other anomalies or physical defects; the cats are healthy and strong, as are the common domestic cats from which they are derived. The Curls are lively and mix moments of great activity with periods of rest or, perhaps, meditation. They are happy and give affectionate head bumps to human companions; they eagerly participate in all aspects of their owner's daily life.

3. Procurl Harem Basil Redbowe, American Curl Longhair. The longer coat does not detract from the characteristic ear curl which typifies this breed.

	Body	Head	Ears	Eyes	Nose	Chin	Legs and Feet	Tail	Coat	Varieties
C.F.A.	Well-balanced and moderately muscled rather than massive; the length is one and one-half times the height. Legs are medium-boned.	A modified wedge without flat planes, moderately longer than wide, smooth transitions.	Large, wide at the base and open, curving back in a smooth arc of at least 90 degrees but not more than 180 degrees. Tips are rounded and flexible. Ear furnishings are desirable.	Walnut-shaped and moderately large.	Moderate in length and straight with a slight rise from the bottom of the eyes to the forehead with a gentle curve to the top of the head.	Firm, in line with nose and upper lip	Medium and rounded feet.	Flexible, wide at base, tapering and equal to body length.	Long hair: Semi-long, fine, silky and lying flat with full and plumed tail. Short hair: soft, silky, lying flat, resilient without plushiness; tail coat is same length as body coat.	All colors and patterns, including all pointed colors and combined with white.

AMERICAN SHORTHAIR

In truth, the roots of the American Shorthair are traced back to Europe. Most believe that the breed's progenitors, in the company of their owners, departed Europe for a new life in the New World some four centuries ago. Having survived the long and difficult Atlantic crossing, they soon adapted to their new homes, proliferated, and began leading their usual life divided between home and street, always hunting small rodents and adventures. Early in this century, someone finally took a good look at this omnipresent American cat and realized that, in truth, it was truly a beautiful cat, very robust, well-proportioned, and had a wonderful disposition. They concluded that it might be worthwhile to establish this cat's best characteristics and elevate it to the distinction of being a national American breed. The first example given the status of belonging to a recognized American breed was born in 1904 from a mating between American and British Shorthairs. Originally identified as the Domestic Shorthair, this working cat of the United States is now proudly recognized as the American Shorthair.

1. The wide black stripes of the Silver Tabby variety stand out sharply against a clear silver background. This strongly built, well-balanced, symmetrical cat has a conformation indicating power, endurance and agility.

2. Gahlee the Golden One, Brown Tabby variety. The squareness of the muzzle marks the head of this true breed of working cat.

3

4

The origins of the American Shorthair, as with the British and European Shorthair breeds, trace back to a common domestic cat. This was a cat that lacked blue blood, but had desirable qualities of strength, a pleasing appearance, intelligence, and sociability. This was a cat for both the home and the farm fields of a gentler time that partially escaped natural selection thanks to its domesticity but still was free to mate as it wished. From these appealing but obscure progenitors, breeders have labored to establish the cat's best characteristics including the strongly built and well balanced body, the good bone structure and well-developed muscles; the thick, dense coat, which becomes thicker in winter to provide protection against even the most intense cold; natural agility, strength, and energy; and an amiable disposition. It is difficult to find a single negative aspect in this breed.

Living with an American Shorthair is not difficult, even for those lacking free time to dedicate as much attention to their companion cat as they might like. The American Shorthair naturally enjoys excellent health, is strong, has no fear of cold, needs no special diet, is independent and well-balanced. It is a home-loving cat and becomes attached to all family members including children. It responds well when called by its owner but will not be overly disturbed if days go by in which it is nearly forgotten. When it wants to play, it seeks out children and romps with them or goes off on its own, amusing itself with a simple paper bag or other items found in its environment.

3. American Shorthair cats with pure white coats may have blue eyes, gold eyes or may be odd-eyed, that is one eye blue and the other gold.

4. Gahlee the Golden One. The distinct tabby markings have been perfected by American Shorthair breeders.

	Body	Head	Ears	Eyes	Nose	Chin	Legs and Feet	Tail	Coat	Varieties
C.F.A.	Solidly built, powerful and muscular with well-developed shoulders, chest, and hindquarters.	Large, with full cheek face. Jaws are strong. Neck is muscular and strong.	Medium size; slightly rounded at the tips.	Large and wide with half-almond-shaped upper lid and a fully rounded curve to the lower lid. Bright, clear, and alert.	Medium length, same width for entire length.	Solid and well-developed with a squared muzzle.	Full, firm and rounded with heavy pads.	Medium length, heavy at base, tapering to an apparently blunt end.	Short, thick, even, and hard in texture.	Solid colors; Shaded; Smoke; Tabby; Parti-Color; and BiColor.

5

6

5. Silver Tabby. In the classic tabby, three long dark stripes run along the spinal column (spinals), a design in the shape of a butterfly appears on the shoulders, and there is a bulls-eye on each flank. The pattern includes necklaces, bracelets, rings on the tail, vest buttons and an intricate 'M' on the forehead. On the face, the stripes are thinner and converge toward the nose; the eyes are sometimes emphasized, as in this example, by a dark line.

6. Carocat's Molly and Me and Carocat's Them There Eyes, Blue Tabby Kittens. Examples of the blue classic tabby, each demonstrates the rich, warm overtones or patina that is a necessary part of this color.

Intense selective breeding has led to the establishment of a large number of well-defined colors and patterns which are easily distinguished. Of these, perhaps the most typical or universally recognized are those with a pattern of dark stripes against a pale background. These are, of course, tabby cats, but the origin of the word has nothing to do with the origin of the cats themselves.

The name tabby traces back to Al-Attabiya, a quarter in the city of Baghdad, where silk was manufactured. The weavers based their patterns on those of cats' coats; and, when sent to Europe, these patterned silks were sold under the name 'tabby'.

The tabby pattern is widespread and common to a great many breeds; however, it was already common long before controlled selective breeding since, the pattern is so well suited to camouflage. In underbrush or on a field, a tabby cat, whether moving or stationary, is difficult to see as it blends so well into the shadows of the plants, bushes, and the grass. For this reason the tabby coat has been "adopted" by many types of wild cats.

The base of the tabby coat is agouti fur in which each hair has two to three bands of a color contrasting with the color at the base of the hair. The result is a "sand-like effect" that is itself a form of camouflage. The tabby pattern can be mackerel (tiger), classic (blotched), spotted, or ticked (as is the Abyssinian).

The original pattern, the one from which all the others derived, is the mackerel. It is defined by dark stripes (not too wide), parallel, continuous, and vertical on the cat's sides. The tail and limbs, both fore and hind, have regularly spaced dark rings; on the head, the stripes between the eyes and ears form an intricate 'M.' More common than the mackerel tabby pattern is the classic tabby which changes broadly from individual to individual. The stripes are always somewhat large which, on the flanks, are spiral in pattern forming a large bulls-eye or blotch instead of the vertical stripes of the mackerel pattern. The typical 'M' appears on the head. In the spotted pattern, the vertical stripes on the flanks are broken into shorter segments forming spots and oblong shaped areas. Finally, in the ticked tabby, the stripes are transitional and confined to the head and tip of the tail.

The American Wirehair is a recent breed whose origins date from 1966 when two kittens with wiry, curly hair were found in Verona, New York in a litter from an American Shorthair. The two kittens, otherwise absolutely normal and healthy, were carefully raised by expert breeders and, when adult, were used in controlled pairings that permitted the rapid establishment of this distinctive phenotypic characteristic. With the exception of the hair, the American Wirehair is similar to its progenitor, the American Shorthair. This is true even for the qualities of strength and health because, fortunately, the genetic modification responsible for the wiry and curly coat is not a source of other anomalies. Because of this cat's recent appearance, and perhaps also because not everyone finds the rough, wiry coat pleasing, the American Wirehair is currently limited to the United States where it has received C.F.A. championship recognition.

1. Bicolor (black with white) American Wirehair.
2. Brown Mackerel Patched Tabby with White.
3. Brown Mackerel Tabby.

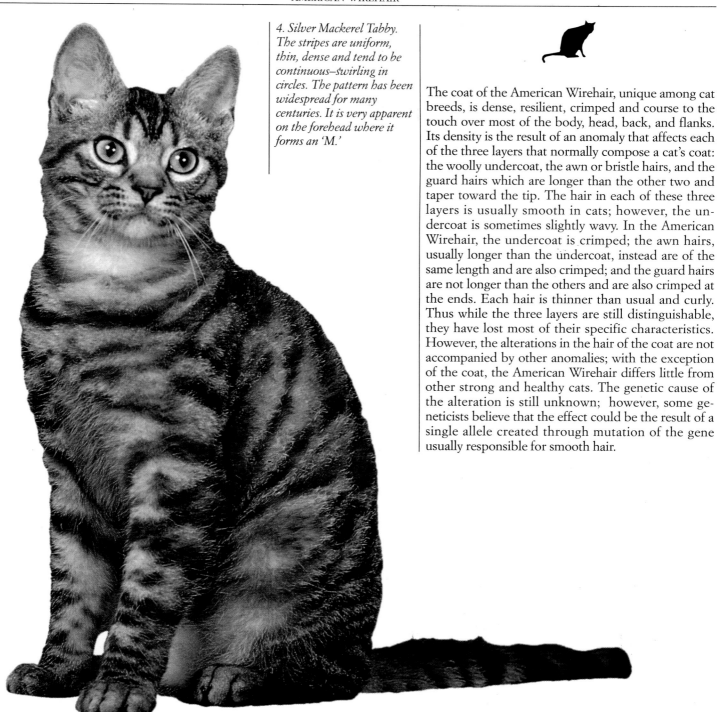

4. *Silver Mackerel Tabby. The stripes are uniform, thin, dense and tend to be continuous—swirling in circles. The pattern has been widespread for many centuries. It is very apparent on the forehead where it forms an 'M.'*

The coat of the American Wirehair, unique among cat breeds, is dense, resilient, crimped and course to the touch over most of the body, head, back, and flanks. Its density is the result of an anomaly that affects each of the three layers that normally compose a cat's coat: the woolly undercoat, the awn or bristle hairs, and the guard hairs which are longer than the other two and taper toward the tip. The hair in each of these three layers is usually smooth in cats; however, the undercoat is sometimes slightly wavy. In the American Wirehair, the undercoat is crimped; the awn hairs, usually longer than the undercoat, instead are of the same length and are also crimped; and the guard hairs are not longer than the others and are also crimped at the ends. Each hair is thinner than usual and curly. Thus while the three layers are still distinguishable, they have lost most of their specific characteristics. However, the alterations in the hair of the coat are not accompanied by other anomalies; with the exception of the coat, the American Wirehair differs little from other strong and healthy cats. The genetic cause of the alteration is still unknown; however, some geneticists believe that the effect could be the result of a single allele created through mutation of the gene usually responsible for smooth hair.

	Body	Head	Ears	Eyes	Nose	Chin	Legs and Feet	Tail	Coat	Varieties
C.F.A.	Medium to large; males are larger than females.	Round with prominent cheek bones and a well-developed muzzle.	Medium, slightly rounded at the tip. Broadly spaced and not too open at the base.	Large, round, bright, and clear. Set well apart.	In profile, the nose shows a gentle, concave curve.	Firm and well-developed. No apparent malocclusion.	Oval and compact.	Proportional to body length; the rounded tip is neither blunt nor pointed.	Springy, tight, medium in length. Individual hairs are crimped, hooked or bent. Whiskers are also curly.	Solid color; Shaded; Smoke; PartiColor; BiColor; and all colors except the pointed (Himalayan) spectrum.

BALINESE

Although called Balinese, this breed has nothing to do with the Island of Bali. It appeared in the United States during the 1950's in litters of Siamese. A single genetic mutation or group of mutations make this breed differ from a Siamese. Initially, the breed was called a Longhair Siamese, but protests from the breeders of traditional Siamese led to its quick renaming. The Balinese has something of the Siamese even though the traits are not always identifiable; the pointed coat colors are typical of the Siamese and often demonstrate a somewhat more pronounced darkening in the mature cat. The coat is of medium length, fine, silky and lacks a downy undercoat. The deep, clear blue eyes are almond-shaped and slant toward the nose in harmony with the lines of the wedge-shaped head and strikingly large ears. Named Balinese because the fluid motions of these lovely semi-longhaired cats reminded an early breeder of Balinese Temple Dancers.

1

1. Princess Mai Dii, 18 month old female Blue Point Balinese. The facial mask, ears, limbs, and tail are of a slate gray. The Balinese is characterized by a physical structure between the heavier, muscular type and extreme thin types. It has a slender neck, relatively thin limbs, a long, tapering tail, triangular wedge-shaped head, large, pointed ears with a wide base, and clear blue eyes slanted in harmony with the over all lines of the head and ears.

2. Grand Champion Purrmatix Mr. wonderful, Blue Point male. A long, svelte body, head the shape of a long tapering wedge, and deep, vivid blue eyes form a striking appearance.

2

The Balinese breed originated in a litter of Siamese kittens; a breeder's expert eye spotted small physical differences among some of the kittens that were potentially interesting including a coat more suited to a longhaired cat than to the smooth short-coated Siamese. Successive crosses between examples with similar morphological characteristics rapidly led to the definition of this new breed; however, the genetic basis of the differences between the Balinese and the Siamese or from any other known breeds remains unknown. Indeed, little or nothing is yet known of the genetics of the Balinese. In terms only of its coat, its affinity for the Himalayan Persian (medium-long coat, more intense coloring in outer areas with this patterned distribution most probably dependent on body temperature) would suggest an identical gene makeup. However, the Balinese' physical structure is completely different—lighter, with longer, thinner limbs—from that of the Himalayan. The body conformation depends on polygenes, groups of genes whose nature is, as yet, controversial and practically unknown; these may interact, along with various other results, with the very genes that determine the characteristics of the coat. For the moment, there is still much to be learned about the genetic makeup of

3. Grand Champion Purrmatix Suzie Q, Chocolate Point female. The coat of the Balinese is of medium length but longer over the neck, on the shoulders, and on the tail; it is fine and silky and lacks an undercoat. Together with the absence of a ruff, the absence of the undercoat, which is usually well-developed and soft in longhair breeds (such as the Persian), constitutes one of the identifying characteristics of the Balinese.

4. Picardy's Tahari.

3

4

	Body	Head	Ears	Eyes	Nose	Chin	Legs and Feet	Tail	Coat	Varieties
C.F.A.	Medium-sized, graceful, long and svelte with shoulders no wider than the hips. Long, slender neck. Long, slim legs.	Medium-size long tapering wedge proportional in size to the body.	Strikingly large, pointed, wide at the base.	Medium-sized and almond-shaped, slightly slanted towards the nose in harmony with wedge and ears. Deep, vivid blue.	Long and straight; a continuation of the forehead; no break.	Fine, wedge shaped.	Dainty, small, and oval.	Long, thin, tapering to a fine point.	Medium length, fine, silky without downy undercoat; longest on the tail. Body is an even color with subtle shading in older cats.	Seal Point, Blue Point, Chocolate Point, and Lilac Point.

If a Balinese is bred to a Siamese, the litter will have all the characteristics of pure Siamese but with short, felt-like coats. This suggests that the effects of the Balinese genes on such physical characteristics as body structure and hair length are masked by the stronger effects of the Siamese genes. According to C.F.A., the cross between a Balinese and a Siamese born, through breeding to Colorpoint Short Hairs producing other colors, with all the characteristics of the Siamese, but with long hair, results in a completely different breed, the Javanese. Breeders and experts, studying to unlock the secrets and inventiveness of genetics, have not reached any firm conclusions in this matter.

5. From left to right: Singapore Ni taan Kesary, 15 day old male, Blue Point; Princess Mai Dii; Surhaya Ni taan Kesary, 15 day old male, Blue Point.

6. Singapore and Surhaya Ni taan Kesary.

7. Surhaya Ni taan Kesary. As with Siamese, the kittens are born with a uniformly pale coat; the outer areas take on darker shadings in a few weeks. Mating between Balinese give litters of 3-4 kittens. The Balinese reaches early sexual maturity often between 6 and 10 months of age. The females are attentive and affectionate mothers never tire of playing with their young and performing their role as "teacher" with assiduous care. The good character of the Balinese is further demonstrated in its relationships with humans; a social animal, it establishes excellent bonds with all the people who live in a house, as well as with guests. However, the Balinese selects a single person as its "preferred owner." As so often happens in matters involving sentiment, the reasons for the choice (which the cat makes absolutely independently and which resists all pressure) are not always immediately clear.

8

9

8. Chmpion Purrmatix Daydreams, Lilac Point. The Balinese is an intelligent animal and adapts equally to life in an apartment or to larger, open areas, including terraces or gardens. Lively, but not overly so, it can always find something of interest in a house irrespective of its sophisticated air, it unhesitatingly hunts rodents or toy surrogates.

9. Grand Champion Cheseboro Beauregard, Lilac Point. The Balinese has little fear and has a healthy, strong composition; it usually requires no particular care except for its long, fine, silky coat, which must be brushed and combed; however, because of the absence of an undercoat, it seldom forms tangles or mats.

BENGAL

The Bengal, which is not recognized by C.F.A., is the most recent of the tabby breeds obtained through processes of genetically planned breedings. The first Bengal was born in the United States from the mating of a female American Shorthair with an Asian leopard (Felis bengalensis...hence the new breed's name). The

aim was that of creating a domestic cat with the appearance and perhaps also some of the behavioral traits of a feral cat. The selection program began in 1963 but was then suspended owing to difficulties in locating fertile males. It was resumed in 1970 and is still being done. No one can say whether or not the characteristics of the breed have yet been established in a definitive way. The behavioral characteristics, among others, are extremely variable from individual to individual and have not yet been refined to complete satisfaction. Irrespective of the ongoing progress, the Bengal still cannot, as yet, be defined as a modern, companion cat suitable for any family. Timorous, it has difficulty in learning basic rules such as not stealing food from the kitchen. At this time, only the T.I.C.A. (The International Cat Association) has set provisional standards for the Bengal.

1. Spotted Tabby variety. The pattern is rare in other breeds, but not unknown. In the Bengal, it is an inheritance from the breed's wild progenitor, the Asian leopard. The markings, of a uniform color with well-defined edges, must be arranged so as not having any semblance of striping. Stripes are permitted, but only on the head, neck, and limbs.

2. Classic (or Blotched) Tabby.

Although elegant and subtle, the Bengal's general physical structure is of a definite muscular type. The fore legs are longer than the hind legs, giving it a dignified posture well-suited to its cautious stride when walking; it always appears to be wary and studied. It is so silent as to be nearly imperceptible. Capable of sudden, lightning leaps, the Bengal is an athletic cat… calling it agile is not enough. It might even seem reckless, but because of its feral ancestry, is full of common sense, is well aware of its abilities, and does not take undue risks. It should be left alone and admired. Naturally, it needs a gymnasium in which to work out such as a large terrace, better still a well protected, large garden with several trees. This is an energy filled animal that must have the opportunity of expending that energy in frequent physical exercise.

3. Black Spotted. Unlike the Egyptian Mau or Ocicat, the spots are not of a uniform color and should be, instead, rosettes. Rosettes are light spots enclosed in a darker outer circle.

4. Spotted on a silver background. Kittens are lively only when they feel completely safe; their fur is rough and a slightly wavy; the pattern and color are not visible for the first 5-6 months.

The Bengal was first christened the Leopardette or small leopard cat, a name that seems perfectly suited to the breed. Those involved in this breeding project still refuse to abandon the original name. The Bengal has the appearance, way of moving, and alert intelligence of a feral cat while, at the same time, having temperament of a domestic cat. It is a wild cat with domestic inclinations; and, while considered a true domestic cat, it must still learn discipline and, most of all, must be developed so as to minimize its tendency to be quite timid. There is nothing surprising in this as wild predators, such as the progenitors of the Bengal, make extreme prudence a way of life. That very prudence is often mistaken for fear. It is highly likely that the Bengal has not yet acquired full trust in humans still seeing them as potential enemies.

Body	Head	Ears	Eyes	Nose	Chin	Legs and Feet	Tail	Coat	Varieties
Large size, muscular, especially in males. Large but fragile bone structure. Legs are medium length, strong, and muscular.	Large, triangular, longer than wide. Strong, muscular neck.	Short, with a wide base and rounded tips.	Oval, large, and not protruding.	Large. Red-brick color.	Strong.	Large, round feet.	Thick, medium length, with a black tip.	Short, spotted black, brown, red, chocolate, or cinnamon on an rufous ground color.	All colors of brown are acceptable. The preferred ground color is golden orange.

BIRMAN

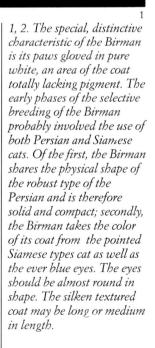

Many years ago, there was a wise man who lived in the mountains of Indochina with a cat which was as white as snow as his only companion. When death came for the holy man, he was sitting meditating beneath the statue of a goddess while the cat lay curled in his lap. The soul of the man entered the body of the cat, and, as a gift, the goddess, with a smile, bestowed the gilt reflection of her own clothes and the blue of her eyes to the cat. However, the cat's paws, still resting on the lap of its beloved owner, remained forever white. So goes only one of the many legends concerning the origin of this breed which is considered to be very ancient and native to southeast Asia. Even so, there are those who claim the breed is the happy result of experiments conducted by an enterprising French breeder during the early 1920's. This breeder is said to have crossed a Persian with a Siamese, obtaining the phenotypic Birman within a few generations. What is certain is that the controlled breeding of the Birman began in France in the early years of this century leading to their first official recognition in 1925.

1, 2. The special, distinctive characteristic of the Birman is its paws gloved in pure white, an area of the coat totally lacking pigment. The early phases of the selective breeding of the Birman probably involved the use of both Persian and Siamese cats. Of the first, the Birman shares the physical shape of the robust type of the Persian and is therefore solid and compact; secondly, the Birman takes the color of its coat from the pointed Siamese types cat as well as the ever blue eyes. The eyes should be almost round in shape. The silken textured coat may be long or medium in length.

3

3. The color of the coat is determined by a combination of five different genes of which only one is always the same: that responsible for the "white gloves." Each of the other four genes can cause different forms (or alleles). The combinations of these various forms create the shadings of color that have established the identities of different varieties.

4. Falstaff dei Ke-Hsi Mansam, 2 year old Seal Point male.

5. Niniane Neit, 2 year old female, Blue Point. Note the semi-long hair on the tail.

6. Jeussi Von Gripsholm, Seal-point adult male. As with the Siamese and the Himalayan Persian, the characteristic distribution of color in the Birman, with some outer areas darker (points) than the rest of the body, is probably an early adaptation of the ancestors of today's cats to differences in body temperature during cold weather. According to this theory, more pigment is located where the body would suffer greater heat loss (during cold temperatures) such as ears, mask, limbs, and tail.

4

5

6

	Body	Head	Ears	Eyes	Nose	Chin	Legs and Feet	Tail	Coat	Varieties
C.F.A.	Long and stocky. Females may be proportionately smaller.	Skull strong, broad and rounded.	Medium in length set as much on the top as the side of the head.	Slightly oval of intense blue.	Medium length and width with Roman shape in profile.	Full with somewhat rounded muzzle & strong, well-developed chin.	Paws are large, round and firm. Even, white gloves on front paws, slightly longer gloves running up the rear of the hind legs (the hock) forming an inverted "V" (the laces).	Medium length.	Medium long to long, silken in texture which does not mat.	Seal Point, Blue Point, Chocolate Point, Lilac Point.

7

The Birman, or "Sacred Cat of Burma," is the best known breed with gloves, or gauntlets; pure white fur must be present on all four paws and in a definite pattern. It must be only to the height of the first joint and thus only on the "end" of the paw. Obtaining cats with this precise characteristic is not easy. The trait depends on a single gene that determines phenotypes in which the color white is present but in an extremely variable measure. The white can vary from being nearly a completely white coat to one which is almost completely colored having only a small white spot (a locket or button, for example). This variation in the amount of white includes all the possible variations available between these two extremes, from almost all the coat to nearly none. The problem is to obtain the right quantity of white and locate it only in the required, special places...only on the paws, and in the correct amount and pattern!

7. From left to right: Falstaff dei Ke-Hsi Mansam; Rebecca del Verbano, Rufus del Verbano, Rubens del Verbano and Rea del Verbano; 3 month old seal Point kittens.

8. Great lovers of home, comfort, and an orderly life, Birmans tend to develop exclusive relationships with their owners and are jealous; they need to sense their owner's affections however fleeting these might be. They show little interest in strangers and are intolerant of other animals, either cats or dogs, that invade their territory.

8

The Bombay was developed in the late 1950s by an American breeder with a clear vision to "create" a cat similar to the Burmese but black instead of brown and with copper eyes instead of yellow. As a first step, the breeder bred a female Burmese to a black male American Shorthair with copper eyes; however, the Bombay, as it exists today, was realized many generations later–after careful and patient selective breeding. The new breed was given a name recalling India, the Bombay; in fact, the cat does resemble a miniature Indian black leopard. And not only because of the color of its coat and eyes, but also because of its elegant, compact physical structure, powerful muscles, agile movements, and the characteristic gait, accompanied, as in wild cats, by a rhythmic swaying of the back. The breed was officially recognized by the C.F. A. in 1976 but is still rare outside the United States, in part, perhaps, as a result of confusion on the part of the world's cat fanciers with the American, British, and European Short Hairs. However, the breed enjoys continued success at cat shows in the United States.

1

2

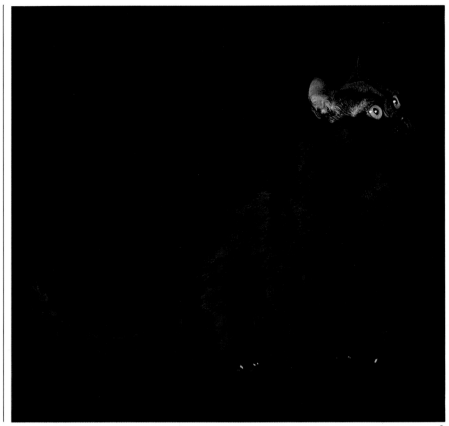

The Bombay has the elegant, supple beauty of the leopard it so resembles, but also the perfect domesticity of an animal bred to be a companion. A tranquil but playful breed, Bombays love everybody. Silent and careful in its movements, it is gentle with all family members, including children, for whom it shows great patience. It is also true that, when it sees its owner sitting at a table reading the paper or writing a letter, it will hop up and lie either on or across the page. The Bombay is sensible and patient, capable of respecting the occupations and humors of its owner, and never an inconvenience. Bombay cats like to play, but they are never wildly hyperactive as are some other breeds; they do play, but with dignity.

1, 2, 3, 4. The coat of the Bombay is shiny, short, and satin-like; although uniformly black, it may include a few white hairs. Kittens are born jet black; however, their coats tend to take on a cinnamon or rusty patina because of the moisture from the licking their mother does to keep them clean. Just as characteristic of the breed as the coat are the rounded, gold to copper colored eyes. The Bombay is best described as being the cat with the black patent leather coat and copper penny eyes.

	Body	Head	Ears	Eyes	Nose	Chin	Legs and Feet	Tail	Coat	Varieties
C.F.A.	Medium, muscular, and neither compact nor rangy with a surprising weight for its size. Legs in proportion to body.	Round without sharp angles and a short, well-developed muzzle but neither pugged nor snubbed in appearance.	Medium in size, broad at the base with slightly rounded tips.	Rounded and set far apart. Color from gold to copper.	Has a visible nose break.	Firm and reflecting a proper bite.	Paws are round.	Medium, straight, neither short nor "whip-like."	Fine, short, satin-like, close-lying, with a shimmering sheen.	Black only (however, an occasional sable color may appear which cannot be shown).

BRITISH SHORTHAIR

Around the middle of the last century, Harrison Weir, the distinguished Englishman remembered in history as the first professional breeder of cats and as the "Father of the Cat Fancy," got the idea that the ordinary shorthaired cat, domestic or street, could be raised to the status of a breed. At the first cat show (based on rigidly defined criteria which Mr. Weir himself had written) held in London in 1871, what had once been taken as a simple house cat was christened with the patriotic name of British Shorthair. Over the years, the popularity of the British Shorthair has experienced varying fortune. At first solid and triumphal, it declined in the early years of this century when the Persian was introduced into Europe, then returned in popularity only to have it decline again during the difficulties of the two world wars. Its popularity was reborn in the early postwar period reinforced by a new breeding program that, making use of the maxim "When your enemy is stronger than you, make him your ally," involved breeding to the Persian. Today, the satisfactory characteristics of the breed are solidly fixed, and the British Shorthair, now reasonably widespread, enjoys a universal popularity.

1

1. *Quetzalcoatl di Fatamorgana, 18 month old Cream Spotted Tabby male. The spotted coat was exhibited as a variety of classic or blotched tabby in the first cat shows; it wasn't until 1966 that it was recognized as a distinct variety.*

2. *Malaxis di Glicini, 3 year old Blue Cream female. The two colors, blue and cream, must be evenly distributed; the borders between the areas of different colors are indistinct or "heathered." The blue-cream was obtained through dilution of the tortoiseshell (red and black). As with that variety, only females can be exhibited.*

2

Currently not officially recognized by the C.F.A., the British Shorthair breed offers, as do a few other breeds, the solid color lilac variety. This is a unique and difficult to describe delicate, very pale, somewhat warm, pinkish-gray shade. It is indirectly derived from black and directly derived from brown. In the first phase of the genetics that produce lilac, the original black pigmentation is completely replaced by brown (the same color that characterizes the Havana Brown breed). The single gene responsible for this is termed by experts as the "allele b" and is found in the genotype of all lilac-color cats, as it is also in the Havana. In the second phase, the brown coloration undergoes what breeders call dilution; rather than being uniformly distributed, the pigment is gathered in granules or clumps leaving each single hair with microscopic areas void of pigment. The result is a decidedly less intense color.

Dilution of color is caused by the "d gene" (the identification of the genetic factor indicating dilution), a mutant form of the gene that controls the deposit of pigment. The "d allele" performs its duty independently of whether the original pigment is brown or, as in this case, black. It is therefore the same allele that, in cats with a gray (or, as experts say, blue) coat transforms the original basic solid black color to the dilute form, blue.

4

3, 4, 5. Achillea de Glicini, 6 month old tortoiseshell female. In the tortoiseshell coat (which is basically black) the relative quantity and distribution of the orange and black can vary from cat to cat. This particular coloration depends on the presence of two different alleles of the same gene, called respectively "o" and "O." Only the heterozygote "Oo" will produce a cat with a tortoiseshell coat. Since the gene in question is located in the female sexual chromosome X, only females, XX can be tortoiseshell. Males that are XY can be tortoiseshell only through rare, accidental chromosomal alterations that affect fertility. Naturally, the females can also be homozygous "oo," with a non-red (orange) coat or "OO", uniformly

	Body	Head	Ears	Eyes	Nose	Chin	Legs and Feet	Tail	Coat	Varieties
C.F.A.	Large to medium size; powerful, with a level back, broad chest, set on short, straight legs.	Round and massive set on a short, thick neck.	Medium, broad at the base, with rounded points.	Large, round, well-opened and set wide apart and level.	Medium and broad. In profile there is a gentle dip.	Well developed.	Paws are round and firm.	Medium in length, thick at base, tapering to a slightly rounded tip.	Short, very dense, well-bodied, resilient to the touch.	Solid color; Tabby, Smoke, PartiColor, Dilute; BiColor; and any color except those showing hybridization with the Himalayan pattern.

6

In 1800, the British Shorthair was still commonly found on the streets and was often semi-feral. Today, as a result of controlled breeding arranged by breeders under the guidance of genetic experts, the breed exhibits the best physical and behavioral characteristics. Among these are the underlying strength suggested by the cat's stocky body structure confirmed by its ironclad good health, and underscored by the breed's character, one of solid composure. The British Shorthair is tough, with great inner strength, capable of facing up to any situation. Its body is compact, well-proportioned and powerful; the strong legs are short to medium in length, the chest broad, the neck is short and thick. Overall, the general body type is that of the so-called muscular type—not as powerful,

therefore, as that of the Persian, which is the robust type, nor as light as that of the Siamese, which is the thin type. Although usually moving with calm deliberation, it is capable of lightning reflexes in times of need. The coat, is short, very dense, well-bodied, resilient and firm to the touch, neither double coated nor woolly. The British coat provides a protective layer that assures adequate protection from both cold and heat and allows the British Shorthair to expose itself to the worst of weather without harm. In fact—and this could not be otherwise—another original trait the breed preserves is that of being an able hunter. Irrespective of the comfortable life offered in our modern homes, the British Shorthair has lost none of its original ability to get by and ably fend for itself. A great number of color varieties are currently recognized, including solids, bicolor (including tortoiseshell), and tricolors. Some of these are so popular, widespread, and well known that they are often

6. Revilo Frantic Fatima, 3 year old blue female. As with all blue cats, the color of the coat is actually a shade of gray, modified with lighter tones from the natural refraction of the light rays. The nose, lips, and paw pads are also blue. The eyes must be gold or copper. A pure blue coat is highly valued and considered typical of the breed which is often called the British Blue. Compared with the Chartreux, the British is less woolly; in fact, the British coat must be neither woolly nor double.

mistaken for separate breeds. Such is the case with the British Tabby Shorthair; some people would be surprised to learn that only two genes (those that codify the agouti and tabby characteristics) separate the tabby from, for example, the black. The black is a splendid cat, completely black, without even the slightest trace of any other color. The coat, therefore, is solidly monochrome, without the stripes of the tabby pattern but also without the bands of color found on each single hair of a coat of the agouti type. As with every other solid-color cat, black is classified as non-agouti. As can easily be imagined, the non-agouti phenotype is derived from a mutation, an accidental modification of the agouti genetic material. Paradoxically, black cats sometimes possess the alleles responsible for tabby striping; however, on a non-agouti coat, striping is never visible. Black is the original solid color, which means that other basic solid colors blue, brown, and lilac were obtained either accidentally or intentionally from black, by way of later mutations or appropriate genetic rearrangements. Together with the solid black, the British Blue Shorthair is very popular and very competitive with the French blue-colored cat, the Chartreux.

The colors and patterns of the coat of many of the varieties of British Shorthairs are common to other breeds, particularly the American and European Shorthairs. This does not mean that an expert might confuse a British with an American or European; the general physical characteristics and various attributes of the coat are different enough to justify their classification into separate breeds. In fact, contrary to what one might think, the characteristics that define

7

7. Quetzalcoatl. This cat exemplifies the solid, robust and well-proportioned physique of the British Shorthair. In the male, the short, thick neck appears almost square and with the medium ears fitting into,

without distorting, the rounded contour of the head, suggests a sense of strength. The tail is wider at the distal end.

8. Mirtillo de Glicini, 3 year old black male. Although perhaps a less sophisticated color than blue, the pure black coat is extraordinary with eyes of gold or copper and showing no trace of green.

8

a breed and make it distinguishable from others usually have little to do with the color of the coat. It should be pointed out, however, that both British and American Shorthairs include a variety with a somewhat singular color and pattern of coat. In Great Britain this is termed the British Tipped. The short, thick undercoat is uniformly white; the outer coat, composed of the awn and guard hairs, is also white, but on the back, flanks, head, and ears many of the single hairs are tipped with a different color. This tipping can be of any of the solid colors; multicolored hairs on a single individual are not permitted. Rings of color may appear on the tail, perhaps an indication of an original tabby pattern. The origins of the tipping is unknown. It may have derived from

some breeding with Persians of which there are tipped varieties (e.g., Chinchilla Silver, Shaded Silver, Shell and Shaded Cameo, etc.); however, nothing rules out the possibility that the trait appeared without the addition of Persian influence through genetic mutations not necessarily identical but with similar macroscopic effects.

Few cats are as adaptable as the British Shorthair. Tranquil, dignified, and independent, it requires no special attention. It has no fear of the cold nor, when in the wild, being a skilled hunter, of hunger. If permitted to conduct its life in relative freedom, it makes itself a silent and discreet presence between the house and garden and creates no problems. It may occasionally bring home gifts of prey as a treat for its human companions. It's best to accept such gifts gracefully, complimenting the cat on its skill; this is only a sign of consideration and a means of consolidating family ties. Even with its pronounced sense of independence, the British Shorthair is capable of

9. Quetzalcoatl's profile reveals the rounded forehead and slightly flat plane on top of the head, a medium, broad nose, and a strong chin. Unlike those on the Bengal, the spots on the spotted British Shorthair are partially distributed along ideal lines that recall the original striping. This is true most of all on the flanks, neck, and limbs. From the genetic point of view, the creation of a red tabby coat requires the mixture of several different genes: one for the agouti coat, one for the tabby pattern, and a third gene, the allele O found only in a single pair of X chromosomes, for the red color.

9

10

11

great loyalty and tenacious affection for all members of the family, including children, without showing preference for one person over another. This may well signify that, way down, the cat does not recognize any owner; rather, it makes its social relations as close as needed on the basis of mutual respect and shared feelings. From this viewpoint, of being an equal to its human friends, the British Shorthair is different from other breeds, particularly those of Oriental origin which tend to select a single person as the exclusive recipient of all their affection. But this is not surprising; in its emotions as in every other aspect of its existence, the British Shorthair never loses its sense of measure or its typically Anglo-Saxon self-control.

10. The British Shorthair is a compact powerful cat with a round head, good width between the ears, round cheeks and round, well opened eyes.

11. Excalibur's Boy George, Blue and White Bicolor.

BURMESE

One legend holds that the Burmese is derived from a shorthair breed of ancient origin that was once venerated as the incarnation of a god in Burmese temples. This legend is supported by an illustration in a book of poems from Thailand that cannot be given a proven date of origin. It was most probably written during the period between 1350 and 1750 and illustrates many patterned cats including one that is unquestionably a Burmese and another that is definitely the pattern we identify as being a Siamese. The illustrations prove that although there is a strong genetic affinity between the two breeds, they were already showing different physical characteristics centuries ago. It also indicates that the two breeds have remained essentially unchanged, thereby suggesting that the process of differentiation that led to the Burmese' and Siamese' being two distinct breeds must have begun prior to this time period. Nonetheless, the Burmese, recognized today by international cat associations, was obtained in the United States in the 1930's from kittens born from the breeding together of a male Siamese and a brown female cat found on the San Francisco waterfront and believed to have traveled there from Burma; many identify the sable brown cats of this breed with the Supilak, or Copper Cat of Siam.

Although Siamese blood

1. Sable Burmese. The physical structure is typically muscular, well proportioned, and elegant. The neck is well developed; the head is pleasingly rounded. The body weight is usually greater than would be expected in a medium-size cat as a result of the muscle mass, which is highly developed, strong, and easily seen beneath the satin-like, glossy, short sable colored coat.

2. The eyes are large, set far apart and have a rounded aperture.

3. At rear: Tjalfes' Biella Rieppe, a 2½ year old female and in the foreground, Kawpaw Sebastian, a 2½ year old male.

runs in the veins of the modern Burmese, the two breeds have been recognized as distinct for hundreds of years. While the body of the Siamese is unequivocally long, tubular and thin, that of the Burmese is medium in size, muscular, and compact in appearance. Its conformation is strong and robust, with particularly well-developed muscles, a broad chest, substantial bone structure, with surprising weight for its size. The head is pleasingly rounded, lacking flat planes with a short, well-developed muzzle as opposed to the straight lines of the Siamese' wedge-shaped head. Overall, in comparison with the physical shape the Siamese, the Burmese gives the general impression of greater strength and solidity.

4. At birth, the coat can appear a café au lait color and have, as in the kitten in the foreground, faintly visible stripes, reminiscent of the tabby pattern. In subsequent months, the color darkens and the stripes generally will disappear. The final coloration appears before the cat reaches sexual maturity. The young are somewhat precocious, very lively, and require constant attention, which is ensured by the tireless and affectionate mother. Maternal behavior is highly developed in the Burmese, so much so that it is extended to the "kittens" of other cats: no cat is as patient and gentle with progeny as the Burmese.

5. Dark sable brown coat.

Although no less lively than the Siamese, the Burmese is less unpredictable and more constant in its affections. Exuberant and full of life, it is curious, intelligent, and inquisitive. It makes friends easily with all members of the family and, generally, does not exhibit a basic distrust of strangers. It loves to play and is always in search of something to capture its attention. Healthy and strong, it is also fearless. Although it adapts well to apartment life, it loves a well supervised terrace, garden, or countryside where it can run about at will and with safety from the problems presented by a modern, urban lifestyle. Its adaptability and ability to respond quickly to change let it face travel or relocation without serious problems. When traveling, rather than curl up and sleep, the Burmese prefers to watch what is happening around it and look at the landscape out the window of its traveling carrier. Occasionally, it will make a comment, a short meow in a decidedly loud voice, no less raucous and sharp than that of its Siamese countryman.

From its owner, the Burmese wants a modicum of availability and lots of affection. The owner should give him a little "quality" time each day, stopping to have a chat, rolling him onto his back and playing with him as if he were still a kitten, cuddling, petting and generally pampering this lovely, short coated cat.

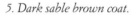

4

5

6

The best-known and most popular variety of Burmese is the sable brown. The color is produced by an allele, a variant of the gene that controls the quantity and distribution of pigment both in the coat and in the iris. The original gene, termed "C" (for colored), corresponds to an intense coloration (black for the fur, yellow-orange for the eyes); the allele in the Burmese instead causes a more shaded and less sharp coloration. Thus, the coat goes from black to a brown or a sable shade, and the eyes become yellow-gold. In the Siamese, a new variant of the original gene, and thus a different allele, accentuates the dilution of the color, making the body color paler. In the coat of the Burmese, the extremities (the mask, ears, and ends of the limbs and tail, or "points") may have coloration that is slightly darker than the rest of the body. This is reminiscent of the darker colored points of the Siamese. However, while the contrast between areas of different pigment is always present and immediately evident in the Siamese, in the Burmese is it barely perceptible and insignificant. This applies to adults; in kittens, the differences in color can be more perceptible.

6. Darinas mi Amore, a sable female. The ears, tilted slightly forward, give the animal and expression of constant alertness. The color may take on slightly darker shadings on the muzzle, which emphasizes, by contrast, the intense yellow of the eyes. Although sable brown is the most popular color, there are other colors. The F.I.F.e. and G.C.C.F.

standards recognize ten colors, while those of the C.F.A. in the United States, are more restricted, accepting only four which including the colors of the Burmese Dilute Division, Champagne, Blue and Platinum.

7. Champion Bayburn's Ice Maiden in Platinum, platinum burmese.

7

	Body	Head	Ears	Eyes	Nose	Chin	Legs and Feet	Tail	Coat	Varieties
C.F.A.	Medium size, muscular, and compact in appearance. Heavier than expected.	Pleasingly rounded with no flat planes; considerable width between the eyes, and a short, broad muzzle.	Medium, spaced well apart, broad at the base; rounded tips, tilted slightly forward.	Large, set far apart with rounded aperture. The color ranges from yellow to gold.	In profile, there is a visible nose break.	Firmly rounded.	Paws are round.	Straight and medium in length.	Fine, glossy, satin-like texture, short and very close lying.	Sable, champagne, blue, and platinum.

BURMILLA

In 1981, the accidental mating of a male Persian Chinchilla and a female Lilac Burmese produced four kittens with black-tipped, short hair that attracted the attention of breeders because of the homogeneity and elegance of the phenotype. The following year, the mating was repeated with the declared aim of establishing a new breed. The breeding program involved crosses between cats from the first five generations followed by further crosses with Chinchilla Persians and, more often, with Burmese, following the general lines of the well-planned program which created the Bombay and Tiffany (a longhaired variety of Burmese) breeds. Early in 1984 the Burmilla Cat Club was inaugurated in Great Britain which now has branches throughout Europe, but not in the United States, where the breed is waiting to be introduced. First presented to the public in cat shows in 1985, the Burmilla is today numbered among the experimental breeds by the F.I.F.e..

1, 2. *According to the Burmilla Cat Club, a Burmilla must exhibit six fundamental phenotypic characteristics: clear contrast between the silvery undercoat and the shading or tipping which is accepted in all the standard colors (plus black, caramel, beige and apricot) permitted for the European Burmese; delicate tabby markings in the same color as the shading or tipping confined to the tail, lower area of the legs, and on the forehead, where they should form a distinct 'M'; thick fur with a rough surface; eyes, nose, and lips outlined by the same color as the shading or tipping; green eyes with rounded lower eye aperture and straight upper aperture, and a terra-cotta colored nose. The Burmilla possesses a tranquil disposition, and is even tempered with an outgoing personality.*

It seems that someone, examining the four kittens—almost Burmese, but not quite—that had been born to a Burmese mother and a Persian Chinchilla father, commented, "Yes, they are distinctly Burmilla." This name, considered rather odd by its inventor, enjoyed immediate success and was adopted for this hybrid breed. It is the coat color and texture that distinguish the Burmilla from its Burmese mother, as it is neither short nor of medium length, and it can be said to be a little longer than that of the Burmese. It is very dense, slightly bristly or rough on the ends; this characteristic, not unpleasant to the touch, results in greater fullness to the cat's appearance. The color can be described as interesting. The base is silvery gray, and delicate tabby stripes appear on the mask, paws, and tail. This "reduced" tabby pattern is similar to that of the Abyssinian; in the Aby, however, the body areas not affected by the striping are agouti instead of being tipped. The general physical appearance of the Burmilla is that of the European Burmese—muscular, but not as compact and heavy-boned as that of the Persian. The head is gently rounded, and the ears, wide at the base and with rounded tips as in the Burmese, are tilted slightly forward; a characteristic that gives the cat a pleasing and appealing expression, one of the distinctive elements of this new breed.

3

3. To understand the genetic basis for the Burmilla's shaded coloration, it is best to begin at the source and take into consideration the coat of the breed's Persian Chinchilla parent. The long hair of the Chinchilla are depigmented resulting in a whitish translucence for most of each hair's length. This is caused by the presence of the "I" gene (for "inhibitor" gene), which inhibits, or suppresses the deposit of pigment in the hair during development. The activity of the "I" gene appears to be controlled by a group of modifying genes, as yet not identified, whose existence has been empirically inferred more than demonstrated by experimentation. Some of these modifying genes facilitate the inhibiting action of the "I" gene thereby strengthening it; however, others counter its action rendering it less effective. This is precisely what occurs in a coat of the shaded type; since the effect of the "I" gene is diminished, the lack of pigmentation is not homogeneous, and its effect is generally reduced. Thus, at least a portion of the hair in the coat ends up with far more pigment than it would have if the color were Chinchilla. The shaded Burmilla genotype shares the "I" gene with that of the Persian Chinchilla but appears to have different modifying genes. It should be noted that the reduced pigmentation appears even more diluted in the Persian because of the extraordinary length of its coat; in the Burmilla, with its shorter coat, the contrast between the distal color and proximal depigmentation of the hair is more evident and more visible. The modifying genes that differentiate the Chinchilla coloration from that of the shaded are also responsible for the subtle distinction between shading and tipping, based both on the relative amount of pigmentation, as well as, depigmentation of each single hair plus the relative frequency of the more or less depigmented hairs.

	Body	Head	Ears	Eyes	Nose	Chin	Legs and Feet	Tail	Coat	Varieties
G.C.C.F.	Medium size, muscular. Broad chest.	Large and rounded. Strong jaws.	Medium size with rounded tips.	Expressive, open, and slightly slanted. Set wide apart. Color from yellow-green to green.	The profile shows a distinct break.	Strong with an even bite.	Paws are oval.	Medium length, elegant, with a rounded tip.	Short, dense, thick, and soft.	Silver, shaded and tipped with points in solid colors and in the Tortoiseshell pattern; black, blue, chocolate, lilac, caramel, beige, and apricot.

CHARTREUX

The Chartreux probably owes its name to the hypothesis concerning its origin which holds that it is a shorthaired breed that arrived in France, probably from Syria, early in the 1500s and was raised in a monastery of Carthusian monks near Paris. Monks and monasteries are said to have played leading roles in the care of ancient feline breeds in centuries past. This was perhaps a reflection of the love and respect with which the religious spirit then looked on all living creatures. According to a second, somewhat more romantic theory, the breed originated on Belle-Île, a small French island in the Bay of Biscay. There a young traveler, struck by the beauty of the isolated cats, brought a pair back with him when he returned to the continent. The cat Fancy program of selective Chartreux breeding and registration began in France between 1925 and 1930.

1

1. Grand Champion Lutece Hymne a la Joie. The Chartreux does not have a normal walk, but has a noble gait similar to that of the wild feline…measured and lacking ostentation.

Agile and precise in its movements, it is a methodical and efficient hunter.

2. Katmanbleu's Isis of Minetbleu

Among the breed's many good qualities is its character. Affectionate, peaceful, and independent, it has no need for excessive attention, but wishes only to be treated with respect and consistency. It needs an available hunting ground, whether in a well protected garden, a basement, or an attic. It performs these hunts, which are invariably crowned with success, according to rhythms inscrutable to humans, alternating them with long periods of apparent laziness curled in a favorite chair. It is silent and affectionate with all family members; in fact, the French nickname this breed the "dog-like" cat since they display an intense devotion to their owners and are very wary of strangers. A very tranquil cat, it is well-suited to those who lead an orderly life and also love tranquillity; however, with its patience and goodwill, it can get along even with owners whose lives are more chaotic.

2

The thick, velvety coat of the Chartreux is any shade of blue-gray in color–from ash to slate with the tips lightly brushed with silver; the color emphasizes clarity and uniformity rather than shade. Of course, what is gray to the layman is blue to the cat Fancy, and in the Chartreux all parts of the cat must be blue including the skin of the nose pad, and lips; the foot pad color is best described as rose-taupe in hue. The color of the coat is derived from black, but rather than being evenly distributed, the pigment is gathered and amassed in irregular granules spread along the structure of each hair. As a result, the black color appears diluted and gray. The cause of this dilution is a single allele, "d," the same that acts in other breeds, thereby causing color dilution. In the Chartreux, the greater the dilution, the paler the gray tones of the coat and the greater the appeal of the specimen. However, clarity and uniformity of color are prized above any specific shade. A blue coat is not the exclusive attribute of the Chartreux; there are blue varieties of the British, European, and American Shorthairs, the Scottish Fold, the Manx, the Persian, the Russian Blue, the Oriental Shorthair, the American Curl, the Korat, etc. In all these breeds, the color of the coat is a result of the same genetic structure, but, of course, the length and consistency of the coat differ from breed to breed, as do the general physical characteristics of the cat.

3. *Katmanbleu's Isis of Minetbleu, female. The general physical shape of the robust Chartreux includes a medium, husky, primitive body type which is neither cobby nor classic. This is most true, however, of the male: in Chartreux the size difference between the sexes is more marked than in some other breeds with the females decidedly smaller and lighter. In particular, the head of the female is less massive and lacks the large jowls which are very characteristic of the male.*

4. *Grane des Petits Lacs, male.*

	Body	Head	Ears	Eyes	Nose	Chin	Legs and Feet	Tail	Coat	Varieties
C.F.A.	Medium-long, robust physique with broad shoulders, massive, dense and muscular. Legs comparatively short and fine-boned.	Rounded and broad, but not a sphere. The jowls (particularly in the adult male) are pronounced.	Medium in height and width, set high on the head…very erect.	Rounded and open, alert and expressive with color range from copper to gold with a clear, deep, brilliant orange preferred.	Straight, medium in length and width with a slight stop at eye level.	Powerful jaw; sweet smiling expression.	Round and dainty; may appear almost dainty compared to body mass.	Moderate length; heavy base tapering to oval tip.	Medium short and slightly woolly in texture; should "break" at neck and flanks.	A single variety in all the shades of blue, from ash to slate-blue, with preference given to clarity and uniformity of color.

CEYLON

The Ceylon arrived in Europe such a short time ago that the number of generations is not yet sufficient for the breed to achieve official recognition. In this instance, at least, the breed's name is faithful to its place of origin; this cat originates on the island of Ceylon (Sri Lanka), where it has been raised as a pet for centuries. Credit for introducing it to the rest of the world goes to an Italian, Paolo Pellegatta, who first imported some examples to Italy in 1984. Officially presented to a commission of F.I.Fe. judges in 1988, its sociable and confident character, in addition to its physical characteristics, immediately stirred great interest and approval. In 1990 it was given a provisional standard by the F.I.Fe., and official recognition will eventually follow; in the meantime, since the basic characteristics of the breed are already well established, breeders are busy working to define the color varieties and establish the genetic base for the coat's highly original coloration. The Ceylon is uniformly agouti on the back, flanks, and neck with tabby striping on the tail, limbs, and head.

1. Raissa, adult female.

2. Ortica, 10 month old blue female.

3. Oshadhi, 6 month old red male. The red and blue coloration appeared spontaneously through a chance combination from the genetic sire's bloodlines. The physical shape is basically of the thin type but is compact and muscular. Size is a characteristic of the breed; the Ceylon is very small, smaller that most other breeds, as is the Singapura. Its small size may well represent an adaptation to the tropical climate (the smaller the body the greater the proportional surface dispersion of heat) and island environment (on islands, selection often favors smaller body sizes than those found in species located on large continents).

The coloration of the coat of the Ceylon is highly unusual. Uniformly agouti on the back, flanks, chest, and neck, it has clear tabby stripes the entire length of the tail, on the limbs (both fore and hind), on the mask and cheeks, and between the eyes. The inhabitants of Ceylon (Sri Lanka) say that the design formed by the stripes on the head is similar to the that on head of the cobra which is sacred to Buddha; as such, the design is considered a good omen. The original color is a tawny shade which has been named manila. Many different shadings of manila exist–from sand to cinnamon, from ginger to coffee. The tabby stripes are in a color that matches that of the rest of the coat; the tip of the tail, however, is always black. The agouti coloration, stripes on the points, and warm manila color are shared by other breeds of cat found in the area adjacent to the Indian Ocean (the Singapura, for example), probably because the overall effect is one of effective camouflage. These are most probably phenotypic traits fixed through natural selection during centuries of life in the wild before becoming a domestic cat. The Ceylon shares with the Abyssinian the uniformly agouti coloration, but does have marked tabby stripes on the outer areas; in the Abyssinian, however, these stripes are absolutely evanescent and are tolerated only on the head and tail.

These considerations have led to the theory that the Ceylon possesses the allele responsible for the distribution of color typical of the Abyssinian, T(a), but is heterozygous with the allele t(b), responsible for the blotched tabby pattern. The allele T(a) would limit the striping to the outer areas of the body, while the t(b) would strengthen their color, increase their extension, and amplify their distribution. It cannot be excluded, however, that other tabby alleles may be part of the Ceylon genotype, either as alternates or in addition to those just described. The Ceylon has not , as yet been seen in the United States; it is neither registered nor recognized by the C.F.A.

4. Ortica.

5. Ofman, 14 month old red (manila) female. In addition to the distribution of color in its coat and its small size, other characteristics of the Ceylon are its large, expressive eyes, and the attentive, thoughtful, calm, and perhaps dreamy gaze. Although lively and active, the Ceylon is adaptable and has an excellent character. Very affectionate with its owners, it is disciplined and clever. Curious, but not invasive, it behaves in a cordial manner with strangers; always self-confident, and not easily disturbed.

	Body	Head	Ears	Eyes	Nose	Chin	Legs and Feet	Tail	Coat	Varieties
F.I.F.E.	From small to medium, finely structured, short and low on its legs.	Well-proportioned with rounded cheeks and marked cheekbones.	Large, wide at the base and set high on the head.	Large, open, with an almond-shaped upper lid and a rounded lower lid. Color from gold to green.	Short with a slight indentation at the level of the eyes.	Well-developed but not overly pronounced.	Small and rounded.	Short, wide at the base and tapering toward a rounded tip.	Short, close-lying, fine, and silky. Clear markings on the abdomen against a golden sand background.	Ticking and pattern: black, blue, red, and lilac, with corresponding varieties of tortoiseshell.

COLORPOINT SHORTHAIR

The Colorpoint Shorthair is the result of breeding between Siamese and other shorthaired breeds, in particular the American Shorthair. These breedings were performed with the intent of enriching the color varieties and patterns in the Siamese style cat. Some cat associations have adopted the position that the amount of non-Siamese blood from these breedings is too large for the Colorpoint to be considered as a Siamese. This question is still unresolved, and the Colorpoint Shorthair

breed has been recognized only by the C.F.A.. In Europe, neither the F.I.F.e. nor the G.C.C.F. recognizes the Colorpoint Shorthair. According to C.F.A. standards, the Colorpoint must have a physical shape of the foreign type, with long, thin bones; the musculature must be strong. The head, wedge-shaped and pointed, characterized by very large ears and almond-shaped, deep, blue eyes. The coat, very close-lying to the body, is of the pointed type; the color tends to darken with age. The physical characteristics and behavioral traits, including unpredictability and extreme vivacity, are in large measure identical, at least along general lines, with those of the Siamese.

1, 2. Colorpoint Seal Lynx Point. The entire length of the tail shows clear tabby stripes. In this and in other varieties subtle shadings in color (absent in this example) are permitted on the flanks, chest, and stomach. The trunk, limbs, neck, and tail are extremely thin and tapered. No adipose tissue is desirable.

The line that divides the Colorpoint from the Siamese is based on color, pattern and a confusing maze of alleles. The Colorpoint Shorthair's colors are not the classic Siamese colors (seal, blue, chocolate, and lilac), and to create them, new alleles and alleles of alleles were added, or replaced, or mixed with the original Siamese genotype. Even so, the distribution of color on the coat, the general physical shape, and the behavioral characteristics of the Colorpoint Shorthair are very similar to those of the Siamese. As with the Siamese, the Colorpoint has the allele "c(s)" which is responsible for the shaded pigmentation of the coat; and similar to the Siamese, the Colorpoint Shorthair's coat is usually (but there are always exceptions!) solid non-agouti, and the pigment is diluted. In fact, in some varieties of Colorpoint Shorthair, the points, meaning the outer areas with more intense color, show the stripes as characteristic of the tabby and are termed Lynx Points; however, the allele responsible for this appears to be missing, or at least has not yet been proven to be present. In other varieties, the colors of the points contrast with the background color to create an overall effect that, on careful consideration, seems quite similar to the tortoiseshell pattern; and, in fact, it is a tortoiseshell for the expected alleles are there. All in all, a puzzle for patient geneticists, it can be stated that breeds derived from the Siamese are complex and genetically unpredictable.

3. Chocolate Tortie Lynx Point. The tabby stripes are clear not only on the tail but also on the limbs and head. The nose pad, pink outlined in cinnamon, is highly valued. The paw pads are cinnamon. The semicircular pink marking at the center of the ears is a characteristic of Lynx Point Colorpoint Shorthairs. The bones are elegant and refined, with hips that are never wider than the shoulders.

	Body	Head	Ears	Eyes	Nose	Chin	Legs and Feet	Tail	Coat	Varieties
C.F.A.	Medium size, tubular, long and svelte. Fine bones and firm muscles. Long, slim legs.	Long tapering wedge. Medium in size and in proportion to the body. Long, slender neck.	Strikingly large and pointed. Wide at the base, continuing the lines of the wedge.	Almond-shaped and of medium size. Color is a deep, vivid blue.	Long and straight without a break.	Medium in size.	Dainty, small, and oval.	Long, thin, tapering to a fine point.	Short, fine textured, glossy; lying close to the body.	Red-Cream Blue-Cream, Lilac-Cream point. Lynx point: seal, chocolate, blue, lilac, red, cream. Seal and Chocolate Tortie Point, and Tortie Lynx point: Seal, Chocolate, Blue-Cream, and Lilac-Cream.

CYMRIC (The Longhaired MANX)

The Cymric, identical to the Manx except for its coat, which is long rather than short, is a relatively recent development. Longhaired Manx have appeared from time to time, which is not surprising when one considers that Manx cats were allowed to breed at random in their native Isle of Man. However, it was in Canada during the 1960's that a pair of registered, pedigreed shorthaired Manx gave birth to several longhaired kittens. The kittens were healthy and excited the interest of Manx breeders; the kittens were later bred which quickly helped to establish the characteristics that mark the variation. The name, Cymric (pronounced Kimrik), is the Celtic word for "Welsh" and was given to these longhaired Manx. The reasoning behind this choice may appear to be fanciful but is based on the fact that the Isle of Man, origin of the Manx breed, is located midway between Ireland and Wales. The characteristics (which are those of the shorthaired Manx with the exception of the hair length) are already well-defined. Even so, the variety is not yet widespread and is essentially confined to North America. Today, the long hair division of the Manx (Cymric) has official recognition only from C.F.A., where it is exhibited as a Division of the Manx Breed.

1

1, 3. Red classic tabby variety. As with all Manx, the physical conformation is robust. The hind legs are longer than the forelegs, producing a typical rise in the line of the back; being very strong, the legs and musculature permit the longhaired Manx to reach great speed in sprints. Usually, its movements are fluid, tranquil, almost phlegmatic.

2, 4. Solid white variety with blue eyes. As in most white cats of other breeds, the eye color can also be copper, or odd-eyed: one copper and the other blue. Practically all solid colors are available and popular today.

2

Irrespective of its undercoat, the Longhaired Manx coat does not have the richness of that of a Persian; even so, it is very soft, pleasant to the touch, and shiny. It forms fewer tangles than that of the Persian and is easier to maintain.

The source of the Cymric's long fur is interesting from the genetic viewpoint. In the Cymric, as in other longhaired breeds, the length of the coat is a result of the presence of an allele, called "l" (representing long hair) that dictates the speed and amount of hair growth. It has been determined that the Manx did not inherit this gene through a breeding with a longhaired cat; the allele was produced in its genotype through a spontaneous mutation of the original 'L' gene. This same mutation had already occurred in the progenitor of all the other longhaired cats. Thus, the "L" allele has undergone the same fate at least twice. these two distinct mutations, independent of each other, modified hair length in the same way by transforming the same allele.

3

5

4

5. Double Champion Loss Tails Cream Spot. Not all Manx are born without a tail; it is not uncommon to find some kittens may have at least a stump or even a complete tail.

Naturally, the most highly valued specimens and, in C.F.A., the only ones admitted in championship shows, are those completely lacking a tail.

	Body	Head	Ears	Eyes	Nose	Chin	Legs and Feet	Tail	Coat	Varieties
C.F.A.	Strong bone structure. Muscular, heavy bone, compact, and well-balanced. Broad chest and slightly rounded back. Males are larger than females. Hind legs longer than front.	Medium in length, round with jowls. Short, thick neck. Well-developed muzzle, slightly longer than wide. Definite whisker break.	Medium size, wide at the base, with rounded tips.	Large, round, and full. All colors are permitted.	Gentle dip from forehead to nose.	Strong.	Heavily boned and muscular; solid paws.	Non-existent in the perfect specimen.	Shorthair: Double, short and dense. Longhair: Silky texture with somewhat hard guard hair, not cottony nor even in length.	All colors and patterns except those showing hybridization with the Himalayan pattern. (See Manx)

EGYPTIAN MAU

In Egyptian the name Mau, an imitation of a cat's meow, sensibly enough means "cat." The Mau is, therefore, truly an Egyptian cat and even possibly the same cat that appears in murals dating back as early as 3000 B. C. It seems probable that the Mau has descended from the cats worshipped by the pharaohs as incarnations of the goddess Bast. Examination of the mummified remains of Egyptian cats has, at least in some cases, suggested cats with more of an affinity to the Mau than to the Abyssinian. Even so, as a separate breed recognized by international cat associations, the Mau came into existence in Italy in 1953. In that year, a noblewoman returned from a trip to Egypt with an adult female, which was then bred to a male Mau which had been brought to Italy through the assistance of the Syrian ambassador. In 1956 the same noblewoman brought the first examples, obtained by crosses of the original mother and father with their progeny, to the United States. There, a breeding program was begun. It was designed to protect and establish the physical characteristics of the Mau, a cat which, more than any other breed, recalls those cats in tomb paintings of ancient Egypt with their slender body shape plus the characteristic spotted coat. The C.F.A. gave official recognition to the Mau in 1958; however, it was not until 1992 that F.I.Fe. gave the breed championship recognition.

1. *Grand Champion Maipet's Shanadu of Kaizie. The trunk is somewhat elongated, the chest broad, the head a slightly rounded wedge shape without flat planes. The hind limbs are proportionately longer than the front giving the appearance of being on tiptoe when standing upright.*

2. *Grand Champion Bacamamdit's Ricohet of Pazlo. Sexual dimorphism is very slight in the Mau; the muscle masses are comparable; however, males do tend to be slightly larger than females.*

The most obvious characteristic of the Egyptian Mau is its spotted tabby coat. In the Mau breed, the ringed tail and striped paws typical of the classic or blotched tabby are accompanied by distinct spots which can be large or small, round, oblong, or irregular-shaped and which are distributed in a random pattern over the body. The spotted coat is not rare among wild cats and also occurs in other domestic cat breeds–the Ocicat and European Shorthair are examples. Diligent and constant work on the part of breeders is necessary in order to maintain this characteristic. The origins of the spotted pattern are not clear today. The Mau may possess in its genotype one or more particular gene responsible for the spotting that are absent in other breeds. A more probable theory holds that the spotted coat is determined by a specific variant of the gene that codifies the classic tabby pattern. This second hypothesis is suggested by the traces of the tabby pattern evident on the head, paws, and tail of the Mau. The Mau is recognized in three color varieties: Silver-charcoal colored markings against a white to pale silver undercoat, Bronze, dark brown-black markings against a warm coppery brown undercoat, and Smoke-jet black markings against a black smoke coat with a white to pale silvery undercoat.

3. International Grand Champion, U.S.A. Champion, and International European Champion Pazlo's Friend of Mr. Cairo, 2 year old male. Three thin, dark stripes, which ideally break into elongated spots, run in a continuous pattern along the spinal column and at its sides. This pattern is characteristic of the classic tabby in which these spinal stripes are wider. The coat's silvery color is derived from black with the introduction of a gene that prevents the deposition of yellow pigment in agouti areas.

	Body	Head	Ears	Eyes	Nose	Chin	Legs and Feet	Tail	Coat	Varieties
C.F.A.	Medium-long and muscular; elegant. A characteristic loose skin flap extends from flank to hind leg at knee.	A slightly rounded wedge without flat planes, medium length.	Medium to large, alert and moderately pointed, continuing the planes of the head; slightly flared with ample width between. May be tufted.	Large and alert, almond-shaped with a slight slant towards the ears. "Gooseberry green" color in adults.	Profile shows a gentle contour with a slight rise from bridge to forehead, even in width when viewed from the front.	Firm.	Legs in proportion to the body. Hind are slighter longer. Small, dainty, slightly oval feet.	Medium-long, thick at base, with slight tapering.	Hair is medium in length with a lustrous sheen. The smoke has silky, fine textured hair, other colors dense and resilient in texture accommodating two or more bands of ticking.	Silver; Bronze; Smoke.

Favored by its overall medium-long and graceful physical shape, the Mau is agile, light, quick, and capable of lightning reflexes. Very lively, and animated by inexhaustible curiosity, it loves movement; a good jumper and great climber, it will conquer one after another of all the available "peaks" in a home (cupboard, dresser, bookshelf, and so on) and will remain (briefly) curled up to enjoy the panoramic view while mentally planning its next assault. That fact is that the Mau likes to keep what is happening around it under control, and, as with any good tactician, it knows that elevated positions are best-suited to this end. It adapts well to life in an apartment provided it is given a small space all its own for its sole use. The vivacity of the Mau begins with the first days of life; Mau kittens may begin to open their eyes at three days, and by the tenth day they are usually toddling about.

4. *Reckmira de Joha, silver female of 2 years, and her kittens of 15 days. By this age the kittens are already capable of moving around alone with alternate long periods of sleep with their first explorations.*

5. *Grand Champion Bacamamdit's Ricochet of Pazlo*

6. *Left, Rishra de Joha, 1 month old silver female; right, Ramses de Joha, bronze male of the same age. The careful breeding of the Mau, both in the past and today, has been directed not only at physical characteristics, but also at character. Intelligent, calm, and gentle, the Mau quickly becomes attached to its owner to whom it shows a strong attachment.*

EUROPEAN SHORTHAIR

The origins of the European Shorthair go back to a common domestic, or, more often, wild, cat that was widespread throughout Europe for many centuries. It was at the end of the last century that this domestic cat was given specific breed status, as well as, an accompanying program of selective breeding designed to produce specific physical and behavioral characteristics. At about the same time, another indigenous cat was elevated to the breed status, the British Shorthair, which some maintain is the same cat as the European. This logic can also be applied to the American Shorthair which many consider to be the same cat as the European. The maintenance of standards for the European has been complicated by the enormous diffusion of the breed and the uncontrolled matings that have resulted. The constant genetic mixing to which the European has been exposed is beneficial in that it naturally selects against problems that can result from crosses among blood relations. This also increases the phenotypic variations (that is, the physical and behavioral characteristics) so much that they come into conflict with the work of breeders trying to establish the most desirable qualities as defined by the written standard which describes the perfect example of this lovely breed.

1. International Grand Champion Askungens Gigant, 2 year old blue classic (blotched) tabby male.

2. Grand Champion Patata, 2 year old tortoiseshell female.

3. International Champion Passepartout, 18 month old black male. Of medium-large size, the European Shorthair has a physical form of the robust type. The compact form, solid bone structure, medium length legs, strong neck, and the round head go together to form a well-proportioned whole. Breeders seek to eliminate extreme physical characteristics without canceling any of the natural feline elegance.

From the behavioral point of view, the European Shorthair displays two fundamental characteristics: the first is an adaptability that permits it to find the best strategies for exploiting, in the most advantageous ways, any environment or situation in which it happens to find itself; the second is the great variety among individual members of the breed due to the natural selection from accidental pairings. Thus, it is difficult to predict the eventual personality of any individual. The frequency of uncontrolled matings between unrelated subjects has assured, however, good health, a strong constitution, and a quick intelligence. The European is a cat that can face any situation. If it is locked outdoors, it will succeed in finding a warm, protected refuge; if an overworked owner forgets to set out its food, it will manage to dine on a rich menu based on mice and other small animals; if a hurried owner shuts it in the broom closet, it will quite easily find a way out, either squeezing out of the window or leaving properly through the door by opening the handle. Even wounds, not so improbable in an animal that enjoys great freedom (most of all in males during the mating season), should not be the cause of undue alarm; thanks to its efficient immune system and assiduous and patient cleaning habits, wounds heal quickly.

4. *Champion Obelix Pink Fuggy, 3 year old cream male.*

5. *Gino, 10 month old blue male.*

6. *International Grand Champion Bogelund's Celestin 2 year old red classic (blotched) tabby* *male. The compactness of the physical structure is emphasized by the strong, well-developed muscles. It's important to guarantee a European Shorthair the opportunity of moving about, exploring, hunting, or playing. The breed's natural disposition toward physical activity should* *be met by providing opportunities for activity. In truth, the European is a healthy, strong, and robust animal full of energy that must be used to assure the maintenance of good, balanced health— not only physical but mental.*

There are a great many varieties of the European Shorthair based on the color and pattern of the coat, and some are particularly interesting. There is, for example, the solid white European, which is not an albino, for it does not lack pigment. The deposition of pigment in its hair (but not its irises!) is blocked by the action of a certain, well-identified gene. White cats can be born with some trace of color on the head, but this is usually lost before reaching sexual maturity. The eyes can be blue, yellow, orange, green, or even one blue and one of another color—the so-called odd-eyed cats. Unfortunately, white cats with two blue eyes are often deaf; those with a single blue eye are often deaf in the ear on the same side. At this point, even readers with the least sense of genetics will conclude that a tie exists between the white color of the coat, the blue iris, and deafness. In fact, these characteristics are all controlled by the same gene.

One variety of the European is called albino, even if it really is not albino. Its irises, in fact, are not pink, as they would be due to the total absence of pigment in a true albino, but are instead light blue. There is some pigment, therefore, even though very little. The genetic configuration of the European albino is still being debated. Awaiting a decision on this matter, this variety is not permitted in shows.

found in the domestic and semi-domestic populations from which the European began.

8. Askungens Gigant. In the European, the combination of different patterns and colors has been favored by the constant genetic roulette resulting from casual pairings. Without doubt, the classic (blotched) tabby pattern is one of the oldest, best known, and widespread; its popularity shows no sign of diminishing. In the European, as in other breeds, the mackerel tabby and spotted tabby are less frequent.

7

8

7. Quarto di Luna di Gens Rubra, 9 month old cream classic (blotched) tabby female. The coat of the European is very thick, dense, and close-lying to the body. Although short, because of the complete development of each of the three layers of hair (woolly | *undercoat, awn hairs, and guard hairs), it guarantees excellent protection from cold and heat. As for the colors and patterns the breed can exhibit, breeders have limited themselves to trying to put into order the extraordinary variety of coloration spontaneously*

	Body	Eyes	Head	Ears	Nose	Chin	Legs and feet	Tail	Coat	Varieties
F.I.F.E.	From medium to large, robust and muscular, but not stocky.	Round, well-distanced, open, located slightly obliquely. Color: green, yellow, orange, blue, or odd-eyed (in cats with white coats).	Face is longer than wide. Well-developed cheeks. Forehead and cranium are rounded. Medium neck.	Of medium size, slightly rounded, located well apart, with tufts.	Straight, medium in length.	Strong.	Strong, solid legs of medium length. Rounded feet.	Medium length, thick at the base with a rounded tip.	Short, thick, compact, and shiny.	Solid and Tortoiseshell in Smoke, Tabby, and Silver Tabby: classic (blotched), mackerel (tiger), and spotted); BiColor, Harlequin, White.

9. Salome, left, and Sacripante di Maga Luci, 50 day old cream classic (blotched) tabby kittens. Reproduction presents no problems for the European Shorthair. Litters are large; the mothers are alert and efficient, and the kittens lively and curious with quick reflexes naturally given to much play.

10. International Grand Champion Odette Sugar Baby 3 year old patched mackerel tabby female. The imposition of the tabby design over the red-and-black tortoiseshell pattern is not rare. The stripes are diluted and broken up, and the pattern is less distinct.

11. Sibilla di Maga Luci, 50 day old patched mackerel tabby female kitten.

The tortoiseshell variety, affectionately known as the tortie, includes only females; this could not be otherwise. The tortie coat has an irregular arrangement of large black, orange, or cream spots, preferably with sharp outlines. This coat color variation depends on the contemporaneous presence and simultaneous activity of a certain gene and its allele. Nothing remarkable up to this point; in fact, every unit of genetic transmission is present in the genotype in double pairs, and the two pairs can be either identical ("homozygous") or replaced by different forms of the same gene ("heterozygous").

The complications begin when one learns that the genetic unit in question is located on one of the sexual chromosomes. It may help to imagine the genetic material as being composed of a series of ladders, which we call chromosomes, on each of which are orderly stacks of the instructions for the construction of an individual. The sexual chromosomes are those ladders that contain, together with others, the instructions for the determination of sex. They are of two types, X and Y. Males possess one X chromosome and one Y; females two X chromosomes (and no Y chromosome). Now, the genetic unit in question is located on the X chromosome. Males, possessing a single X chromosome, will have available a single version of the gene for the tortie coat. As such, the male can never be a tortie. Females, on the other hand, having two X chromosomes, can have both the necessary versions: the original gene on one of the X chromosomes, and its allele on the other. And thus they can be torties. On occasion, a tortie male is produced; however, these 'sports' are most generally sterile.

12, 13. Quirinus, adult brown classic (blotched) tabby male. The European Shorthair greatly resembles the British Shorthair in terms of its physical appearance, the quality of its coat, its character, the available varieties, and even its origins. Indeed, the F.I.Fe. standards for a great number of varieties give identical descriptions for the British and the European. Not surprisingly, distinguishing specimens from the two breeds can sometimes be anything but easy. In some cases (but only some!) the fur of the European is more coarse or stiff and almost bristly, while that of the British is always crisp but soft. The cheeks of the European are less fully rounded than those of the British; the tail is generally a little longer; and, finally, the character is more variable. In the final analysis, what most differentiates the European from the British Shorthair is that the latter displays greater homogeneity of phenotypic characteristics, both physical and behavioral. Without doubt, even today the European is less subject than its English colleague to the rigors of selection guided by breeders.

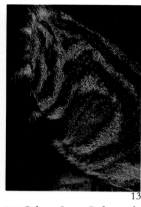

14. Odette Sugar Baby with 50 day old kittens, a patched tabby (left) and a cream. One reason breeding programs are applied less rigorously to the European than to the British and American Shorthairs is that the noble versions of the common street cat enjoy greater esteem in the Anglo-Saxon world while hardly awakening interest among the European public. Things are quite different among professionals, however, and European Shorthairs invariably meet with great approval at European shows and competitions. Perhaps the breed's good qualities should be advertised more effectively, or perhaps what is needed is a new taste for simplicity—which is so often full of deeper meaning.

Spotted tabby coats can be found in the European Shorthair constituting a distinct variety apart from the others. The general configuration of the coat is the same as for the Mau: spots arranged on the back and flanks, with stripes on the mask, between the ears, on the paws, and on the tail. Unlike the Mau, however, in the European the size, density, and distribution of the spots, as well as the frequency, width, and distribution of the stripes, can vary greatly even from individual to individual. Nothing rules out the possibility that careful breeding may create greater regularity.

15

16

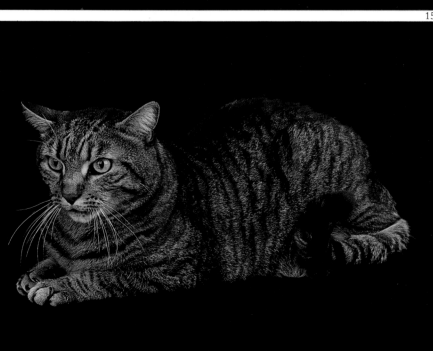

17

15. European Prize Vickie, brown mackerel tabby adult male. The head of the European is strong but well-proportioned to the rest of the body; nearly oval in shape, it has pronounced cheek bones in proportion to the length of the muzzle. The forehead and cranium are rounded, and the cheeks are well-developed, most of all in males. The nose is short, straight, and of medium length; the chin is solid, definite, not too strong or prominent. The eyes are large, round, and slightly oval, set well apart, with a wide range of colors.

16. Bogelund's Iris, 7 month old classic patched tabby female.

17. Vickie. As with its British and American counterparts, the European Shorthair is particularly prized for its lively intelligence. Like all other phenotypic characteristics, its intelligence is the result of natural selection and has evolved over the course of centuries, from wild cats to semi-domestic cats or strays, developing gifts of intuition, quick understanding of situations, and inventiveness in finding solutions to problems (in a sense, a "street smart cat"). Today, the European is a cat with a strong personality, highly independent, autonomous in the direction of its own existence, in its decisions and affections. A European will not settle for being an ornament, toy, or pet constantly available to the wishes and caprices of its owner. The European has its own life and intends to live it without interference. This does not mean that it is not affectionate, that it does not enjoy and return caresses, that it does not want and seek out the nearness of humans—just the opposite is true. The owner who shows respect for his European and treats it in a balanced and affectionate manner will find a faithful lifelong companion.

18. Ofiura, left, and Ofelia del Mare, 4 year old calico females.

19. Calico kittens. The European is thought to be a direct descendent of *Felis libyca*, the African wild cat, still living although threatened with extinction, which is presumed to have been (but this is not positively proven) the progenitor of all domestic cats. The first testimony of the existence of domestic cats comes from Egyptian tomb art; from Egypt, the domestic cat, by then the distinct species *F. catus*, spread to Greece and then the Roman Empire and throughout Europe. The theory that the domestic cat is derived from *F. libyca*, and not, for example, from the European wild cat *F. silvestris* is based on comparative anatomical-osteological studies, as well as the consideration that the process of domestication in all likelihood began in a physical environment (steppes, plains) colonized by *F. libyca*, but not by its cousin *silvestris*.

18

BiColor cats are perhaps the most widespread. One of the two colors is always white, while the other can be black, or black diluted with blue, or chocolate. One might be led to think that the white zones are controlled by the same gene responsible for the depigmentation in solid white cats. But no. This is due to a completely different gene, which acts not like the first, which impedes the deposition of pigment, but in a far more drastic way by impeding the synthesis of pigment.

The size of the white areas can vary in all forms ranging from the two extremes of a coat totally without white and a coat that is totally white. In the latter case, the specimen is indistinguishable from a solid white cat, but belongs to the bicolor variety. Such is the power of genes.

19

EXOTIC

The Exotic is a new breed having been created in the United States during the 1960's by interbreeding longhaired Persians with American Shorthairs, along with a small added dose of Burmese. The genetic plan was designed to create a cat with the physical structure of the Persian (which until then had no equivalent among shorthaired cats), but having a short coat or at least one of intermediate length. The results were very satisfying; the Exotic joins an unquestionably robust body with a highly original coat, not truly short nor semi-long either, very soft and of excellent quality. To maintain the desired characteristics, the breeding programs involve frequent breedings with Persians. The first official recognition was given in 1966; today, the breed is recognized by all the major international cat associations. Already widespread in the United States, the Exotic is gradually conquering Europe, where it is becoming more and more familiar to the public.

1. *Grand Champion and National Winner Jovan Ypes Stripes, 3 year old red tabby female. Rather than lying close, the fur stands out from the body.*

2. *Mashad Shadow Light, 4 month old classic patched tabby female. The Exotic is now available in all the colors and patterns of the Persian.*

3. *Grand Champion Jovan Charlie Brown, brown classic tabby. The head and "full-relief" muzzle, almost perfectly round, constitute one of the distinctive characteristics of the breed. In reality, the compact, round head and snub-nose are also typical of the Persian; however, the shorthair of the Exotic serves to emphasize these characteristics.*

4. *Jaffna Smemoranda, 3 month old classic patched tabby female.*

5. *Jaffna Shoking Johnny, 3 month old red tabby male. The frequent breedings with Persians, necessary to maintain the qualities of the coat and type, occasionally lead to the birth of a longhaired Exotic kitten.*

	Body	Head	Ears	Eyes	Nose	Chin	Legs and feet	Tail	Coat	Varieties
C.F.A.	Large or medium, of cobby type, low on the legs, broad and deep through the chest. Equally massive across shoulders and rump, short, well rounded middle piece, level back.	Round and massive with great breadth of skull, round face, short neck.	Small, round tipped, set far apart and low on the head.	Brilliant in color, large, round and full; set level and far apart giving a sweet expression.	Short, snub and broad, with "break" centered between the eyes.	Full, well-developed, and firmly rounded, reflecting proper bite.	Legs are short, thick, strong; forelegs straight; paws large, round and firm.	Short, but in proportion to body length; carried straight, at an angle lower than the back.	Medium length, dense, plush, full of life; stands out from body due to thick undercoat.	All colors and patterns of the Persian.

6

Some of the Exotic's behavioral traits resemble those of the Persian. As with the Persian, it loves home life, comfort, the warmth of a living room, and long naps on the couch. It senses no need for a terrace, much less a garden. It feels perfectly at ease within the walls of a home and, helped by its own gentleness, which extends to a form of tolerance, succeeds in forming good relationships with all those around it. Affectionate and sweet, it is easily won over by a friendly pat, compliment, or a simple caress. It avoids complications and change, but when necessary can confront them philosophically. It is a good observer with a pensive character. Astonishingly, it is a good hunter and will chase toys with great verve.

7

8

9

10

6. *Jaffna Se Same Chip Brown.*

7. *Jaffna Smemoranda, left, and Jovan Charlie Brown, right.*

8. *Mashad Shadow Light.*

9. *Mashad Stron Minder, 4 month old brown classic tabby male.*

10. *Champion Rigoletto, 18 month old cream classic tabby male .*

11. *Blue classic (blotched) tabby. There are several reasons for the growing popularity of the Exotic. On the practical side, the short coat requires less attention and care than a long coat; a daily brushing and occasional bath are more than enough. The Exotic is thus a 'tailored' Persian suitable for people with little time on their hands. Beyond the beauty of its physical structure and unique coat, the Exotic is healthy and strong. The Exotic's trump card, however, is its character, to which breeders have dedicated great attention. Well-balanced, the Exotic is generally constant and predictable. Polite, gentle, and discreet, the Exotic is, at the same time, lively and full of spirit. An innate and infallible sense of restraint permits the Exotic to adapt well to any acceptable environment.*

12. *Swift Wind Bacardi of Frangelica, (blue cream and white) dilute calico.*

11

12

HAVANA BROWN

A Havana Brown accidentally occurred in England in 1952 when a black "shorthair" Persian had a brief fling with a Chocolate Point Siamese. When the outraged owners protested, the female merely smiled to herself because she knew her fleeting affair would lead to the birth of a single kitten, but an extraordinary one–a female. When the owners saw her, they were amazed. Slightly embarrassed, they withdrew their protests and excused themselves, and when the female became an adult they rushed to find another Chocolate Siamese to mate with her. The story then takes on the tones of a mystery, with the rest of the formula a secret. There was the suspected participation of a Russian Blue, other crosses were made in secret, closed doors, and "no comment" when asked. The ultimate result of all this effort was a medium-sized, elegant shorthaired Havana Brown named for its color which resembles the famous Havana cigar. This name, however, led to confusion about the breed's country of origin; a few years later the English tried to change the cat's breed name to Chestnut Brown. This effort failed since the breed was already well-established and identified as the Havana Brown. Thus, the Havana is still the Havana, and the English are resigned to having it mistaken as a breed that originated in Cuba. The breed has been officially

1, 2. Nike Nova Karitka, 11 month old female. The distinctive characteristics of the Havana are the shape of the muzzle and ears, the intelligent, lively face, and the color of its coat. The head must be longer than wide with a distinct muzzle. The muzzle appears almost square with a well-developed chin. The ears are large, round tipped, and wide-set. Males are larger than females.

recognized by the C.F.A. and G.C.C.F., but not the F.I.Fe. In the United States, other Havana bloodlines were developed following the same genetic principles including using Chocolate Point Siamese and Russian Blues as a starting point.

The Havana Brown is characterized by its solid, non-agouti coat of rich, warm brown. Unlike the blue of the Chartreux, for example, the brown of the Havana is not the result of a dilution of black. Rather, it is derived from a densely and uniformly distributed pigment that is chocolate in color rather than black. A single allele, known as 'b' (for brown) is responsible for the substitution of the original pigment with the brown color. (A variant of this has recently appeared on the scene that causes a lighter color with shadings in a tabby design that are visible only under good light.)

Spirited, but never impetuous, elegant and graceful in its movements, the Havana is a great player. Capable of amusing itself alone with any object that attracts its attention, it is also amenable to playing with its owner. Often a clown, the Havana has been known to play games such as 'Hide and Seek', jumping out from behind a wall or door to see the surprise this trick produces with its owner. And, for the Havana there is only one owner, a single person to whom the cat remains faithful as a discreet but constant companion, without ever abandoning itself to great shows of affection. From this point of view, the Havana is moderate and requests moderation in return. Although lively and having a strong physical build that would favor life outdoors, the Havana is adaptable to apartment life. It becomes fond of home and although intrigued by change, prefers a regular schedule.

3. Nike Nova Karitka. The eyes, always attentive, must be of any vivid and level shade of green, the deeper the color, the better. The coat is short to medium in length, smooth and lustrous.

	Body	Head	Ears	Eyes	Nose	Chin	Legs and feet	Tail	Coat	Varieties
C.F.A.	Torso is medium length, firm and muscular. Males are larger than females.	Longer than wide, viewed from above with a pronounced break behind both whisker pads.	Large, round tipped, little hair inside or outside.	Medium size, oval-shaped aperture, wide-set, brilliant, and open. Vivid green.	Vertically aligned with the chin; distinct stop at the eyes.	Well-developed and more square than round, heightening the illusion of a square muzzle.	Stands relatively high on straight legs. Females have slim, dainty legs. Oval paws.	Medium length, slender, tapering at end, but neither "whip-like" nor blunt.	Short to medium in length, smooth, lustrous; a rich, even shade of warm brown.	Varieties: Brown with color tending to red-brown (mahogany).

JAPANESE BOBTAIL

The Japanese Bobtail is an ancient breed indigenous to Japan, its country of origin where it is greatly loved. Well-represented in pictorial screens and classical wood block prints including those of Hiroshige. This breed is often referred to in both classical and contemporary literature. The tri-colored Bobtail, known as the Mi-ke, (white with black and red spots) is believed to bring good luck to any home in which it resides. In modern Japan, good luck statuettes are made that show the cat seated with one paw raised in a polite salute (the Maneki Neko). These statuettes are often placed in the windows or prominently displayed on the premises of businesses in order to bring patrons and ensure success. Members of religious orders have often contributed to the protection and maintenance of feline breeds, as have military men who have played an important role in spreading cat breeds from their country of origin throughout the rest of the world. It was at the end of World War II that the Bobtail was brought to the United States by returning American soldiers. The Bobtail did not receive a uniformly warm reception in the West; some people criticized its "bobbed" tail; others, however, were intrigued and fascinated. They worked with the breed and imported others to assure that the breed was successful with an adequate gene pool from which to draw.

1. *Jari Akai, 20 month old white and red bicolor male .*

2. *Kemage Sokuza Ni of Aerostar, black and white bicolor. The coat of the Bobtail originally had a vast range of colors and patterns. However, the examples with no more than three colors distributed in large solid-colored marks were the most highly prized by the Japanese.*

As its name indicates, the Bobtail is a partially tailed cat. Unlike the Manx, the cat from the Isle of Man which can be completely tail-less, the Bobtail has a definite tail. The tail, however, should consist of one or more curves, angles or kinks or any combination thereof; the furthest extension of the tail from the body should be no longer than three inches. The tail may be flexible or rigid and should be of a size and shape that harmonizes with the rest of the cat. It is usually curved in shape, may have a slight straight section next to the rump before the beginning to curl (a delayed bobtail), and is covered with fur thereby producing the appearance of a pom-pom or bunny tail. The genetic reason for this characteristic, a malformation, is not known. Any relationship to Manx tail-lessness has been genetically ruled out. However, kittens with bobbed tails, such as those of the Japanese Bobtail, are sometimes born to non pedigree domestic cats; therefore, the characteristic is probably the result of a relatively fre-

3. Grand Champion Mari Cho's Hoseki. The coat of the Longhair Bobtail is medium long to long without noticeable undercoat. It requires minimal attention, a brushing no more than once a week in part because shedding is almost nonexistent. Crossing of a bobtail with a long-tailed cat produces kittens with long tails which carry the bobtail gene; however, breeding two Bobtails together results in Bobtail kittens. Both the female and the male are excellent parents; they are also very sociable with other cats often preferring to live in large groups even when the available space is limited.

quent mutation with effects limited to the tail. This characteristic is well established in the Bobtail so that breeders have no difficulty maintaining it.

The Bobtail has an excellent character and easily adapts to apartment life as well as to the great outdoors. Vivacious, curious, and active, it also loves the comforts of home and long periods of relaxation. Like many Oriental cats, it has a strong personality and likes to make decisions on its own. It is an intelligent, interactive, and attentive animal. A Bobtail will be at least moderately affectionate with everyone in the family. They do not require much care. The three golden rules for creating a good relationship with a Bobtail are:

1) Respect its individuality;

2) Give it attention, show interest, talk to it a little;

3) Prepare a tasty treat containing some fish for it from time to time. (After all, this is a cat from Japan; it should surprise no one that fish is often its favorite food).

3

	Body	Head	Ears	Eyes	Nose	Chin	Legs and feet	Tail	Coat	Varieties
C.F.A.	Medium in size; torso is long, lean and elegant, but not tubular. Muscular and harmoniously proportioned (well-balanced).	Forms a nearly perfect equilateral triangle with gentle curving lines and high cheekbones.	Large, upright and expressive, wide set but at right angles to the head; not flared.	Large, oval rather than round, wide open, alert. Color should harmonize with the coat.	Long, well-defined by parallel lines from tip to brow with a gentle dip at eye level or below.	Fairly broad and rounding into the whisker break.	Legs in proportion and long, slender and high but not dainty or fragile. The hind legs are noticeably longer than the forelegs. Oval paws.	Unique to the breed, curved and harmonizing with the cat.	Shorthair: Medium length, soft, and silky, without a noticeable undercoat. Longhair: Medium-long to long; soft and silky, without a noticeable undercoat. Frontal ruff desirable.	Tricolors (black, red, and white). BiColor; Solids, Dilutes; tabby, PartiColor, OJBC.

JAVANESE

The Javanese was recently created in the United States; therefore, the name given the breed has nothing to do with its geographical origin. One of the foundation cats of today's Javanese was a kitten born from the cross of a Balinese with a Colorpoint Shorthair that had all the characteristics of the Siamese, except for coat length and color. As of this writing, the breed has been officially recognized by the C.F.A. and F.I.Fe. but not the G.C.C.F. According to C.F.A. standards, the Javanese differs from the Balinese only in the color of its coat, and eye color is accepted only in deep vivid blue. However, according to F.I.Fe. standards, the Javanese shares the principal phenotypic characteristics of the Oriental Shorthair, including green eyes, uniform coloring of the coat, and differs in the length of its fur, which is long rather than short. Both associations recognize a large number of varieties based on coat color and pattern.

1. Grand Premier Zinzani Fourth Horseman, blue lynx point, 8 months old. The Javanese is characterized by an overall physical appearance that is heavier and more muscular than that of its relative the Siamese, but no less graceful and elegant. The limbs are long and relatively thin, but at the same time muscular; the hind legs are slightly longer than the fore, favoring great speed in spurts. All in all, the body suggests agility more than strength. The Javanese displays three principal distinctive characteristics: the long coat, as in the Balinese; the pointed-type coloration, as in the Balinese or Siamese; and the color of the eyes, a splendid green and intense, as in the Oriental Shorthair.

2. Grand Champion Hunnapurr Diamond Jim of Balique

3. *Grand Premier Zinzani Fourth Horseman. The Javanese adapts perfectly to life in an apartment, but if given the chance will make full use of a terrace or garden as a hunting ground and gymnasium to keep fit. Very lively, the Javanese loves to show off, whether in the open or not, in spectacular performances of acrobatic skills. It does so without becoming invasive or endangering precious knickknacks. This cat requires a small personal space, which does not always or necessarily coincide with the basket specially set aside for its naps. Its owner must willingly respect the site chosen by the cat.*

4. *Seal-Tortie lynx point. The Javanese shares not only some physical characteristics with the* Balinese, *but also various behavioral traits. In particular, as in the Balinese, the maternal behavior of the Javanese is well-developed: the mothers are attentive, assiduous, and gentle. In the first days after giving birth they do not like to see their kittens picked up and taken away from the basket, even for a moment. When the kittens later begin to stand and take off on their first explorations of the vast world around them, the mother never lets them completely out of her sight. This does not indicate excessive apprehension on the part of the mother, who will actually interfere only in the case of true need. The Javanese is a polite and pleasant pet: independent to the right degree, it is sociable and affectionate, without ever losing its reserved dignity.*

	Body	Head	Ears	Eyes	Nose	Chin	Legs and feet	Tail	Coat	Varieties
C.F.A.	Long-lined and elegant. Medium size, shoulders no wider than the hips. Long, slender neck.	Medium size, well-proportioned; can be inscribed in a triangle.	Large, pointed, wider at the base.	Medium size, neither sunken nor protruding. Almond shaped and slightly slanted. Color: vivid, luminous green.	Long and straight, without stop.	Medium size with a narrow muzzle.	Long, thin paws; small, oval feet.	Very long and thin, ends in a point.	Long and fine, silky, without woolly undercoat. Medium length; longer on the neck, shoulders, and tail. Uniform color.	Solid colors; Tortoiseshell in solid colors; Silver; Golden; Smoke, Tabby, Silver Tabby in colors: solids and tortoiseshell.

KORAT

The Korat is an ancient breed of a shorthaired cat named after a former province of Thailand where the breed is believed to have originated. Pictures of this ancient breed are found, together with those of Siamese and Burmese, in a poetic text, the Smud Khoi, illustrated early in the 14th century. Some people even claim that the Korat is the progenitor of the Siamese, but, as of now, this theory is unconfirmed. Today, as in the past, this cat is considered a symbol of

prosperity in Thailand and is revered as a lucky charm often given to both newlyweds and important people. There seems to be a widespread tendency in the Far East to raise cats to the rank of benign, minor divinities: there are, as examples, the Japanese Bobtail, also considered a good luck charm; the Sacred Cat of Burma, once sacred in Burmese temples; and the Siamese, always welcome in palaces and places of worship. The Korat first appeared in Europe around the end of the last century. It was presented at cat shows in London awakening curiosity and mild interest. In 1959 a pair was brought to the United States where, in 1965, the breed was first given official recognition. The F.I.Fe. recognized the breed in 1972.

1, 2. Si-sawat, the name of the Korat in the Thai language, can be roughly translated as "gray-green" or "gray-silver." In fact, the coat of the Korat is a uniform blue-silver, tipped with silver. Notwithstanding its particular silvery shading, this color alone would not be enough to distinguish the Korat from the other blue breeds or varieties such as the Chartreux or the British Shorthair. A part of that which sets the Korat apart is the silver halo effect produced by the coat's silver tipping; completely lacking an undercoat, the coat is short in length, close-lying to the body, glossy and fine, and tends to 'break' over the spine as the cat moves. Much more obvious to the casual observer is this breed's unmistakable heart-shaped head, and the large, luminous, round, well-spaced eyes. A little oversized for the cat's face, and very luminous and ever-so singular and distinctive. Finally, there is the tail, which gently tapers to a rounded tip.

Characteristics of the Korat include the beautiful silver blue coat, originally derived from black following dilution, and the large, luminous, well-rounded, green eyes. But perhaps even more singular and worthy of note are its personality and character. A tranquil animal, the Korat prefers a serene environment. Excessive activity, noise, and the coming and going of strangers are not for this cat. It is a cat for an apartment and becomes devoted to its home. In fact, it seems forever intent on studying and evaluating its surroundings and events–or perhaps those things which may soon occur. Although very much a house cat, it is not a cat given to easy naps and certainly cannot be accused of laziness. Ever vigilant and attentive, it closely follows the course of family life, however humdrum. Delicately affectionate and dedicated to its owners, the Korat becomes unexpectedly aroused when faced with unknown cats. It will not permit any invasion of its territory; the home is his or hers, and the cat (or dog) that incautiously or accidentally invades that territory may be in danger. But it is sweet with its owner with whom it shares each moment of the day and to whom it remains faithful for life.

3

4

5

3, 4, 5. The Korat requires little grooming other than being given a warm, clean place of its own. The diet should include a high protein intake balanced with other feline nutritional requirements; care must be taken to avoid dampness and chilling to which most breeds are somewhat susceptible. Appropriate inoculations and vaccinations are a must!

	Body	Head	Ears	Eyes	Nose	Chin	Legs and Feet	Tail	Coat	Varieties
C.F.A.	Semi-cobby, neither compact nor svelte; muscular with a feeling of hard-coiled spring power. Back carried in a curve.	Heart-shaped when viewed from the front or looking down over the back of the head.	Large, with rounded tip, a large flare at the base, and set high on the head.	Large, round, and luminous. Particularly prominent and over-sized for the face. Green, amber caste acceptable.	Slight stop between forehead and nose which has a lion-like downward curve just above the leather.	Medium size.	Legs are well proportioned to the body; oval paws.	Medium length; heavier at the base, tapering to a rounded tip.	Single, short in length, glossy, fine and close lying.	Only silver-blue.

MAINE COON

The origin of the Maine Coon Cat is uncertain. The breed's name, of course, suggests its American roots, and the breed is said to be derived from a cross between an American domestic cat, not yet recognized as a distinct breed at that time, and an Angora. (Popular folk tradition held that the breed was descended from a breeding between a cat and a raccoon, a genetically impossible proposition.) The addition of Persian blood can be excluded since the Maine Coon Cat was already an established breed long before the arrival of any Persians, which was around the beginning of this century. The arrival of the "Persian era," however, marked a change in the history of the Maine Coon; up until that time, it was admired at shows and was fairly widespread. Then, over the span of just a few years, the Maine Coon was forced to give way to its longer haired rival, the Persian, contenting itself with a secondary and decreasing role in the eyes and affections of the cat loving public. Today, a renewed interest in semi-longhair breeds has raised the status of the Maine Coon, rapidly returning it to its former popularity. This large, working breed of cat has superb qualities, both physically and in temperament.

1. Heavy and shaggy, the Maine Coon's coat appears to lack undercoat. This compromises neither its beauty nor its warmth; if anything, this coat makes it easier for an owner to skip the daily brushing on occasion without a sense of guilt. In truth, a weekly brushing is often sufficient; however, care must be taken when the cat is shedding and the loss of fur is heavy so that the cat does not ingest excessive quantities of fur during its self-cleaning. During the shedding period, the fur remains long only on the tail, and the Maine Coon may temporarily resemble a shorthair.

2. Blazing Saddles, tabby and white bicolor kitten.

The Maine Coon is a cat for everyone. Sweet and well behaved with anyone who treats it gently, it is affectionate with the entire family but elects a single person its beloved owner. Tranquil, discreet, and independent, it loves home and creature comforts but is happy to have the use of a garden. Robust and of good health, it has no fear of the open air or the cold. It is made-to-order for tranquil environments, but will readily adapt to more active situations. This is a truly appealing cat that knows how best to make itself a well-loved member of the family.

3. Grand Champion Nooget's Renault Blanc. The Maine Coon is one of the largest domestic cat breeds. The physical structure is robust, long and with all parts in proportion so as to create a well-balanced rectangular appearance. The legs are substantial, wide set, of medium length and in proportion to the body. Given the mass of the body, one might expect the head to be heavy, but instead it is exquisitely designed and undeniably elegant. The head is medium in width and medium long with a square muzzle. This distinctive muzzle is framed by a frontal ruff. The pronounced cheek bones, firm chin, large, well-tufted ears, and oblique setting of large, expressive eyes give

the cat's expression an extraordinary intensity.
4. Red (left) and cream classic (blotched) tabby kittens.

5. Omero, 11 month old brown mackerel tabby male

	Body	Head	Ears	Eyes	Nose	Chin	Legs and feet	Tail	Coat	Varieties
C.F.A.	Medium to large, muscular and broad chested. Elongated but rectangular in appearance.	Medium in width and length with a square muzzle and high cheekbones.	Large, well-tufted, wide at base, tapering to appear pointed; set high and well apart.	Large, expressive, wide set. Slightly oblique setting. All colors acceptable.	Medium length, with a slight concavity when viewed in profile.	Firm and in line with the nose and upper lip.	Legs substantial, wide set, medium length, proportional to body. Paws large, round, and well-tufted.	Long, wide at base, and tapering. Fur long and flowing .	Heavy and shaggy, longer on stomach and britches, shorter over shoulders; silky and falling smoothly.	All colors including the varieties with white in any proportion but not Siamese pattern or derivative colors therefrom (chocolate or lilac).

The Maine Coon owes its name to its resemblance to the raccoon, a feral animal widespread in the North American forests that also has a long, thick tabby-like coat. The points of resemblance between the cat and the raccoon include size, the solid and robust body structure, and the coat–short on the head, with tufts in the ears, progressively longer on the neck, decidedly longer, thicker, and somewhat shaggy on the rest of the body–and the magnificent plumed tail. The short fur on the head, which constitutes one of the distinctive characteristics of the Maine Coon, is not appreciated by everyone; many people prefer more uniformly long fur, such as that of the Persian. There is a precise genetic reason for this difference among breeds; the Maine Coon lacks certain genes, known as "modifiers," that control the length of the fur including that on the head and neck. The Maine Coon has a somewhat comparable general physical shape (other than the Maine Coon's long body) to the Persian (robust type, heavy-boned, muscular legs, and a broad chest), but its head is not round like that of the Persian, and its muzzle is certainly not snub-nosed.

6

7

6. Nunki, 18 month old male.

7. Orange, 11 month old female .

8. Kittens: the one at left and the only one sitting are cream; the two in the middle are classic red tabbies; and the one at right is a silver patched tabby.

Development is particularly slow in Maine Coon cats, who reach maturity at about 3 to 4 years of age. Reproduction poses no problems although the litters may be small. The females are good mothers, attentive and affectionate; for their part, the kittens tend to be tranquil and very obedient.

8

MANX

This is one of the few breeds whose origins are well known, and its likely history can be reconstructed more easily than in most other cases. The Manx is tailless, an unmistakable trait that makes it immediately recognizable. Although the name Manx stands for "cat of the Isle of Man," the first Manx of which we have any trace lived in Asia Minor. It is believed that the Phoenicians, who traded with distant lands, brought the breed to the Far East where it acclimatized well and multiplied. From there, probably on commercial ships, it reached Europe. The story continues that in 1588, a Spanish galleon (part of the Spanish Armada) had several of these cats on board when it sank off the coast of Ireland near the Isle of Man. Some of the cats swam ashore, landing on the island to which they owe their name. Isolated on the island, they became widespread and were adopted and protected by the inhabitants who contributed to the preservation of the breed's characteristics by making sure for many centuries that other (tailed) cats did not interbreed with them. The Manx Club on the Isle of Man was founded in 1901. Since the cat's reproduction is usually overseen by experts, the spread of the Manx is limited; even so, the breed enjoys great popularity and has become a symbol of the Isle of Man throughout the world.

1, 2, 3. Grand Champion Raspoutine de Maneki-Neko, 5 year old brown mackerel tabby and white male. CFA show rules permit only specimens that do not have even the slightest hint of a tail, called "rumpies" by experts, or those who have a slight rise of bone at the end of the spine (rumpy risers).

Together with its long hair variant, formerly identified as the Cymric, the Manx is the only completely tailless breed of cat. Not all Manx are tailless (rumpies); some have a small protuberance which may even be a small stump (called stumpies), and yet others have a fully functional tail (tailies). Show cats, however, must not have any tail whatsoever. Where the tail would normally be, there is a dimple over which the fur is sometimes tufted producing the impression of a fan or pom-pom. Without doubt, the absence of the tail is a striking and singular characteristic producing a particular harmony to the overall rounded, circular physical appearance of the animal. This is a breed which demands that those working with it have a sound background in genetics so as to assure the production of healthy, robust specimens of the breed. Improper breeding can produce unacceptable results. Fortunately, thanks to the efforts of knowledgeable breeders, such anomalies are rare.

4

4, 5. Champion Osyris dei Capricci, classic patched tabby and white female. This rumpy female has a particularly sophisticated coat color. Her calico patterned coat includes three colors: white, red, and black. The simultaneous presence of red and black is a result of the synergetic actions of two different alleles of the same gene located on the female XX chromosomes; therefore, only females can be calico. In the cat pictured, the calico colors are overlaid on a classic tabby pattern of black stripes on a silver background. Note the length of the hind legs, which add agility and an overall sense of strength.

5

Cats without tails often appear at random in otherwise normal litters, but only in the Manx has this characteristic been engendered and maintained over time. How did the Manx lose its tail? On the Isle of Man there are those who relate a delightful, mythical story. At the time of the Great Flood, the Manx cats arrived at the Ark breathless and late just as Noah was about to cast off. With a final desperate and mighty leap, the Manx made it aboard just a fraction of a second before Noah slammed shut the last door…on the cats' tails. The Manx howled, yanked, and were safe inside—but their tails had been lost forever. Others claim that things happened differently: The Manx, they say, yanked and yanked and pulled its tail free from the door and in fact kept it firmly attached for many centuries to come until a vain, and somewhat primitive, warrior decided to decorate his helmet with a nice cat's tail. For the cats,

this was a baleful moment; the tail looked so handsome that all the warrior's brothers-in-arms set off across the island in search of cats and their tails. The cats soon realized that this new fashion would become widespread, and that a cat tail would become obligatory on the helmet of every warrior. Fighting, arguing, and hiding were out of the question. So with the force of desperation, the mother cats themselves bit off the tails of their kittens saving them the far greater pain of losing their tails as adults and at the same time leaving the ill-bred warriors sorely disappointed.

6. Grand Premier Tarahill's This One's 4 Robin, Red Classic (blotched) Tabby. Manx with a partial tail are called stumpies and are not permitted in shows, nor are those with an almost normal tail which are called tailies. It is impossible to predict how many rumpies, stumpies, and tailies will be born in a litter.

6

	Body	Head	Ears	Eyes	Nose and Chin	Legs and feet	Tail	Coat	Colors	Varieties
C.F.A.	Solid, compact, medium in size with sturdy bone structure. Broad chest, short back, rounded rump.	Medium in length, round, prominent cheeks, well developed muzzle, round whisker pads.	Medium size in proportion to head, wide at the base, set slightly outward forming the shape of a cradle's rocker when viewed from the rear.	Large, round and full, set at a slight angle toward the nose. Color conforms to coat color requirements.	In profile, there is a gentle dip from the forehead to the nose. Chin: Strong.	Heavily boned, front legs short and set well apart; hind legs much longer. Muscular paws neat and round.	Appearing to be absolutely tailless in the perfect specimen.	Shorthair: double coat is short and dense. Long hair double coat is medium in length, dense and well-padded over the main body.	All colors and coat patterns are permitted, including all varieties with white with the exception of those showing evidence of hybridization.	Shorthair and Longhair (see CYMRIC).

7. *The absence of a tail is caused by a specific gene, termed M (for Manx). A variant of the M, known as m, exists that has no effect. Since every unit of genetic transmission is present by two pairs in the genetic material (or genotype) of each individual, it is possible to have genotypes with two M genes (MM), with a single M gene and an m allele (Mm), or with two m alleles (mm). Manx cats are exclusively of the Mm genotype. Individuals of the MM genotype die in the uterus, for a double "dose" of the M gene is lethal; mm individuals have a normal tail and thus cannot be considered show Manx.*

8. *Brerbit Record dei Capricci, 8 month old male.*

Maintaining the Manx breed is not easy. No matter how carefully matings are controlled, a percentage of kittens will be lost to genetically related intrauterine defects (as with all breeds); furthermore, about one third of the kittens in each litter are born with a normal or partial tail and are thus excluded from the Championship competition. It is almost impossible to predict how many of the kittens will be born completely tailless. To strengthen the breed, breeders make periodic crosses with fully tailed Manx.

8

NORWEGIAN FOREST CAT

The Norwegian Forest Cat is a feline with ancient origins. It appears in Norwegian mythology and folk sagas and often plays a primary role in Nordic fables. The enchanted cat of these fables, with its long, thick tail, appears and disappears amid the trees of Norwegian forests; it sees what men cannot see and walks where men can never hope to go. At the beginning of this century the breed had weakened, probably as a result of frequent inbreeding; local breeders then began a program of selective breeding that was a prelude to the introduction of the Norwegian Forest Cat to the rest of the world. It was first presented at a cat show in Oslo, Norway, shortly before the Second World War; however, the first official Cat Fancy recognition was not given until 1977. Today, the breed enjoys increasing interest and admiration, although it is still relatively limited in number outside its own country.

1. *Harek Ganpesgaen's, 2 year old brown tabby and white male. Distinctive characteristics include the dense and abundant fur and the thick neck ruff. Even more distinctive is the shape of the head, which can be inscribed in a triangle, with its singular, long and straight profile. The eyes are large and almond shaped, set slightly at the oblique; their color does not necessarily harmonize with the color of the coat. The overall impression, in part due to the influence of the breed's name, is that the head and muzzle could easily belong to a small feral cat.*

2. *International Champion Oline del Valhalla, 1 year old female. This female, slightly smaller in size than the male, lacks a neck ruff.*

The Norwegian Forest Cat adapts to apartment life surprisingly well–surprising because everything about the cat makes it appear to be made for large open spaces and for an independent, free life. While it is in fact a fine hunter, intelligent, attentive, and cautious, it nonetheless is a fine companion cat. The Norwegian knows its hunting territory, which it explores systematically; it knows its prey and studies its habits; and it knows its own abilities. This is not a cat given to reckless moves. While hunting is one of its favorite activities, it enjoys home life and the company of human beings. Regardless of its wild appearance, it is, in fact, a social cat; it loves caresses, compliments, acts of attention, shared games, and intimate chats. Tolerant of strangers, if not absolutely friendly with them, it shows a deep and tenacious affection for its owner. Except during the mating season, it will willingly accept the presence of other cats as long as they don't disturb its personal territory. And it is able to get along easily with dogs after earning their respect in the inevitable initial skirmishes. It is a cat of great character, therefore, and without doubt, fully domesticated. Even so, perhaps in response to certain atavistic instincts, it is very happy if given a properly sheltered and well protected place outdoors, perhaps one that is also somewhat hidden.

3. *Bicolor kittens: black and white at left, blue and white at right. The females are excellent mothers–courageous, tireless, and perfectly capable of caring for both themselves and their young without human assistance.*

4. *From the left: Obo Herze Felis Jubatus, 1 year old male; Noblesse Av Trollsfjord, 10 month old female; Champion Gloria Av Trollsfjord, 15 month old female. In recent years, breeders have succeeded in* obtaining a wide range of colors and coat patterns. The combinations of tabby and white are particularly popular. Sometimes, as in the case of this male, a white spot located on the throat emphasizes the thick neck ruff.

5. *Oline del Valhalla.*

With an ancient breed such as the Norwegian Forest Cat, natural selection has had enough time to work out extraordinary adaptations to the environment, beginning with the breed's physical characteristics. To survive in a sub-Arctic climate, this cat has evolved a notable, large and imposing physical size (the bigger the body volume, the less internal heat is lost through the body's surface) and a double coat in which the undercoat, particularly rich and abundant, holds in body heat while the surface fur, of medium length, keeps rain and snow from reaching and wetting the undercoat. Heavy tufts of fur at the ears protect this particularly exposed area from the cold. The body shape is moderate in length with substantial bone structure and is powerful in appearance. The legs are medium with the hind legs being longer than the front; the paws, which appear to "toe out" when viewed from the front, are large, round, and heavily tufted between the toes thereby permitting the cat to walk comfortably over the snow. Because of its exceptionally strong claws, it can climb any tree to any height and has even been known to climb rocky walls. It is wonderfully agile and tireless as well as resistant to cold, fatigue, or hunger. It moves silently and carefully and without useless expenditure of energy; but, when necessary, the Norwegian shows itself capable of swift and powerful movements.

6. *The feral intensity of the countenance is particularly valued in the Norwegian Forest Cat.*

6

	Body	Head	Ears	Eyes	Nose	Chin	Legs and Feet	Tail	Coat	Varieties
C.F.A.	Large and imposing, solidly muscled, well balanced, moderate in length, substantial bone structure. Females may be more refined and smaller.	Triangular shaped; neck short and heavily muscled.	Medium to large, broad at base, set as much on the side as on the top of the head.	Large, almond shaped, set at a slight angle with the outer corner higher than inner corner. All colors are permitted.	Straight from brow ridge to tip of the nose without a break in the line.	Firm and in line with front of the nose. Gently rounded in profile.	Medium, with the hind legs longer than the fore; heavily muscled thighs. Paws large, round and heavily tufted.	Long and bushy; guard hairs desirable.	Double, long guard hairs desired. Full frontal bib, mutton chops, and britches highly desirable. Texture is relatively silky.	All colors including varieties with white in any proportion, but not Siamese markings nor chocolate nor lilac colors.

OCICAT

The Ocicat is a new breed, created by American breeders who successfully exploited the potential offered by a kitten with a singular spotted coat that resulted from the pairing of two "Siamese ." None of the characteristics of the parents would have led anyone to expect a kitten with a spotted coat: the father was a Chocolate point—he had chocolate-colored points—and the mother was a rare, experimental, unrecognized Abyssinian point, with points in the warm color of the original Abyssinian coat. During the initial period of its existence, the new breed was mixed not just with Siamese blood but also with Abyssinian and American Shorthair. As a result, the breed's general physical shape gradually went from being the tubular body type of the Siamese to a shorter, more compact body type. The most obvious characteristic of the Ocicat is its spectacular spotted coat. Indeed, the breed owes its name to this coat; Ocicat is based on ocelot (Felis pardalis), the medium-size wild cat widespread in Central and South America that is characterized by its splendid spotted coat. Although young, the breed has won recognition from the major international cat associations.

The typical coat of the Ocicat is really a spotted tabby. A few other breeds share this characteristic: the Egyptian Mau, the European, British, the Oriental Shorthair, and Oriental Longhair. The Ocicat's spots are larger and spread farther apart than those of the Egyptian Mau; they also tend to be a little less circular and a little more elongated resembling a thumb print; also, the color contrast with the agouti background is usually more marked. The more spots, the better; in fact, one of the challenges in breeding this cat is to produce spotting which continues across the sides of the body and on down the thighs and legs. On the sides of the body, the spots often arrange themselves in an implied rosette or "broken" classic tabby bull's eye pattern. This solid, hard, and rather long bodied, but never coarse, spotted cat is as lively and impetuous as its relative the Siamese. An athletic cat, it is important that it have a good deal of available space and an owner who supports it and who leaves it free to move about. The Ocicat needs an environment filled with things to capture its attention, intrigue it, and serve as the excuse for a new game. It gets along well with other domestic animals (which often become companions in games and frolics) and with humans; but, as with many other cats of Siamese derivation, the Ocicat becomes particularly and exclusively attached to a single person.

1. *Example of exceptional spotting.*

2. *Chocolate Ocicat.*

3. *Chocolate Ocicat. As with the Egyptian Mau and other shorthair spotted cats, the spots are located primarily on the back and flanks: along the entire length of the limbs, on the* tail (*most of all toward the distal end*), *on the ventral side of the neck, on the chest, and on the head between the ears. The spots are often replaced by striping reminiscent of the mackerel tabby pattern; however, they are less uniform and more discontinuous. This has led to the hypothesis that the* spotted pattern may be derived from an original mackerel by way of fragmentation of the stripes. Two different theories exist concerning the genetic basis of the hypothesized fragmentation of tabby stripes in the Ocicat; the "interrupted stripes" pattern may be the result of a tabby allele *created through accidental genetic mutation and different from those responsible, respectively, for the tiger (mackerel) pattern T, the classic pattern t(b), and the Abyssinian ticked tabby T(a). According to the second theory, the functionality of the allele is by itself responsible for the mackerel tabby T and is* modified by one or more modifier genes that are different and independent of the tabby alleles.

	Body	Head	Ears	Eyes	Nose	Chin	Legs and Feet	Tail	Coat	Varieties
C.F.A.	Medium to large, solid, hard, and rather long bodied.	A modified wedge shape showing a slight curve from muzzle to cheek; muzzle is broad and well defined with a suggestion of squareness.	Moderately large and set at a 45° angle, neither too high nor too low; tufts are a bonus.	Large, almond-shaped, angling slightly upwards toward the ears. All colors except blue are permitted.	A visible, but gentle rise from the bridge of the nose to the brow.	Strong with a firm jaw.	Well muscled, medium long, powerful, proportional. Paws are oval and compact.	Fairly long, medium-slim with only a slight taper; dark tip.	Short, smooth and satiny with lustrous sheen, tight and close lying, but with ticking.	Spotted in the colors tawny, chocolate, cinnamon, blue, lavender, fawn, silver, chocolate silver, cinnamon silver, blue silver, lavender silver, and fawn silver.

ORIENTAL SHORTHAIR

In the 1960s, this breed was recognized in Great Britain and was named the Foreign Shorthair; when recognized in the United States ten years later, it was renamed as the Oriental Shorthair. Notwithstanding its recent recognition, the breed's origins are ancient; originally from Thailand as were the Siamese, Burmese, and Korat, it is a Siamese in every sense except having a coat lacking all point markings (the characteristic darker coloration on the mask, ears, legs, and tail which identifies the Siamese). The name Foreign was invented by breeders in England in the 1920's when solid-colored Siamese were excluded from the original Siamese breed. Overshadowed by the popularity of the Siamese in the first half of this century, the Oriental Shorthair has recently spawned new interest and a heightened standing among breeders as well as the general public. The breeding program is designed to produce the breed's phenotypic characteristics, physical and behavioral, which are increasingly similar to those of the Siamese, with the exception of the distribution of color on the coat and the color of the eyes. Crosses between Siamese or Colorpoint Shorthairs and Orientals produce mixed litters with some kittens of the Siamese or Colorpoint phenotype and others of the Oriental; however, those which appear to be Siamese are not accepted for the Championship

1. Ace-of-Hearts, 7 month old Ebony female. This variety is included among the solid colors, with an undercoat and top coat of the same color. The eyes can be light green as in this cat, or a darker shade of green.

2. European Champion Ramses von der Spitzleithe, 1 year and 8 month old blue male. In the Oriental Shorthair, the coat is short and close-lying, fine-textured and glossy. The general physical shape, indistinguishable from that of the Siamese, perfectly fits the description of a svelte cat with long tapering lines, lithe but muscular.

3

4

3, 4. Buena Suerta Catmandu. The body of the Oriental Shorthair is long and svelte, a distinctive combination of fine bones and firm muscle, with shoulders no wider than the hips. Muscle tone is crucial, for from it depends a good deal of agile and alert appearance that distinguishes the breed. The head of the Oriental Shorthair, not unlike that of the Siamese, must be a long tapering wedge in form; the muzzle must be fine and wedge-shaped, the ears strikingly large, pointed, wide at the base and continuing the lines of the wedge. The eyes are slanted towards the nose in harmony with the lines of the wedge and ears, almond-shaped, and medium in size. The females are quite fertile. The kittens, somewhat precocious, are very lively and should be watched over closely. The females become particularly restless when in heat, and their usual meows can turn into sharp howls.

5. Okonor-Menyet, 1 year old chocolate spotted tabby female.

5

Show bench as Siamese but are relegated to the Any Other Variety (AOV) status where they can be used for further Oriental breeding. The longhair variant is provisionally accepted by CFA.

Everyone knows that most cats do not like any form of physical restriction. However, there are exceptions, and the Oriental Shorthair is among them, sharing this characteristic with the Siamese from which it is derived. Because of this singular trait, Oriental Shorthairs can be trained to wear a collar and to follow their owner on a leash. Such docility is surprising in an animal known for its exuberant, capricious, and sometimes unpredictable character. It may, however, be a reflection of another of its special characteristics: adaptability. As with the Siamese, the Oriental Shorthair is capable of quickly adjusting to changes in its environment or to changes in habits and schedule. This characteristic makes this cat one of the few that can be taken on trips without the risk of excessive harm to its physical and psychological health. However, whatever the environment and whatever the changes might be, it is important that the Oriental always be able to sense the reassuring presence of its owner who constitutes its fundamental reference point.

Like the Siamese, the Oriental Shorthair is long-lived but delicate. The incidence of illness from colds, infections and gastrointestinal disturbances can sometimes be greater than in other breeds. However, effective prevention involves only small matters of care, such as avoiding exposure either to sudden changes in temperature or to excessively frigid climates, a proper diet, and assuring that the animal has ample exercise.

In 1994, CFA provisionally recognized the long hair variant of the Oriental Shorthair and named the breed the Oriental Longhair. It is likely that the Oriental Longhair will be accorded full Championship recognition soon. Other than length of coat, the standards and color variants for both breeds are identical. However, in terms of breeding, the Oriental Shorthair can be bred to other Oriental Shorthairs, Colorpoint Shorthairs or Siamese; the Oriental Longhair, in addition, can use the Oriental Shorthair, the Javanese and the Balinese as outcross breeds.

7

6. Kan Kinya, blue-eyed white.

7. Grand Champion, Kee Wee Kristy of Felitan. The Oriental is a very lively cat, always active, full of energy, and capable of sudden bursts of vitality. Therefore, it must have the opportunity to move, run, rove about, and to perform physical exercise at its pleasure. The ideal environment for the Oriental Shorthair includes at least an enclosed terrace, but a walled, covered garden would be even better. Full of curiosity, it loves to explore, and its expeditions of world discovery will take it far from home if left to wander on its own…something certainly neither suggested nor desirable.

8. Ace-of-Hearts.

8

9. *The Oriental Shorthair's complex character is doubtless a result of the breed's close relationship to the Siamese. It is fickle and not overly social, neither with other animals nor with humans. It usually selects a single person with whom it establishes an intense and exclusive relationship. It is capable of deep affection, but perhaps precisely for this reason is very sensitive and requires a great deal of personal attention. It cannot be forced; although it demonstrates marked "psychological" dependence on its owner. It is independent in planning its daily routine and impulsive in its show of affection. Thus, rather than to try to force it into a game or a caress, it's better to let the cat come on its own to seek one or the other…even more so since it is a master of the of art of making itself understood. Finally, its mood swings, sudden as those of the Siamese, must be respected. All in all, it has a strong, fascinating personality that no owner can ever claim to understand fully. One thing is certain; with an Oriental Shorthair, life is never monotonous.*

9

	Body	Head	Ears	Eyes	Nose	Chin	Legs and Feet	Tail	Coat	Varieties
C.F.A.	Long and svelte, fine bones and firm muscles, tubular body, and a long, slender neck.	Long tapering wedge; straight lines to the tips of the ears forming a triangle.	Strikingly large, pointed, wide at the base.	Almond-shaped, medium size, neither protruding nor recessed. Slanted towards the nose; color, green; whites may have blue, green or odd-eyed color.	Long and straight, continuation of forehead with no break.	Medium size.	Long, slim legs; small, dainty and oval paws.	Long, thin at base and tapered to a fine point.	Short, fine textured, glossy, lying close to the body.	Both Shorthair and Longhair; many colors are recognized, divided in five groups: the solid, shaded, smoke, tabby, and parti-color classes.

PERSIAN

Although its origins are certainly ancient, the Persian (indeed, longhaired cats in general) was unknown in Europe until approximately 1520. Later, in the 17th century, an Italian traveler to Asia, Pietro della Valle, brought an example from Persia to Italy, where the breed, considered extraordinary and precious, was jealously cared for and guarded. A century later another explorer, the Frenchman Nicolas de Pereisc, brought new specimens from Turkey. In the first half of the 19th century, some of the Persians raised in Italy were brought, it seems secretly, to France and England, where they were crossed with the Persians of Turkish descent, marking the birth of the modern Persian. In 1871 a breeding program was organized by English breeders; in its initial period it involved crosses with Angora cats, which improved the quality of the coat. At the same time, systematic work began on expanding the range of possible colors and coat patterns.

1

1. Rajiv degli Ingauni, 7 month old red classic tabby male .

2. American Grand Champion and European Champion Kueen Kognac, 6 year old black male. The fundamental requirements of a Persian are a body of *the cobby type; long fine and silky fur; an ample ruff and luxurious tail; a round head with small rounded ears and large, round eyes; an accentuated* *stop or "break", and a short, snub nose along with a firmly rounded chin.*

2

3

4

5

3. *South Paw Bless My Soul, copper eyed white.*

4. *Spectacular red Persian; note the outstanding copper eye color.*

5. *Quick-cream dei Graffiti, 5 month old cream female. The first truly cream examples were obtained in about 1920. Prior to that time, the color was defined as Fawn and lacked the clarity of today's pale cream Persian cats. The color must be perfectly sound along the entire length of each single hair and on the entire body. Examples that meet these requisites are decidedly rare. The nose leather and paw pads should be pink.*

6. *Red and white bicolor.*

On the following pages:

7, 8. *Champion Kikicat's Joseph of McReid.*

9. *Red Classic (blotched) tabby with excellent markings of deep, rich red on a red ground color.*

6

	Body	Head	Ears	Eyes	Nose	Chin	Legs and Feet	Tail	Coat	Varieties
C.F.A.	Of cobby type, low on the legs, broad, massive, with a level back. Short, thick neck.	Round and massive, with great breadth of skull, round face and underlying bone structure.	Small, round tipped, set far apart and low on the head.	Large, round, brilliant in color, set level and far apart.	Short, snub and broad, with "break" centered between the eyes.	Full, well developed, firmly rounded. Jaws broad and powerful.	Legs, short thick and strong, forelegs straight; paws large, round and firm.	Short, but in proportion to body length; carried at an angle lower than back.	Long and thick, standing off from the body; of fine texture, glossy and full of life.	Divided into seven groupings: Solid Color, Shaded, Smoke, Tabby, Parti-Color, Bi-Color and Himalayan.

Varieties with tipped coats are characterized by coats of solid color that have a haze of different color on the tips of the hairs. The result is a shading or shadowy haze that runs across the coat; it becomes darker if the fur is flattened and almost imperceptible if, instead, the fur is pushed back in the opposite direction uncovering the lighter base. This effect is the result of a single gene, I (from inhibitor), that, as its name would suggest, partially inhibits the deposition of pigment so that the color appears only on the tips of some of the hairs.

Tipped coats can be chinchilla, shaded, smoke, parti-color, bi-color, or tabby. The tipping may be black, blue, red, chocolate, lilac, or combinations thereof (e.g., tortoiseshell, blue-cream, etc.) According to the intensity of the pigmentation on the distal ends of the hairs, the colors are divided into the chinchilla or shell (lightest amount of tipping), shaded (intermediate tipping), and the smoke, the most heavily tipped.

Kittens with either chinchilla or shaded coats, and sometimes smoke, show traces of their original classic or mackerel tabby pattern that usually disappears as the coat grows thereby diffusing the pattern. This phenomenon is linked to their origins, the tabby Persian.

8

9

11

10. *Champion Beaudee's Poppin' Fresh cream and white bicolor.*

11. *Grand Champion Johaelan's Dapper Dan, white. It is important that the white coat be pristine white and not have even the slightest yellow staining.*

12. *Grand Champion South Paw Cloudburst of Fancy Fluff.*

It is said that no breed has a coat comparable to that of the Persian. This is a question of taste, of course, but no one can fail to recognize that the qualitative characteristics of the Persian coat are unequaled today. The coat can reach lengths of between 6 and 8 inches; the innermost layer of undercoat, which in other breeds is shorter than the two outer layers (awn and guard hairs), is just as long in the Persian. Furthermore, each of the three layers is thick, rich, and fully developed. The hairs are strong and regular in structure; those of the two outer layers have the characteristic apical swelling that makes them stronger and thicker. The coat is naturally lost during the spring shedding, but the loss is not as drastic and total as occurs, for example, in the Angora. Also characteristic are the abundant ruff, which is called, more simply, the collar or frill, and the bushy tail or brush. The full tail is carried without a curve and at an angle lower than the back.

12

The length of the coat depends on the presence in the genetic material of the individual cat of an allele termed l (from long hair). All longhaired cats, whether Persian or not, contain the pair ll in their genotype. Its role is that of accelerating the growth of the hairs so that they reach a greater length than normal during the period of growth available to them which remains fixed in all breeds of cats.

The uniformity of the length of the hair on various body areas and the abundance of the hair are controlled by a group of "modifying" genes that are unrelated to the l allele and that are present in different measure in the genetic material of the various longhaired breeds. If the richness of the hair or the length of the hair in the same areas of the body differs between two breeds, it means that the breeds possess different modifying genes.

13

13. *Grand Champion Bar-B Lucky Red Prime, red tabby male.*

14. *Shaded silver Persian.*

14

15. *Copacats Bobbie, 8 month old cream and white Bi-Color female. In bicolor varieties, one of the two colors must be white. In the Bi-Colors, as a preferred minimum, the cat should have white feet, legs, undersides, chest, and muzzle; less white than this minimum should be penalized proportionately.*

16. *Grand Champion Victoria's Just Happnin, dilute calico. The calico coat is characterized by patches of white, black, and red with clearly defined borders; in the dilute calico, the black is diluted to blue, and the red to cream. As in any other case of dilution, the d allele is responsible for the reduced pigmentation. The name calico is derived from the popular printed cotton material; the English originally preferred the name chintz, but that term has fallen out of use. It seems that the first calico examples were obtained in England early in this century from breedings of solid-color Persians to non pedigree females of no precise breed but with attractive tortoiseshell coats (black with red and cream patching). Today's calico is the fruit of more than twenty years of selective breeding; the feet, legs, undersides, chest and muzzle should be white; the patches of color should be distributed on the head and back in accordance with a bilateral symmetry. Initially not overly appreciated, perhaps because of its humble origins, the calico variety today enjoys the favor of both experts and the public.*

15

16

17

17. *Bolo's Turning Up the Juice, red and white bicolor.*

18. *Grrand Champion Victoria's Just Happnin.*

19. *International Champion Min-Amun Sen di Meneftha, two year old black and white Bi-Color male.*

20. *Questione di Feeling, 3 month old van calico female. As with bi-colors, the presence of white areas depends on an allele called S (from spotted). However, while the van is necessarily a homozygous SS, in non-van bi-colors the S can find itself in the heterozygotic condition (Ss). It is not known if a certain genetic mechanism exists with the role of confining the deposition of pigment to certain body areas (such as the head and tail).*

18

19

Without doubt, the most visible of the physical characteristics that distinguish the Persian is the coat, but far more important to an expert eye is the breed's general physical shape or conformation which is crucial and more determinant than any other aspect of the breed. It must be of the cobby type, having a solid body with heavy bone structure (including the female), massive across the shoulders and deep through the chest, and with short, straight, thick legs and large, round, firm paws. The back does not arch but is level. It should be possible to inscribe the body within a rectangle. The tail is short but in proportion to the length of the body; the neck is short and thick, and the head is round and massive with great breadth of skull. The jaws are broad and powerful with full cheeks adding to the overall round shape of the head. The nose is short, snub and broad with a "break" centered between the eyes. The ears are small, round tipped, not unduly open at the base, set far apart and low on the head. The eyes are brilliant in color, large, round and full. The shape of the head of one Persian variety is reminiscent of that of a Pekinese dog and so it is called Peke-face; the Peke-face Persian occurs only in the colors red and red tabby. Some of the Persian characteristics can be found in other breeds that were crossed with the Persian relatively recently; however, only in a good pedigreed Persian are they all united. There are also some characteristics that are absolutely unique to the breed; among these is the structure of the head and, most of all, the overall appearance of the Persian head.

20

21. *Exceptional Tortoise-shell Persian of superb type, color and style.*

22. *Champion Kikicat's Joseph of McReid..*

23. *Rudy degli Estensi, 4 month old cream and white van male (a dilution of red).*

21

22

The fascination of a Persian focuses on its thick coat and rich ruff. However, the exceptional length of the coat and its particular structure, with the internal layer and outer layers of equal length, favors the formation of knots and makes careful and frequent combing or brushing a necessity. Beginning with the sixth week of life, when the longer hair begins to grow, a daily brushing with a soft brush or a careful combing, so as not to break the hairs, is absolutely necessary, not only to protect the cat's beauty but also its health and hygiene. A long, thick coat presents an ideal home for fleas, for example, and even cats that live in an apartment are not immune to the danger of a possible infestation. Furthermore, swallowing too much hair during its natural licking and grooming can cause health problems (hair balls.) At intervals, based on the cat's type of life and the needs of its coat, a good shampooing in lukewarm water is required. The soap should be of a neutral pH, and the cat should be thoroughly rinsed and completely dried.

23

24. *Grand Premier Kitty Charm's Imari, Blue Cream Persian. The blue-cream is the dilute version of the tortoiseshell. One must avoid confusing these two varieties with those included in the bicolor class; with bi-colors, one of the two colors is always white. Unlike bi-color cats, tortoiseshell and blue-cream examples lack white patches. In blue-cream coats, the patches of color should have clearly defined borders but may shade from one to the next. Even when they have borders, however, because of the length of the coat, the overall effect is of a mixture between the two colors. It is, however, important that the well defined cream patches appear both on the body and the extremities. Pale cream is usually preferred to the more intense cream tones ("hot" cream.) As with the calico, the tortoiseshell coat, and also its dilute version, can exist only on females. The presence at same time of black and red patches is, in fact, a phenotypic characteristic tied to the female sex. Tortoiseshell and blue-cream examples can be obtained through crosses of individuals of different varieties. The number of possible combinations is high, and, naturally, only a certain percentage of the kittens in any given litter will have the coloration in question.*

24

25. Pansy patch Charmin of Angtini, dilute van calico.

26. Grand Champion Grand Premier Mystichill Mighty High, blue cream.

27.Palmetto's Walking in High Cotton, black smoke.

Well-suited to apartment life, Persians do not need open spaces. And for various reasons, this is all to the good. First of all, if a Persian spent part of the day romping in a garden, or even only on a terrace, the care of its coat would become a complex enterprise, and the danger of fleas in warmer climes would be increased exponentially. Secondly, prolonged exposure to the sun can damage the quality and color of the coat; the effects are disastrous for solids and noticeable even in varieties with more colors. Shaded Persians have been known to get a sun burn. Finally, despite its robust physical appearance, the Persian is a somewhat delicate animal, probably because of artificial selection over the past century by breeders as opposed to the random system of nature. For example, while its thick coat makes it intolerant of overly hot environments, this same coat is still not enough to protect the cat from catching a chill caused by sudden changes in temperature. It must therefore be watched over attentively, with every effort made to provide a constant "micro climate." Care must also be given to its diet which should be balanced and should include protein, vitamins and minerals.

At first glance, a Persian often appears haughty, aloof, and indifferent, and as if it thought nothing were worthy of its attention, much less a mere, mortal human. That, however, is truly not the case; in its motionless silence, the cat is carefully studying its surroundings recording, gathering, and cataloging information for later evaluation. The Persian ponders. An intelligent animal, analytical and prudent, it needs time to think things through. Through its continuous inspection, it slowly familiarizes itself with its environment, other cats, and humans. It is not impulsive; however, as mutual familiarity and understanding between it and its environment grow, it becomes more extroverted and begins to display the other half of its personality–graciousness, sweetness, and controlled cheerfulness. It is thoughtful, discreet, radiant, and friendly. It enjoys company and has the capacity for a deep, abiding affection. And in its affection, it is loyal, pure, and tenacious, without ever losing its aristocratic aplomb. This is a cat with which one can establish a rich and intense relationship comprised of glances, physical closeness, and shared understanding. A small companion, the Persian is ever-faithful over the years.

28

28. Jimilene Buttons and Bows, Himalayan Blue Point..

29. The many varieties of Persian available today include the Blue Point example in this photograph, as well as various tonalities of brown, lilac, red, and cream. The more sophisticated coats have tortoiseshell or tabby points. The eyes are always blue, although the intensity of the blue varies; indeed, it seems that the gene responsible for the dilution of the pigment may affect the color not only of the coat but also of the iris, even more so if found together with the gene responsible for the Siamese-type coloration. Nonetheless, the eye color

29

RAGDOLL

The Ragdoll owes it name to its behavior of going limp in one's arms when picked up, relaxing all its muscles and becoming as floppy as its namesake, the rag doll. This longhair breed was created in the 1960's in Southern California through reported crosses of white Persian, a Seal Point Birman, and Burmese. The breed was first recognized in the United States in 1965. Although not well known in Europe, its popularity there is growing. From the Persian, the Ragdoll has inherited its heavy bone, its tranquil character, and its perfect suitability to apartment life; from the Burmese it has its coloration, which is darker on the points (limbs, tail, face, ears), and from the Birman, its white. The coat is medium to long, plush and silky and is longest around the neck and outer edges of the face. The coat is of a non-matting texture. The breed is currently only shown as an "Exhibition only" entry at CFA shows.

1. Quadruple Grand Champion TLC Marco Polo, blue bicolor.

2. Double Grand Champion Purrlins Sir Varnseworth. The Ragdoll is a large cat; an adult male can weigh from 18 to 22 pounds; females average about half that. The "white gloves," similar to those of the Birman to which the Ragdoll is related, and white pattern of the bi-color Ragdoll are considered a distinctive characteristic. The coat is accepted in four colors based on the Siamese colors of seal, blue, chocolate, and lilac. CFA currently allows only the Bi-Color pattern to be exhibited.

	Body	Head	Ears	Eyes	Nose	Chin	Legs and Feet	Tail	Coat	Varieties
G.C.C.F.	Elongated with a full, broad chest, equally massive across shoulders and hips.	A medium sized, broad, modified wedge with a flat plane between the ears. Rounded, medium length muzzle.	Medium size, wide at base, rounded tip; set to continue the lines of the modified wedge.	Large, oval, and sapphire blue. Wide set.	There is a medium break between the eyes; the nose leather must be pink.	Well developed and strong.	Legs medium to medium long, strong boned; paws large, round and well tufted.	Long in proportion to the body; medium at base with slight taper.	Medium long to long, plush and silky.	Bi-color in seal, blue, chocolate, and lilac. Mask to have a white inverted "V", stomach and all four legs, feet and ruff to be white.

REX (CORNISH REX)

Cats with curly rather than smooth coats were once considered aberrations. Such cats were discounted by breeding programs until 1950, when a female in Cornwall with Siamese blood gave birth to a curly-coated kitten in an otherwise normal litter. The cat was bred back with its mother, producing curly kittens which became the foundation of a new breed and attracted world interest in cats with curly coats. On at least three occasions since then, otherwise normal litters have included cats with curly coats as a result of spontaneous mutation (and not as a result of pairing with the Cornish breed). All three cases led to a new breed– Oregon Rex, Devon Rex, and German Rex (the names derived from their place of origin). Although the Rex breed is a recent arrival, intense and careful breeding has led to the recognition of a great number of varieties. The Cornish Rex was given official recognition in 1967; the breed is still more widespread and popular in the United States than in Europe.

1

2

3

1, 2, 3. Cornish Rex is clearly of the curved, lithe body type. Indeed, in the Rex, the physical characteristics of the curves seem exaggerated to the point of extremity. The body is small to medium with a long and slender torso; the back is typically held naturally arched with the lower line of the body approaching the upward curve. The legs are very long and slender, hips and hindquarters are well muscled, and the neck is long and slender. The breed's curly coat reminded early breeders of the curly coat of the Rex rabbit, thereby giving the breed its name.

4, 5. Simply Rex Overtop, black and white van bi-color. The head of the Rex is comparatively small and narrow; it is egg shaped with large ears which are full from the base, erect and alert, and set high on the head. The distribution of the color in the van type, characteristic of the Turkish Van for which it is named, requires a solid white coat with the exception of patches of color that must be located on the extremities with one or two small body spots acceptable. At this time it is genetically impossible to manipulate or control the distribution of color versus white; one must trust to luck, and each litter is a surprise.

The Cornish and other Rex breeds (German and Devon) share a unique characteristic: their curly coat. The coat of a normal cat, whether short or long, is composed of three layers of hair: the woolly internal undercoat, the awn hairs in the middle, and the external guard hairs. The length of the hair increases progressively from the undercoat to the guard hairs. Each single hair of the awn and guard hairs has a characteristic apical swelling. In the Cornish Rex, as in the German, the outermost layer of guard hairs is completely absent or is indistinguishable from the awn hairs immediately under it. The apical swelling, normally found in each hair of the awn coat, is also absent or is found only in some of the hairs or is so minor as to be barely perceptible. Furthermore, both the undercoat and the awn hairs are decidedly shorter than normal. The overall result is a very short coat, curly or wavy, and very soft to the touch. Even the whiskers are shorter than normal, and curly.

4

5

	Body	Head	Ears	Eyes	Nose	Chin	Legs and Feet	Tail	Coat	Varieties
C.F.A.	Small to medium, torso long and slender, not tubular; heavy, muscular hindquarters. The back is naturally arched.	Relatively small and narrow, egg shaped, 1/3 longer than wide. High and prominent cheekbones.	Large, full from the base, set high on the head.	Medium to large in size, oval in shape. The color harmonizes with the coat; blue or odd-eyed (white cats). Blue in the "Sia-Rex".	The profile is composed of two convex arcs: the forehead is rounded, the nose break is smooth and mild; the Roman nose has a high, prominent bridge.	Strong and well developed.	Very long, and slender legs; dainty, slightly oval paws.	Long and slender tapering toward the end and extremely flexible.	Short, extremely soft, silky and completely free of guard hair. A tight, uniform marcel wave lies close to the body over the entire cat.	All coat colors are recognized, including varieties that include white in any proportion.

The length of a cat's hair depends on two factors: speed and time of growth. The speed of growth is less in shorthair cats than in longhair cats; the time of growth is fixed; it is the same for all breeds. In the Cornish Rex, as in the Devon and German, the speed of growth is abnormally slow. The hair grows very slowly, and, since the period available for its growth is limited, it does not succeed in reaching normal length. This diminished speed of growth involves the guard hairs more than the other two types of hair to the point that their development is either impeded altogether or they become indistinguishable from the awn hairs. A single allele causes the modifications of the coat in the Cornish Rex, identified as the R allele (from Rex).

As its physical build would suggest, the Rex is agile, active, quick, and, in fact, the breed is known not just for its curly coat but also for its inexhaustible vivacity. Continuously active and very playful, it makes legitimate claims to acrobatic skills. Even so, it does not disdain the warmth and comforts of home and is well-suited for apartment life–provided it can transform the home into its own personal gymnasium. Equally energetic in its affection, it becomes tied to its owner in an almost domineering way and seeks to play an important role in his or her life. To stay beside its owner, it is willing to follow along on a leash during walks outside the home. The Rex is an animal of habit and prefers a life of regular rhythms; changes and surprises may stimulate its curiosity but are just as likely to be a source of displeasure.

6. Left to right: Simply Rex Odissey, 3 month old cream and white bi-color male; Simply Rex Oblige, 3 month old calico female; Simply Rex Overtop (the same cat in picture 4 on page 115.) Since the Rex is a lively, highly active cat as an adult, you can just imagine how Rex kittens must play. They are, to say the very least, wild, and give their parents more than a few problems. All the varieties of color known in other breeds have been produced in the Rex, including the Siamese pattern and colors. The breed's thin coat may not completely mask the folds of skin, visible most of all around the armpits and hind legs. These folds should not appear excessive, and the skin should not seem loose. Care for the coat involves no great challenges, but brushes, which could break or otherwise damage the hairs, should not be used; instead use a flannel mitt. A few good strokes across the coat will remove any dead hair and make the coat shiny. Shedding is almost nonexistent.

6

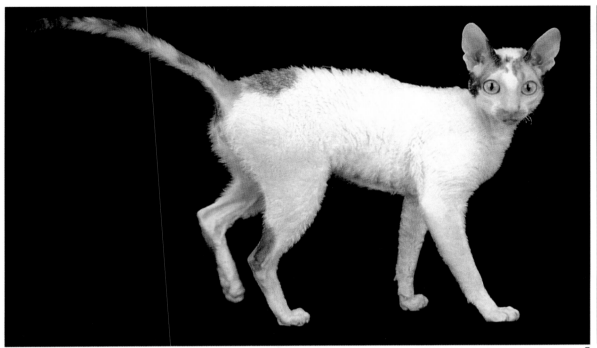

7

8

9

7, 8. *Simply Rex Nassau, 11 month old dilute calico (Harlequin) female. The Harlequin pattern differs from the van pattern in that the patches of color are more numerous and rather than being confined to the head, tail, and front area of the back, they are also located, usually, asymmetrically, on other areas of the body including the limbs and all along the back.*

9. *Simply Rex Oblige, left, and Simply Rex Overtop, right.*

10. *Grand Champion Blu Sprs Magdalene.*

10

REX (DEVON REX)

The Devon Rex appeared in Devonshire, England, in 1960, ten years after the birth of the first Rex, the progenitor of the Cornish breed. The establishment of the Cornish breed had convinced breeders that cats with curly shorthair coats were of interest and should no longer be considered aberrations. Therefore the curly-haired Devon kitten was greeted with enthusiasm, particularly since its arrival was completely unrelated to the Cornish breed. In fact, its curly coat was not derived from a pairing with a Cornish but from a different spontaneous genetic mutation. The work of breeders and geneticists has since proven that the genetic base of the curly coat is different in the two breeds. The quality of the coat in the Devon breed is different from that of the Cornish. The breed, however, is the object of ongoing interest, although perhaps less for the general public than for those who particularly like to show and breed cats.

1. Kwe-Ni Van Manding, brown tabby. The Devon is similar to the Cornish because of its wavy coat. Other than that, the two breeds are totally dissimilar. The Devon's body is hard and muscular, slender, of medium length, broad in the chest and medium fine in boning. The unique head with large eyes, short muzzle, prominent cheekbones, and huge, low-set ears combine to create a characteristic elfin look. Harmony of form, stylish, modern curves and the distinctive coat provide interest and originality to the Rex breeds. Aided by their lively and playful character, they are very appealing cats. A side note: those who are allergic to most cats because of dander may find that the Rex breeds do not affect their allergies.

2. Obelix Prince Rex, blue tabby.

At first glance, the coat of the Devon Rex does not seem different from that of other Rex breeds...very short and curly. However, unlike the Cornish and German Rex, the Devon Rex has all three of the types of hair that normally make up a cat's coat. Even so, the two outermost layers (awn and guard hairs) are quite different from the norm. In fact, the hairs are usually without the end swelling that confers thickness and strength and they present an extremely irregular structure with an unpredictable alternation of thick and thin areas. The hairs in these areas are fragile and often break. The hair of Devons breaks so easily (primarily from the mechanical action of the cat's tongue during its daily personal cleaning) that it is not rare to find certain areas, particularly on the stomach, that are completely hairless until the next shedding and new coat growth cycle. The whiskers suffer the same fate, for beginning with the first months of life they are so fragile that they are invariably either absent or reduced to stumps. It thus happens that the coat of the Devon can be less thick, uniform, and pleasing to the touch than that of the Cornish. Delicacy and attention are required, of course, in the care of the coat; brushes should be banned and replaced by the use of a soft flannel mitt.

3. Champion Carlozio's Raymond Gold, 1 year old seal point male.

4, 5. Champion Carlozio's Raphael Gold, 1 year old male. Not unlike the Cornish Rex, the Devon is a good eater, but sometimes has a tendency to overeat and gain weight. Its diet must therefore be carefully controlled, and it must be prevented from making raids in the kitchen. As with all other Rex, a Devon cannot be permitted to be overweight. Furthermore, it is important that the skin should remain firm and tight so as to reduce to a minimum the inevitable folds of skin, often clearly visible because of the sometimes sparse coat.

	Body	Head	Ears	Eyes	Nose	Chin	Legs and Feet	Tail	Coat	Varieties
C.F.A.	Hard and muscular, slender and of medium length; broad in the chest with medium fine boning.	A modified wedge with a short muzzle and pronounced cheekbones. Forehead curves back to a flat skull; the neck is medium long and slender.	Strikingly large, wide at the base, and set very low on the head.	Large and wide set, oval in shape. Intense color appropriate to coat color and pattern.	In profile, the nose has a strongly marked stop.	Strong, well developed with a short muzzle; prominent whisker pads.	Long and slim legs; paws are small and oval.	Long, fine and tapering, well covered with short fur.	Well covered with soft, fine, full bodied and rexed fur longest on body and tail.	All coat colors are recognized including those varieties that include white in any proportion.

6. Pulsatilla degli Efli, 10 month old female. The name given this cat says much about the character of the Devon. The pulsatilla is a medicinal herb that favors the reflexes, and indeed few cats are more lively than the Devon. Hyperactive, fearless, and endlessly playful, the Devon amuses itself endlessly in every sort of activity, well aware that its owner can never hope to catch it by the hair and make it give up its pranks. Intelligent and curious, it is an entertaining cat. But it is also demanding, not only because it must be kept under control, but also because it needs a lot of affection and attention which it returns with a deep and enduring attachment.

7. 2 month old kittens.

8. Razaby Sugarbaby Blu, silver chocolate patched tabby.

Like the Cornish Rex, the short coat in the Devon Rex is the result of a slowed rate of hair growth. However, the gene whose mutation is responsible for the phenomenon is different in the two breeds. A cross between a Devon and a Cornish results in kittens with quite normal hair (which might seem odd to the public at large, but not to geneticists.)

The extreme tendency to break, characteristic of the Devon coat, seems to depend on a group that genes that have nothing whatsoever to do with the gene responsible for the slowed rate of growth.

REX (German Rex)

Aside from the Cornish and Devon Rex there is a third type of cat with curly short hair, which first appeared in Germany. The German Rex is not recognized by CFA as a separate breed for registration or show. The first of this breed was "discovered" in 1951 when it was already a few years old, and it is not improbable that this was actually the first true Rex. The coat of the German Rex is without the outer guard hairs; the awn hairs and undercoat are far shorter than normal, just as in the Cornish. However, differences can be found if one examines the coats of the German and Cornish closely. In the German, but not the Cornish, the awn hairs are a little thicker than those of the undercoat, and the apical swelling, usually absent in the Cornish, is almost always present in the German. Overall, in the German the awn hairs are more developed and uniform.

1, 2. German Rex, solid black. When breeders tried a cross between German and Cornish Rex, they obtained kittens that the German breeders considered German, but which the English saw as Cornish. Putting aside national pride, this means really only one thing: from the genetic point of view, the German and Cornish breeds are identical. The allele responsible for the short, curly coat is the same in the two breeds. However, there is no doubt that the German Rex also has some odd genetic twist (probably a group of modifying genes that act in a synergetic way) that encourages the development of the awn hairs, making its coat thicker and more uniform than that of the Cornish Rex.

	Body	Head	Ears	Eyes	Nose	Chin	Legs and Feet	Tail	Coat	Varieties
F.I.F.E.	Medium size and length, strong and muscular; neither solid nor fat.	Rounded, broad between the ears. Pronounced cheekbones.	Of medium size, wide at the base, slightly rounded.	Of medium size, well open. Well distanced from the nose and located somewhat toward the outside. Color conforms to that of the coat.	Has a slight bump at the base.	Strong.	Thin legs of medium length; small oval paws.	Medium length, wide at the base and rounded at the tip.	Silky, short, with a tendency to waviness. Absence of long, coarse hairs. Curly whiskers.	Not recognized by CFA. However, all coat colors are produced, including varieties that include white in any proportion.

RUSSIAN BLUE

As its name indicates, this blue-coated cat seems to be of Russian origin; it is said to have arrived in England in the mid 19th century aboard a Russian merchant ship from the port of Archangel for which reason it is also known as the Archangel Cat. This story becomes slightly blurred when one realizes that some people call this breed the Spanish Blue or Maltese Cat. One can conclude that this is a cat that has traveled a great deal, and many of the regions it has visited have apparently wished to claim it as their own. Oddly enough, England is not among these claimants, even though it was English breeders who developed the breed and first showed it. The breed suffered a great deal during the two world wars; in attempts to protect it, English and Swedish breeders made much use of Siamese blood with results that later proved to be nearly disastrous. Only in the 1960s were breeders successful in reproducing the cat's original type. In order to maintain the breed's distinctive characteristics, reproduction must be controlled by experts.

2

The Russian Blue is the ideal cat for those who lead a regular, quiet life; perhaps more accurately, quiet, regular people are ideal for the Russian Blue. This is an animal that detests noise, confusion, change, or surprises. Its paradise consists of an armchair near a radiator or a warm fire, where it can be left in peace for an entire winter and moved only with the first warm day of spring. And yet, perhaps to live up to its name, this sleepy lazybones can stand up to cold and inclement weather. It is an affectionate cat, gentle and sensitive; never insistent, never in any way overbearing. It is capable, however, of being there at the right moment and of anticipating its owner's intentions in an instant. Even its "meow" is thoughtful, discreet, almost silent, or perhaps musical. This is one of those cats to which one finds oneself suddenly deeply attached without knowing exactly how it all came about.

3

1. Grand Premier Roxanastasia's Nickoli Lobachevsky, Russian Blue kitten

2. The blue coat of the Russian Blue is an even, bright blue throughout with the lighter shades of blue preferred; guard hairs are distinctly silver-tipped. Only in the Russian Blue, in fact, is the point of each single guard hair slightly lighter in color than the base. This is a form of light ticking that creates a fine contrast with the color of the eyes, which are vivid green particularly valued for their intensity. Although recognized by the major international cat associations, the Russian Blue is not widespread today

and is best known to experts and cat professionals. The general public easily confuses this magnificent breed with other blue-coated cats.

3. Grand Premier Roxanastasia's Nickoli Lobachevsky.

	Body	Head	Ears	Eyes	Nose	Chin	Legs and Feet	Tail	Coat	Varieties
C.F.A.	Fine boned, long, firm and muscular; lithe and graceful in outline but not tubular in appearance.	A smooth medium wedge neither long nor short, and with flat planes. Long slender neck.	Rather large and wide at base; set far apart, as much on the side as on the top of the head.	Set wide apart; aperture rounded in shape. Vivid green in color.	Medium in length; a straight line in profile without break.	Perpendicular with end of nose and with level under-chin.	Long, fine boned legs; small, slightly rounded paws.	Long but in proportion with the body, tapering from a moderately thick base.	Short, dense, fine and plush, the double coat stands out from the body due to its density. It has a distinct soft and silky feel. Color is an even bright blue with silver-tipped guard hairs.	Recognized only in Blue. Some countries recognize the White and Black Russians.

4, 5. *Faberge's Mariska of Satineque.*

6. *Ikon Silme of Elde.*

At least three different breeds of cat are characterized by a blue coat: the Chartreux, the Korat, and the Russian Blue. Although the color of their coat is similar, the good examples of the different breeds of blue cats are not difficult to tell apart. For example, one could compare between the Russian Blue and the Chartreux. The coat of the Russian Blue has a silvery sheen because of almost imperceptible tipping, and its appearance and feel bring to mind mink. The coat of the Chartreux has a consistency similar to that of the otter, being medium short in length and slightly woolly in texture. Their general physical structure is completely different; irrespective of its somewhat large size, the Russian Blue is fine boned, long, firm, muscular, lithe and graceful in outline without being tubular in appearance, making it very different from the sturdy, robust, strong boned, solid and dense Chartreux. The shape of the head of the Russian Blue constitutes one of the distinctive characteristics of the breed; given the cat's general physical shape one would expect that the head would be thin, long and triangular. Instead, it is a smooth medium wedge with the top of the skull flat in profile continuing at a slight downward angle in a straight line to the tip of the nose and completely lacking the rounded, broad head and characteristic large jowls of the Chartreux.

7. Fee Rosa Glauca. With a physical structure that is both elegant and muscular, the Russian Blue achieves a balanced compromise between the lithe Oriental type and the more cobby body typical of the European and American Shorthair cats.

8. Grand Champion Roxanastasia's Bela Karolyi.

9. Faberge's Mariska of Satineque.

6   7

8   9

SCOTTISH FOLD

The first historical evidence of cats with folded or pendulous ears dates to 1796 and comes from China. In that year, an English sailor is said to have brought an example with him on his return trip to Europe. Another case is reported in 1938, again in China. However, as its name indicates, the Scottish fold that we know today was born in Pertshire, Scotland. In 1961 a female kitten with folded ears was discovered in a litter of otherwise normal, common, domestic cats. The folded ear characteristic was then fixed through breeding with common domestic cats and British Shorthairs. The development of the breed, however, and the stabilization of its phenotypic peculiarities was accomplished more by American breeders than by English. All bona fide Scottish Fold cats trace their pedigree to Susie, the first fold-ear cat discovered by the founders of the breed, William and Mary Ross. So far, official recognition has been given only by the C.F.A.. Extremely popular in the United States, the Scottish Fold is still relatively rare in Europe. Its diffusion is probably compromised by the moderate difficulties involved in reproduction, which can be achieved only through crosses between a Scottish Fold and an American or British Shorthair producing litters of no more than 2-4 kittens of which only a few (on average about half) have the characteristic folded ears. Interestingly, GCCF does not recognize this indigenous cat of the United Kingdom.

The ears of the Scottish Fold get their distinctive folded shape from an allele called F(d) (from folded). F(d) is the result of a mutation of the gene f(d), which has no effect on the shape of the ears and is possessed by all cats with normal ears. The Scottish Fold has a pair of F(d), and one of the original gene f(d); cats with normal ears have two pairs of f(d) and are thus said to be homozygous for f(d). Cats that are homozygous F(d), thus possessing two pairs of the variant F(d), must generally face serious problems: they are congenitally affected by an abnormal development of the epiphysis, an endocrine gland, which can cause several consequences, including the difficulty or impossibility of walking. To avoid the birth of kittens with this problem, Scottish Folds must generally not be mated to other other folded ear Scottish Folds. Reproduction of the breed is trusted to crosses with American or British Shorthairs; half of the kittens in each litter usually have normal ears, the other half will be Scottish Folds.

1. Scottish Fold silver tabby and white .
2. Red classic tabby. Contrary to what one might imagine, the Scottish Fold's folded ears cause no problems to its hearing or hygiene. As with any breed of cat, a weekly cleaning is enough. The folded ears are certainly an anomaly but in no sense an impairment; the Scottish Fold is a strong, healthy cat that requires no special care.

3. Longhaired brown mackerel tabby. The hair of the Scottish Fold can be short or, as in this example, long.
4. Calico.

5. Brown mackerel tabby and white. The Scottish Fold is a highly social animal, both with humans and with other domestic animals. Calm, sweet, and affectionate, thanks to its balanced character, it has no fear of children with whom it shows itself to be patient and gentle.

The most striking characteristic of the Scottish Fold is its small ears folded forward and downward, set in a caplike fashion to expose the rounded cranium; the ear tips are also rounded. This characteristic does not appear before the fourth week of age and takes on its final appearance within the first three months. Other details contribute to the singular appearance of the Scottish Fold: first of all there are its eyes, which are truly round, large, and wide open; its head is also well rounded with a particularly short, strong neck. The cat should stand firm on a well padded body without any hint of thickness or lack of mobility due to short coarse legs. The tail is medium to long in proportion to the body; it is important that the tail be flexible, preferably long and tapering. All in all, the impression is of a "fully round," compact, solid, and undeniably cute and appealing cat. The Scottish Fold is irresistible. If it seems downhearted, it is enough just to catch its eye and then it will become immediately attentive, stand up straight, pull in its tail, turn its head to the side, aim its folded ears at the speaker and look at him or her with its eyes wide open. How could anyone resist smiling?

	Body	Head	Ears	Eyes	Nose	Chin	Legs and Feet	Tail	Coat	Varieties
C.F.A.	Medium, rounded, and even from shoulder to pelvic girdle; medium bone structure.	Well-rounded, blending into a short neck.	Folded forward and downward, set in a cap-like fashion to expose the rounded cranium.	Wide open, large, round and well separated; color corresponds to that of the coat.	Short, with a gentle curve; a brief stop is permitted.	Firm chin and jaw.	No hint of thickness or lack of mobility due to short, coarse legs. Toes neat and well rounded.	From medium to long, in proportion to the body. Flexible and tapering.	Recognized in both Shorthair and Longhair variants.	Accepted in all colors, patterns, and with white except those showing evidence of hybridization with the Himalayan pattern.

SIAMESE

The Siamese is named for Siam, the former name of Thailand, source of the first examples to reach Europe. The breed is certainly very ancient; a cat with the basic characteristics of the modern Siamese appears in a Thai poetry text created between 1350 and 1750. There are even earlier illustrations that show a feline, perhaps wild, with the physical shape of the Siamese, but with a striped coat. The Siamese was introduced to Europe only around the end of the last century. In 1880 the King of Siam gave two pairs of Siamese to the English consul-general in Bangkok. These were taken to London and presented to the public in a show the following year where they were identified as the Royal cat of Siam and enjoyed enormous success. In 1890, the first Siamese arrived in the United States, the result of another gift from the King of Siam, this to an American friend. The era of the Siamese had fully begun.

1. Champion Black Thai's Victoria, seal point. The long, tapering head is in harmony with the general physical shape of the svelte type. The chin is square but not heavy and is in line with the tip of the nose. The chin and jaws of males are stronger than those of females.

2. Chocolate point.

The Siamese is an intelligent, highly original cat with a striking personality and an inscrutable inner life, sudden changes of humor, and unpredictable changes in behavior. It is very sensitive; one must be careful in responding to its requests, which are themselves not always explicit. It should be treated with balance and deep respect. It requires patience, dedication, and loads of affection; even when it seems aloof, it wants to sense the nearby presence of its owner. Thus, a Siamese is the proper pet only for someone who is sure to dedicate all the affection and time necessary. A neglected Siamese is capable of letting itself slowly die, but a Siamese given plenty of attention more than returns the affection and will follow its beloved owner everywhere.

	Body	Head	Ears	Eyes	Nose	Chin	Legs and Feet	Tail	Coat	Varieties
C.F.A.	Medium size, graceful, long and svelte, a distinctive combination of fine bones and firm muscles; a long, slender neck.	Long, tapering wedge, medium in size, proportional, triangular.	Strikingly large, pointed, wide at the base, continuing the lines of the wedge.	Medium size, almond-shaped. Deep. vivid blue.	Long and straight , a continuation of the forehead with no break.	Medium size; a fine, wedge shaped muzzle.	Legs long and slim; paws dainty, small and oval.	Long, thin, tapering to a fine point.	Short, fine textured, glossy, lying close to body. Definite contrast between body color and points.	Seal Point, Blue Point, Chocolate Point, Lilac Point.

Almost two centuries of controlled breeding were required to put an end to the thorny question of the Siamese cat's tail. The question was whether it should be long, short, or a corkscrew ("curled" has a more elegant sound). According to some, the short tail, was a distinctive sign of the original Asiatic Siamese and should have been maintained in homage to tradition. Indeed, it seems probable that the progenitors of today's Siamese had a twisted or kinked tail. A legend tells how the princesses of Siam were in the habit of entrusting their rings to Siamese cats who used their tails as a sort of ring holder. Since the rings fell off straight, thin tails the diligent custodians themselves curved their tails so that the rings, once slipped on, could no longer slide off. The breeders of today, however, pay little heed to such legends and consider the short or "curled" tail an anomaly to be eliminated. The tail, therefore, must be long, thin, and tapering (like those that were of no use to the princesses of Siam). Today, only cats with long tails and with no visible knots, kinks or abnormalities are accepted for show.

3. Champion J. Bar's Deli Delight of Siminn, seal point.

4. Left, Champion Petisfois En Plus D'Exquis, blue point. Right, Grand Champion Petitfois Dangerous, seal point.

5. Premier Morningbrook So Solomon, chocolate point.

5

The Siamese cats that arrived in the West between 1880 and 1890 were not precisely the Siamese we know today; the original body structure was more cobby; the head was small and round rather than triangular; and the eyes were located so as to make the cats appear slightly cross-eyed. Even so, the Siamese rapidly earned vast popularity. At the beginning of this century, in the 1920s, Siamese cats were so fashionable that the demand exceeded the supply, and breeders, overwhelmed by requests, abandoned strict breeding programs and permitted a great deal of inbreeding. The result was catastrophic; the breed was greatly weakened, and the mortality rate in utero as well as among kittens and even adults—already high in an animal as delicate as the Siamese—rose to dizzying heights. The breed was at serious risk. Whether they wished to or not, the breeders were forced to return to a carefully planned breeding program, producing fewer cats but respecting the laws of nature. The splendid and regal animal that we know today was in reality born only after the crisis of the 1920's.

6

6, 7. The ears are very large, well spaced, wide at the base, and pointed. Looked at straight on, the head must be perfectly inscribable within a triangle with the base above and the point at the nose; the outer borders of the ears must form an extension of the two sides of the triangle. The ears, therefore, emphasize and extend the wedge shape of the head.

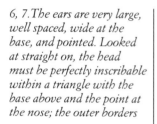

7

132

Physical characteristics are not the only unique aspect of the Siamese. Pages and pages have been written about the character of the Siamese, and feline literature abounds with anecdotes, analyses, interpretations, advice, warnings, pleas, opinions, and declarations, all designed to cast at least some light on the fascinating mystery of the breed. Meanwhile, the Siamese, well aware of the trepidation with which his admirers approach him, does with them as he wishes. Lively, indeed exuberant, full of life and overflowing with energy, he occasionally gives in to absolute explosions of vitality that seriously endanger knick-knacks, teapots and cups, photograph holders, exotic plants, curtains, pillows, even furniture (considered by the Siamese as ideal for sharpening claws). Thus we have the first rule: acquire a Siamese only if you have a properly Siamese-proofed area. The breed's vitality also shows up in exuberant sexual activity; during the mating season, both males and females are extremely restless (more than usual), and express themselves in piercing, almost continuous loud vocalizations, and, impulsive as they are, do not think twice about leaping out an open window and disappearing across the rooftops or down the street in search of their amorous dreams. So the second rule: acquire a Siamese only if you are of a tranquil nature and are endowed with nerves of steel.

8. Champion Begbie's Barry Blue Bear, blue point. In the Siamese as in all breeds with elegant bones and lithe bodies, the musculature is not strong, firm and elastic. For this reason, it is essential that there not be any accumulations of adipose fat. Unfortunately, by 2-3 years of age, even the best examples tend to gain weight. Furthermore, the body coat usually darkens with age.

8

9. The Blue Point has a bluish white body color which contrasts with the deep blue point color. The nose leather is slab colored.

10. The chocolate point Siamese is noted for its ivory colored body which is free of shading; points of a milk chocolate color are warm in tone.

The head of the Siamese is a long, tapering wedge, medium in size and in good proportion with the body. The total wedge starts at the nose and flares out in straight lines to the tips of the ears forming a triangle. The eyes must be placed no less than the width of an eye apart; they are almond-shaped, medium sized and slanted toward the nose in harmony with lines of the wedge and ears. Occasionally, this eye set will produce the appearance of the cat's having crossed eyes…an undesirable trait. One legend relates that Siamese cats were entrusted with guarding an ancient vase of great value in a temple (Siamese cats often appear as guardians of precious objects in popular tradition). The cats watched over the vase so long, staring at it fixedly and intensely, that their eyes remained forever crossed. Today, crossed eyes are considered a defect; breeders have generally corrected it.

11

11. *Typical, elegant, high style Siamese cat demanded or the modern show bench.*

On the coat of the Siamese, which is short, fine-textured, close lying and glossy, areas of intense coloration stand out. These areas, located on the mask, ears, legs, feet, and tail, are the points. These are not spots; they do not have clearly defined borders but are instead so delicately shaded that they blend into the lighter, uniform contrasting color of the coat that covers the rest of the body. In the area of the points, as elsewhere, the coat of the Siamese is of the non agouti type; each single hair has a solid coloration that is not broken by stripes of color. This is a characteristic of all solid coats. In fact, the coat of the Siamese begins as one solid color. The gene that causes the solid color is called the C (from colored) gene; a variant of this gene, the allele c(s), controls the coloration of the Siamese type. Other alleles of the C gene are known: C(b), for example, causes the dark brown color of the Burmese. Given the power of genes, one would expect that the concentration of color on the points would also depend on some piece of genetic material with a cryptic abbreviation. Instead, for once, this is not the case. Temperature is the cause; the lower the body temperature, the greater the deposition of pigment. In outer areas, as, for example, on the ears, the loss of body heat is greatest; thus, the body temperature is lower and the color is darker. Given that the loss of heat increases with the drop in environmental temperature, Siamese raised in cold areas tend to have particularly dark points. However, the relationship between environmental temperature, loss of body heat, and pigmentation of the points is not absolute and exhibits variations, sometimes large, from individual to individual.

12, 13. The seal point tabby genotype differs from the chocolate only in that the pair of bb alleles is replaced by the B gene, which, in both homozygous BB and in heterozigotic Bb, effects the synthesis of black pigment rather than chocolate. By acting on the color of the pigment and its dilution one can obtain blue, lilac, or other colored tabby patterns. The same goes for the rest of the non-tabby pointed coat.
Regardless of variety, Siamese (and Colorpoint Shorthairs) are born without pigment; the synthesis of pigment begins only after a few days of life.

12

13

In this case, the breed's name truly reflects its place of origin, for Singapura is the Malaysian name for the island of Singapore, and this is the cat of Singapore. Domestic by vocation, wild by necessity, its origins are lost in time. The Western world became aware of it only in 1974, when something in its appearance or behavior attracted the attention of two vacationing Americans. The first pair arrived in the United States in 1975; new cats were imported in 1980. The breed is still relatively rare, both in the United States and in Europe. Even so, the Singapura has many good qualities that should increase its standing with the general public: it is small but strong and enjoys good health, thanks in part to the natural selection it underwent during its years on its own. Capable of self-sufficiency when needed, it has a gentle character and is social both with humans and other cats. Discreet and never invasive, it maintains its taste for playing through its entire life.

1. The Singapura is the smallest breed of cat. Even so, it is solid and muscular. Agile and quick, it keeps its trim body even at an advanced age thanks in part to its ability to adjust its diet to its energy needs. The ticked coat is similar to that of the Abyssinian in that each hair has an ivory-color base and ticking of a warm brown color. Small barring appears on the inner area of the front legs and on the back knee only. The very large eyes have an appealing sloe-eyed look.

2. Grand Champion Nuance Rimba's Peaches of Squire.

It must be admitted that this little cat reminds most observers of its larger, wild cousin, the American cougar. It has many appealing features including its pastel coloring and distinctive visage. The breed is characterized by its alert expression, its healthy, small to medium-sized muscular body and noticeably large eyes and ears. The coat is fine and short and lies close to the body; the tail is thin, but not whip-like, and ends in a blunt, dark colored tip. The cat has a sepia agouti coat with its characteristic dark brown ticking on a warm, old ivory ground color. The broad muzzle, chin, chest, and stomach are the color of unbleached muslin. Capable of adapting to any situation, of taking care of itself and wriggling out of the most difficult situations, the Singapura has a very peaceful temperament and a natural inclination to home life. It is as if it wanted only to rest after the years of living on the streets of Singapore. Mild, patient, discreet, and affectionate, it is a cat in search of security and protection. It has the air of a wild cat just picked up off the street and brought into a warm house full of good cooking smells–amazed and uncertain, it is as though it doesn't believe its own eyes. And the final result is that it brings out the tenderness in everyone.

3. Singapore Gin Sling. The Singapura is a peaceful cat. This trait comes from its innate prudence, a quality acquired during the long years of life in the wild, as well as its marked friendliness, which is fed by its inexhaustible curiosity. One characteristic of the Singapura is the way it approaches strangers: at first it maintains its distance, but its curiosity gradually takes over, finally becoming so irresistible that it makes a few cautious maneuvers that bring it closer to the stranger. At that point, a little petting is

3

	Body	Head	Ears	Eyes	Nose	Chin	Legs and Feet	Tail	Coat	Varieties
C.F.A.	Small to medium size. Moderately stocky and muscular.	Rounded skull with definite whisker break. Medium-short broad muzzle. Short, thick neck.	Large, slightly pointed, wide open at the base.	Large, almond-shaped, brilliant and wide open. Hazel, green, or yellow in color.	A blunt nose with a very slight stop well below eye level.	Well developed.	Heavy, muscular legs tapering to small, short, oval feet.	Thin but not whip like. Blunt tip.	Fine, very short, and close-lying.	Only sepia agouti.

SNOWSHOE

The Snowshoe traces its ancestry to a kitten born in the 1970's in the United States. Both the sire and the dam were Siamese; however, the kitten was not only pointed, but was also marked with white on its legs, face and the underside of its body. This distinctive coloration was maintained by a careful breeding program which included controlled mating with the American Shorthair. Today's shorthaired Snowshoe is characterized by its pointed coat and areas of pure white which include the face, the underside of the body, and the paws. Of particular note are the white gloves on the front paws, which must be symmetrical and confined to the lower part of the paw. Ideally, the white markings on the front paws end at the first joint, forming a straight line. On the rear legs, the white extends up the back of the leg, ending in a pointed shape called the lance. This cat is noted for the colorful display of its golden-beige coat with either seal brown or slate gray-blue points and white accents on its underside, its face, and each of its four paws.

1. Seal Snowshoe. The coat is thick and glossy but not particularly silky in feel. There is a sharp contrast between the body coloring, the points, and the areas of white. The cat is medium to large in size with the females slightly smaller.

2. Kittens. Seal Point and Blue Point are the only two colors recognized at this time.

Body	Head	Ears	Eyes	Nose	Chin	Legs and Feet	Tail	Coat	Varieties
Solid in structure; strong and muscular.	Medium size as wide as it is long; gently rounded planes, high cheekbones.	Medium in size with slightly rounded tips; wide at the base.	Large, neither rounded nor slanted, wide set, spaced slightly apart; dark blue	Medium in length.	Well-developed forming a perpendicular line with the nose. Cheeks: Well-developed in the males (stud jowls).	Strong legs; paws are oval and compact. Paws must be white.	Medium to long; thick at the base, narrowing to a point at the end.	Short and dense	Seal Point and Blue Point.

SOMALI

Though its name would indicate an origin in Somalia, this breed first appeared in the United States; it was named "Somali" because it was derived from an Abyssinian, and Somalia is geographically nearby. The breed originated early in the 20th century in litters of Abyssinians. Its expansion was originally restricted by the small number of breeders involved, but the Somali's popularity was given a boost in 1978 when the breed was officially recognized by the C.F.A. The Somali was presented to the European public soon after and met with a favorable response, obtaining recognition from the F.I.Fe. and G.C.C.F.. Today, the Somali's popularity is on the increase throughout the world although many professionals and ordinary cat fanciers seem to prefer its progenitor, the Abyssinian. The truth is that the agouti coloration, which constitutes the dominant characteristic of the coat in both breeds, is more easily appreciated on the Abyssinian's shorter, resilient coat than on the Somali's medium length coat.

1

2

3

1. Champion Fifala's Swampfox, blue Somali. The Somali body type strikes a medium between the extremes of the cobby and the svelte, lengthy types.

2, 3. At birth, the coat is usually darker than it will appear in the adult; it reaches full development and takes on its final color after 2 years.

4. Champion Lynn-Lee's Sunday of Catipaws, red Somali.

5. Suspance di Gens Rubra, 45 day old female.

Even from the behavioral point of view, the Somali has preserved the basic characteristics of the Abyssinian. It needs a little space at its disposition and a feeling of freedom. Despite its medium-length coat, however, it does not tolerate the cold well; during the winter it should be let out only during the warmer hours of the day. Curious and intelligent, it is a good observer. Before establishing a close and positive relationship with its owner, it wants to know him or her deeply, gradually growing more familiar one small step at a time. Loyally affectionate, the Somali retains a somewhat independent character.

The Somali is an Abyssinian with a medium long coat; its double coat is very soft, extremely fine and silky—the more dense, the better. Except for its length, the coat has all the standard Abyssinian characteristics; it is uniformly agouti on the body with possible traces of an evanescent tabby pattern on the head and tail. Unlike the Abyssinian, the Somali has the particular genetic makeup that in longhaired breeds of cats increases the speed of hair growth, but it does not possess the modifying genes that would render the coat particularly rich and thick. A colorful cat, the Somali is accepted in the Abyssinian colors Ruddy, Red, Blue and Fawn.

4

5

	Body	Head	Ears	Eyes	Nose	Chin	Legs and Feet	Tail	Coat	Varieties
C.F.A.	Medium long, lithe, and graceful; back is slightly arched, no tuck up.	A modified, slightly rounded wedge without flat planes.	Large, alert, moderately pointed, broad; tufts desirable.	Almond shaped, large, brilliant, expressive with dark lid skin; gold or green in color.	Showing a gentle contour and with a slight rise from the bridge to the forehead.	Full and rounded.	In proportion to the torso; oval and compact feet.	Having a full brush, thick at base and slightly tapering.	Medium length, soft, extremely fine, double coated; preference given ruff and breeches.	Ruddy, Red, Blue, Fawn.

SPHYNX

The Sphynx (one glance is enough to understand the name) is derived from several hypotrichous—meaning with very short, almost absent, hair—kittens born in an otherwise normal litter from a female Siamese. This occurrence in Canada in 1966 is only one known instance of this mutation; a similar mutation had already happened in Mexico at the end of the last century. In that case, the kittens awakened interest in breeders, were crossed with their parents and with one another, and led to a new breed, the Mexican Hairless, recognized only in its country of origin. Other cases have occurred independently of one another in Australia, Morocco, and France. The genetic basis for this absence of hair has been studied only in the Canadian Sphynx and in the French hairless cats. The breeding of hairless cats raises several ethical questions. The almost total absence of hair is, without doubt, a serious anomaly, constantly countered in nature as a maladaptive mutation. Perhaps in this case man should limit himself to scientific interest and put a brake on his attraction to that which is unusual.

1, 2. Gadget des Nesmes, one and one-half year old male. The Sphynx is a medium-size cat with a relatively light bone structure and well-developed musculature. The nearly total absence of hair is not its sole characteristic. Among its other distinguishing traits are its richly folding skin; found on the stomach, paws which seem to have been subjected to twisting torsion. It has thick and strong knees on its forelegs, paws with elongated toes, enormous ears which are very wide at the base and, as with the eyes, spaced far apart. The head has pronounced and protruding cheekbones. All together, the appearance is quite surprising and really seems to have little to do with the average cat.

There is hair on the Sphinx, but it is almost invisible; it is impossible to speak of inner, middle and outer layers of the coat, of undercoat, awn hairs, and guard hairs. The coat of the Sphynx, or better its down, is very short, sparse and is not organized in layers. The cat's skin is clearly visible on the muzzle, ears, paws, and tail and feels, in these areas, similar to suede. The normal temperature of the Sphynx is slightly higher than that of other domestic breeds making it very warm to the touch. Even the whiskers are short and irregular. As in other cases in which man has sought to fix characteristics that natural selection would have eliminated, the life of the Sphynx is not easy. This breed is highly sensitive to cold, to abrupt changes in temperature, to dampness and to humidity. To make up for the increased energy lost to thermo-regulation, it must eat a great deal and often; also it wounds easily (a coat protects against blows) and reproduction is complex. The Sphynx is an extremely delicate animal even though the nearly complete absence of hair is not accompanied by any other obvious physical anomalies. In the Canadian Sphynx, the reduction of the coat to a minimum is caused by a gene known as h(r); in the French Sphynx, a different gene, known as h, appears to be involved. The exact mechanism by which the development of the hair is so greatly inhibited is not clear.

3, 4. The absence of hair of the Sphynx does not exempt its owner from caring for its hygiene and appearance. The skin of the Sphynx perspires and must be cleaned regularly using a delicate cleansing solution; some owners use warm milk for this purpose. The large ears easily become dirty and should be carefully cleaned with cotton swabs. The Sphynx requires a constant temperature and should rarely be permitted out doors. Since it is very lively and would enjoy playing in a garden in the company of its owner to whom it becomes firmly attached, the Sphinx needs extra attention and affection; it wants to sense the constant presence of its owner. It develops an emotional co-dependency on its owner, following him everywhere, seeking to take part in all his activities, and requiring continuous assurances from a glance, a word, or a caress. This is truly an unique animal.

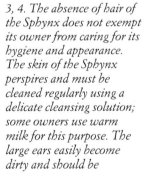

	Body	Head	Ears	Eyes	Nose	Chin	Legs and Feet	Tail	Coat	Varieties
	Medium size and small boned with compact muscles and a "barrel" chest.	Neither round nor wedge-shaped. Longer than wide.	Large and rounded at the tips.	Lemon-shaped and set back.	Short with a slight stop well below eye level.	Normal.	Long, thin legs; the feet have long toes.	Long and tapering.	Nearly nude except for a light down on the face, ears, legs, tail, and paws.	Most colors.

TIFFANY

This new breed is the result of a precise plan to create a cat with the physical shape of a Burmese and the long hair of a Persian. The first experimental crosses between Burmese and Persians took place in the United States and produced encouraging results; the kittens enjoyed excellent health, survived well into adulthood, and reproduced easily. Furthermore, they exhibited a relative phenotypic homogeneity with only limited variations within each generation and among later generations. Re-breeding the cats from the first generations led to a rapid increase in the percentage of kittens in each litter that exhibited the desired phenotypic characteristics and led to the rapid fixing of these characteristics. When the probability of obtaining all Tiffany kittens in the fifth generation appraoched 100 percent, the breeding program introduced new outcrosses to Burmese and Persian phenotypes in order to limit the dangerous effects of inbreeding and to guarantee the new breed a large and rich gene pool.

1, 2. In the Tiffany, as in its Persian progenitor, the length of hair is a result of its speed of growth; simply put, in longhaired cats the coat grows more rapidly than in Shorthairs. This increased speed of growth is caused by a pair of alleles called l (from long). The activity of the l allele is, however, regulated by modifying genes, and these are different in the Tiffany and Persian. In the Tiffany, the speed of growth, although increased, is slower than it is in the Persian. As a result, the coat of the Tiffany is semi-long, a characteristic that makes its care easier without in any way compromising its richness and softness. Nonetheless, the coat requires daily care.

Not recognized by C.F.A., the Tiffany is a longhair variant of the Burmese. Between the Tiffany and the Burmese there is only one different allele; the gene that controls the speed of hair growth is present in the Tiffany in the l form responsible for the rapid growth of longhaired cats; in the Burmese, it appears in the L form responsible for the diminished rate of growth common to shorthair cats. From its Burmese progenitor, the Tiffany gets its physical shape, its outgoing nature, and its endless curiosity. However, in the Tiffany, the vivacity and independence typical of shorthair cats are tempered by the breed's Persian influence which is revealed not only in the long hair but also in its mildness of character and gentle personality. Thus, without any particular effort on the part of breeders, the Tiffany displays the best behavioral traits of the Burmese and the Persian.

3, 4. Initially, the Tiffany was known only in sable, the color of the Burmese. However, the brown of the Tiffany is slightly lighter than the sable brown of the Burmese, as if the pigmentation were less decided and more shaded. Not surprisingly, at birth Tiffany kittens appear not really brown but a light coffee color; with age, the color gradually darkens until assuming the final coloration around the sixth or seventh month of life. With a brown Tiffany, the foot pads must be brown, and the color of the hairless skin must match that of the coat. This also applies in the more recent varieties, the standards for which have at the moment been set only by the G.C.C.F. in England even though the breed was created in the United States. Aside from its coat, the special characteristics of the Tiffany include its muscular physical structure with rounded lines, its head, which is more round than that of the Burmese, its ears which are pricked slightly forward, and its round, slightly oblique set eyes.

	Body	Head	Ears	Eyes	Nose	Chin	Legs and Feet	Tail	Coat	Varieties
G.C.C.F.	Medium size, muscular, with a broad chest.	Large and round. Strong, rounded muzzle.	Medium size with rounded tips.	Expressive, well open and positioned slightly on the oblique. Well spaced and of a golden-green or green color.	In profile there is a visible break.	Well developed with no sign of malocclusion	Proportional legs of medium length; oval feet.	Medium length, elegant, bushy.	Semi-long and silky.	Solid colors; tortoiseshell in the colors black, blue, chocolate, and lilac and Burmese variants of the same colors, including silver.

TONKINESE

The Tonkinese is one of the many breeds that have been given attractive but completely unfounded exotic names because of their relationship with other Oriental breeds. The Tonkinese, as a matter of fact, has nothing whatsoever to do with the Gulf of Tonkin; it was first produced in North America between 1950 and 1970 through the combined efforts of American and Canadian breeders who wanted to combine the high style Siamese with the more moderate and muscular Burmese selecting what they considered to be the best of each of these two famous breeds. The resulting breed, the Tonkinese, was created

to fill the gap which occurred when the old fashioned, moderate, round (apple) headed Siamese was greatly modified through selective breeding to produce the modern, high style, racy looking, tubular bodied, wedge-shaped headed cats of today's show type Siamese. The first official recognition was conferred in 1978 by the C.F.A.; European cat associations have yet to recognize this breed. For the moment, the Tonkinese is far more popular in the United States than in Europe even though it is always given a warm welcome at cat shows by both the public and experts.

1. Platinum Mink variety. From the genetic point of view, the pigmentation of the coat of the Tonkinese is the fruit of the concerted activity of two different alleles of the same gene. Of these, one, known as c(s) (from Siamese coloration) comes from the Siamese progenitor; the other, c(b) (from Burmese color) comes from the Burmese progenitor. The two alleles, joined in a co-dominant relationship, work side by side without difficulty to control the quantity and distribution of pigment.

2. Champagne Mink.
3. Blue Mink.
4. Natural Mink.

Since the Tonkinese was created by crossing a Siamese and a Burmese, its coat is pointed like the Siamese. In the Natural Mink coloration, for example, the base color of its coat is midway between the seal point of the Siamese and the dark sable brown of the Burmese; it is a medium brown with contrasting dark brown points. The contrast between the points and the rest of the coat is less marked than it is in the Siamese, but still must be evident. The color of the Tonkinese coat ranges from the medium brown of the Natural Mink, through buff-cream in the Champagne Mink, soft blue-gray with warm overtones in the Blue Mink, to pale, slivery gray with warm overtones in the Platinum Mink; the corresponding point colors are dark brown, medium brown, slate blue or frosty gray respectively. Most of the phenotypic characteristics of the Tonkinese are midway between those of the original two breeds. The body of the American style Burmese is compact and surprisingly heavy for its size, while the Siamese is known for its long, elegant, tubular body with its high style lines and long, fine-boned legs. The body of the Tonkinese strikes a balance between these two extremes; its legs are fairly slim but more solid and muscular, and the head is a modified wedge that is slightly longer than wide but less narrow and pointed than that of the Siamese.

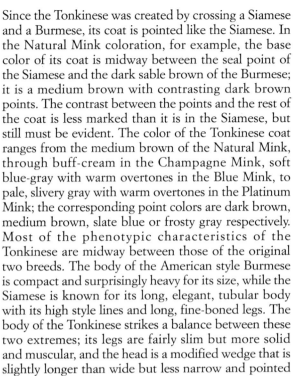

4

	Body	Head	Ears	Eyes	Nose	Chin	Legs and Feet	Tail	Coat	Varieties
C.F.A.	Medium size, torso of medium length; well-developed muscles but without coarseness.	Modified wedge shape, longer than wide. High cheekbones and blunt muzzle.	Medium size with oval tips, broad at the base. The skin may be visible through the hair.	Open, almond-shaped, slanted. Color is aqua, a definitive characteristic of the breed.	With slight stop at eye level.	In profile, the tip aligns with the tip of the nose on the same vertical plane.	Fairly slim and proportional to the body; paws more oval than round .	Tapering and proportional in length to the body.	Medium short, close-lying, fine, soft and silky with lustrous sheen.	Natural Mink; Champagne Mink; Blue Mink; Platinum Mink.

TURKISH ANGORA

Before 1500, longhaired cats were unknown in Europe, and the first documented report of a longhaired cat is dated 1520. The cat was white and came from Ankara, Turkey. Ankara has given its name to more than one breed of longhaired mammal–not only the Angora cat, but also the Angora goat and Angora rabbit (which provides the famous yarn known as angora wool). It is a possibility that the climate of the region favored the selection of animals with longer hair who were thereby well protected from the cold. However, the Angora cat's beauty did not help it maintain its fame over the centuries. Supplanted in popularity by the Persian, the Angora nearly became extinct. The breed survived only because a few examples were kept on display in the Ankara zoo. In the early 1960's, an American couple obtained permission to take a few Angora cats to the United States where breeding and selection began. The breed is not, as yet, universally recognized.

1

2

1. No Ruz Lily, a ten month old amber eyed white female. During the second half of this century, breeders created Angora colors other than white. Today there are black, blue, red, and cream Angora cats, as well as tabbies, smokes Parti-colors, bi-colors, and variations with white. No one can deny, however, that the most popular variety is still the white, not only because it typifies the original breed, but also because the white coat, without any trace of color or yellowish cast, is a superbly striking.

2. Champion/Premier Ziya Cadenza of Silverlock, Distinguished Merit.

3. Lacking an undercoat, the coat is less thick and less dense than in other breeds of semi-long or long hair cats; on the other hand, this quality also reduces knots and tangles making combing and brushing much easier.

3

	Body	Head	Ears	Eyes	Nose	Chin	Legs and Feet	Tail	Coat	Varieties
C.F.A.	Medium size, balance and fineness of bone more important than size; torso long and slender, firmly muscular.	Small to medium in size; a medium long smooth wedge.	Large, wide at base, pointed and tufted; set close together, high on the head, vertical and erect.	Large, almond-shaped, slanting slightly upward; open. May be blue, amber, or odd-eyed.	Medium in length; two planes formed by flat top head and line of nose; no break.	Firm, gently rounded.	Long, the hind legs longer than the front; paws are small, round and dainty.	Long and tapering from wide base to narrow end; full brush.	Single coat, full tail and ruff finely textured with silk-like sheen; "britches" on hind legs.	Solid colors, smoke, tabby, Parti-color, Bi-color, and combinations including with white.

The coat of the Angora, unlike the Persian, lacks undercoat, presumably the result of a different set of the modifying genes that control its richness. But the major difference between the two cats is their overall physical shape which is long and slender in the torso in the Angora and cobby in the Persian. In addition, the contrast continues with the Angora's body structure which is fine boned and medium sized with shoulders which are the same width as the hips; the legs are long. The Angora's head is small to medium in size and is a medium long, smooth wedge. Its ears are large, wide at the base and set close together, vertically and high on the head. The plume-like tail is long and tapers from a wide base to a narrow end.

4, 5. No Ruz Lily. The Angora cats maintained in the Ankara zoo were, and certainly had good reason to be, suspicious and semi-wild. Today, thanks to the efforts of breeders, the Angora is a friendly and gentle companion. Lively, happy, and playful at any age, it is a real extrovert who loves to be around humans and is interested in their activities. Rather quiet, it is sweet and affectionate with its owner. With its undeniable beauty and good character, and the fact that its coat does not require excessive care, this ancient breed's popularity will continue to grow. Popular in the United states, the Angora is still relatively rare in Europe where it more familiar to experts than to the public at large.

The true Angora cat, the ancient, almost legendary progenitor of the Persian, has a single coat which is finely textured and has a silk-like sheen. The tail and ruff should be long and full, and the "britches" should be apparent on the hind legs. The summer season results in a drastic loss of coat; the cats, when out of coat, look quite different, and their body structure, usually camouflaged by their coat, is readily apparent. As with many solid-color, white cats (for example, the white Persian), the white coat is often accompanied by deafness if either one or both of the eyes are blue (the cat will be deaf on the blue-eyed side if it is an odd-eyed white.)

TURKISH VAN

This breed, without a doubt ancient, traces its origin to the region of Turkey's Lake Van from which it takes its name. Its long hair, predominantly white, suggests family ties to the other famous breed of Turkish cat, the Angora; however, this connection has not been proven. The Turkish Van arrived in England in 1955. Although the Persian was still reigning supreme among longhaired cats, the Van awakened a certain amount of interest and was appreciated for the quality of its coat, its characteristic coloration, and for its overall physical shape. The breed was given official recognition in England in 1969 and in the rest of the world the following year. Although the Van is a healthy cat and reproduces without difficulty, its popularity has been limited by the difficulty in producing examples with the correct characteristic distribution of the areas of color on its otherwise pristine, white coat. Their breeding is best accomplished by experienced and patient cat experts. The results, when correct, bring enormous satisfaction.

1, 2. Ava Von Ararat, 10 month old white female with brownish-red markings and amber eyes. The distribution of color characteristic to the Van enjoys great popularity and has been "exported" to other breeds. But this is not the only characteristic that makes the Van a superb cat; equally important is its sturdy and muscular physical shape. The body is moderately long, broad and deep chested; the head is a substantially broad wedge with gentle contours and a slight dip in the nose below eye level which produces an aristocratic profile. The coat is semi-long with a cashmere-like texture completely without undercoat, a characteristic it shares with the Angora. This feature is appreciated by owners who have fewer mats or tangles with which to contend when taking comb and brush in hand.

The distribution of color on the Turkish Van is unmistakable. It is this distinctive color distribution which was adopted by other breeds as the currently, well-known, beautiful Van pattern. Except for the tail, which has colored bands, and a few, usually two, colored markings on the forehead, and one or two small colored body spots, the coat is entirely chalk white. From the genetic point of view, the Turkish Van is no different from any other bi-color cat. This means that the presence and distribution of the colored areas are controlled by a single gene, called S. It seems that the S gene decrees that the marks will exist, but does not specify exactly how many, how large, and where they will be located. This is the reason that creating cats with only limited colored markings, and locating them exclusively in certain pre-established areas, is a tremendous challenge. Producing a Van in keeping with the established color standard is not easy. It is hoped, however, that, someday, an increased knowledge of cat genetics will permit the identification and use, for example, of some new "modifying" gene involved in "positioning" the colored markings.

3. In this cat, the same as on the preceding page, the marks have a reddish tone; however due to the effect of dilution, the red has been transformed into its dilute color, cream.

4. Rikki Tikki Tavi is a 4 month old cream marked male. The dilution is complimented by the color of the eyes, which are a pale gold. In the Van, the distribution and quality of the color are well defined even at birth.

3

4

The Turkish Van is said to love water. And, in truth, it does not struggle when given a bath. However, this may be nothing more than a philosophical acceptance of one more of life's inevitable ills. Nor is this such an odd notion as the Turkish Van is a peaceful, obedient, and sufficiently intelligent cat which is quickly capable of developing a trust for its human companion. Even so, the bath should be performed with care; irrespective of the apparent strength of the cat and its thick coat, it is a delicate animal that easily catches cold, as do all cats. Therefore, it requires attention and care, which it will repay with delicate demonstrations of affection directed at all members of the family, but most of all at the person it selects for its special companion.

5. Rikki Tikki Tavi.

6, 7. Ava Von Ararat with her Titian Red marks. Although sweet and affectionate with their owners, Van cats may be quite aggressive with other cats. Combative and daring, they can become involved in furious battles in which they fight to the end and *usually win. Given freedom of movement, a group of Van cats is likely to form a compact social group, a true pack. As can be imagined, these somewhat wild aspects of the Van's character do not facilitate its involvement in shows nor in breeding programs.*

5

6

7

	Body	Head	Ears	Eyes	Nose	Chin	Legs and Feet	Tail	Coat	Varieties
C.F.A.	Moderately long, sturdy, broad, muscular and deep chested; males substantially larger than females.	Substantially broad wedge with gentle contours.	Moderately large to large, set fairly high and well apart, tips slightly rounded.	Moderately large, rounded aperture, set at a slant. Amber, blue, or odd-eyed in color.	Has a slight dip below eye level.	Firm, in line with nose and upper lip, rounded muzzle.	Moderately long, muscular legs taper to rounded moderately large feet.	Long, in proportion to body, with a brush appearance.	Semi-long with cashmere-like texture; coat is seasonal… shorter in summer; substantially longer and thicker in winter.	Chalk white with solid, tabby, PartiColor or any other color markings except those indicating hybridization with the Himalayan pattern.

THE CAT FANCIERS' ASSOCIATION INC.

SHOW STANDARDS

ABYSSINIAN

■ POINT SCORE

HEAD (25)	
Muzzle	6
Skull	6
Ears	7
Eye Shape	6
BODY (30)	
Torso	15
Legs and Feet	10
Tail	5
COAT (10)	
Texture	10
COLOR (35)	
Color	15
Ticking	15
Eye Color	5

GENERAL: the overall impression of the ideal Abyssinian would be a colorful cat with a distinctly ticked coat, medium in size and regal in appearance. The Abyssinian is lithe, hard and muscular, showing eager activity and a lively interest in all surroundings. Well balanced temperamentally and physically with all elements of the cat in proportion.
HEAD: a modified, slightly rounded wedge without flat planes; the brow, cheek, and profile lines all showing a gentle contour. A slight rise from the bridge of the nose to the forehead, which should be of good size, with width between the ears and flowing into the arched neck without a break. MUZZLE: not sharply pointed or square. The chin should be neither receding nor pro-

truding. Allowance should be made for jowls in adult males.
EARS: alert, large, and moderately pointed; broad, and cupped at base and set as though listening. Hair on ears very short and close lying, preferably tipped with black or dark brown on a ruddy Abyssinian, chocolate-brown on a red Abyssinian, slate blue on the blue Abyssinian, or light cocoa brown on a fawn Abyssinian.
EYES: almond shaped, large, brilliant, and expressive. Neither round nor oriental. Eyes accentuated by fine dark line, encircled by light colored area.
BODY: medium long, lithe and graceful, but showing well developed muscular strength without coarseness. Abyssinian conformation strikes a medium between the extremes of the cobby and the svelte lengthy type. Proportion and general balance more to be desired than mere size.
LEGS and FEET: proportionately slim, fine boned. The Abyssinian stands well off the ground giving the impression of being on tip toe. Paws small, oval, and compact. Toes: five in front and four behind.
TAIL: thick at base, fairly long and tapering.
COAT: soft, silky, fine in texture, but dense and resilient to the touch with a lustrous sheen. Medium in length but long enough to accommodate two or three dark bands of ticking.

PENALIZE: off-color pads. Long narrow head, short round head. Barring on legs, dark broken necklace markings, rings on tail. Coldness or grey tones in the coat.

DISQUALIFY: white locket, or white

anywhere other than nostril, chin, and upper throat area. Kinked or abnormal tail. Dark unbroken necklace. Grey undercoat close to the skin extending throughout a major portion of the body. Any black hair on red Abyssinian. Incorrect number of toes. Any color other than the four accepted colors.

ABYSSINIAN COLORS
Coat color: warm and glowing. Ticking: distinct and even, with dark colored bands contrasting with lighter colored bands on the hair shafts. Undercoat color clear and bright to the skin. Deeper color shades desired, however intensity of ticking not to be sacrificed for depth of color. Darker shading along spine allowed if fully ticked. Preference given to cats UNMARKED on the undersides, chest, and legs; tail without rings. Facial Markings: dark lines extending from eyes and brows, cheekbone shading, dots and shading on whisker pads are all desirable enhancements. Eyes accentuated by fine dark line, encircled by light colored area. Eye color: gold or green, the more richness and depth of color the better.

RUDDY: coat ruddy brown (burnt-sienna), ticked with various shades of darker brown or black; the extreme outer tip to be the darkest, with orange-brown undercoat. Tail tipped with black. The underside and inside of legs to be a tint to harmonize with the main color. Nose leather: tile red. Paw pads: black or brown, with black between toes, extending slightly beyond the paws.

RED: coat rich, warm glowing red,

ticked with chocolate-brown, the extreme outer tip to be dark, with red undercoat. Tail tipped with chocolate-brown. The underside and inside of legs to be a tint to harmonize with the main color. Nose leather: rosy pink. Paw pads: pink, with chocolate-brown between toes, extending slightly beyond the paws.

BLUE: coat warm beige, ticked with various shades of slate blue, the extreme outer tip to be the darkest, with blush beige undercoat. Tail tipped with slate blue. The underside and inside of legs to be a tint to harmonize with the main color. Nose leather: old rose. Paw pads: mauve, with slate blue between toes, extending slightly beyond the paws.

FAWN: coat warm rose-beige, ticked with light cocoa brown, the extreme outer tip to be the darkest, with blush beige undercoat. Tail tipped with light cocoa brown. The underside and inside of legs to be a tint to harmonize with the main color. Nose leather: salmon. Paw pads: pink with light cocoa brown between the toes, extending slightly beyond the paws.
Abyssinian allowable outcross breeds: none.

AMERICAN CURL

■ POINT SCORE

HEAD (20)	
Shape & Size	8
Profile	6
Muzzle	4
Chin	2
EARS (30)	
Degree of Curl	10
Shape & Size	10
Placement	8
Furnishings	2
EYES (10)	
Shape & Size	6
Placement	3
Color	1
BODY (25)	
Torso & Neck	9
Size & Boning	6
Legs & Feet	5
Tail Length	5
COAT AND COLOR (15)	
Silky Texture	6
Minimal Undercoat	4
Body Coat Length	2
Tail Coat Length	2
Color	1

GENERAL: the distinctive feature of the American Curl, first noted in Southern California in 1981, is their uniquely attractive curled ears. Shulamith, the first American Curl, was first noted in Southern California in 1981. Selective breeding began in

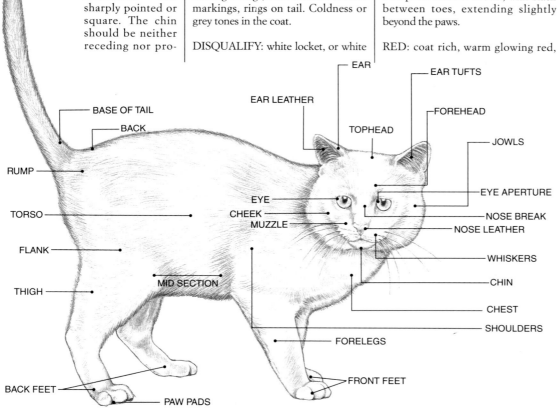

EAR
EAR TUFTS
EAR LEATHER
FOREHEAD
TOPHEAD
JOWLS
BASE OF TAIL
BACK
RUMP
EYE APERTURE
TORSO
EYE
NOSE BREAK
CHEEK
MUZZLE
NOSE LEATHER
FLANK
WHISKERS
CHIN
MID SECTION
THIGH
CHEST
SHOULDERS
BACK FEET
FORELEGS
FRONT FEET
PAW PADS

1983. Curls are well balanced, moderately muscled, slender rather than massive in build. Females weigh 5 to 8 pounds, males weigh 7 to 10 pounds. Proper proportion and balance are more important than size. Allowance is to be made for normal male characteristics. They are alert, active, with gentle, even dispositions.

HEAD: Shape: modified wedge without flat planes, moderately longer than wide, smooth transitions. Profile: nose moderate in length and straight, slight rise from bottom of eyes to forehead, gentle curve to top of head, flowing into neck, without a break. Size: medium in proportion to body. Muzzle: rounded with gentle transition, no pronounced whisker break. Chin: firm, in line with nose and upper lip.

EARS: Degree: minimum 90 degree arc of curl, not to exceed 180 degrees. Firm cartilage from ear base to at least 1/3 of height. Shape: wide at base and open, curving back in smooth arc when viewed from front and rear. Tips rounded and flexible. Size: moderately large. Placement: erect, set equally on top and side of head. Furnishings: desirable. Note: when Curls are alert with ears swiveled toward front, lines following curve of ear through tips should point to center of base of skull.

EYES: Shape: walnut, oval on top and round on bottom. Placement: set on slight angle between base of ear and tip of nose one eye width apart. Size: moderately large. Color: clear, brilliant, no relation to coat color except blue eyes required in colorpoint class.

BODY: Torso Shape: semi-foreign rectangle, length one and one-half times height at shoulder, medium depth of chest and flank. Size: intermediate, with allowances for larger males. Musculature: moderate strength and tone, flexible. Tail: flexible, wide at base, tapering; equal to body length. Legs: length medium in proportion to body, set straight when viewed from front or rear. Medium boning, neither fine nor heavy. Neck: medium. Feet: medium and rounded.

COAT & COLOR: Longhair Division: Texture: fine, silky, laying flat. Undercoat: minimal. Coat length: semilong. Tail coat: full and plumed. Color: all colors accepted as listed. Shorthair Division: Texture: soft, silky, laying flat, resilient without a plush dense feel. Undercoat: minimal. Coat length: short. Tail coat: same length as body coat. Color: all colors accepted as listed.

PENALIZE: Ears: low set; abrupt change of direction without smooth curve; pinch, horizontal or vertical crimp; interior surface which appears corrugated. Body: tubular or cobby. Excessive size. Nose: deep nose break. Coat: Longhair Division: heavy undercoat; heavy ruff; coarse or cottony texture. Shorthair Division: heavy undercoat, coarse texture; dense or plush coats.

DISQUALIFY: extreme curl in adult where tip of ear touches back of ear or head. Straight or severely mismatched ears. Thick or calcified ears. Lack of firm cartilage in base of ear. Tail faults.

AMERICAN CURL COLORS

WHITE: pure glistening white. Nose leather and paw pads: pink.

BLACK: dense coal black, sound from roots to tip of fur. Free from any tinge of rust on tips or smoke undercoat. Nose leather: black. Paw pads: black or brown.

BLUE: blue, lighter shade preferred, one level tone from nose to tip of tail. Sound to the roots. A sound darker shade is more acceptable than an unsound lighter shade. Nose leather and paw pads: blue.

RED: deep, rich, clear, brilliant red; without shading, markings, or ticking. Lips and chin the same color as coat. Nose leather and paw pads: brick red.

CREAM: one level shade of buff cream, without markings. Sound to the roots. Lighter shades preferred. Nose leather and paw pads: pink.

CHOCOLATE: rich, warm chocolate-brown, sound from roots to tip of fur. Nose leather and paw pads: brown.

LILAC: rich, warm lavender with a pinkish tone, sound and even throughout. Nose leather and paw pads: pink.

CHINCHILLA SILVER: undercoat pure white. Coat on back, flanks, head, and tail sufficiently tipped with black to give the characteristic sparkling silver appearance. Legs may be slightly shaded with tipping. Chin, ear tufts, stomach, and chest, pure white. Rims of eyes, lips, and nose outlined with black. Nose leather: brick red. Paw pads: black.

SHADED SILVER: undercoat white with a mantle of black tipping shading down from sides, face, and tail from dark on the ridge to white on the chin, chest, stomach, and under the tail. Legs to be the same tone as the face. The general effect to be much darker than a chinchilla. Rims of eyes, lips, and nose outlined with black. Nose leather: brick red. Paw pads: black.

CHINCHILLA GOLDEN: undercoat rich warm cream. Coat on back, flanks, head, and tail sufficiently tipped with black to give golden appearance. Legs may be slightly shaded with tipping. Chin, ear tufts, stomach, and chest, cream. Rims of eyes, lips, and nose outlined with black. Nose leather: deep rose. Paw pads: black.

SHADED GOLDEN: undercoat rich warm cream with a mantle of black tipping shading down from the sides, face, and tail from dark on the ridge to cream on the chin, chest, stomach, and under the tail. Legs to be the same tone as the face. The general effect to be much darker than a chinchilla. Rims of eyes, lips, and nose outlined with black. Nose leather: deep rose. Paw pads: black.

SHELL CAMEO (Red Chinchilla): undercoat white, the coat on the back, flanks, head, and tail to be sufficiently tipped with red to give the characteristic sparkling appearance. Face and legs may be very slightly shaded with tipping. Chin, ear tufts, stomach, and chest, white. Nose leather, rims of eyes and paw pads: rose.

SHADED CAMEO (Red Shaded): undercoat white with a mantle of red tipping shading down the sides, face, and tail from dark on the ridge to white on the chin, chest, stomach, and under the tail. Legs to be the same tone as face. The general effect to be much redder than the shell cameo. Nose leather, rims of eyes and paw pads: rose.

SHELL TORTOISESHELL: undercoat white. Coat on the back, flanks head, and tail to be delicately tipped in black with well-defined patches of red and cream tipped hairs as in the pattern of the tortoiseshell. Face and legs may be slightly shaded with tipping. Chin, ear tufts, stomach, and chest, white to very slightly tipped. Blaze of red or cream tipping on face is desirable.

SHADED TORTOISESHELL: undercoat white. Mantle of black tipping and clearly defined patches of red and cream tipped hairs as in the pattern of the tortoiseshell. Shading down the sides, face, and tail from dark on the ridge to slightly tipped or white on the chin, chest, stomach, legs, and under the tail. The general effect is to be much darker than the shell tortoiseshell. Blaze of red or cream tipping on the face is desirable.

BLACK SMOKE: white undercoat, deeply tipped with black. Cat in repose appears black. In motion the white undercoat is clearly apparent. Points and mask black with narrow band of white at base of hairs next to skin which may be seen only when fur is parted. Nose leather and paw pads: black.

BLUE SMOKE: white undercoat, deeply tipped with blue. Cat in repose appears blue. In motion the white undercoat is clearly apparent. Points and mask blue, with narrow band of white at base of hairs next to skin which may be seen only when fur is parted. Nose leather and paw pads: blue.

CAMEO SMOKE (Red Smoke): white undercoat, deeply tipped with red. Cat in repose appears red. In motion the white undercoat is clearly apparent. Points and mask red, with narrow band of white at base of hairs next to skin which may be seen only when fur is parted. Nose leather, rims of eyes, and paw pads: rose.

CHOCOLATE SMOKE: white undercoat, deeply tipped with chocolate. Cat in repose appears chocolate. In motion the white undercoat is clearly apparent. Points and mask chocolate with narrow band of white at base of hairs next to skin which may be seen only when fur is parted. Nose leather and paw pads: chocolate.

LAVENDER SMOKE: white undercoat, deeply tipped with lavender. Cat in repose appears lavender. In motion the white undercoat is clearly apparent. Points and mask lavender, with narrow band of white at base of hairs next to skin which may be seen only when fur is parted. Nose leather and paw pads: lavender.

CREAM SMOKE: white undercoat, deeply tipped with cream. Cat in repose appears cream. In motion the white undercoat is clearly apparent. Points and mask cream, with narrow band of white at base of hairs next to skin which may be seen only when fur is parted. Nose leather, rims of eyes, and paw pads: pink.

SMOKE TORTOISESHELL: white undercoat, deeply tipped with black with clearly defined unbrindled patches of red and cream tipped hairs as in the pattern of the tortoiseshell. Cat in repose appears tortoiseshell. In motion the white undercoat is clearly apparent. Face and ears tortoiseshell pattern with narrow band of white at the base of the hairs next to the skin that may be seen only when fur is parted. Blaze of red or cream tipping on face is desirable.

CHOCOLATE TORTOISESHELL SMOKE: white undercoat, deeply tipped with chocolate tortoiseshell. Cat in repose appears chocolate tortoiseshell. In motion the white undercoat is clearly apparent. Points and mask chocolate tortoiseshell with narrow band of white at base of hairs next to skin which may be seen only when fur is parted. Nose leather and paw pads: mottled with pink on nose and paws.

BLUE-CREAM SMOKE: white undercoat deeply tipped with blue, with clearly defined patches of cream as in the pattern of the blue-cream. Cat in repose appears blue-cream. In motion the white undercoat is clearly apparent. Face and ears blue-cream pattern with narrow band of white at the base of the hair next to the skin that may be seen only when fur is parted. Blaze of cream tipping on face is desirable.

CLASSIC TABBY PATTERN: markings dense, clearly defined, and broad. Legs evenly barred with bracelets coming up to meet the body markings. Tail evenly ringed. Several unbroken necklaces on neck and upper chest, the more the better. Frown marks on forehead form an intricate letter "M." Unbroken line runs back from outer corner of eye. Swirls on cheeks. Vertical lines over back of head extend to shoulder markings which are in the shape of a butterfly with both upper and lower wings distinctly outlined and marked with dots inside outline. Back markings consist of a vertical line down the spine from butterfly to tail with a vertical stripe paralleling it on each side, the three stripes well separated by stripes of the ground color. Large solid blotch on each side to be encircled by one or more unbroken rings. Side markings should be the same on both sides. Double vertical rows of buttons on chest and stomach.

MACKEREL TABBY PATTERN: markings dense, clearly defined, and all narrow pencillings. Legs evenly barred with narrow bracelets coming up to meet the body markings. Tail barred. Necklaces on neck and chest distinct, like so many chains. Head barred with an "M" on the forehead. Unbroken lines running back from the eyes. Lines running down the head to meet the shoulders. Spine lines run together to form a narrow saddle. Narrow pencillings run around body.

PATCHED TABBY: a patched tabby (torbie) is an established silver, brown, or blue tabby with patches of red and/or cream.

SPOTTED TABBY PATTERN: markings on the body to be spotted. May vary in size and shape with preference given to round, evenly distributed spots. Spots should not run together in a broken mackerel pattern. A dorsal stripe runs the length of the body to the tip of the tail. The stripe is ideally composed of spots. The markings on the face and forehead shall be typically tabby markings. Underside of the body to have "vest buttons." Legs and tail are barred.

TICKED TABBY PATTERN: body hairs to be ticked with various shades of marking color and ground color. Body when viewed from top to be free from noticeable spots, stripes, or blotches, except for darker dorsal shading. Lighter underside may show tabby markings. Face, legs, and tail must show distinct tabby striping. Cat must have at least one distinct necklace.

BROWN PATCHED TABBY: ground color brilliant coppery brown with classic or mackerel tabby markings of dense black with patches of red and/or cream clearly defined on both body and extremities; a blaze of red and/or cream on the face is desirable. Lips and chin the same shade as the rings around the eyes.

BLUE PATCHED TABBY: ground color, including lips and chin, pale bluish ivory with classic or mackerel tabby markings of very deep blue affording a good contrast with ground color. Patches of cream clearly defined on both body and extremities; a blaze of cream on the face is desirable. Warm fawn overtones or patina over the whole.

SILVER PATCHED TABBY: ground color, including lips and chin, pale silver with classic or mackerel tabby markings of dense black with patches of red and/or cream clearly defined on both body and extremities. A blaze of red and/or cream on the face is desirable.

SILVER TABBY (classic, mackerel): ground color, including lips and chin, pale, clear silver. Markings dense black. Nose leather: brick red. Paw pads: black.

RED TABBY (classic, mackerel): ground color red. Markings deep, rich red. Lips and chin red. Nose leather and paw pads: brick red.

BROWN TABBY (classic, mackerel): ground color brilliant coppery brown. Markings dense black. Lips and chin the same shade as the rings around the eyes. Back of leg black from paw to heel. Nose leather: brick red. Paw pads: black or brown.

BLUE TABBY (classic, mackerel): ground color, including lips and chin, pale bluish ivory. Markings a very deep blue affording a good contrast with ground color. Warm fawn overtones or patina over the whole. Nose leather: old rose. Paw pads: rose.

CREAM TABBY (classic, mackerel): ground color, including lips and chin, very pale cream. Markings of buff or cream sufficiently darker than the ground color to afford good contrast, but remaining within the dilute color range. Nose leather and paw pads: pink.

BLUE SILVER and CREAM SILVER TABBIES: tabby pattern with colors and leathers same as for corresponding shaded colors.

CHOCOLATE SILVER TABBY: ground color, including lips and chin, is silver. Markings rich chestnut. Nose leather: chestnut or pink rimmed with chestnut. Paw pads: cinnamon.

LAVENDER SILVER TABBY: ground color, including lips and chin, a cold clear silver. Markings sound lavender. Nose leather: lavender or pink rimmed with lavender. Paw pads: lavender-pink.

CAMEO TABBY (classic, mackerel): ground color off-white. Markings red. Nose leather and paw pads: rose.

TORTOISESHELL: black with unbrindled patches of red and cream. Patches clearly defined and well broken on both body and extremities. Blaze of red or cream on face is desirable.

CALICO: white with unbrindled patches of black and red. As a preferred minimum, the cat should have white feet, legs, undersides, chest, and muzzle. Less white than this minimum should be penalized proportionately. Inverted "V" blaze on face desirable.

DILUTE CALICO: white with unbrindled patches of blue and cream. As a preferred minimum the cat should have white feet, legs, undersides, chest, and muzzle. Less white than this minimum should be penalized proportionately. Inverted "V" blaze on face desirable.

BLUE-CREAM: blue with patches of solid cream. Patches clearly defined and well broken on both body and extremities.

BI-COLOR: black and white, blue and white, red and white, or cream and white. As a preferred minimum, the cat should have white feet, legs, undersides, chest, and muzzle. Less white than this minimum should be penalized proportionately. Inverted "V" blaze on face desirable. Cats with no more than a locket and/or button do not qualify for this color class. Such cats shall be judged in the color class of their basic body color with no penalty for such locket or button.

VAN BI-COLOR: Black and white, red and white, blue and white, or cream and white. White cat with color confined to the extremities; head, tail, and legs. One or two small colored patches on body allowable.

VAN CALICO: white cat with unbrindled patches of black and red confined to the extremities; head, tail, and legs. One or two small colored patches on body allowable.

VAN DILUTE CALICO: white cat with unbrindled patches of blue and cream confined to the extremities; head, tail, and legs. One or two small colored patches on body allowable.

(NOTE: cats having more than two small body spots should be shown in the regular bi-color class.)

TABBY AND WHITE: white with colored portions, the colored portions of the cat to conform to the currently established classic, mackerel, patched, ticked and spotted tabby color standards. As a preferred minimum, the cat should have white feet, legs, undersides, chest, and muzzle. Less white than this minimum should be penalized proportionately. Inverted "V" blaze on face desirable.

SEAL POINT: body even pale fawn to cream, warm in tone, shading gradually into lighter color on the stomach and chest. Points deep seal brown. Nose leather and paw pads: same color as points. Eye color: blue.

CHOCOLATE POINT: body ivory with no shading. Points milk-chocolate color, warm in tone. Nose leather and paw pads: cinnamon pink. Eye color: blue.

BLUE POINT: body bluish white, cold in tone, shading gradually to white on stomach and chest. Points blue. Nose leather and paw pads: slate blue. Eye color: blue.

LILAC POINT: body glacial white with no shading. Points frosty grey with pinkish tone. Nose leather and paw pads: lavender pink. Eye color: blue.

LILAC-LYNX POINT: body glacial white. Body shading may take form of ghost striping. Points: frosty grey with pinkish tone bars, distinct and separated by lighter background color; ears frosty grey with pinkish tone, paler thumbprint in center. Nose leather: lavender-pink permitted, pink edged in lavender-pink preferred. Paw pads: lavender-pink. Eye color: blue.

LILAC-CREAM POINT: body glacial white; mottling, if any, in the shade of the points. Points: frosty grey with pinkish tone, uniformly mottled with pale cream; a blaze is desirable. Nose leather and paw pads: lavender-pink; flesh or coral pink mottling desirable. Eye color: blue.

LILAC-CREAM LYNX POINT: body glacial white. Body shading may take form of ghost striping and/or cream mottling. Points: frosty grey with pinkish tone bars, distinct and separated by lighter background color; ears frosty grey with pinkish tone, paler thumbprint in center. Uniform mottling of cream overlays the markings of the points. Nose leather: lavender-pink permitted, pink edged in lavender-pink preferred, flesh or coral pink mottling may be present. Paw pads: lavender-pink, or lavender-pink mottled with flesh or coral pink. Eye color: deep vivid blue. NOTE: these cats resemble lynx points more than tortie points.

FLAME (RED) POINT: body creamy white. Points deep orange flame to deep red. Nose leather and paw pads: flesh or coral pink. Eye color: blue.

CREAM POINT: body creamy white with no shading. Points buff cream with no apricot. Nose leather and paw pads: flesh pink or salmon coral. Eye color: blue.

CREAM LYNX POINT: body clear white. Body shading may take form of ghost striping. Points: bars of pale buff cream to light pinkish cream, distinct and separated by lighter background color; ears pale buff cream to light pinkish cream, paler thumbprint in center. Nose leather and paw pads: flesh to coral pink. Eye color: blue.

TORTIE POINT: body creamy white or pale fawn. Points seal with unbrindled patches of red and/or cream. Blaze of red or cream on face is desirable. Nose leather and paw pads: seal brown with flesh and/or coral pink mottling to conform with colors of points. Eye color: blue.

CHOCOLATE-TORTIE POINT: body ivory, may be mottled in older cats. Points: warm milk-chocolate uniformly mottled with red and/or cream; a blaze is desirable. Nose leather and paw pads: cinnamon; flesh or coral pink mottling desirable. Eye color: blue.

CHOCOLATE-TORTIE LYNX POINT: body ivory. Body shading may take form of ghost striping and/or cream mottling. Points: warm milk-chocolate bars, distinct and separated by lighter background color; ears warm milk-chocolate with paler thumbprint in center. Uniform mottling of red and/or cream overlays the markings of the points. Nose leather: cinnamon permitted, pink edged in cinnamon preferred, flesh or coral pink mottling may be present. Paw pads: cinnamon, or cinnamon mottled with flesh or coral pink. Eye color: blue. NOTE: these cats resemble lynx points more than tortie points.

BLUE-CREAM POINT: body bluish white or creamy white, shading gradually to white on the stomach and chest. Points blue with patches of cream. Nose leather and paw pads: slate blue, pink, or a combination of slate blue and pink. Eye color: blue.

CHOCOLATE LYNX POINT: body ivory. Body shading may take form of ghost striping. Points: warm milk-chocolate bars, distinct and separated by lighter background color; ears warm milk-chocolate with paler thumbprint in center. Nose leather: cinnamon permitted, pink edged in cinnamon preferred. Paw pads: cinnamon. Eye color: blue.

SEAL LYNX POINT: points beige-brown ticked with darker brown tabby markings. Body color pale cream to fawn, warm in tone. Mask must be clearly lined with dark stripes vertical on forehead with classic "M" on forehead, horizontal on cheeks and dark spots on whisker pads clearly outlined in dark color edges. Inner ear light with thumbprint on outer ear. Markings dense, clearly defined and broad. Legs evenly barred with bracelets. Tail barred. No striping or mottling on body, but consideration to be given to shading in older cats. Nose leather: seal or brick red. Paw pads: seal. Eye color: blue.

BLUE LYNX POINT: points light, silvery blue, ticked with darker blue tabby markings. Body color bluish white, cold in tone. Mask must be clearly lined with dark stripes vertical on forehead with classic "M" on forehead, horizontal on cheeks and dark spots on whisker pads clearly outlined in dark color edges. Inner ear light with thumbprint on outer ear. Markings dense, clearly defined and broad. Legs evenly barred with bracelets. Tail barred. No striping or mottling on body, but consideration to be given to shading in older cats. Nose leather: blue or brick red. Paw pads: blue. Eye color: blue.

TORTIE-LYNX POINT: points beige-brown with dark brown tabby markings and patches of red. Body color creamy white or pale fawn. Mask must be clearly lined with dark stripes vertical on forehead with clas-

sic "M" on forehead, horizontal on cheeks and dark spots on whisker pads clearly outlined in dark color edges. Inner ear light with thumbprint on outer ear. Markings dense, clearly defined and broad. Legs evenly barred with bracelets. Tail barred. Nose leather and paw pads: seal brown and/or flesh or coral pink. Eye color: blue.

BLUE-CREAM LYNX POINT: points blue with darker blue tabby markings and patches of cream. Body color bluish white, cold in tone. Mask must be clearly lined with dark stripes vertical on forehead with classic "M" on forehead, horizontal on cheeks and dark spots on whisker pads clearly outlined in dark color edges. Inner ear light with thumbprint on outer ear. Markings dense, clearly defined and broad. Legs evenly barred with bracelets. Tail barred. Nose leather and paw pads: slate blue and/or pink. Eye color: blue.

OACC (Other American Curl Colors): all accepted pointed colors with white. Any other color or pattern.

American Curl allowable outcross breeds - domestic longhair or shorthair for litters born before 1/1/2010.

AMERICAN SHORTHAIR

■ POINT SCORE
HEAD (including size and shape of eyes, ear shape, and set and structure of nose)   30
TYPE (including shape, size, bone, and length of tail)   25
COAT   15
COLOR   20
(Tabby pattern = 10 points; Color =10 points)
EYE COLOR   10

GENERAL: the American Shorthair is a true breed of working cat. The conformation should be adapted for this with no part of the anatomy so exaggerated as to foster weakness. The general effect should be that of a strongly built, well balanced, symmetrical cat with conformation indicating power, endurance, and agility.
SIZE: medium to large. No sacrifice of quality for sake of size. Females may be less massive in all respects than males.
PROPORTIONS: slightly longer than tall. (Height is profile measure from top of shoulder blades to ground. Length is profile measure from tip of breastbone to rear tip of buttocks.) Viewed from side, body can be divided into three equal parts: from tip of breastbone to elbow, from elbow to front of hindleg, and from

front of hindleg to rear tip of buttocks. Length of tail is equal to distance from shoulder blades to base of tail.
HEAD: large, with full-cheeked face giving the impression of an oblong just slightly longer than wide. Sweet, open expression. Viewed from front, head can be divided in two equal parts; from base of ears to middle of eyes and from middle of eyes to chin tip.
EARS: medium size, slightly rounded at tips and not unduly open at base. Distance between ears, measured from lower inner corners, twice distance between eyes.
FOREHEAD: viewed in profile, forehead forms smooth, moderately convex continuous curve flowing over top of head into neck. Viewed from front, there is no dome between ears.
EYES: large and wide with upper lid shaped like half an almond (cut lengthwise) and lower lid shaped in a fully rounded curve. At least width of one eye between eyes. Outer corners set very slightly higher than inner corners. Bright, clear and alert.
NOSE: medium length, same width for entire length. Viewed in profile, gentle concavely curved rise from bridge of nose to forehead.
MUZZLE: squared. Definite jowls in mature males.
JAWS: strong and long enough to successfully grasp prey. Both level and scissors bites considered equally correct. (In level bite, top and bottom front teeth meet evenly. In scissors bite, inside edge of top front teeth touch outside edge of lower front teeth.)
CHIN: firm and well-developed, forming perpendicular line with upper lip.
NECK: medium in length, muscular and strong.
BODY: solidly built, powerful, and muscular with well-developed shoulders, chest, and hindquarters. Back broad, straight and level. Viewed in profile, slight slope down from hip bone to base of tail. Viewed from above, outer lines of body parallel.
LEGS: medium in length and bone, heavily muscled. Viewed from rear, all four legs straight and parallel with paws facing forward.
PAWS: firm, full and rounded, with heavy pads. Toes: five in front, four behind .
TAIL: medium long, heavy at base, tapering to abrupt blunt end in appearance but with normal tapering final vertebrae.
COAT: short, thick, even and hard in texture. Regional and seasonal variation in coat thickness allowed. Coat dense enough to protect from moisture, cold, and superficial skin injuries.

PENALIZE: excessive cobbiness or ranginess. Very short tail.

DISQUALIFY: cats showing evidence of hybridization resulting in the colors chocolate, sable, lavender, lilac, point-restricted (i.e. Siamese-type markings) or unpatterned agouti (i.e. Abyssinian-type ticked tabby). Any appearance of hybridization with any other breed – including long or fluffy fur, deep nose break, bulging eye set, brow ridge. Kinked or abnormal tail. Locket or button (white spots on colors not specifying same). Incorrect number of toes. Undershot or overshot bite. Tongue persistently protruding. Obesity or emaciation. Any feature so exaggerated as to foster weakness.

AMERICAN SHORTHAIR COLORS

WHITE: pure glistening white. Nose leather and Paw pads: pink. Eye color: deep blue or brilliant gold. Odd-eyed whites shall have one blue and one gold eye with equal color depth.

BLACK: dense coal black, sound from roots to tip of fur. Free from any tinge of rust on tips or smoke undercoat. Nose leather: black. Paw pads: black. Eye color: brilliant gold.

BLUE: blue, lighter shade preferred, one level tone from nose to tip of tail. Sound to the roots. A sound darker shade is more acceptable than an unsound lighter shade. Nose leather and Paw pads: blue. Eye color: brilliant gold.

RED: deep, rich, clear, brilliant red; without shading, markings, or ticking. Lips and chin the same color as coat. Nose leather and Paw pads: brick red. Eye color: brilliant gold.

CREAM: one level shade of buff cream without markings. Sound to the roots. Lighter shades preferred. Nose leather and Paw pads: pink. Eye color: brilliant gold.

CHINCHILLA SILVER: undercoat pure white. Coat on back, flanks, head, and tail sufficiently tipped with black to give the characteristic sparkling silver appearance. Legs may be slightly shaded with tipping. Chin and ear tufts, stomach and chest, pure white. Rims of eyes, lips and nose outlined with black. Nose leather: brick red. Paw pads: black. Eye color: green.

SHADED SILVER: undercoat white with a mantle of black tipping shading down from sides, face, and tail from dark on the ridge to white on the chin, chest, stomach, and under the tail. Legs to be the same tone as the face.

The general effect to be much darker than a chinchilla. Rims of eyes, lips, and nose outlined with black. Nose leather: brick red. Paw pads: black. Eye color: green.

SHELL CAMEO (Red Chinchilla): undercoat white, the coat on back, flanks, head, and tail to be sufficiently tipped with red to give the characteristic sparkling appearance. Face and legs may be very slightly shaded with tipping. Chin, ear tufts, stomach, and chest white. Nose leather, Rims of eyes, and Paw pads: rose. Eye color: brilliant gold.

SHADED CAMEO (Red Shaded): undercoat white with a mantle of red tipping shading down the sides, face, and tail from dark on the ridge to white on the chin, chest, stomach, and under the tail. Legs to be the same tone as face. The general effect to be much redder than the shell cameo. Nose leather, Rims of eyes, and Paw pads: rose. Eye color: brilliant gold.

BLACK SMOKE: white undercoat, deeply tipped with black. Cat in repose appears black. In motion the white undercoat is clearly apparent. Points and mask black with narrow band of white at base of hairs next to skin which may be seen only when fur is parted. Nose leather and Paw pads: black. Eye color: brilliant gold.

BLUE SMOKE: white undercoat, deeply tipped with blue. Cat in repose appears blue. In motion the white undercoat is clearly apparent. Points and mask blue, with narrow band of white at base of hairs next to skin which may be seen only when fur is parted. Nose leather and Paw pads: blue. Eye color: brilliant gold.

CAMEO SMOKE (Red Smoke): white undercoat, deeply tipped with red. Cat in repose appears red. In motion the white undercoat is clearly apparent. Points and mask red with narrow band of white at base of hairs next to skin which may be seen only when fur is parted. Nose leather, Rims of eyes, and Paw pads: rose. Eye color: brilliant gold.

TORTOISESHELL SMOKE: white undercoat deeply tipped with black with clearly defined, unbrindled patches of red and cream tipped hairs as in the pattern of the tortoiseshell. Cat in repose appears tortoiseshell. In motion the white undercoat is clearly apparent. Face and ears tortoiseshell pattern with narrow band of white at the base of the hairs next to skin which may be seen only when fur is parted. White ear tufts. Blaze of red or cream tipping on face is desirable. Eye color: brilliant gold.

BLUE CHINCHILLA SILVER: undercoat pure white. Coat on back, flanks and tail sufficiently tipped with blue to give the characteristic sparkling silver appearance. Legs may be slightly shaded with tipping. Chin and ear tufts, stomach and chest, pure white. Rims of eyes, lips and nose outlined with blue. Nose leather: old rose. Paw pads: blue or old rose. Eye color: green.

BLUE SHADED SILVER: undercoat white with a mantle of blue tipping shading down from sides, face and tail from dark on the ridge to white on the chin, chest, stomach and under the tail. Legs to be the same tone as the face. The general effect to be much darker than a blue chinchilla. Rims of eyes, lips and nose outlined with blue. Nose leather: old rose. Paw pads: old rose or blue. Eye color: green.

CREAM SHELL CAMEO (cream Chinchilla): undercoat white, the coat on back, flanks, head and tail to be sufficiently tipped with cream to give the characteristic sparkling appearance. Face and legs may be very slightly shaded with tipping. Chin, ear tufts, stomach and legs white: Nose leather, rims of eyes and paw pads: pink. Eye color: brilliant gold.

CREAM SHADED CAMEO (Cream Shaded): undercoat white with a mantle of cream tipping shading down the sides, face and tail from dark on the ridge to white on the chin, chest, stomach, and under the tail. Legs to be the same tone as face. The general effect to be much more cream than the cream shell cameo. Nose leather, rims of eyes, and paw pads: pink. Eye color: brilliant gold.

BLUE CREAM SMOKE: white undercoat deeply tipped with blue with clearly defined, unbrindled patches of cream tipped hairs as in the pattern of the blue cream. Cat in repose appears blue cream. In motion, the white is clearly apparent. Face and ears blue cream pattern with narrow band at the base of the hairs next to the skin which may be seen only when the fur is parted. White ear tufts. Blaze of cream tipping on face is desirable. Eye color: brilliant gold.

BLUE SILVER TABBY (Pewter Tabby): ground color, including lips and chin, pale, clear bluish silver. Markings sound blue. Nose leather: blue or old rose trimmed with blue. Paw pads: blue. Eye color: green or hazel.

BLUE SILVER PATCHED TABBY (Pewter Patched Tabby): ground color, including lips and chin, pale, clear bluish silver with classic or

mackerel tabby markings of deep blue with patches of cream clearly defined on both body and extremities. A blaze of cream on the face is desirable. Eye color: green or hazel.

Cream cameo tabby (Dilute Cameo): ground color off white. Markings cream. Nose leather and paw pads: pink. Eye color: brilliant gold.

SMOKE AND WHITE (including vans): White with unbrindled portions which have a white undercoat deeply tipped in color (black, blue, red, cream, tortoiseshell, cameo). The cat in repose appears white and black (white & blue, white & red etc.), in motion the white undercoat may be apparent. As a preferred minimum, the cat should have white feet, legs, undersides, chest and muzzle. Less white than this minimum should be penalized proportionately. An inverted "V" blaze is desirable.

BLACK SMOKE AND WHITE: white with portions of black smoke. Eye color: brilliant gold

Blue Smoke and White: white with portions of blue smoke. Eye color: brilliant gold.

Tortoiseshell Smoke and White: white with portions of tortoiseshell smoke. Eye color: brilliant gold.

Shell Cameo and White: white with portions of shell cameo. Eye color: brilliant gold.

Shaded Cameo and White: white with portions of shaded cameo. Eye color: brilliant gold.

Smoke Cameo and White: white with portions of smoke cameo. Eye color: brilliant gold.

CLASSIC TABBY PATTERN: markings dense, clearly defined, and broad. Legs evenly barred with bracelets coming up to meet the body markings. Tail evenly ringed. Several unbroken necklaces on neck and upper chest, the more the better. Frown marks on forehead form an intricate letter "M." Unbroken line runs back from outer corner of eye. Swirls on cheeks. Vertical lines over back of head extend to shoulder markings which are in the shape of a butterfly with both upper and lower wings distinctly outlined and marked with dots inside outline. Back markings consist of a vertical line down the spine from butterfly to tail with a vertical stripe paralleling it on each side, the three stripes well separated by stripes of the ground color. Large solid blotch on each side to be encircled by one or more unbroken rings. Side markings should be the same on both sides. Double vertical rows of buttons on chest and stomach. Hocks: to be the same color as markings.

MACKEREL TABBY PATTERN: markings dense, clearly defined, and all narrow pencillings. Legs evenly barred with narrow bracelets coming up to meet the body markings. Tail barred. Necklaces on neck and chest distinct, like so many chains. Head barred with an "M" on the forehead. Unbroken lines running back from the eyes. Lines running down the head to meet the shoulders. Spine lines run together to form a narrow saddle. Narrow pencillings run around body. Hocks: to be the same color as markings.

PATCHED TABBY PATTERN: a patched tabby (torbie) is an established silver, brown, or blue tabby with patches of red and/or cream.

BROWN PATCHED TABBY: ground color brilliant coppery brown with classic or mackerel tabby markings of dense black with patches of red and/or cream clearly defined on both body and extremities; a blaze of red and/or cream on face is desirable. Lips and chin the same shade as the rings around the eyes. Eye color: brilliant gold.

BLUE PATCHED TABBY: ground color, including lips and chin, pale bluish ivory with classic or mackerel tabby markings of very deep blue affording a good contrast with ground color. Patches of cream clearly defined on both body and extremities; a blaze of cream on the face is desirable. Warm fawn overtones or patina over the whole. Eye color: brilliant gold.

SILVER PATCHED TABBY: ground color, including lips and chin, pale silver with classic or mackerel tabby markings of dense black with patches of red and/or cream clearly defined on both body and extremities. A blaze of red and/or cream on the face is desirable. Eye color: brilliant gold, green or hazel.

SILVER TABBY (classic, mackerel): ground color, including lips and chin, pale, clear silver. Markings dense black. The silver tabby genetically is a shaded cat expressing the agouti pattern, therefore the undercoat should be white. Nose leather: brick red. Paw pads: black. Eye color: green or hazel.

RED TABBY (classic, mackerel): ground color red. Markings deep rich red. Lips and chin to match the color around the eyes. Nose leather and Paw pads: brick red. Eye color: brilliant copper.

BROWN TABBY (classic, mackerel): ground color brilliant coppery brown. Markings dense black. Lips and chin the same shade as the rings around the eyes. Back of legs black from paw to heel. Nose leather: brick red. Paw pads: black or brown. Eye color: brilliant gold.

BLUE TABBY (classic, mackerel): ground color, including lips and chin, pale bluish ivory. Markings a very deep blue affording a good contrast with ground color. Warm fawn overtones or patina over the whole. Nose leather: old rose. Paw pads: rose. Eye color: brilliant gold.

CREAM TABBY (classic, mackerel): ground color, including lips and chin, very pale cream. Markings of buff or cream sufficiently darker than the ground color to afford good contrast but remaining within the dilute color range. Nose leather and Paw pads: pink. Eye color: brilliant gold.

CAMEO TABBY (classic, mackerel): ground color off-white. Markings red. The cameo tabby genetically is a shaded cat expressing the agouti pattern, therefore the undercoat should be white. Nose leather and Paw pads: rose. Eye color: brilliant gold.

TABBY AND WHITE (including Vans)*: white with colored portions, the colored portions conform to the currently established tabby classes; mackerel and classic. As a preferred minimum, the cat should have white feet, legs, undersides, chest and muzzle. Less white than this minimum should be penalized proportionately. An inverted "V" blaze is desirable.

SILVER TABBY AND WHITE (classic, mackerel): white with portions of silver tabby Eye color: brilliant gold, green or hazel.

SILVER PATCHED TABBY AND WHITE: white with portions of silver patched tabby. Eye color: brilliant gold, green or hazel.

CAMEO TABBY AND WHITE (classic, mackerel): white with portions of cameo tabby. Eye color: brilliant gold.

BROWN TABBY AND WHITE (classic, mackerel) white with portions of brown tabby. Eye color: brilliant gold.

BROWN PATCHED TABBY AND WHITE: white with portions of brown patched tabby. Eye color: brilliant gold.

BLUE TABBY AND WHITE (classic, mackerel): white with portions of blue tabby. Eye color: brilliant gold.

BLUE PATCHED TABBY AND WHITE: white with portions of blue patched tabby and white. Eye color: brilliant gold.

RED TABBY AND WHITE: (classic, mackerel) white with portions of red tabby. Eye color: brilliant gold.

CREAM TABBY AND WHITE (classic, mackerel): white with portions of cream tabby. Eye color: brilliant gold.

*Van is the term for a cat who is white with the additional colored portions confined to the head, tail and legs. One or two small portions of color on the body are allowable.

TORTOISESHELL: black with unbrindled patches of red and cream. Patches clearly defined and well broken on both body and extremities. Blaze of red or cream on face is desirable. Eye color: brilliant gold.
Chinchilla shaded tortoiseshell (shell tortoiseshell): undercoat pure white. Coat on back, flanks, head and tail sufficiently tipped with black and well-defined patches of red and/or cream as in the pattern of the tortoiseshell to give the characteristic sparkling appearance. The cat is in appearance a chinchilla silver with patches of red tipping. Blaze of cream or red tipping desirable. Eye color: green or brilliant gold.
Shaded tortoiseshelL: undercoat white. Mantle of black tipping and clearly defined patches of red and cream tipped hairs as in the pattern of the tortoiseshell. Blaze of red or cream tipping on face is desirable. Eye color: green or brilliant gold.
Dilute chinchilla shaded tortoiseshell (Dilute Shell Tortoiseshell): undercoat pure white. Coat on back, flanks, head and tail sufficiently tipped with blue and well-defined patches of cream as in the pattern of the blue cream to give the characteristic sparkling appearance. The cat is in appearance a dilute chinchilla silver with patches of cream tipping. Blaze of cream tipping desirable. Eye color: green or brilliant gold.
Dilute shaded tortoiseshell: undercoat white. Mantle of blue tipping and clearly defined patches of cream tipped hairs as in the pattern of the blue cream. Blaze of cream tipping on face is desirable. Eye color: green or brilliant gold.

CALICO: white with unbrindled patches of black and red. White predominant on underparts. Eye color: brilliant gold.

DILUTE CALICO: white with unbrindled patches of blue and cream. White predominant on underparts. Eye color: brilliant gold.

BLUE-CREAM: blue with patches of solid cream. Patches clearly defined and well broken on both body and extremities. Eye color: brilliant gold.

BI-COLOR: white with unbrindled portions of black, white with unbrindled portions of blue, white with unbrindled portions of red, or white with unbrindled portions of cream. Eye color: gold, the more brilliant the better.

VAN BI-COLOR: black and white, red and white, blue and white, or cream and white. White cat with color confined to the extremities; head, tail, and legs. One or two small colored patches on body allowable.

VAN CALICO: white cat with unbrindled patches of black and red confined to the extremities; head, tail, and legs. One or two small colored patches on body allowable.

VAN BLUE-CREAM AND WHITE: white cat with unbrindled patches of blue and cream confined to the extremities; head, tail, and legs. One or two small colored patches on body allowable.
American Shorthair allowable outcross breeds: none.

■ POINT SCORE

HEAD (including size and shape of eyes, ear shape and set)	25
TYPE (including shape, size, bone and length of tail)	20
COAT	45
COLOR and EYE	10

GENERAL: the American Wirehair is a spontaneous mutation. The coat, which is not only springy, dense, and resilient, but also coarse and hard to the touch, distinguishes the American Wirehair from all other breeds. Characteristic is activity, agility, and keen interest in its surroundings.
HEAD: in proportion to the body. Underlying bone structure is round with prominent cheekbones and well-developed muzzle and chin. There is a slight whisker break.
NOSE: in profile the nose shows a gentle concave curve.
MUZZLE: well-developed. Allowance for jowls in adult males.
CHIN: firm and well-developed with no apparent malocclusion.
EARS: medium, slightly rounded at tips, set wide and not unduly open at the base.
EYES: large, round, bright, and clear. Set well apart. Aperture has slight upward tilt.
BODY: medium to large. Back level, shoulders and hips same width, torso well-rounded and in proportion. Males larger than females.
LEGS: medium in length and bone, well-muscled and proportionate to body.
PAWS: oval and compact. Toes, five in

front and four behind.
TAIL: in proportion to body, tapering from the well-rounded rump to a rounded tip, neither blunt nor pointed.
COAT: springy, tight, medium in length. Individual hairs are crimped, hooked, or bent, including hair within the ears. The overall appearance of wiring and the coarseness and resilience of the coat is more important than the crimping of each hair. The density of the wired coat leads to ringlet formation rather than waves. That coat, which is very dense, resilient, crimped, and coarse, is most desirable, as are curly whiskers.

PENALIZE: deep nose break. Long or fluffy fur.

DISQUALIFY: incorrect coat. Kinked or abnormal tail. Incorrect number of toes. Evidence of hybridization resulting in the colors chocolate, lavender, the Himalayan pattern, or these combinations with white.

AMERICAN WIREHAIR COLORS
WHITE: pure glistening white. Nose leather and Paw pads: pink. Eye color: deep blue or brilliant gold. Odd-eyed whites shall have one blue and one gold eye with equal color depth.

BLACK: dense coal black, sound from roots to tip of fur. Free from any tinge of rust on tips or smoke undercoat. Nose leather: black. Paw Pads: black or brown. Eye color: brilliant gold.

BLUE: blue, lighter shade preferred, one level tone from nose to tip of tail. Sound to the roots. A sound darker shade is more acceptable than an unsound lighter shade. Nose leather and Paw pads: blue. Eye color: brilliant gold.

RED: deep, rich, clear, brilliant red, without shading, markings or ticking. Lips and chin the same color as coat. Nose leather and Paw pads: brick red. Eye color: brilliant gold.

CREAM: one level shade of buff cream, without markings. Sound to the roots. Lighter shades preferred. Nose leather and Paw pads: pink. Eye color: brilliant gold.

CHINCHILLA SILVER: undercoat pure white. Coat on back, flanks, head, and tail sufficiently tipped with black to give the characteristic sparkling silver appearance. Legs may be slightly shaded with tipping. Chin and ear tufts, stomach and chest, pure white. Rims of eyes, lips, and nose outlined with black. Nose leather: brick red. Paw pads: black. Eye color: green or blue-green.

SHADED SILVER: undercoat white with a mantle of black tipping shading down from sides, face and tail from dark on the ridge to white on the chin, chest, stomach, and under the tail. Legs to be the same tone as the face. The general effect to be much darker than a chinchilla. Rims of eyes, lips, and nose outlined with black. Nose leather: brick red. Paw pads: black. Eye color: green or blue-green.

SHELL CAMEO (Red Chinchilla): undercoat white, the coat on the back, flanks, head, and tail to be sufficiently tipped with red to give the characteristic sparkling appearance. Face and legs may be very slightly shaded with tipping. Chin, ear tufts, stomach, and chest white. Nose leather, Rims of eyes, and Paw pads: rose. Eye color: brilliant gold.

SHADED CAMEO (Red Shaded): undercoat white with a mantle of red tipping shading down the sides, face, and tail from dark on the ridge to white on the chin, chest, stomach, and under the tail. Legs to be the same tone as face. The general effect to be much redder than the shell cameo. Nose leather, Rims of eyes, and Paw pads: rose. Eye color: brilliant gold.

BLACK SMOKE: white undercoat, deeply tipped with black. Cat in repose appears black. In motion the white undercoat is clearly apparent. Points and mask black with narrow band of white at base of hairs next to skin which may be seen only when the fur is parted. Nose leather and Paw pads: black. Eye color: brilliant gold.

BLUE SMOKE: white undercoat, deeply tipped with blue. Cat in repose appears blue. In motion the white undercoat is clearly apparent. Points and mask blue, with narrow band of white at base of hairs next to skin which may be seen only when fur is parted. Nose leather and Paw pads: blue. Eye color: brilliant gold.

CAMEO SMOKE (Red Smoke): white undercoat, deeply tipped with red. Cat in repose appears red. In motion the white undercoat is clearly apparent. Points and mask red with narrow band of white at base of hairs next to skin which may be seen only when fur is parted. Nose leather, Rims of eyes, and Paw pads: rose. Eye color: brilliant gold.

CLASSIC TABBY PATTERN: markings dense, clearly defined, and broad. Legs evenly barred with bracelets coming up to meet the body markings. Tail evenly ringed. Several unbroken necklaces on neck and upper chest, the more the better. Frown marks on forehead form an intricate letter "M." Unbroken line runs back from outer

corner of eye. Swirls on cheeks. Vertical lines over back of head extend to shoulder markings which are in the shape of a butterfly with both upper and lower wings distinctly outlined and marked with dots inside outline. Back markings consist of a vertical line down the spine from butterfly to tail with a vertical stripe paralleling it on each side, the three stripes well separated by stripes of the ground color. Large solid blotch on each side to be encircled by one or more unbroken rings. Side markings should be the same on both sides. Double vertical rows of buttons on chest and stomach.

MACKEREL TABBY PATTERN: markings dense, clearly defined, and all narrow pencillings. Legs evenly barred with narrow bracelets coming up to meet the body markings. Tail barred. Necklaces on neck and chest distinct, like so many chains. Head barred with an "M" on the forehead. Unbroken lines running back from the eyes. Lines running down the head to meet the shoulders. Spine lines run together to form a narrow saddle. Narrow pencillings run around body.

SILVER TABBY (classic, mackerel): ground color, including lips and chin, pale, clear silver. Markings dense black. Nose leather: brick red. Paw pads: black. Eye color: green or hazel.

RED TABBY (classic, mackerel): ground color red. Markings deep, rich red. Lips and chin red. Nose leather and Paw pads: brick red. Eye color: brilliant gold.

BROWN TABBY (classic, mackerel): ground color brilliant coppery brown. Markings dense black. Lips and chin the same shade as the rings around the eyes. Back of leg black from paw to heel. Nose leather: brick red. Paw pads: black or brown. Eye color: brilliant gold.

BLUE TABBY (classic, mackerel): ground color, including lips and chin, pale bluish ivory. Markings a very deep blue affording a good contrast with ground color. Warm fawn overtones or patina over the whole. Nose leather: old rose. Paw pads: rose. Eye color: brilliant gold.

CREAM TABBY (classic, mackerel): ground color, including lips and chin, very pale cream. Markings of buff or cream sufficiently darker than the ground color to afford good contrast, but remaining within the dilute color range. Nose leather and Paw pads: pink. Eye color: brilliant gold.

CAMEO TABBY (classic, mackerel): ground color off-white. Markings red.

Nose leather and Paw pads: rose. Eye color: brilliant gold.

TORTOISESHELL: black with unbrindled patches of red and cream. Patches clearly defined and well-broken on both body and extremities. Blaze of red or cream on face is desirable. Eye color: brilliant gold.

CALICO: white with unbrindled patches of black and red. White predominant on underparts. Eye color: brilliant gold.

DILUTE CALICO: white with unbrindled patches of blue and cream. White predominant on underparts. Eye color: brilliant gold.

BLUE-CREAM: blue with patches of solid cream. Patches clearly defined and well-broken on both body and extremities. Eye color: brilliant gold.

BI-COLOR: white with unbrindled patches of black, white with unbrindled patches of blue. White with unbrindled patches of red, or white with unbrindled patches of cream. Eye color: gold, the more brilliant the better.

OWC (Other Wirehair Colors): any other color or pattern with the exception of those showing evidence of hybridization resulting in the colors chocolate, lavender, the Himalayan pattern, or these combinations with white. Eye color: appropriate to the color of the cat.
American Wirehair allowable outcross breeds: American Shorthair.

BALINESE

■ POINT SCORE

HEAD (20)	
Long flat profile	6
Wedge, fine muzzle, size	5
Ears	4
Chin	3
Width between eyes	2
EYES (5)	
Shape, size, slant, and placement	5
BODY (30)	
Structure and size, including neck	12
Muscle tone	10
Legs and Feet	5
Tail	3
COAT (20)	
Length	10
Texture	10
COLOR (25)	
Body color	10
Point color (matching points of dense color, proper foot pads and nose leather)	10
Eye color	5

GENERAL: the ideal Balinese is a svelte cat with long tapering lines, very lithe but strong and muscular. Excellent physical condition. Neither flabby nor bony. Not fat. Eyes clear. Because of the longer coat the Balinese appears to have softer lines and less extreme type than other breeds of cats with similar type.

HEAD: long, tapering wedge. Medium size in good proportion to body. The total wedge starts at the nose and flares out in straight lines to the tips of the ears forming a triangle, with no break at the whiskers. No less than the width of an eye between the eyes. When the whiskers and face hair are smoothed back, the underlying bone structure is apparent. Allowance must be made for jowls in the stud cat.
SKULL: flat. In profile, a long straight line should be felt from the top of the head to the tip of the nose. No bulge over the eyes. No dip in nose.
NOSE: long and straight. A continuation of the forehead with no break.
MUZZLE: fine, wedge-shaped.
CHIN and JAW: medium size. Tip of chin lines up with tip of nose in the same vertical plane. Neither receding nor excessively massive.
EARS: strikingly large, pointed, wide at base, continuing the lines of the wedge.
EYES: almond shaped. Medium size. Neither protruding nor recessed. Slanted towards the nose in harmony with lines of wedge and ears. Uncrossed.
BODY: medium size. Graceful, long, and svelte. A distinctive combination of fine bones and firm muscles. Shoulders and hips continue same sleek lines of tubular body. Hips never wider than shoulders. Abdomen tight. The male may be somewhat larger than the female.
NECK: long and slender.
LEGS: bone structure long and slim. Hind legs higher than front. In good proportion to body.
PAWS: dainty, small, and oval. Toes: five in front and four behind.
TAIL: bone structure long, thin, tapering to a fine point. Tail hair spreads out like a plume.
COAT: medium length, fine, silky without downy undercoat lying close to the body, the coat may appear shorter than it is. Hair is longest on the tail.
COLOR: Body: even, with subtle shading when allowed. Allowance should be made for darker color in older cats as Balinese generally darken with age, but there must be definite contrast between body color and points. Points: mask, ears, legs, feet, tail dense and clearly defined. All of the same shade. Mask covers entire face including whisker pads and is connected to ears by tracings. Mask

should not extend over top of head. No ticking or white hairs in points.

PENALIZE: lack of pigment in the nose leather and/or paw pads in part, or in total. Crossed eyes. Palpable and/or visible protrusion of the cartilage at the end of the sternum. Soft or mushy body.

DISQUALIFY: any evidence of illness or poor health. Weak hind legs. Mouth breathing due to nasal obstruction or poor occlusion. Malocclusion resulting in either undershot or overshot chin. Emaciation. Kink in tail. Eyes other than blue. White toes and/or feet. Incorrect number of toes. Definite double coat (i.e., downy undercoat).

BALINESE COLORS

SEAL POINT: body even pale fawn to cream, warm in tone, shading gradually into lighter color on the stomach and chest. Points deep seal brown. Nose leather and Paw pads: same color as points. Eye color: deep vivid blue.

CHOCOLATE POINT: body ivory with no shading. Points milk-chocolate color, warm in tone. Nose leather and Paw pads: cinnamon-pink. Eye color: deep vivid blue.

BLUE POINT: body bluish white, cold in tone, shading gradually to white on stomach and chest. Points deep blue. Nose leather and Paw pads: slate-colored. Eye color: deep vivid blue.

LILAC POINT: body glacial white with no shading. Points frosty grey with pinkish tone. Nose leather and Paw pads: lavender-pink. Eye color: deep vivid blue.

Balinese allowable outcross breeds: Siamese.

BENGAL

There are currently no CFA standards for this breed.

BIRMAN

(Sacred Cat of Burma)

■ POINT SCORE
HEAD, BODY, TYPE & COAT (65)
   Head (including boning, nose, jaw, chin profile, ear & eye shape & set.) 30
   Body/Type (including boning, stockiness elongation, legs, tail.) 25
   Coat (including length, texture, ruff.)   10

COLOR – INCLUDING EYE COLOR (35)
   Color except gloves (including body color, point color, eye color.) 15
   Gloves (including front & rear gloves, laces & symmetry)   20

GENERAL: a cat of mystery and legend, the Birman is a color pointed cat with long silky hair and four pure white feet. It is strongly built, elongated and stocky, neither svelte nor cobby. The distinctive head has strong jaws, firm chin, medium length Roman nose with nostrils set low on the nose leather. There should be good width between the ears, which are medium in size. The blue, almost round eyes are set well apart, giving a sweet expression to the face.
HEAD: skull strong, broad, and rounded. There is a slight flat spot just in front of the ears.
NOSE: medium in length and width, in proportion to size of head. Roman shape in profile. Nostrils set low on the nose leather.
PROFILE: the forehead slopes back and is slightly convex. The medium length nose, which starts just below the eyes, is Roman in shape (which is slightly convex), with the nostrils set low on the nose leather. The chin is strong, with the lower jaw forming a perpendicular line with the upper lip.
CHEEKS: full with somewhat rounded muzzle. The fur is short in appearance about the face, but to the extreme outer area of the cheek the fur is longer.
JAWS: heavy.
CHIN: strong and well-developed.
EARS: medium in length. Almost as wide at the base as tall. Modified to a rounded point at the tip; set as much to the side as into the top of the head.
EYES: almost round with a sweet expression. Set well apart, with the outer corner tilted VERY slightly upward. Blue in color, the deeper blue the better.
BODY: long and stocky. Females may be proportionately smaller than males.
LEGS: medium in length and heavy.
PAWS: large, round, and firm. Five toes in front, four behind.
TAIL: medium in length, in pleasing proportion to the body.
COAT: medium long to long, silken in texture, with heavy ruff around the neck, slightly curly on stomach. This fur is of such a texture that it does not mat.

COLOR EXCEPT GLOVES: Body: even, with subtle shading when allowed. Strong contrast between body color and points. Points except gloves: mask, ears, legs, and tail dense and clearly defined, all of the same shade. Mask covers entire face including whisker pads and is connected to ears by tracings. No ticking or white hair in points. Golden Mist: desirable

in all points colors is the "golden mist," a faint golden beige cast on the back and sides. This is somewhat deeper in the seal points, and may be absent in kittens.

GLOVES: Front paws: front paws have white gloves ending in an even line across the paw at, or between, the second or third joints. (The third joint is where the paw bends when the cat is standing.) The upper limit of white should be the metacarpal (dew) pad. (The metacarpal pad is the highest up little paw pad, located in the middle of the back of the front paw, above the third joint and just below the wrist bones.) Symmetry of the front gloves is desirable. Back paws: white glove covers all the toes, and may extend up somewhat higher than front gloves. Symmetry of the rear gloves is desirable. Laces: the gloves on the back paws must extend up the back of the hock, and are called laces in this area. Ideally, the laces end in a point or inverted "V" and extend 1/2 to 3/4 of the way up the hock. Lower or higher laces are acceptable, but should not go beyond the hock. Symmetry of the two laces is desirable. Paw pads: pink preferred, but dark spot(s) on paw pad(s) acceptable because of the two colors in pattern. Note: ideally, the front gloves match, the back gloves match, and the two laces match. Faultlessly gloved cats are a rare exception, and the Birman is to be judged in all its parts, as well as the gloves.

PENALIZE: white that does not run across the front paws in an even line. Persian or Siamese type head. Delicate bone structure. White shading on stomach and chest. Lack of laces on one or both back gloves. White beyond the metacarpal (dew) pad. (The metacarpal pad is the highest up little paw pad, located in the middle of the back of the front paw, above the third joint and just below the wrist bones.)

DISQUALIFY: lack of white gloves on any paw. Kinked or abnormal tail. Crossed eyes. Incorrect number of toes. Areas of pure white in the points, if not connected to the gloves and part of or an extension of the gloves. Paw pads are part of the gloves. Areas of white connected to other areas of white by paw pads (of any color) are not cause for disqualification. Discrete areas of point color in the gloves, if not connected to point color of legs (exception, paw pads). White on back legs beyond the hock.

BIRMAN COLORS

SEAL POINT: body even pale fawn to cream, warm in tone, shading gradually to lighter color on the stomach and chest. Points, except for gloves, deep seal brown. Gloves pure white. Nose leather: same color as points. Paw pads: pink. Eye color: blue, the deeper and more violet the better.

BLUE POINT: body bluish white to pale ivory, shading gradually to almost white on stomach and chest. Points, except for gloves, deep blue. Gloves pure white. Nose leather: slate-color. Paw pads: pink. Eye color: blue, the deeper and more violet the better.

CHOCOLATE POINT: body ivory with no shading. Points, except for gloves, milk-chocolate color, warm in tone. Gloves pure white. Nose leather: cinnamon-pink. Paw pads: pink. Eye color: blue, the deeper and more violet the better.

LILAC POINT: almost white. Points, except for gloves, frosty grey with pinkish tone. Gloves pure white. Nose leather: lavender-pink. Paw pads: pink. Eye color: blue, the deeper and more violet the better.
Birman allowable outcross breeds: None.

BOMBAY

■ POINT SCORE
HEAD AND EARS (25)

Roundness of head	7
Full face and proper profile	7
Ears	7
Chin	4
EYES (5)	
Placement and shape	5
BODY (20)	
Body	15
Tail	5
COAT (20)	
Shortness	10
Texture	5
Close lying	5
COLOR (30)	
Body color	20
Eye color	10

GENERAL: due to its short jet black, gleaming coat and bright gold to vivid copper eyes, combined with a solid body and a sweet facial expression, the ideal Bombay has an unmistakable look of its own. It is a medium-sized cat, well-balanced, friendly, alert, and outgoing; muscular and having a surprising weight for its size. The body and tail should be of medium length, the head round with medium-sized, wide-set ears, a visible nose break, large rounded wide-set eyes, and be of excellent proportions and carriage.
HEAD: the head should be pleasingly rounded with no sharp angles. The face should be full with considerable breadth between the eyes, tapering

slightly to a short, well-developed muzzle. In profile there should be a visible nose break; however, it should not present a "pugged" or "snubbed" look.
EARS: the ears should be medium in size and set well apart on a rounded skull, alert, tilting slightly forward, broad at the base, and with slightly rounded tips.
CHIN: the chin should be firm, neither receding nor protruding, reflecting a proper bite.
EYES: set far apart with rounded aperture.
BODY: medium in size, muscular in development, neither compact nor rangy. Allowance is to be made for larger size in males.
LEGS: in proportion to the body and tail.
PAWS: round. Toes, five in front, four in back.
TAIL: straight, medium in length; neither short nor "whippy."
COAT: fine, short, satin-like texture; close-lying with a shimmering patent leather sheen.

PENALIZE: excessive cobbiness or ranginess.

DISQUALIFY: kinked or abnormal tail. Lockets or spots. Incorrect number of toes. Nose leather or Paw pads other than black. Green eyes. Improper bite. Extreme break that interferes with normal breathing and tearing of eyes.

BOMBAY COLOR

COLOR: the mature specimen should be black to the roots. Kitten coats should darken and become more sleek with age. Nose leather and paw pads: black. Eye color: ranging from gold to copper, the greater the depth and brilliance the better.
Bombay allowable outcross breeds: Black American Shorthair, Sable Burmese.

BRITISH SHORTHAIR

■ POINT SCORE
HEAD (25)

Muzzle and Chin	5
Skull	5
Ears	5
Neck	5
Eye shape	5
BODY (35)	
Torso	20
Legs and Paws	10
Tail	5
COAT (20)	
Texture, length, and density	20
COLOR (20)	
Eye color	5
Coat color	15

GENERAL: the British Shorthair is compact, well-balanced and powerful, showing good depth of body, a full broad chest, short to medium strong legs, rounded paws, tail thick at base with a rounded tip. The head is round with good width between the ears, round cheeks, firm chin, medium ears, large round and well-opened eyes, and a medium broad nose. The coat is short and very dense. Females are less massive in all respects with males having larger jowls. This breed is slow to mature.
HEAD: round and massive. Round face with round underlying bone structure well set on a short thick neck. The forehead should be rounded with a slight flat plane on the top of the head. The forehead should not slope.
NOSE: medium, broad. In profile there is a gentle dip.
CHIN: firm and well-developed.
MUZZLE: distinctive, well-developed, with a definite stop beyond large, round whisker pads.
EARS: ear set is important. Medium in size, broad at the base, rounded at the tips. Set far apart, fitting into (without distorting) the rounded contour of the head.
EYES: large, round, well opened. Set wide apart and level.
BODY: medium to large, well knit and powerful. Level back and a deep broad chest.
LEGS: short to medium, well-boned and strong. In proportion to the body. Forelegs are straight.
PAWS: round and firm. Toes: five in front and four behind.
TAIL: medium length in proportion to the body, thicker at base, tapering slightly to a rounded tip.
COAT: short, very dense, well bodied, resilient and firm to the touch. Not double coated or woolly.
COLOR: for cats with special markings: 5 points for coat color and 10 points for markings. Shadow tabby markings in solid color, smoke, bicolor, or calico kittens are not a fault.

PENALIZE: definite nose stop. Overlong or light undercoat. Soft coat. Rangy body. Weak chin.*

DISQUALIFY: incorrect eye color, green rims in adults. Tail defects. Long or fluffy coat. Incorrect number of toes. Locket or button. Improper color or pigment in nose leather and/or paw pads in part or total. Any evidence of illness or poor health. Any evidence of wryness of jaw, poor dentition (arrangement of teeth), or malocclusion.*
*The above listed penalties and disqualifications apply to all British Shorthair cats. Additional penalties and disqualifications are listed under colors.

BRITISH SHORTHAIR COLORS
WHITE: pure white, untipped with yellow. Eye color: deep sapphire blue, gold, or copper. Odd-eyed whites shall have one deep sapphire blue and one gold eye with equal color depth. Nose leather and paw pads: pink.

BLACK: jet black to roots, no rusty tinge, no white hair anywhere. Nose leather: black. Paw pads: black or brown. Eye color: gold or copper with no trace of green.

BLUE: light to medium blue, lighter shade preferred, very level in color. Sound medium shade more acceptable than an unsound lighter shade. No tabby markings or white anywhere. Nose leather and paw pads: Blue. Eye color: gold or copper.

CREAM: rich cream, lighter shades preferred, level in color, sound to the roots. No white anywhere. Nose leather and paw pads: pink. Eye color: gold or copper. *

DISQUALIFY: Heavy tabby markings.

BLACK SMOKE: white or pale silver undercoat, deeply tipped with black. Cat in repose appears black. In motion the white or silver undercoat is clearly apparent. Nose leather and paw pads: black. Eye color: gold or copper.

BLUE SMOKE: white or pale silver undercoat, deeply tipped with blue. Cat in repose appears blue. In motion the white or silver undercoat is clearly apparent. Nose leather and paw pads: blue. Eye color: gold or copper.

CLASSIC TABBY PATTERN: markings dense, clearly defined, and broad. Legs evenly barred with bracelets coming up to meet the body markings. Tail evenly ringed. Several unbroken necklaces on neck and upper chest, the more the better. Frown marks on forehead form an intricate letter "M." Unbroken line runs back from outer corner of eye. Swirls on cheeks. Vertical lines over back of head extend to shoulder markings which are in the shape of a butterfly with both upper and lower wings distinctly outlined and marked with dots inside outline. Back markings consist of a vertical line down the spine from butterfly to tail with a vertical stripe paralleling it on each side, the three stripes well separated by stripes of the ground color. Large solid blotch on each side to be encircled by one or more unbroken rings. Side markings should be the same on both sides. Double vertical rows of buttons on chest and stomach. *

PENALIZE: brindling.

DISQUALIFY: white anywhere.

MACKEREL TABBY PATTERN: markings dense, clearly defined, and all narrow pencillings. Legs evenly barred with narrow bracelets coming up to meet the body markings. Tail barred. Necklaces on neck and chest distinct, like so many chains. Head barred with an "M" on the forehead. Unbroken lines running back from the eyes. Lines running down the head to meet the shoulders. Spine lines run together to form a narrow saddle. Narrow pencillings run around body. *

PENALIZE: brindling.

DISQUALIFY: white anywhere.

SPOTTED TABBY PATTERN: good, clear spotting is essential. The spots can be round, oblong, or rosette-shaped. Any of these are of equal merit but the spots, however shaped or placed, shall be distinct. Head: as classic tabby. Body and Legs: good, clear spotting essential. Tail: spots or broken rings desirable. Color: silver with black spots, brown with black spots, red with deep rich red spots. Any other recognized ground color acceptable with appropriate spotting. Eye color: as for classic tabby. Nose leather and paw pads: as for classic tabby. *

PENALIZE: solid spine color line, brindling, markings not distinct and separate.

DISQUALIFY: white anywhere.

SILVER TABBY: ground color, including lips and chin, pale clear silver. Markings dense black. Nose leather: brick red. Paw pads: black. Eye color: green or hazel.

RED TABBY: ground color red, including lips and chin. Markings deep, rich red. Nose leather and paw pads: brick red. Eye color: gold or copper.

BROWN TABBY: ground color brilliant coppery brown. Markings dense black. Lips and chin of same shade as the rings around the eyes. Back of leg black from paw to heel. Nose leather: brick red. Paw pads: black or brown. Eye color: gold or copper.

BLUE TABBY: ground color, including lips and chin, pale bluish ivory. Markings a very deep blue affording a good contrast with ground color. Warm fawn overtones or patina over the whole. Nose leather: old rose. Paw pads: rose. Eye color: gold or copper.

CREAM TABBY: ground color, including lips and chin, very pale cream. Markings of buff or cream sufficiently darker than the ground color to afford good contrast, but remaining within the dilute color range. Nose leather and paw pads: pink. Eye color: gold or copper.

TORTOISESHELL: black and rich red to be softly mingled, with both colors clearly defined over the whole animal but without any obvious patches of either color, with the exception of a short, narrow blaze which is permissible. While a single shade of rich red is desirable, the presence of two shades of red should not be heavily penalized. Nose leather and paw pads: pink and/or black. Eye color: gold or copper. *

PENALIZE: tabby markings, unbroken color on paws. Unequal balance of color.

DISQUALIFY: white anywhere.

CALICO: patches of black and rich red on white, equally balanced. Colors to be brilliant and absolutely free from brindling or tabby markings. The tri-color patching should cover the top of the head, ears, cheeks, back, tail, and part of the flanks. Patches to be clear and defined. White blaze desirable. Nose leather and paw pads: pink and/or black. Eye color: gold or copper. *

PENALIZE: brindling, tabby markings, unbroken color on paws. Unequal balance of color.

DISQUALIFY: white predominating.

DILUTE CALICO: patches of blue and cream on white, equally balanced. Colors to be brilliant and absolutely free from brindling or tabby markings. The tri-color patching should cover the top of the head, ears, cheeks, back, tail, and part of the flanks. Patches to be clear and defined. White blaze desirable. Nose leather and paw pads: blue and/or pink. Eye color: gold or copper. *Penalize brindling, tabby markings, unbroken color on paws. Unequal balance of color.

DISQUALIFY: white predominating.

BLUE-CREAM: blue and cream to be softly mingled, not patched. Nose leather and paw pads: blue and/or pink. Eye color: gold or copper. *
PENALIZE: tabby markings, unbroken color on paws. Solid patches of color.

DISQUALIFY: white anywhere.

BI-COLOR: black and white, blue and white, red and white, or cream and white. White blaze desirable. Eye color: gold or copper. *
PENALIZE: brindling or tabby markings.
DISQUALIFY: white predominating.
OBSHC (Other British Shorthair Colors): any other color or pattern with the exception of those showing evidence of hybridization resulting in the colors chocolate, lavender, the himalayan pattern, or these combinations with white. Eye color: appropriate to the dominant color of the cat. British Shorthair allowable outcross breeds: none.

BURMESE

■ POINT SCORE
HEAD, EARS, and EYES (30)

Roundness of head	7
Breadth between eyes and Full face	6
Proper profile (includes Chin)	6
Ear set, placement, and size	6
Eye placement and shape	5

BODY, LEGS, FEET, and TAIL (30)

Torso	15
Muscle tone	5
Legs and Feet	5
Tail	5

COAT (10)

Short	4
Texture	4
Close lying	2

COLOR (30)

Body color.	25
Eye color.	5

GENERAL: the overall impression of the ideal Burmese would be a cat of medium size with substantial bone structure, good muscular development and a surprising weight for its size. This together with expressive eyes and a sweet expression presents a totally distinctive cat which is comparable to no other breed. Perfect physical condition, with excellent muscle tone. There should be no evidence of obesity, paunchiness, weakness, or apathy.
HEAD, EARS, and EYES: head pleasingly rounded without flat planes whether viewed from the front or side. The face is full with considerable breadth between the eyes and blends gently into a broad, well-developed short muzzle that maintains the rounded contours of the head. In profile there is a visible nose break. The chin is firmly rounded, reflecting a proper bite. The head sits on a well-developed neck. The ears are medium in size, set well apart, broad at the base and rounded at the tips. Tilting slightly forward, the ears contribute to an alert appearance. The eyes are large, set far apart, with rounded aperture.
BODY: medium in size, muscular in

development, and presenting a compact appearance. Allowance to be made for larger size in males. An ample, rounded chest, with back level from shoulder to tail.
LEGS: well proportioned to body.
PAWS: round. Toes: five in front and four behind.
TAIL: straight, medium in length.
COAT: fine, glossy, satin-like texture; short and very close lying.

PENALIZE: distinct barring on either the front or rear outer legs. Trace (faint) barring permitted in kittens and young adults.

DISQUALIFY: kinked or abnormal tail, lockets or spots. Blue eyes. Incorrect nose leather or paw pad color. Malocclusion of the jaw that results in a severe underbite or overbite that visually prohibits the described profile and/or malformation that results in protruding teeth or a wry face or jaw. Distinct barring on the torso.

BURMESE COLORS
SABLE: the mature specimen is a rich, warm, sable brown; shading almost imperceptibly to a slightly lighter hue on the underparts but otherwise without shadings, barring, or markings of any kind. (Kittens are often lighter in color.) Nose leather and paw pads: brown. Eye color: ranges from gold to yellow, the greater the depth and brilliance the better. Green eyes are a fault.

CHAMPAGNE: the mature specimen should be a warm honey beige, shading to a pale gold tan underside. Slight darkening on ears and face permissible but lesser shading preferred. A slight darkening in older specimens allowed, the emphasis being on evenness of color. Nose leather: light warm brown. Paw pads: warm pinkish tan. Eye color: ranging from yellow to gold, the greater the depth and brilliance the better.

BLUE: the mature specimen should be a medium blue with warm fawn undertones, shading almost imperceptibly to a slightly lighter hue on the underparts, but otherwise without shadings, barring or markings of any kind. Nose leather and paw pads: Slate gray. Eye color: ranging from yellow to gold, the greater the depth and brilliance the better.

PLATINUM: the mature specimen should be a pale, silvery gray with pale fawn undertones, shading almost imperceptibly to a slightly lighter hue on the underparts, but otherwise without shadings, barring or markings of any kind. Nose leather and paw pads: lavender-pink. Eye color: ranging from

yellow to gold, the greater the depth and brilliance the better.
Burmese allowable outcross breeds: none.

EUROPEAN BURMESE

(Eligible for Championship Competition at International Division Shows ONLY, otherwise Miscellaneous Class)

■ POINT SCORE
HEAD and EARS	25
eye shape and color	20
body shape, legs, feet, tail	20
COAT	
color and texture	30
CONDITION and PRESENTATION	5

GENERAL: the European Burmese is an elegant cat of foreign type, which is positive and individual to the breed. Any suggestion of either Siamese type or the cobbiness of the British Shorthair must be regarded as a fault.
HEAD: the top of the head is slightly rounded, with good breadth between the ears, having wide cheekbones and tapering to a short blunt wedge.
NOSE: definite nose break.
JAW: wide at the hinge. Strong lower jaw.
CHIN: strong.
EYES: set well apart. Large and lustrous. The top line of the eyes show a straight oriental slant toward the nose, the lower line is rounded.
EARS: medium in size. Set well apart on the skull. Broad at the base with slightly rounded tips. The outer line of the ears continue the shape of the upper part of the face. This may not be possible in mature males who have developed fullness of cheeks. In profile, ears have a slight forward tilt.
BODY: medium in length and size. Hard and muscular. Heavier than appearance indicates. Chest should be strong and rounded in profile, the back straight from the shoulder to the rump.
LEGS: rather slender and in proportion to the body. Hind legs slightly longer than the front.
FEET: small and oval.
TAIL: medium length, not thick at the base and tapering slightly to a rounded tip.
COAT: short, fine lying close to the body. Satin-like in texture, almost without undercoat. Very glossy.

PENALIZE: jaw pinch, oriental eye shape, round eyes. Pigmentation spots on nose leather of a red or cream European Burmese.

DISQUALIFY: green eye color. White patches or a noticeable number of white hairs. Visible tail kink. Too much tabby markings on a red or cream European Burmese.

EUROPEAN BURMESE COLORS
COLOR: in all colors the underparts of the body will be slightly paler than the back. In kittens and adolescents allowance should be made for faint tabby barring and overall a lighter color than adults. In all adults of all varieties there should be no bars or shading: the points may show a little contrast.

EYE COLOR for all varieties: all shades of yellow to amber, golden yellow preferred. Alert and bright.

BROWN: rich, warm, seal brown. Very dark color bordering on black is incorrect. Nose leather: rich brown. Paw pads: brown.

BLUE: soft, silver blue-gray with a warm tone. Nose leather and paw pads: blue-gray.

CHOCOLATE: warm milk-chocolate; overall evenness of color very desirable. Nose leather: warm, chocolate brown. Paw pads: brick pink shading to chocolate.

LILAC: pale, delicate dove-gray with a slightly pink cast. Nose leather and paw pads: lavender-pink.

RED: warm, orange apricot. Slight tabby markings may be found on the face and small indeterminate markings elsewhere (except on side and belly) are permissible in an otherwise excellent cat. Nose leather and paw pads: brick red.

CREAM: rich cream. Slight tabby markings may be found on the face and small indeterminate markings elsewhere (except on side and belly) are permissible in an otherwise excellent cat. Nose leather and paw pads: pink.

SEAL TORTIE: the colors of red and seal brown distributed in well defined patches over the whole body, including the extremities. The red can show various shades of the color; the colors must be pure and bright. A blaze on the face is desirable. No tabby markings in the red parts. The distribution of patches is of less importance than the other details of the color. Nose leather and paw pads: seal brown, pink or a mixture of both.

BLUE TORTIE: pale tones of blue-gray and cream distributed in patches over the whole body, including the extremities. The distribution of the patches is of less importance than the other details of the color. Nose leather and paw pads: pink, blue-gray, or a mixture of both.

CHOCOLATE TORTIE: milk chocolate patched with red, including the extremities. No tabby barring in the red parts. The distribution of the patches is of less importance than the other details of the color. Nose leather and paw pads: milk chocolate, pink or a mixture of both.

LILAC TORTIE: lilac and pale cream distributed in patches over the whole body including the extremities. No tabby barring in the cream parts. The distribution of the patches is of less importance than the other details of the color. Nose leather and paw pads: lavender-pink, or lavender-pink patched with pink.
European Burmese allowable outcross breeds: none.

BURMILLA

There are currently no CFA standards for this breed.

CEYLON

There are currently no CFA standards for this breed.

CHARTREUX

■ POINT SCORE
HEAD (35)	
Shape and size	6
Profile/nose	5
Muzzle	5
Ear shape and size	5
Ear placement	5
Eye shape and size	5
Neck	4
BODY (30)	
Shape and size	8
Legs and feet	8
Boning	5
Musculature	5
Tail	4
COAT (20)	
Texture	15
Length	5
COLOR (15)	
Coat Color	10
Eye Color	5

GENERAL: the Chartreux is a sturdy French breed coveted since antiquity for its hunting prowess and its dense, water repellent fur. Its husky, robust type is sometimes termed primitive, neither cobby nor classic. Though amply built, Chartreux are extremely supple and agile cats; refined, never coarse nor clumsy. Males are much larger than females and slower to mature. Coat texture, coat color and eye color are affected by sex, age and natural factors which should not penalize.

The qualities of strength, intelligence and amenability, which have enabled the Chartreux to survive the centuries unaided, should be evident in all exhibition animals and preserved through careful selection.
HEAD and NECK: rounded and broad but not a sphere. Powerful jaw; full cheeks, with mature males having larger jowls. High, softly contoured forehead; nose straight and of medium length/width; with a slight stop at eye level. Muzzle comparatively small, narrow and tapered with slight pads. Sweet, smiling expression. Neck short and heavy set.
EARS: medium in height and width; set high on the head; very erect posture.
EYES: rounded and open; alert and expressive. Color range is copper to gold; a clear, deep, brilliant orange is preferred.
BODY and TAIL: robust physique: medium-long with broad shoulders and deep chest. Strong boning; muscle mass is solid and dense. Females are medium; males are large. Tail of moderate length; heavy at base; tapering to oval tip. Lively and flexible.
LEGS and FEET: legs comparatively short and fine-boned; straight and sturdy. Feet are round and medium in size (may appear almost dainty compared to body mass).
COAT: medium-short and slightly woolly in texture (should break like a sheepskin at neck and flanks). Resilient undercoat; longer, protective topcoat. NOTE: degree of woolliness depends on age, sex and habitat, mature males exhibiting the heaviest coats. Silkier, thinner coat permitted on females and cats under two years.

PENALIZE: severe nose break, snubbed or upturned nose, broad, heavy muzzle, palpable tail defect, eyes too close together giving angry look.

DISQUALIFY: white locket, visible tail kink, green eyes; any signs of lameness in the hindquarters.

CHARTREUX COLOR

COLOR: any shade of blue-gray from ash to slate; tips lightly brushed with silver. Emphasis on color clarity and uniformity rather than shade. Preferred tone is a bright, unblemished blue with an overall iridescent sheen. Nose leather is slate gray; lips blue; paw pads are rose-taupe. Allowance made for ghost barring in kittens and for tail rings in juveniles under two years of age.
Chartreux allowable outcross breeds: none.

COLORPOINT SHORTHAIR

■ **POINT SCORE**

HEAD (20)

Long flat profile	6
Wedge, fine muzzle, size	5
Ears	4
Chin	3
Width between eyes	2

EYES (10)

Shape, size, slant, and placement	10

BODY (30)

Structure and size, including Neck	12
Muscle tone	10
Legs and Feet	5
Tail	3

COAT 10

COLOR (30)

Body color	10
Point color (matching points of dense color, proper foot pads and nose leather)	10
Eye color	10

GENERAL: a medium size, refined and svelte cat with long tapering lines, very lithe, but muscular. Males may be proportionately larger. Excellent physical condition, neither flabby nor bony. Eyes clear. Not fat.

HEAD: long tapering wedge. Medium in size in good proportion to body. The total wedge starts at the nose and flares out in straight lines to the tips of the ears forming an approximate equilateral triangle, with no break at the whiskers. No less than the width of an eye between the eyes. When the whiskers are smoothed back, the underlying bone structure is apparent. Allowance must be made for jowls in the stud cat.

SKULL: flat. In profile, a long straight line is seen from the top of the head to the tip of the nose. No bulge over eyes. No dip in nose.

NECK: long and slender.

NOSE: long and straight. A continuation of the forehead with no break.

MUZZLE: fine, wedge shaped.

EARS: strikingly large, pointed, wide at base, continuing the lines of the wedge.

EYES: almond shaped. Medium size. Neither protruding nor recessed. Slanted towards the nose in harmony with lines of wedge and ears. Uncrossed.

CHIN and JAW: medium in size. Tip of chin lines with tip of nose in the same vertical plane. Neither receding nor excessively massive.

BODY: medium size, long, and svelte. A distinctive combination of fine bones and firm muscles. Shoulders and hips continue same sleek lines of tubular body. Hips never wider than shoulders. Abdomen tight.

LEGS: long and slim. Hind legs higher than front. In good proportion to body.

PAWS: dainty, small, and oval. Toes: five in front and four behind.

TAIL: long, thin, tapering to a fine point.

COAT: short, fine textured, glossy. Lying close to body.

COLOR: Body: subtle shading is permissible, but clear color is preferable. Allowance should be made for darker color in older cats as Colorpoint Shorthairs generally darken with age, but there must be definite contrast between body color and points. Points: mask, ears, feet, legs, and tail dense and clearly defined. All of the same shade. Mask covers entire face including whisker pads and is connected to ears by tracings. Mask should not extend over the top of the head. No white hairs in points.

PENALIZE: pigmentation of nose leather and/or paw pads which is not consistent with the cat's particular color description. Palpable and/or visible protrusion of the cartilage at the end of the sternum.

DISQUALIFY: any evidence of illness or poor health. Weak hind legs. Mouth breathing due to nasal obstruction or poor occlusion. Emaciation. Visible kink. Eyes other than blue. White toes and/or feet. Incorrect number of toes. Malocclusion resulting in either undershot or overshot chin.

COLORPOINT SHORTHAIR COLORS

RED POINT: body clear white with any shading in the same tone as points. Points: bright apricot to deep red, deeper shades preferred, with lack of barring desirable. Nose leather and paw pads: flesh or coral pink. Eye color: deep vivid blue.

CREAM POINT: body clear white with any shading in the same tone as points. Points: pale buff cream to light pinkish cream, lack of barring desirable. Nose leather and paw pads: flesh to coral pink. Eye color: deep vivid blue.

SEAL LYNX POINT: body cream or pale fawn, shading to lighter color on stomach and chest. Body shading may take form of ghost striping or ticking. Points: seal brown bars, distinct and separated by lighter background color; ears seal brown with paler thumbprint in center. Nose leather: seal brown permitted, pink edged in seal brown preferred. Paw pads: seal brown. Eye color: deep vivid blue.

CHOCOLATE LYNX POINT: body ivory. Body shading may take form of ghost striping or ticking. Points: warm milk-chocolate bars, distinct and separated by lighter background color; ears warm milk-chocolate with paler thumbprint in center. Nose leather: cinnamon permitted, pink edged in cinnamon preferred. Paw pads: cinnamon. Eye color: deep vivid blue.

BLUE LYNX POINT: body bluish white to platinum grey, cold in tone, shading to lighter color on stomach and chest. Body shading may take form of ghost striping or ticking. Points: deep blue-grey bars, distinct and separated by lighter background color; ears deep blue-grey with paler thumbprint in center. Nose leather: slate-colored permitted, pink edged in slate preferred. Paw pads: slate-colored. Eye color: deep vivid blue.

LILAC LYNX POINT: body glacial white. Body shading may take form of ghost striping or ticking. Points: frosty grey with pinkish tone bars, distinct and separated by lighter background color; ears frosty grey with pinkish tone, paler thumbprint in center. Nose leather: lavender-pink permitted, pink edged in lavender-pink preferred. Paw pads: lavender-pink. Eye color: deep vivid blue.

RED LYNX POINT: body white. Body shading may take form of ghost striping or ticking. Points: deep red bars, distinct and separated by lighter background color; ears deep red, paler thumbprint in center. Nose leather and paw pads: flesh or coral pink. Eye color: deep vivid blue.

CREAM LYNX POINT: body clear white. Body shading may take form of ghost striping or ticking. Points: bars of pale buff cream to light pinkish cream, distinct and separated by lighter background color; ears pale buff cream to light pinkish cream, paler thumbprint in center. Nose leather and paw pads: flesh to coral pink. Eye color: deep vivid blue.

SEAL-TORTIE POINT: body pale fawn to cream, shading to lighter color on stomach and chest. Body color may be mottled with cream in older cats. Points: seal brown, uniformly mottled with red and/or cream. Nose leather and paw pads: seal brown; flesh or coral pink mottling desirable. Eye color: deep vivid blue.

CHOCOLATE-TORTIE POINT: body ivory, may be mottled in older cats. Points: warm milk-chocolate uniformly mottled with red and/or cream. Nose leather and paw pads: cinnamon; flesh or coral pink mottling desirable. Eye color: deep vivid blue.

BLUE-CREAM POINT: body bluish white to platinum grey, cold in tone, shading to lighter color on stomach and chest. Body color may be mottled in older cats. Points: deep blue-grey uniformly mottled with cream. Nose leather and paw pads: slate-colored; flesh or coral pink mottling desirable. Eye color: deep vivid blue.

LILAC-CREAM POINT: body glacial white; mottling, if any, in the shade of the points. Points: frosty grey with pinkish tone, uniformly mottled with pale cream. Nose leather and paw pads: lavender-pink; flesh or coral pink mottling desirable. Eye color: deep vivid blue.

SEAL-TORTIE LYNX POINT: body cream or pale fawn, shading to lighter color on stomach and chest. Body shading may take form of ghost striping or ticking and/or cream mottling. Points: seal brown bars, distinct and separated by lighter background color; ears seal brown with paler thumbprint in center. Uniform mottling of red and/or cream overlays the markings of the points. Nose leather: seal brown permitted, pink edged in seal brown preferred, flesh or coral pink mottling may be present. Paw pads: seal brown, or seal brown mottled with flesh or coral pink. Eye color: deep vivid blue. NOTE: these cats resemble lynx points more than tortie points.

CHOCOLATE-TORTIE LYNX POINT: body ivory. Body shading may take form of ghost striping or ticking and/or cream mottling. Points: warm milk-chocolate bars, distinct and separated by lighter background color; ears warm milk-chocolate with paler thumbprint in center. Uniform mottling of red and/or cream overlays the markings of the points. Nose leather: cinnamon permitted, pink edged in cinnamon preferred, flesh or coral pink mottling may be present. Paw pads: cinnamon, or cinnamon mottled with flesh or coral pink. Eye color: deep vivid blue. NOTE: these cats resemble lynx points more than tortie points.

BLUE-CREAM LYNX POINT: body bluish white to platinum grey, cold in tone, shading to lighter color on stomach and chest. Body shading may take form of ghost striping or ticking and/or cream mottling. Points: deep blue-grey bars, distinct and separated by lighter background color; ears deep blue-grey with paler thumbprint in center. Uniform mottling of cream overlays the markings of the points. Nose leather: slate-colored permitted, pink edged in slate preferred, flesh or coral pink mottling may be present. Paw pads: slate-colored, or slate mottled with flesh or coral pink. Eye color: deep vivid blue. NOTE: these cats resemble lynx points more than tortie points.

LILAC-CREAM LYNX POINT: body glacial white. Body shading may take form of ghost striping or ticking and/or cream mottling. Points: frosty grey with pinkish tone bars, distinct and separated by lighter background color; ears frosty grey with pinkish tone, paler thumbprint in center. Uniform mottling of cream overlays the markings of the points. Nose leather: lavender-pink permitted, pink edged in lavender-pink preferred, flesh or coral pink mottling may be present. Paw pads: lavender-pink, or lavender-pink mottled with flesh or coral pink. Eye color: deep vivid blue. NOTE: these cats resemble lynx points more than tortie points. Colorpoint Shorthair allowable outcross breeds: Siamese.

CORNISH REX

see Rex (Cornish Rex)

DEVON REX

see Rex (Devon Rex)

CYMRIC

see Manx: Longhair

EGYPTIAN MAU

■ POINT SCORE

HEAD (20)	
Muzzle	5
Skull	5
Ears	5
Eye Shape	5
BODY (25)	
Torso	10
Legs and Feet	10
Tail	5
COAT (5)	
Texture and length	5
PATTERN	25
COLOR (25)	
Eye color	10
Coat color	15

GENERAL: the Egyptian Mau is the only natural domesticated breed of spotted cat. The Egyptian's impression should be one of an active, colorful cat of medium size with well developed muscles. Perfect physical condition with an alert appearance. Well balanced physically and temperamentally. Males tend to be larger than females.
HEAD: a slightly rounded wedge without flat planes, medium in length. Not full-cheeked. Profile showing a gentle contour with slight rise from the bridge of the nose to the forehead. Entire length of nose even in width when viewed from the front. Allowance must be made for jowls in

adult males.
MUZZLE: should flow into existing wedge of the head. It should be neither short nor pointed. The chin should be firm, not receding or protruding.
EARS: medium to large, alert and moderately pointed, continuing the planes of the head. Broad at base. Slightly flared with ample width between the ears. Hair on ears short and close lying. Inner ear a delicate, almost transparent, shell pink. May be tufted.
EYES: large and alert, almond shaped, with a slight slant towards the ears. Skull apertures neither round nor oriental.
BODY: medium long and graceful, showing well developed muscular strength. Loose skin flap extending from flank to hind leg knee. General balance is more to be desired than size alone. Allowance to be made for muscular necks and shoulders in adult males.
LEGS and FEET: in proportion to body. Hind legs proportionately longer, giving the appearance of being on tip-toe when standing upright. Feet small and dainty, slightly oval, almost round in shape. Toes: five in front and four behind.
TAIL: medium long, thick at base, with slight taper.
COAT: hair is medium in length with a lustrous sheen. In the smoke color the hair is silky and fine in texture. In the silver and bronze colors, the hair is dense and resilient in texture and accommodates two or more bands of ticking separated by lighter bands

PENALIZE: short or round head. Pointed muzzle. Small, round or oriental eyes. Cobby or oriental body. Short or whip tail. If no broken necklaces. Pencillings in spotting pattern on torso. Poor condition. Amber cast in eye color in cats over the age of 1 1/2 years.

DISQUALIFY: lack of spots. Blue eyes. Kinked or abnormal tail. Incorrect number of toes. White locket or button distinctive from other acceptable white-colored areas in color sections of standard.
MAU PATTERN
(Common to all colors)
PATTERN: markings on torso are to be randomly spotted with variance in size and shape. The spots can be small or large, round, oblong, or irregular shaped. Any of these are of equal merit but the spots, however shaped or whatever size, shall be distinct. Good contrast between pale ground color and deeper markings. Forehead barred with characteristic "M" and frown marks, forming lines between the ears which continue down the

back of the neck, ideally breaking into elongated spots, along the spine. As the spinal lines reach the rear haunches, they meld together to form a dorsal stripe which continues along the top of the tail to its tip. The tail is heavily banded and has a dark tip. The cheeks are barred with "mascara" lines; the first starts at the outer corner of the eye and continues along the contour of the cheek, with a second line, which starts at the center of the cheek and curves upwards, almost meeting below the base of the ear. On the upper chest there are one or more broken necklaces. The shoulder markings are a transition between stripes and spots. The upper front legs are heavily barred but do not necessarily match. Spotting pattern on each side of the torso need not match. Haunches and upper hind legs to be a transition between stripes and spots, breaking into bars on the lower leg. Underside of body to have "vest buttons" spots; dark in color against the correspondingly pale ground color.

EGYPTIAN MAU COLORS

EYE COLOR: light green "gooseberry green." Amber cast is acceptable only in young adults up to 11/2 years of age.

SILVER: pale silver ground color across the head, shoulders, outer legs, back, and tail. Underside fades to a brilliant pale silver. All markings charcoal color with a white to pale silver undercoat, showing good contrast against lighter ground colors. Back of ears grayish-pink and tipped in black. Nose, lips, and eyes outlined in black. Upper throat area, chin, and around nostrils pale clear silver, appearing white. Nose leather: brick red. Paw pads: black with black between the toes and extending beyond the paws of the hind legs.

BRONZE: warm coppery brown ground color across head, shoulders, outer legs, back, and tail, being darkest on the saddle and lightening to a tawny-buff on the sides. Underside fades to a creamy ivory. All markings dark brown-black with a warm coppery brown undercoat, showing good contrast against the lighter ground color. Back of ears tawny-pink and tipped in dark brown-black. Nose, lips, and eyes outlined in dark brown, with bridge of nose brown. Upper throat area, chin, and around nostrils pale creamy white. Nose leather: brick red. Paw pads: black or dark brown, with same color between toes and extending beyond the paws of the hind legs.

SMOKE: pale silver ground color

across head, shoulders, legs, tail, and underside. All markings jet black with a white to pale silver undercoat, with sufficient contrast against ground color for pattern to be plainly visible. Nose, lips, and eyes outlined in jet black. Upper throat area, chin, and around nostrils lightest in color. Nose leather: black. Paw pads: black with black between the toes and extending beyond the paws of the hind legs.
Egyptian Mau allowable outcross breeds: none.

EUROPEAN SHORTHAIR

There are currently no CFA standards for this breed.

EXOTIC

■ POINT SCORE

HEAD (including size and shpae of eyes; ear shape and set)	30
TYPE (including shape, size, bone, and length of tail)	20
COAT	10
BALANCE	5
REFINEMENT	5
COLOR	20
EYE COLOR	10

In all tabby varieties, the 20 points for color are to be divided 10 for markings and 10 for color. In all "with white" varieties (calico, dilute calico, bi-color, van bi-color, van calico, van dilute calico, and tabby and white), the 20 points for color are to be divided 10 for "with white" pattern and 10 for color.

GENERAL: the ideal Exotic should present an impression of a heavily boned, well balanced cat with a sweet expression and soft, round lines. The large, round eyes set wide apart in a large round head contribute to the overall look and expression. The thick, plush coat softens the lines of the cat and accentuates the roundness in appearance.
HEAD: round and massive, with great breadth of skull. Round face with round underlying bone structure. Well set on a short, thick neck.
NOSE: short, snub, and broad, with "break" centered between the eyes.
CHEEKS: full.
JAWS: broad and powerful.
CHIN: full, well-developed, and firmly rounded, reflecting a proper bite.
EARS: small, round tipped, tilted forward, and not unduly open at the base. Set far apart, and low on the head, fitting into (without distorting) the rounded contour of the head.
EYES: brilliant in color, large, round, and full. Set level and far apart, giving a sweet expression to the face.
BODY: of cobby type, low on the legs, broad and deep through the chest, equal-

ly massive across the shoulders and rump, with a well-rounded midsection and level back. Good muscle tone, with no evidence of obesity. Large or medium in size. Quality the determining consideration rather than size.

LEGS: short, thick, and strong. Forelegs straight.

PAWS: large, round, and firm. Toes carried close, five in front and four behind .

TAIL: short, but in proportion to body length. Carried without a curve and at an angle lower than the back.

COAT: dense, plush, soft and full of life. Standing out from the body due to a rich, thick undercoat. Medium in length. Acceptable length depends on proper undercoat. Cats with a ruff or tail-feathers (long hair on the tail) shall be transferred to the AOV class.

DISQUALIFY: locket or button. Kinked or abnormal tail. Incorrect number of toes. Any apparent weakness in the hind quarters. Any apparent deformity of the spine. Deformity of the skull resulting in an asymmetrical face and/or head. Crossed eyes. For pointed cats, disqualify for white toes, eye color other than blue.*

*The above listed disqualifications apply to all Exotic cats. Additional disqualifications are listed under "Colors."

EXOTIC COLORS

WHITE: pure glistening white. Nose leather and paw pads: pink. Eye color: deep blue or brilliant copper. Odd-eyed whites shall have one blue and one copper eye with equal color depth.

BLACK: dense coal black, sound from roots to tip of fur. Free from any tinge of rust on tips or smoke undercoat. Nose leather: black. Paw pads: black or brown. Eye color: brilliant copper.

BLUE: blue, lighter shade preferred, one level tone from nose to tip of tail. Sound to the roots. A sound darker shade is more acceptable than an unsound lighter shade. Nose leather and paw pads: blue. Eye color: brilliant copper.

RED: deep, rich, clear, brilliant red; without shading, markings, or ticking. Lips and chin the same color as coat. Nose leather and paw pads: brick red. Eye color: brilliant copper.

CREAM: one level shade of buff cream, without markings. Sound to the roots. Lighter shades preferred. Nose leather and paw pads: pink. Eye color: brilliant copper.

CHOCOLATE: rich, warm chocolate-brown, sound from roots to tip of fur. Nose leather and paw pads: brown. Eye color: brilliant copper.

LILAC: rich, warm lavender with a pinkish tone, sound and even throughout. Nose leather and paw pads: pink. Eye color: brilliant copper.

CHINCHILLA SILVER: undercoat pure white. Coat on back, flanks, head, and tail sufficiently tipped with black to give the characteristic sparkling silver appearance. Legs may be slightly shaded with tipping. Chin, ear tufts, stomach, and chest, pure white. Rims of eyes, lips, and nose outlined with black. Nose leather: brick red. Paw pads: black. Eye color: green or blue-green. Disqualify for incorrect eye color, incorrect eye color being copper, yellow, gold, amber, or any color other than green or blue-green .

SHADED SILVER: undercoat white with a mantle of black tipping shading down from sides, face, and tail from dark on the ridge to white on the chin, chest, stomach, and under the tail. Legs to be the same tone as the face. The general effect to be much darker than a chinchilla. Rims of eyes, lips, and nose outlined with black. Nose leather: brick red. Paw pads: black. Eye color: green or blue-green. Disqualify for incorrect eye color, incorrect eye color being copper, yellow, gold, amber, or any color other than green or blue-green.

CHINCHILLA GOLDEN: undercoat rich warm cream. Coat on back, flanks, head, and tail sufficiently tipped with black to give golden appearance. Legs may be slightly shaded with tipping. Chin, ear tufts, stomach, and chest, cream. Rims of eyes, lips, and nose outlined with black. Nose leather: deep rose. Paw pads: black. Eye color: green or blue-green. Disqualify for incorrect eye color, incorrect eye color being copper, yellow, gold, amber, or any color other than green or blue-green.

SHADED GOLDEN: undercoat rich warm cream with a mantle of black tipping shading down from the sides, face, and tail from dark on the ridge to cream on the chin, chest, stomach, and under the tail. Legs to be the same tone as the face. The general effect to be much darker than a chinchilla. Rims of eyes, lips, and nose outlined with black. Nose leather: deep rose. Paw pads: black. Eye color: green or blue-green. Disqualify for incorrect eye color, incorrect eye color being copper, yellow, gold, amber, or any color other than green or blue-green.

SHELL CAMEO (Red Chinchilla): undercoat white, the coat on the back, flanks, head, and tail to be sufficiently tipped with red to give the characteristic sparkling appearance. Face and legs may be very slightly shaded with tipping. Chin, ear tufts, stomach, and chest, white. Nose leather, rims of eyes and paw pads: rose. Eye color: brilliant cop-

per.

SHADED CAMEO (Red Shaded): undercoat white with a mantle of red tipping shading down the sides, face, and tail from dark on the ridge to white on the chin, chest, stomach, and under the tail. Legs to be the same tone as face. The general effect to be much redder than the shell cameo. Nose leather, rims of eyes and paw pads: rose. Eye color: brilliant copper.

SHELL TORTOISESHELL: undercoat white. Coat on the back, flanks, head, and tail to be delicately tipped in black with well-defined patches of red and cream tipped hairs as in the pattern of the tortoiseshell. Face and legs may be slightly shaded with tipping. Chin, ear tufts, stomach, and chest, white to very slightly tipped. Blaze of red or cream tipping on face is desirable. Eye color: brilliant copper.

SHADED TORTOISESHELL: undercoat white. Mantle of black tipping and clearly defined patches of red and cream tipped hairs as in the pattern of the tortoiseshell. Shading down the sides, face, and tail from dark on the ridge to slightly tipped or white on the chin, chest, stomach, legs, and under the tail. The general effect is to be much darker than the shell tortoiseshell. Blaze of red or cream tipping on the face is desirable. Eye color: brilliant copper.

BLACK SMOKE: white undercoat, deeply tipped with black. Cat in repose appears black. In motion the white undercoat is clearly apparent. Points and mask black with narrow band of white at base of hairs next to skin which may be seen only when fur is parted. Nose leather and paw pads: black. Eye color: brilliant copper.

BLUE SMOKE: white undercoat, deeply tipped with blue. Cat in repose appears blue. In motion the white undercoat is clearly apparent. Points and mask blue, with narrow band of white at base of hairs next to skin which may be seen only when fur is parted. Nose leather and paw pads: blue. Eye color: brilliant copper.

CREAM SMOKE: white undercoat, deeply tipped with cream. Cat in repose appears cream. In motion the white undercoat is clearly apparent. Points and mask cream, with narrow band of white at base of hairs next to skin which may be seen only when fur is parted. Nose leather and paw pads: pink. Eye color: brilliant copper.

CAMEO SMOKE (Red Smoke): white undercoat, deeply tipped with red. Cat in repose appears red. In motion the white undercoat is clearly apparent. Points and mask red, with narrow band of white at

base of hairs next to skin which may be seen only when fur is parted. Nose leather, rims of eyes, and paw pads: rose. Eye color: brilliant copper.

SMOKE TORTOISESHELL: white undercoat, deeply tipped with black with clearly defined unbrindled patches of red and cream tipped hairs as in the pattern of the tortoiseshell. Cat in repose appears tortoiseshell. In motion the white undercoat is clearly apparent. Face and ears tortoiseshell pattern with narrow band of white at the base of the hairs next to the skin that may be seen only when fur is parted. Blaze of red or cream tipping on face is desirable. Eye color: brilliant copper.

BLUE-CREAM SMOKE: white undercoat deeply tipped with blue, with clearly defined patches of cream as in the pattern of the blue-cream. Cat in repose appears blue-cream. In motion the white undercoat is clearly apparent. Face and ears blue-cream pattern with narrow band of white at the base of the hair next to the skin that may be seen only when fur is parted. Blaze of cream tipping on face is desirable. Eye color: brilliant copper.

SMOKE AND WHITE: white with colored portions, the colored portions of the cat to conform to the currently established smoke color standards. As a preferred minimum, the cat should have white feet, legs, undersides, chest, and muzzle. Less white than this minimum should be penalized proportionally. Inverted "V" blaze on face desirable. Eye color: brilliant copper.

VAN SMOKE AND WHITE: white cat with colored portions confined to the extremities; head, tail, and legs. The colored portions conform to the currently established smoke color standards. One or two small colored patches on body allowable. Eye color: brilliant copper.

CHOCOLATE TORTOISESHELL: rich, warm chocolate brown with patches of red. Patches clearly defined and well broken on both body and extremities. Nose leather and paw pads: brown and/or brick red. Eye color: brilliant copper.

LILAC-CREAM: rich, warm pinkish toned lavender with patches of cream. Patches clearly defined and well broken on both body and extremities. Nose leather and paw pads: pink. Eye color: brilliant copper.

CLASSIC TABBY PATTERN: markings dense, clearly defined, and broad. Legs evenly barred with bracelets coming up to meet the body markings. Tail evenly ringed. Several unbroken necklaces on neck and upper chest, the more the better. Frown marks on forehead form an intricate letter "M." Unbroken line runs back from outer corner of eye. Swirls on cheeks. Vertical lines over back of head extend to shoulder markings which are in the shape of a butterfly with both upper and lower wings distinctly outlined and marked with dots inside outline. Back markings consist of a vertical line down the spine from butterfly to tail with a vertical stripe paralleling it on each side, the three stripes well separated by stripes of the ground color. Large solid blotch on each side to be encircled by one or more unbroken rings. Side markings should be the same on both sides. Double vertical rows of buttons on chest and stomach.

MACKEREL TABBY PATTERN: markings dense, clearly defined, and all narrow pencillings. Legs evenly barred with narrow bracelets coming up to meet the body markings. Tail barred. Necklaces on neck and chest distinct, like so many chains. Head barred with an "M" on the forehead. Unbroken lines running back from the eyes. Lines running down the head to meet the shoulders. Spine lines run together to form a narrow saddle. Narrow pencillings run around body.

PATCHED TABBY: a patched tabby (torbie) is an established silver, brown, or blue tabby with patches of red and/or cream.

BROWN PATCHED TABBY: ground color brilliant coppery brown with classic or mackerel tabby markings of dense black with patches of red and/or cream clearly defined on both body and extremities; a blaze of red and/or cream on the face is desirable. Lips and chin the same shade as the rings around the eyes. Eye color: brilliant copper.

BLUE PATCHED TABBY: ground color, including lips and chin, pale bluish ivory with classic or mackerel tabby markings of very deep blue affording a good contrast with ground color. Patches of cream clearly defined on both body and extremities; a blaze of cream on the face is desirable. Warm fawn overtones or patina over the whole. Eye color: brilliant copper.

SILVER PATCHED TABBY: ground color, including lips and chin, pale silver with classic or mackerel tabby markings of dense black with patches of red and/or cream clearly defined on both body and extremities. A blaze of red and/or cream on the face is desirable. Eye color: brilliant copper or hazel.

SILVER TABBY (classic, mackerel): ground color, including lips and chin,

pale, clear silver. Markings dense black. Nose leather: brick red. Paw pads: black. Eye color: green, brilliant copper, or hazel.

BLUE SILVER TABBY (classic, mackerel): ground color pale bluish silver. Markings sound blue. Undercoat white. Lips and chin the same shade as the rings around the eyes. Nose leather: blue or old rose trimmed with blue. Paw pads: blue or old rose. Eye color: green, hazel, or brilliant copper.

BLUE SILVER PATCHED TABBY (classic, mackerel): ground color pale bluish silver with patches of cream on both body and extremities. Markings sound blue. Undercoat white. Lips and chin the same shade as the rings around the eyes. Nose leather: blue or old rose trimmed with blue and/or pink. Paw pads: blue or old rose and/or pink. Eye color: green, hazel, or brilliant copper.

RED TABBY (classic, mackerel): ground color red. Markings deep, rich red. Lips and chin the same shade as the rings around the eyes. Nose leather and paw pads: brick red. Eye color: brilliant copper.

BROWN TABBY (classic, mackerel): ground color brilliant coppery brown. Markings dense black. Lips and chin the same shade as the rings around the eyes. Back of leg black from paw to heel. Nose leather: brick red. Paw pads: black or brown. Eye color: brilliant copper.

BLUE TABBY (classic, mackerel): ground color, including lips and chin, pale bluish ivory. Markings a very deep blue affording a good contrast with ground color. Warm fawn overtones or patina over the whole. Nose leather: old rose. Paw pads: rose. Eye color: brilliant copper.

CREAM TABBY (classic, mackerel): ground color, including lips and chin, very pale cream. Markings of buff or cream sufficiently darker than the ground color to afford good contrast, but remaining within the dilute color range. Nose leather and paw pads: pink. Eye color: brilliant copper.

CAMEO TABBY (classic, mackerel): ground color off-white. Markings red. Nose leather and paw pads: rose. Eye color: brilliant copper.

PEKE-FACE RED and PEKE-FACE RED TABBY: the peke-face cat should conform in color and general type to the standard set forth for the red and red tabby cat; however, allowance should be made for the slightly higher placement of the ears to conform with the underlying bone structure of the

head which differs greatly from that of the standard Exotic. The nose should be short, depressed and indented between the eyes. The muzzle should be wrinkled. Eyes should be large, round and set wide apart. The horizontal break, which is located between the usual nose break and the top dome of the head, runs straight across the front of the head creating half-moon boning above the eyes and an additional horizontal indentation located in the center of the forehead bone structure. This bone structure results in a very round head with a strong chin. Eye color: brilliant copper.

TORTOISESHELL: black with unbrindled patches of red and cream. Patches clearly defined and well broken on both body and extremities. Blaze of red or cream on face is desirable. Eye color: brilliant copper.

CALICO: white with unbrindled patches of black and red. As a preferred minimum, the cat should have white feet, legs, undersides, chest, and muzzle. Less white than this minimum should be penalized proportionately. Inverted "V" blaze on face desirable. Eye color: brilliant copper.

DILUTE CALICO: white with unbrindled patches of blue and cream. As a preferred minimum the cat should have white feet, legs, undersides, chest, and muzzle. Less white than this minimum should be penalized proportionately. Inverted "V" blaze on face desirable. Eye color: brilliant copper.

BLUE-CREAM: blue with patches of solid cream. Patches clearly defined and well broken on both body and extremities. Eye color: brilliant copper.

BI-COLOR: black and white, blue and white, red and white, or cream and white. As a preferred minimum, the cat should have white feet, legs, undersides, chest, and muzzle. Less white than this minimum should be penalized proportionately. Inverted "V" blaze on face desirable. Eye color: brilliant copper.

VAN BI-COLOR: Black and white, red and white, blue and white, or cream and white. White cat with color confined to the extremities; head, tail, and legs. One or two small colored patches on body allowable. Eye color: brilliant copper.

VAN CALICO: white cat with unbrindled patches of black and red confined to the extremities; head, tail, and legs. One or two small colored patches on body allowable. Eye color: brilliant copper.

VAN DILUTE CALICO: white cat

with unbrindled patches of blue and cream confined to the extremities; head, tail, and legs. One or two small colored patches on body allowable. Eye color: brilliant copper.

(NOTE: cats having more than two small body spots should be shown in the regular bi-color class.)

TABBY AND WHITE: white with colored portions, the colored portions of the cat to conform to the currently established classic, mackerel and patched tabby color standards. As a preferred minimum, the cat should have white feet, legs, undersides, chest, and muzzle. Less white than this minimum should be penalized proportionately. Inverted "V" blaze on face desirable. Eye color: to conform to the established tabby pattern requirements.

VAN TABBY AND WHITE: white cat with colored portions confined to the extremities; head, tail, and legs. The colored portions conform to the currently established classic, mackerel and patched tabby color standards. One or two small colored patches on body allowable. Eye color: to conform to the established tabby pattern requirements.

SEAL POINT: body even pale fawn to cream, warm in tone, shading gradually into lighter color on the stomach and chest. Points deep seal brown. Nose leather and paw pads: same color as points. Eye color: deep vivid blue.

CHOCOLATE POINT: body ivory with no shading. Points milk-chocolate color, warm in tone. Nose leather and paw pads: cinnamon pink. Eye color: deep vivid blue.

BLUE POINT: body bluish white, cold in tone, shading gradually to white on stomach and chest. Points blue. Nose leather and paw pads: slate blue. Eye color: deep vivid blue.

LILAC POINT: body glacial white with no shading. Points frosty grey with pinkish tone. Nose leather and paw pads: lavender pink. Eye color: deep vivid blue.

LILAC-CREAM POINT: body glacial white with no shading. Points lilac with patches of cream. Nose leather and paw pads: lavender pink, pink or a combination of lavender pink and pink. Eye color: deep vivid blue.

FLAME (RED) POINT: body creamy white. Points deep orange flame to deep red. Nose leather and paw pads: flesh or coral pink. Eye color: deep vivid blue.

CREAM POINT: body creamy white

with no shading. Points buff cream with no apricot. Nose leather and paw pads: flesh pink or salmon coral. Eye color: deep vivid blue.

TORTIE POINT: body creamy white or pale fawn. Points seal with unbrindled patches of red and/or cream. Blaze of red or cream on face is desirable. Nose leather and paw pads: seal brown with flesh and/or coral pink mottling to conform with colors of points. Eye color: deep vivid blue.

CHOCOLATE-TORTIE POINT: body ivory with no shading. Points chocolate with unbrindled patches of red and/or cream. Nose leather and paw pads: chocolate with flesh and/or coral pink mottling to conform with the point color. Eye color: deep vivid blue.

BLUE-CREAM POINT: body bluish white or creamy white, shading gradually to white on the stomach and chest. Points blue with patches of cream. Nose leather and paw pads: slate blue, pink, or a combination of slate blue and pink. Eye color: deep vivid blue.

SEAL LYNX POINT: points beige-brown ticked with darker brown tabby markings. Body color pale cream to fawn, warm in tone. Mask must be clearly lined with dark stripes vertical on forehead with classic "M" on forehead, horizontal on cheeks and dark spots on whisker pads clearly outlined in dark color edges. Inner ear light with thumbprint on outer ear. Markings dense, clearly defined and broad. Legs evenly barred with bracelets. Tail barred. No striping or mottling on body, but consideration to be given to shading in older cats. Nose leather: seal or brick red. Paw pads: seal. Eye color: deep vivid blue.

BLUE LYNX POINT: points light, silvery blue, ticked with darker blue tabby markings. Body color bluish white, cold in tone. Mask must be clearly lined with dark stripes vertical on forehead with classic "M" on forehead, horizontal on cheeks and dark spots on whisker pads clearly outlined in dark color edges. Inner ear light with thumbprint on outer ear. Markings dense, clearly defined and broad. Legs evenly barred with bracelets. Tail barred. No striping or mottling on body, but consideration to be given to shading in older cats. Nose leather: blue or brick red. Paw pads: blue. Eye color: deep vivid blue.

FLAME (RED) LYNX POINT: points deep orange flame ticked with deep red tabby markings. Body color creamy white. Mask must be clearly lined with dark stripes vertical on forehead with classics "M" on forehead, horizontal on cheeks and dark spots on whisker pads

clearly outlined in dark color edges. Inner ear light with thumbprint on outer ear. Markings dense, clearly defined and broad. Legs evenly barred with bracelets. Tail barred. Nose leather and paw pads: flesh or coral pink. Eye color: deep vivid blue.

CREAM LYNX POINT: points pale cream ticked with dark cream tabby markings. Body color creamy white, significantly lighter in tone than the points. Mask must be clearly lined with dark stripes vertical on forehead with classics "M" on forehead, horizontal on cheeks and dark spots on whisker pads clearly outlined in dark color edges. Inner ear light with thumbprint on outer ear. Markings dense, clearly defined and broad. Legs evenly barred with bracelets. Tail barred. Nose leather and paw pads: flesh or coral pink. Eye color: deep vivid blue.

TORTIE-LYNX POINT: points beige-brown with dark brown tabby markings and patches of red. Body color creamy white or pale fawn. Mask must be clearly lined with dark stripes vertical on forehead with classic "M" on forehead, horizontal on cheeks and dark spots on whisker pads clearly outlined in dark color edges. Inner ear light with thumbprint on outer ear. Markings dense, clearly defined and broad. Legs evenly barred with bracelets. Tail barred. Nose leather and paw pads: seal brown and/or flesh or coral pink. Eye color: deep vivid blue.

BLUE-CREAM LYNX POINT: points blue with darker blue tabby markings and patches of cream. Body color bluish white, cold in tone. Mask must be clearly lined with dark stripes vertical on forehead with classic "M" on forehead, horizontal on cheeks and dark spots on whisker pads clearly outlined in dark color edges. Inner ear light with thumbprint on outer ear. Markings dense, clearly defined and broad. Legs evenly barred with bracelets. Tail barred. Nose leather and paw pads: slate blue and/or pink. Eye color: deep vivid blue.

CHOCOLATE LYNX POINT: points milk-chocolate ticked with darker chocolate tabby markings. Body color ivory. Mask must be clearly lined with dark stripes vertical on forehead with classic "M" on forehead, horizontal on cheeks and dark spots on whisker pads clearly outlined in dark color edges. Inner ear light with thumbprint on outer ear. Markings dense, clearly defined and broad. Legs evenly barred with bracelets. Tail barred. Nose leather and paw pads: cinnamon pink. Eye color: deep vivid blue.

LILAC LYNX POINT: points pale

frosty grey with pinkish tone ticked with darker lilac tabby markings. Body color glacial white. Mask must be clearly lined with dark stripes vertical on forehead with classic "M" on forehead, horizontal on cheeks and dark spots on whisker pads clearly outlined in dark color edges. Inner ear light with thumbprint on outer ear. Markings dense, clearly defined and broad. Legs evenly barred with bracelets. Tail barred. Nose leather and paw pads: lavender pink. Eye color: deep vivid blue.

CHOCOLATE-TORTIE LYNX POINT: points milk-chocolate ticked with darker chocolate tabby markings and patches of red. Body color ivory. Mask must be clearly lined with dark stripes vertical on forehead with classic "M" on forehead, horizontal on cheeks and dark spots on whisker pads clearly outlined in dark color edges. Inner ear light with thumbprint on outer ear. Markings dense, clearly defined and broad. Legs evenly barred with bracelets. Tail barred. Nose leather and paw pads: cinnamon pink and/or coral pink. Eye color: deep vivid blue.

LILAC-CREAM LYNX POINT: points pale frosty grey with pinkish tone ticked with darker lilac tabby markings and patches of cream. Body color glacial white. Mask must be clearly lined with dark stripes vertical on forehead with classic "M" on forehead, horizontal on cheeks and dark spots on whisker pads clearly outlined in dark color edges. Inner ear light with thumbprint on outer ear. Markings dense, clearly defined and broad. Legs evenly barred with bracelets. Tail barred. Nose leather and paw pads: lavender pink and/or coral pink. Eye color: deep vivid blue.
Exotic allowable outcross breeds: Persian.

HAVANA BROWN

■ POINT SCORE

HEAD (33)	
Shape	8
Profile/Stop	8
Muzzle	8
Chin	4
Ear	5
EYES (10)	
Shape & Size	5
Color	5
COLOR (22)	
Coat Color	20
Paw Pads, Nose Leather & Whiskers	2
COAT	10
BODY AND NECK	15
LEGS AND FEET	5
TAIL	5

GENERAL: the overall impression of

the ideal Havana Brown is a cat of medium size with a rich, solid color coat and good muscle tone. Due to its distinctive muzzle shape, coat color, brilliant and expressive eyes and large forward tilted ears, it is comparable to no other breed.
HEAD: when viewed from above, the head is longer than it is wide, narrowing to a rounded muzzle with a pronounced break on both sides behind the whisker pads. The somewhat narrow muzzle and the whisker break are distinctive characteristics of the breed and must be evident in the typical specimen. When viewed in profile, there is a distinct stop at the eyes; the end of the muzzle appears almost square; this illusion is heightened by a well-developed chin, the profile outline of which is more square than round. Ideally, the tip of the nose and the chin form an almost perpendicular line. Allowance to be made for somewhat broader heads and stud jowls in the adult male. Allow for sparse hair on chin, directly below lower lip.
EARS: large, round-tipped, cupped at the base, wide-set but not flaring; tilted forward giving the cat an alert appearance. Little hair inside or outside.
EYES: Shape: aperture oval in shape. Medium sized; set wide apart; brilliant, alert and expressive. Color: any vivid and level shade of green; the deeper the color the better.
BODY AND NECK: torso medium in length, firm and muscular. Adult males tend to be larger than their female counterparts. Overall balance and proportion rather than size to be determining factor. The neck is medium in length and in proportion to the body. The general conformation is mid-range between the short-coupled, thick set and svelte breeds.
LEGS AND FEET: the ideal specimen stands relatively high on its legs for a cat of medium proportions in trunk and tail. Legs are straight. The legs of females are slim and dainty; slenderness and length of leg will be less evident in the more powerfully muscled, mature males. Hind legs slightly longer than front. Paws are oval and compact. Toes: five in front and four behind.
TAIL: medium in length and in proportion to the body; slender, neither whip-like nor blunt; tapering at the end. Not too broad at the base.
COAT: short to medium in length, smooth and lustrous.

DISQUALIFY: kinked tail, locket or button, incorrect number of toes, any eye color other than green, incorrect color of whiskers, nose leather or paw pads.

HAVANA BROWN COLOR

COLOR: a rich and even shade of warm brown throughout; color tends toward red-brown (mahogany) rather than black-brown. Nose leather: brown with a rosy flush. Paw pads: rosy toned. Whiskers: brown, complementing the coat color. ALLOW FOR GHOST TABBY MARKINGS IN KITTENS AND YOUNG ADULTS. Havana Brown allowable outcross breeds: none.

JAPANESE BOBTAIL

■ POINT SCORE

HEAD	20
TYPE	30
TAIL	20
COLOR and MARKINGS	20
COAT	10

GENERAL: the Japanese Bobtail should present the overall impression of a medium sized cat with clean lines and bone structure, well-muscled but straight and slender rather than massive in build. The unique set of its eyes, combined with high cheek bones and a long parallel nose, lend a distinctive Japanese cast to the face, especially in profile, quite different from the other oriental breeds. Its short tail should resemble a bunny tail with the hair fanning out to create a pom-pom appearance which effectively camouflages the underlying bone structure of the tail.

HEAD: although the head appears long and finely chiseled, it forms almost a perfect equilateral triangle (the triangle does not include the ears) with gentle curving lines, high cheekbones, and a noticeable whisker break, the nose long and well-defined by two parallel lines from tip to brow with a gentle dip at, or just below, eye level. Allowance must be made for jowls in the stud cat.

EARS: large, upright, and expressive, set wide apart but at right angles to the head rather than flaring outward, and giving the impression of being tilted forward in repose.

MUZZLE: fairly broad and rounding into the whisker break; neither pointed nor blunt.

EYES: large, oval rather than round, but wide and alert; set into the skull at a rather pronounced slant when viewed in profile. The eyeball shows a shallow curvature and should not bulge out beyond the cheekbone or the forehead.

BODY: medium in size, males proportionately larger than females. Torso long, lean and elegant, not tubular, showing well developed muscular strength without coarseness. No inclination toward flabbiness or cobbiness. General balance of utmost importance.

LEGS: in keeping with the body, long, slender, and high, but not dainty or fragile in appearance. The hind legs noticeably longer than the forelegs, but deeply angulated to bend when the cat is standing relaxed so that the torso remains nearly level rather than rising toward the rear. When standing, the cat's forelegs and shoulders form two continuous straight lines, close together.

PAWS: oval. Toes: five in front and four behind.

COAT (SHORTHAIR): medium length, soft and silky, but without a noticeable undercoat.

COAT (LONGHAIR): length medium-long to long, texture soft and silky, with no noticeable undercoat in the mature adult. Frontal ruff desirable. Coat may be shorter and close lying over the shoulders, gradually lengthening toward the rump, with noticeable longer hair on the tail and rear britches. Ear and toe tufts desirable. Coat should lie so as to accent the lines of the body.

TAIL: the tail is unique not only to the breed, but to each individual cat. This is to be used as a guideline, rather than promoting one specific type of tail out of the many that occur within the breed.

The tail must be clearly visible and is composed of one or more curves, angles, or kinks or any combination thereof. The furthest extension of the tail bone from the body should be no longer than three inches. The direction in which the tail is carried is not important. The tail may be flexible or rigid and should be of a size and shape that harmonizes with the rest of the cat.

COLOR: in the bi-colors and tri-colors (MI-KE) any color may predominate with preference given to bold, dramatic markings and vividly contrasting colors. In the solid color cat the coat color should be of uniform density and color from the tip to the root of each hair and from the nose of the cat to the tail. Nose leather, paw pads, and eye color should harmonize generally with coat color. Blue eyes and odd eyes are allowed.

PENALIZE: short round head, cobby build.

DISQUALIFY: tail bone absent or extending too far beyond body. Tail lacking in pom-pom or fluffy appearance. Delayed bobtail effect (i.e., the pom-pom being preceded by an inch or two of normal tail with close-lying hair rather than appearing to commence at the base of the spine).

JAPANESE BOBTAIL COLORS

WHITE: pure glistening white.

BLACK: dense, coal black, sound from roots to tip of fur. Shiny and free from any tinge of rust on tips.

RED: deep, rich, clear, brilliant red, the deeper and more glowing in tone the better.

BLACK AND WHITE.

RED AND WHITE (including tabby)

MI-KE (Tri-Color): black, red, and white (red areas may have tabby striping or spotting).

TORTOISESHELL: black, red, and cream.

OTHER JAPANESE BOBTAIL COLORS (OJBC): Include the following categories and any other color or pattern or combination thereof except coloring showing the evidence of hybridization resulting in the colors chocolate, lavender, point-restricted (i.e., Siamese marking) or un-patterned agouti (i.e., Abyssinian coloring), or these combinations with white. "Patterned" categories denote and include any variety of tabby striping or spotting with or without areas of solid (unmarked) color, with preference given to bold, dramatic markings and rich, vivid coloring.

OTHER SOLID COLORS: Blue or Cream. TABBY COLORS: Red Tabby, Brown Tabby, Blue Tabby, Cream Tabby, Silver Tabby. PATCHED TABBY COLORS: Brown Patched Tabby, Blue Patched Tabby, Silver Patched Tabby. OTHER PARTI-COLORS: Blue-Cream. Other Bi-Colors: Blue and White or Cream and White. TABBY AND WHITE COLORS: Brown Tabby and White, Blue Tabby and White, Cream Tabby and White, or Silver Tabby and White. PATCHED TABBY AND WHITE COLORS: Brown Patched Tabby and White, Blue Patched Tabby and White, Silver Patched Tabby and White. PARTI-COLOR AND WHITE COLORS: Tortoiseshell and White or Blue-Cream and White. OTHER TRI-COLORS: Dilute Mi-ke (Blue Cream and White), Patched Tabby and White (Brown Tabby, Red Tabby, and White), Dilute Patched Tabby and White (Blue Tabby, Cream Tabby, and White).

Japanese Bobtail allowable outcross breeds: none.

JAVANESE

■ POINT SCORE

HEAD (20)	
Long flat profile	6
Wedge, fine muzzle, size	5
Ears	4
Chin	3
Width between eyes	2
EYES (5)	
Shape, size, slant, and placement	5
BODY (30)	
Structure and size, including neck	12
Muscle tone	10
Legs and Feet	5
Tail	3
COAT (20)	
Length	10
Texture	10
COLOR (25)	
Body color	10
Point color (matching points of dense color, proper foot pads and nose leather)	10
Eye color	5

GENERAL: the ideal Javanese is a svelte cat with long tapering lines, very lithe but strong and muscular. Excellent physical condition. Neither flabby nor bony. Not fat. Eyes clear. Because of the longer coat the Javanese appears to have softer lines and less extreme type than other breeds of cats with similar type.

HEAD: long, tapering wedge. Medium size in good proportion to body. The total wedge starts at the nose and flares out in straight lines to the tips of the ears forming a triangle, with no break at the whiskers. No less than the width of an eye between the eyes. When the whiskers and face hair are smoothed back, the underlying bone structure is apparent. Allowance must be made for jowls in the stud cat.

SKULL: flat. In profile, a long straight line should be felt from the top of the head to the tip of the nose. No bulge over the eyes. No dip in nose.

NOSE: long and straight. A continuation of the forehead with no break.

MUZZLE: fine, wedge-shaped.

CHIN and JAW: medium size. Tip of chin lines up with tip of nose in the same vertical plane. Neither receding nor excessively massive.

EARS: strikingly large, pointed, wide at base, continuing the lines of the wedge.

EYES: almond shaped. Medium size. Neither protruding nor recessed. Slanted towards the nose in harmony with lines of wedge and ears. Uncrossed.

BODY: medium size. Graceful, long, and svelte. A distinctive combination of fine bones and firm muscles. Shoulders and hips continue same sleek lines of tubular body. Hips never wider than shoulders. Abdomen tight. The male may be somewhat larger than the female.

NECK: long and slender.

LEGS: bone structure long and slim. Hind legs higher than front. In good proportion to body.

PAWS: dainty, small, and oval. Toes: five in front and four behind.

TAIL: bone structure long, thin, tapering to a fine point. Tail hair spreads out like a plume.

COAT: medium length, fine, silky, without downy undercoat, lying close to the body, the coat may appear shorter than it is. Hair is longest on the tail.

COLOR: Body even, with subtle shading when allowed. Allowance should be made for darker color in older cats as Javanese generally darken with age, but there must be definite contrast between body color and points. Points: mask, ears, legs, feet, tail dense and clearly defined. All of the same shade. Mask covers entire face including whisker pads and is connected to ears by tracings. Mask should not extend over top of head. No ticking or white hairs in points.

PENALIZE: lack of pigment in the nose leather and/or paw pads in part or in total, except as allowed in the color definitions for lynx and tortie points. Crossed eyes. Palpable and/or visible protrusion of the cartilage at the end of the sternum. Soft or mushy body.

DISQUALIFY: any evidence of illness or poor health. Weak hind legs. Malocclusion resulting in either undershot or overshot chin. Mouth breathing due to nasal obstruction or poor occlusion. Emaciation. Kink in tail. Eyes other than blue. White toes and/or feet. Incorrect number of toes. Definite double coat (i.e., downy undercoat).

JAVANESE COLORS

RED POINT: body clear white with any shading in the same tone as points. Points: bright apricot to deep red, deeper shades preferred, with lack of barring desirable. Nose leather and paw pads: flesh or coral pink. Eye color: deep vivid blue.

CREAM POINT: body clear white with any shading in the same tone as points. Points: pale buff cream to light pinkish cream, lack of barring desirable. Nose leather and paw pads: flesh to coral pink. Eye color: deep vivid blue.

SEAL LYNX POINT: body cream or pale fawn, shading to lighter color on stomach and chest. Body shading may take form of ghost striping. Points: seal brown bars, distinct and separated by lighter background color; ears seal brown with paler thumbprint in center. Nose leather: seal brown permitted, pink edged in seal brown preferred. Paw pads: seal brown. Eye color: deep vivid blue.

CHOCOLATE LYNX POINT: body ivory. Body shading may take form of ghost striping. Points: warm milk-chocolate bars, distinct and separated by lighter background color; ears warm milk-chocolate with paler thumbprint in center. Nose leather: cinnamon permitted, pink edged in cinnamon preferred. Paw pads: cinnamon. Eye color: deep vivid blue.

BLUE LYNX POINT: body bluish white to platinum grey, cold in tone, shading to lighter color on stomach and chest. Body shading may take form of ghost striping. Points: deep blue-grey bars, distinct and separated by lighter background color; ears deep blue-grey with paler thumbprint in center. Nose leather: slate-colored permitted, pink edged in slate preferred. Paw pads: slate-colored. Eye color: deep vivid blue.

LILAC LYNX POINT: body glacial white. Body shading may take form of ghost striping. Points: frosty grey with pinkish tone bars, distinct and separated by lighter background color; ears frosty grey with pinkish tone, paler thumbprint in center. Nose leather: lavender-pink permitted, pink edged in lavender-pink preferred. Paw pads: lavender-pink. Eye color: deep vivid blue.

RED LYNX POINT: body white. Body shading may take form of ghost striping. Points: deep red bars, distinct and separated by lighter background color; ears deep red, paler thumbprint in center. Nose leather and paw pads: flesh or coral pink. Eye color: deep vivid blue.

CHOCOLATE-TORTIE LYNX POINT: body ivory. Body shading may take form of ghost striping and/or cream mottling. Points: warm milk-chocolate bars, distinct and separated by lighter background color; ears warm milk-chocolate with paler thumbprint in center. Uniform mottling of red and/or cream overlays the markings of the points. Nose leather: cinnamon permitted, pink edged in cinnamon preferred, flesh or coral pink mottling may be present. Paw pads: cinnamon, or cinnamon mottled with flesh or coral pink. Eye color: deep vivid blue. NOTE: these cats resemble lynx points more than tortie points.

BLUE-CREAM LYNX POINT: body bluish white to platinum grey, cold in tone, shading to lighter color on stomach and chest. Body shading may take form of ghost striping and/or cream mottling. Points: deep blue-grey bars, distinct and separated by lighter background color; ears deep blue-grey with paler thumbprint in center. Uniform mottling of cream overlays the markings of the points. Nose leather: slate-colored permitted, pink edged in slate preferred, flesh or coral pink mottling may be present. Paw pads: slate-colored, or slate mottled with flesh or coral pink. Eye color: deep vivid blue. NOTE: these cats resemble lynx points more than tortie points.

LILAC-CREAM LYNX POINT: body glacial white. Body shading may take form of ghost striping and/or cream mottling. Points: frosty grey with pinkish tone bars, distinct and separated by lighter background color; ears frosty grey with pinkish tone, paler thumbprint in center. Uniform mottling of cream overlays the markings of the points. Nose leather: lavender-pink permitted, pink edged in lavender-pink preferred, flesh or coral pink mottling may be present. Paw pads: lavender-pink, or lavender-pink mottled with flesh or coral pink. Eye color: deep vivid blue. NOTE: these cats resemble lynx points more than tortie points.

CREAM LYNX POINT: body clear white. Body shading may take form of ghost striping. Points: bars of pale buff cream to light pinkish cream, distinct and separated by lighter background color; ears pale buff cream to light pinkish cream, paler thumbprint in center. Nose leather and paw pads: flesh to coral pink. Eye color: deep vivid blue.

SEAL-TORTIE LYNX POINT: body cream or pale fawn, shading to lighter color on stomach and chest. Body shading may take form of ghost striping and/or cream mottling. Points: seal brown bars, distinct and separated by lighter background color; ears seal brown with paler thumbprint in center. Uniform mottling of red and/or cream overlays the markings of the points. Nose leather: seal brown permitted, pink edged in seal brown preferred, flesh or coral pink mottling may be present. Paw pads: seal brown, or seal brown mottled with flesh or coral pink. Eye color: deep vivid blue. NOTE: these cats resemble Lynx points more than tortie points.

SEAL-TORTIE POINT: body pale fawn to cream, shading to lighter color on stomach and chest. Body color may be mottled with cream in older cats. Points: seal brown, uniformly mottled with red and/or cream; a blaze is desirable. Nose leather and paw pads: seal brown; flesh or coral pink mottling desirable. Eye color: deep vivid blue.

CHOCOLATE-TORTIE POINT: body ivory, may be mottled in older cats. Points: warm milk-chocolate uniformly mottled with red and/or cream; a blaze is desirable. Nose leather and paw pads: cinnamon; flesh or coral pink mottling desirable. Eye color: deep vivid blue.

BLUE-CREAM POINT: body bluish white to platinum grey, cold in tone, shading to lighter color on stomach and chest. Body color may be mottled in older cats. Points: deep blue-grey uniformly mottled with cream; a blaze is desirable. Nose leather and paw pads: slate-colored; flesh or coral pink mottling desirable. Eye color: deep vivid blue.

LILAC-CREAM POINT: body glacial white; mottling, if any, in the shade of the points. Points: frosty grey with pinkish tone, uniformly mottled with pale cream; a blaze is desirable. Nose leather and paw pads: lavender-pink; flesh or coral pink mottling desirable. Eye color: deep vivid blue.

Javanese allowable outcross breeds: Balinese, Colorpoint Shorthair, or Siamese for litters born before May 1, 2000.

KORAT

■ POINT SCORE

HEAD (25)	
Broad head	5
Profile	4
Breadth between eyes	4
Ear set and placement	4
Heartshape	5
Chin and Jaw	3
EYES (15)	
Size	5
Shape	5
Placement	5
BODY (25)	
Body	15
Legs and Feet	5
Tail	5
COAT (10)	
Short	4
Texture	3
Close lying	3
COLOR (25)	
Body color	20
Eye color	5

GENERAL: the Korat is a rare cat even in Thailand, its country of origin, and because of its unusually fine disposition, is greatly loved by the Thai people who regard it as a "good luck" cat. Its general appearance is of a silver blue cat with a heavy silver sheen, medium sized, hard-bodied, and muscular. All smooth curves with huge eyes, luminous, alert, and expressive. Perfect physical condition, alert appearance.

HEAD: when viewed from the front, or looking down from just back of the head, the head is heartshaped with breadth between and across the eyes. The eyebrow ridges form the upper curves of the heart, and the sides of the face gently curve down to the chin to complete the heartshape. Undesirable: any pinch or narrowness,

173

especially between or across the eyes.
PROFILE: well-defined with a slight stop between forehead and nose which has a lion-like downward curve just above the leather. Undesirable: nose that appears either long or short in proportion.
CHIN and JAW: strong and well-developed, making a balancing line for the profile and properly completing the heartshape. Neither overly squared nor sharply pointed, nor a weak chin that gives the head a pointed look.
EARS: large, with a rounded tip and large flare at base, set high on head, giving an alert expression. Inside ears sparsely furnished. Hairs on outside of ears extremely short and close.
BODY: semi-cobby, neither compact nor svelte. The torso is distinctive. Broad chested with good space between forelegs. Muscular, supple, with a feeling of hard coiled spring power and unexpected weight. Back is carried in a curve. The males tend to be larger than females.
LEGS: well-proportioned to body. Distance along back from nape of neck to base of tail appears to be equal to distance from base of tail to floor. Front legs slightly shorter than back legs.
PAWS: oval. Toes: five in front and four behind.
TAIL: medium in length, heavier at the base, tapering to a rounded tip. Non-visible kink permitted.
EYES: large and luminous. Particularly prominent with an extraordinary depth and brilliance. Wide open and oversized for the face. Eye aperture, which shows as well-rounded when fully open, has an Asian slant when closed or partially closed. Undesirable: small or dull looking eyes.
COAT: single. Hair is short in length, glossy and fine, lying close to the body. The coat over the spine is inclined to break as the cat moves.

DISQUALIFY: visible kink. Incorrect number of toes. White spot or locket. Any color but silver blue.

KORAT COLOR

COLOR: silver blue all over, tipped with silver, the silver should be sufficient to produce a silver halo effect. The hair is usually lighter at the roots with a gradient of blue which is deepest just before the tips which are silver. Without shading or tabby markings. Where the coat is short, the sheen of the silver is intensified. Undesirable: coats with silver tipping on only the head, legs and feet. Nose leather and lips: dark blue or lavender. Paw pads: dark blue ranging to lavender with a pinkish tinge. Eye color: luminous

green preferred, amber cast acceptable. Kittens and adolescents have yellow or amber to amber-green eyes. Color is not usually true until the cat is mature, usually two to four years of age.
Korat allowable outcross breeds: none.

MAINE COON CAT

■ POINT SCORE

HEAD (30)

Shape	15
Ears	10
Eyes	5

BODY (35)

Shape	20
Neck	5
Legs and Feet	5
Tail	5

COAT	20

COLOR (15)

Body color	10
Eye color	5

GENERAL: originally a working cat, the Maine Coon is solid, rugged, and can endure a harsh climate. A distinctive characteristic is its smooth, shaggy coat. With an essentially amiable disposition, it has adapted to varied environments.
HEAD SHAPE: medium in width and medium long in length with a squareness to the muzzle. Allowance should be made for broadening in older studs. Cheekbones high. Chin firm and in line with nose and upper lip. Nose medium long in length; slight concavity when viewed in profile.
EARS: large, well-tufted, wide at base, tapering to appear pointed. Set high and well apart.
EYES: large, expressive, wide set. Slightly oblique setting with slant toward outer base of ear.
NECK: medium long.
BODY SHAPE: muscular, broad-chested. Size medium to large. Females generally are smaller than males. The body should be long with all parts in proportion to create a well-balanced rectangular appearance with no part of the anatomy being so exaggerated as to foster weakness. Allowance should be made for slow maturation.
LEGS and FEET: legs substantial, wide set, of medium length, and in proportion to the body. Paws large, round, well-tufted. Five toes in front; four in back.
TAIL: long, wide at base, and tapering. Fur long and flowing.
COAT: heavy and shaggy; shorter on the shoulders and longer on the stomach and britches. Frontal ruff desirable. Texture silky with coat falling smoothly .

PENALIZE: a coat that is short or overall even.

DISQUALIFY: delicate bone structure. Undershot chin. Crossed eyes. Kinked tail. Incorrect number of toes. Buttons, lockets, or spots.

MAINE COON CAT COLORS

EYE COLOR: eye color should be shades of green, gold, or copper, though white cats may also be either blue or odd-eyed. There is no relationship between eye color and coat color.
Solid Color Class

WHITE: pure glistening white. Nose leather and paw pads: pink.

BLACK: dense coal black, sound from roots to tip of fur. Free from any tinge of rust on tips or smoke undercoat. Nose leather: black. Paw pads: black or brown.

BLUE: one level tone from nose to tip of tail. Sound to the roots. Nose leather and paw pads: blue.

RED: deep, rich, clear, brilliant red; without shading, markings, or ticking. Lips and chin the same color as coat. Nose leather and paw pads: brick red.
CREAM: one level shade of buff cream, without markings. Sound to the roots. Nose leather and paw pads: pink.
Tabby Color Class

CLASSIC TABBY PATTERN: markings dense, clearly defined, and broad. Legs evenly barred with bracelets coming up to meet the body markings. Tail evenly ringed. Several unbroken necklaces on neck and upper chest, the more the better. Frown marks on forehead form an intricate letter "M." Unbroken line runs back from outer corner of eye. Swirls on cheeks. Vertical lines over back of head extend to shoulder markings which are in the shape of a butterfly with both upper and lower wings distinctly outlined and marked with dots inside outline. Back markings consist of a vertical line down the spine from butterfly to tail with a vertical stripe paralleling it on each side, the three stripes well separated by stripes of the ground color. Large solid blotch on each side to be encircled by one or more unbroken rings. Side markings should be the same on both sides. Double vertical rows of buttons on chest and stomach.

MACKEREL TABBY PATTERN: markings dense, clearly defined, and all narrow pencillings. Legs evenly barred with narrow bracelets coming up to meet the body markings. Tail barred. Necklaces on neck and chest

distinct, like so many chains. Head barred with an "M" on the forehead. Unbroken lines running back from the eyes. Lines running down the head to meet the shoulders. Spine lines run together to form a narrow saddle. Narrow pencillings run around body.

PATCHED TABBY PATTERN: a patched tabby (torbie) is an established silver, brown, or blue tabby with patches of red and/or cream.

SILVER TABBY (classic, mackerel, patched): ground color pale, clear silver. Markings dense black. White trim around lip and chin allowed. Nose leather: brick red desirable. Paw pads: black desirable.

BLUE-SILVER TABBY: Ground color pale, clear silver. Markings a deep blue affording a good contrast with ground color. White trim around lip and chin allowed. Nose leather: old rose desirable. Paw pads: rose desirable.

RED TABBY (classic, mackerel): ground color red. Markings deep, rich red. White trim around lip and chin allowed. Nose leather and paw pads: brick red desirable.

BROWN TABBY (classic, mackerel, patched): ground color brilliant coppery brown. Markings dense black. Back of leg black from paw to heel. White trim around lip and chin allowed. Nose leather and paw pads: black or brown desirable.

BLUE TABBY (classic, mackerel, patched): ground color pale bluish Ivory. Markings a very deep blue affording a good contrast with ground color. Warm fawn overtones or patina over the whole. White trim around lip and chin allowed. Nose leather: old rose desirable. Paw pads: rose desirable.

CREAM TABBY (classic, mackerel): ground color very pale cream. Markings of buff or cream sufficiently darker than the ground color to afford good contrast but remaining within the dilute range. White trim around lip and chin allowed. Nose leather and paw pads: pink desirable.

CAMEO TABBY (classic, mackerel): ground color off-white. Markings red. White trim around lip and chin allowed. Nose leather and paw pads: rose desirable.
Tabby with White Class

TABBY WITH WHITE: color as defined for tabby with or without white on the face. Must have white on bib, belly, and all four paws. White on one-third of body is desirable. Colors accepted are silver, red, brown, blue, cream, or cameo.

VAN TABBY: white with color confined to the extremities: head, tail, and legs. One or two small colored patches on body allowable. Tabby pattern to be present in the colored markings.

PATCHED TABBY WITH WHITE (torbie with white): color as described for patched tabby (torbie) but with distribution of white markings as described in tabby with white. Color as described for patched tabby (torbie) with or without white on face. Must have white on bib, belly, and all four paws. White on one-third of body desirable. Colors accepted are silver, brown, or blue.

BLUE SILVER TABBY AND WHITE: color as defined for tabby with or without white on the face. Must have white on bib, belly and all four paws. White on one-third of the body is desirable.

PARTI-COLOR CLASS

TORTOISESHELL: black with unbrindled patches of red and cream. Patches clearly defined and well broken on both body and extremities. Blaze of red or cream on face is desirable.

TORTOISESHELL WITH WHITE: color as defined for tortoiseshell with or without white on the face. Must have white on bib, belly, and all four paws. White on one-third of body is desirable.

CALICO: white with unbrindled patches of black and red. White predominant on underparts.

DILUTE CALICO: white with unbrindled patches of blue and cream. White predominant on underparts.

BLUE-CREAM: blue with patches of solid cream. Patches clearly defined and well broken on both body and extremities.

BLUE-CREAM WITH WHITE: color as defined for blue-cream with or without white on the face. Must have white on bib, belly. and all four paws. White on one-third of the body is desirable.

BI-COLOR: a combination of a solid color with white. The colored areas predominate with the white portions being located on the face, chest, belly, legs, and feet. Colors accepted are red, black, blue, or cream.

VAN BI-COLOR: white with color confined to the extremities: head, tail,

and legs. One or two small colored patches on body allowable.

Other Maine Coon Colors Class

CHINCHILLA SILVER: undercoat pure white. Coat on back. flanks, head, and tail sufficiently tipped with black to give the characteristic sparkling silver appearance. Legs may be slightly shaded with tipping. Chin, ear tufts, stomach, and chest, pure white. Rims of eyes, lips, and nose outlined with black. Nose leather: brick red. Paw pads: black.

SHADED SILVER: undercoat white with a mantle of black tipping shading down from sides, face, and tail from dark on the ridge to white on the chin, chest, stomach, and under the tail. Legs to be the same tone as the face. The general effect to be much darker than a chinchilla. Rims of eyes, lips, and nose outlined with black. Nose leather: brick red. Paw pads: black.

SHELL CAMEO (Red Chinchilla): undercoat white, the coat on the back, flanks, head, and tail to be sufficiently tipped with red to give the characteristic sparkling appearance. Face and legs may be very slightly shaded with tipping. Chin, ear tufts, stomach, and chest white. Nose leather, rims of eyes and paw pads: rose.

SHADED CAMEO (Red Shaded): undercoat white with a mantle of red tipping shading down the sides, face, and tail from dark on the ridge to white on the chin, chest, stomach, and under the tail. Legs to be the same tone as face. The general effect to be much redder than the Shell Cameo. Nose leather, rims of eyes and paw pads: rose.

BLACK SMOKE: white undercoat, deeply tipped with black. Cat in repose appears black. In motion the white undercoat is clearly apparent. Points and mask black with narrow band of white at base of hairs next to skin which may be seen only when fur is parted. Light silver frill and ear tufts. Nose leather and paw pads: black.

BLUE SMOKE: white undercoat, deeply tipped with blue. Cat in repose appears blue. In motion the white undercoat is clearly apparent. Points and mask blue with narrow band of white hairs next to skin which may be seen only when fur is parted. White frill and ear tufts. Nose leather and paw pads: blue.

CAMEO SMOKE (Red Smoke): white undercoat, deeply tipped with red. Cat in repose appears red. In motion the white undercoat is clearly apparent. Points and mask red with narrow band

of white at base of hairs next to skin which may be seen only when fur is parted. Nose leather, rims of eyes and paw pads: rose.

BLUE-CREAM SMOKE: white undercoat, deeply tipped with blue, with clearly defined patches of cream as in the pattern of the blue-cream. Cat in repose appears blue-cream. In motion, the white undercoat is clearly apparent. Face and ears blue-cream pattern with narrow band of white at the base of the hairs next to the skin which may be seen only when the fur is parted. White ruff and ear tufts. Blaze of cream on face is desirable.

TORTIE SMOKE: white undercoat, deeply tipped with black with clearly defined unbrindled patches of red and cream. Cat in repose appears tortoiseshell. In motion the white undercoat is clearly apparent. Face and ears tortoiseshell pattern with narrow band of white at the base of the hairs next to the skin that may be seen only when fur is parted. White ruff and ear tufts. Blaze of red or cream on face is desirable.

SMOKE WITH WHITE: Color as defined for smokes with or without white on the face. Must have white on bib, belly, and all four paws. White on one-third of the body is desirable.

OMCCC (Other Maine Coon Cat Colors): any other color with the exception of those showing hybridization resulting in the colors chocolate, lavender, the Himalayan pattern, or these combinations with white.

Maine Coon Cat allowable outcross breeds: none.

MANX

■ POINT SCORE

HEAD and EARS	25
EYES	5
BODY	25
TAILLESSNESS	5
LEGS and FEET	15
COAT – LENGTH	10
Texture	10
COLOR and MARKINGS	5

GENERAL: the overall impression of the Manx cat is that of roundness; round head with firm, round muzzle and prominent cheeks; broad chest; substantial short front legs; short back which arches from shoulders to a round rump; great depth of flank and rounded, muscular thighs. The Manx should be alert, clear of eye, with a glistening, clean, well-groomed coat. They should be surprisingly heavy when lifted. Manx may be slow to mature and allowance should be made in young cats.

HEAD & EARS: round head with prominent cheeks and a jowly appearance (more evident in adult males) that enhances the round appearance of the breed. In profile, head is medium in length with a gentle dip from forehead to nose. Well developed muzzle, very slightly longer than it is broad, with a strong chin. Definite whisker break with large, round whisker pads. Short, thick neck. Ears wide at the base, tapering gradually to a rounded tip. Medium in size in proportion to the head, widely spaced and set slightly outward. When viewed from behind, the ear set resembles the rocker on a cradle. The furnishings of the ears are sparse in Shorthair Manx and full furnishings for Longhair Manx.

EYES: large, round and full. Set at a slight angle toward the nose (outer corners slightly higher than inner corners). Ideal eye color conforms to requirements of coat color.

BODY: solidly muscled, compact and well-balanced, medium in size with sturdy bone structure. The Manx is stout in appearance with broad chest and well-sprung ribs. The constant repetition of curves and circles give the Manx the appearance of great substance and durability, a cat that is powerful without the slightest hint of coarseness. Males may be slightly larger than females.

Flank (fleshy area of the side between the ribs and hip) has greater depth than in other breeds, causing considerable depth to the body when viewed from the side.

The short back forms a smooth, continuous arch from shoulders to rump, curving at the rump to form the desirable round look. Length of back is in proportion to the entire cat, height of hindquarters equal to length of body. Males may be somewhat longer. Because the Longhair Manx has longer coat over the rump area and breeches, the body may appear longer.

TAILLESSNESS: appearing to be absolute in the perfect specimen. A rise of bone at the end of the spine is allowed and should not be penalized unless it is such that it stops the judge's hand, thereby spoiling the tailless appearance of the cat. The rump is extremely broad and round.

LEGS & FEET: heavily boned, forelegs short and set well apart to emphasize the broad, deep chest. Hind legs much longer than forelegs, with heavy, muscular thighs and substantial lower legs. Longer hind legs cause the rump to be considerably higher than the shoulders. Hind legs are straight when viewed from behind. Paws are neat and round with five toes in front and four behind.

COAT LENGTH - Shorthair: double coat is short and dense with a well-padded quality due to the longer, open outer coat and the close cottony undercoat. Coat may be thinner during the summer months.

COAT TEXTURE - Shorthair: texture of outer guard hairs is somewhat hard, appearance is glossy. A softer coat may occur in whites and dilutes due to color/texture gene link but should not be confused with the silky texture found in the Longhair Manx.

COAT LENGTH - Longhair: the double coat is of medium length, dense and well padded over the main body, gradually lengthening from the shoulders to the rump. Breeches, abdomen and neck-ruff is usually longer than the coat on the main body. Cheek coat is thick and full. The collar like neck-ruff extends from the shoulders, being bib-like around the chest. Breeches should be full and thick to the hocks in the mature cat. Lower leg and head coat (except for cheeks) should be shorter than on the main body and neck-ruff, but dense and full in appearance. Toe tufts and ear tufts are desirable. All things being equal in type, preference should be given to the cat showing full coating.

COAT TEXTURE LONGHAIR: coat is soft and silky, falling smoothly on the body yet being full and plush due to the double coat. Coat should have a healthy glossy appearance. Allowance to be made for seasonal and age variations.

TRANSFER TO AOV: definite, visible tail joint. Long, silky coat on the Shorthair Manx or short, hard coat on the Longhair Manx.

PENALIZE: on the Longhair Manx, coat that lacks density, has a cottony texture or is of one overall length.

DISQUALIFY: evidence of poor physical condition; incorrect number of toes; evidence of hybridization; evidence of weakness in the hindquarters.

MANX COLORS

WHITE: pure glistening white. Nose leather and paw pads: pink. Eye color: deep blue or brilliant copper. Odd-eyed whites shall have one blue and one copper eye with equal color depth.

BLACK: dense coal black, sound from roots to tip of fur. Free from any tinge of rust on tips. Nose leather: black. Paw pads: black or brown. Eye color: brilliant copper.

BLUE: blue, lighter shade preferred, one level tone. Sound to the roots. A sound darker shade is more acceptable than an unsound lighter shade. Nose

leather and paw pads: blue. Eye color: brilliant copper.

RED: deep, rich, clear, brilliant red; without shading, markings, or ticking. Lips and chin the same color as coat. Nose leather and paw pads: brick red. Eye color: brilliant copper.

CREAM: one level shade of buff cream without markings. Sound to the roots. Lighter shades preferred. Nose leather and paw pads: pink. Eye color: brilliant copper.

CHINCHILLA SILVER: undercoat pure white. Coat on back, flanks, and head sufficiently tipped with black to give the characteristic sparkling silver appearance. Legs may be slightly shaded with tipping. Chin, stomach, and chest, pure white. Rims of eyes, lips, and nose outlined with black. Nose leather: brick red. Paw pads: black. Eye color: green or blue-green.

SHADED SILVER: undercoat white with a mantle of black tipping shading down from sides and face from dark on the ridge to white on the chin, chest, and stomach. Legs to be of the same tone as the face. The general effect to be much darker than a chinchilla. Rims of eyes, lips, and nose outlined with black. Nose leather: brick red. Paw pads: black. Eye color: green or blue-green.

BLACK SMOKE: white undercoat, deeply tipped with black. Cat in repose appears black. In motion the white undercoat is clearly apparent. Points and mask black with narrow band of white at base of hairs next to skin which may be seen only when fur is parted. Nose leather and paw pads: black. Eye color: brilliant copper.

BLUE SMOKE: white undercoat, deeply tipped with blue. Cat in repose appears blue. In motion the white undercoat is clearly apparent. Points and mask blue with narrow band of white at base of hairs next to skin which may be seen only when fur is parted. Nose leather and paw pads: blue. Eye color: brilliant copper.

CLASSIC TABBY PATTERN: markings dense, clearly defined, and broad. Legs evenly barred with bracelets coming up to meet the body markings. Several unbroken necklaces on neck and upper chest, the more the better. Frown marks on forehead form an intricate letter "M." Unbroken line runs back from outer corner of eye. Swirls on cheeks. Vertical lines over back of head extend to shoulder markings which are in the shape of a butterfly with both upper and lower wings distinctly outlined and marked with dots inside outline. Back markings consist of a vertical

line from butterfly down the entire spine with a vertical stripe paralleling it on each side, the three stripes well separated by stripes of the ground color. Large solid blotch on each side to be encircled by one or more unbroken rings. Side markings should be the same on both sides. Double vertical rows of buttons on chest and stomach.

MACKEREL TABBY PATTERN: markings dense, clearly defined, and all narrow pencillings. Legs evenly barred with narrow bracelets coming up to meet the body markings. Necklaces on neck and chest distinct, like so many chains. Head barred with an "M" on the forehead. Unbroken lines running back from the eyes. Lines running down the head to meet the shoulders. Spine lines run together to form a narrow saddle. Narrow pencillings run around body.

PATCHED TABBY PATTERN: a patched tabby (torbie) is an established silver, brown, or blue tabby with patches of red and/or cream.

BROWN PATCHED TABBY: ground color brilliant coppery brown with classic or mackerel tabby markings of dense black with patches of red and/or cream clearly defined on both body and extremities. A blaze of red and/or cream on the face is desirable. Lips and chin the same shade as the rings around the eyes. Eye color: brilliant copper.

BLUE PATCHED TABBY: ground color, including lips and chin, pale bluish ivory with classic or mackerel tabby markings of very deep blue affording a good contrast with ground color. Patches of cream clearly defined on both body and extremities. A blaze of cream on the face is desirable. Warm fawn overtones or patina over the whole. Eye color: brilliant copper.

SILVER PATCHED TABBY: ground color, including lips and chin, pale silver with classic or mackerel tabby markings of dense black with patches of red and/or cream clearly defined on both body and extremities. A blaze of red and/or cream on the face is desirable. Eye color: brilliant copper or hazel.

SILVER TABBY (classic, mackerel): ground color, including lips and chin, pale clear silver. Markings dense black. Nose leather: brick red. Paw pads: black. Eye color: green or hazel.

RED TABBY (classic, mackerel): ground color red. Markings deep, rich red. Lips and chin red. Nose leather and paw pads: brick red. Eye color: brilliant copper.

BROWN TABBY (classic, mackerel): ground color brilliant coppery brown.

Markings dense black. Lips and chin the same shade as the rims around the eyes. Back of leg black from paw to heel. Nose leather: brick red. Paw pads: black or brown. Eye color: brilliant copper.

BLUE TABBY (classic, mackerel): ground color, including lips and chin, pale bluish ivory. Markings a very deep blue affording a good contrast with ground color. Warm fawn overtones or patina over the whole. Nose leather: old rose. Paw pads: rose. Eye color: brilliant copper.

CREAM TABBY (classic, mackerel): ground color, including lips and chin, very pale cream. Markings buff or cream sufficiently darker than the ground color to afford good contrast but remaining within the dilute color range. Nose leather and paw pads: pink. Eye color: brilliant copper.

TORTOISESHELL: black with unbrindled patches of red and cream. Patches clearly defined and well broken on both body and extremities. Blaze of red or cream on face is desirable. Eye color: brilliant copper.

CALICO: white with unbrindled patches of black and red. White predominant on underparts. Eye color: brilliant copper, odd-eyed, or blue-eyed.

DILUTE CALICO: white with unbrindled patches of blue and cream. White predominant on underparts. Eye color: brilliant copper, odd-eyed, or blue-eyed.

BLUE-CREAM: blue with patches of solid cream. Patches clearly defined and well broken on both body and extremities. Eye color: brilliant copper.

BI-COLOR: white with unbrindled patches of black, white with unbrindled patches of blue, white with unbrindled patches of red, or white with unbrindled patches of cream. Cats with no more than a locket and/or button do not qualify for this color class. Such cats shall be judged in the color class of their basic color with no penalty for such locket and/or button. Eye color: brilliant copper, odd-eyed, or blue-eyed.

OMC (Other Manx Colors): any other color or pattern with the exception of those showing hybridization resulting in the colors chocolate, lavender, the Himalayan pattern, or these combinations with white. Eye color: appropriate to the predominant color of the cat. Manx allowable outcross breeds: none.

NORWEGIAN FOREST CAT

■ POINT SCORE

HEAD (50)

Nose profile	10
Muzzle	10
Ears	10
Eye shape	5
Eye set	5
Neck	5
Chin	5

BODY (30)

Torso	10
Legs/feet	10
Boning	5
Tail	5
COAT LENGTH/TEXTURE	5
COLOR/PATTERN	5
CONDITION	5
BALANCE	5

GENERAL: the Norwegian Forest Cat is a sturdy cat with a distinguishing double coat and easily recognizable body shape. It is a slow maturing breed, attaining full growth at approximately five years of age.

HEAD: triangular shaped, where all sides are of equal length as measured from the outside of the base of the ear to the point of the chin. The neck is short and heavily muscled.

NOSE PROFILE: straight from the brow ridge to the tip of the nose without a break in the line. The flat forehead continues into a gentle curved skull and neck.

CHIN: the chin is firm and should be in line with the front of the nose. It is gently rounded in profile.

MUZZLE: part of the straight line extending toward the base of ear without pronounced whisker pads and without pinch.

EARS: medium to large, rounded at the tip, broad at base, set as much on the side of the head as on top of the head, alert, with the cup of the ear pointing a bit sideways. The outsides of the ears follow the lines from the side of the head down to the chin. Ears are heavily tufted. Lynx tips are desirable but not required.

EYES: large, almond shaped, well-opened and expressive, set at a slight angle with the outer corner higher than the inner corner.

BODY: solidly muscled and well-balanced, moderate in length, substantial bone structure, with powerful appearance showing a broad chest and considerable girth without being fat. Flank has great depth. Males should be large and imposing; females may be more refined and may be smaller.

LEGS: medium with hind legs longer than front legs, making the rump higher than the shoulders. Thighs are heavily muscled; lower legs are substantial. When viewed from the rear, back legs are straight. When viewed from the front the paws appear to be "toe out."

Large round, firm paws with heavy tufting between toes.

TAIL: long and bushy. Broader at the base. Desirable length is equal to the body from the base of tail to the base of neck. Guard hairs desirable.

COAT: is double, long guard hairs desired. Long all over body and tail except at back of neck. Full frontal bib, mutton chops and britches highly desirable. May be shorter and less dense in warmer half of year. Texture is relatively silky with multi-colored hairs somewhat firmer than solid hairs. Undercoat and belly hair is of softer and finer texture than guard hairs.

PATTERNS: every color and pattern is allowable with the exception of those showing hybridization resulting in the colors chocolate, lavender/lilac, the Himalayan pattern, or these combinations with white.

DISQUALIFY: severe break in nose, square muzzle, whisker pinch, long rectangular body, cobby body.

NORWEGIAN FOREST CAT COLORS

EYE COLOR: eye color should be shades of green, gold, or green-gold. White cats may have blue or odd eyes.

NOSE LEATHER AND PAW PADS: any color or combination of colors, not necessarily related to coat color except where so noted. Cats with white on feet may have pink paw pads or they may be bi- or multi-colored.

BUTTONS AND LOCKETS: allowable on any color and/or pattern. Cats with no more than two white spots, whether buttons or lockets, shall be judged as the color of their basic color/pattern. Cats with more than two white spots, whether buttons or lockets, shall be judged as a bicolor, parti-color, or "and white" whichever is appropriate.

WHITE: pure glistening white. Nose leather and paw pads: pink desirable.

BLACK: dense coal black, sound from roots to tip of fur. Nose leather: black desirable. Paw pads: black desirable.

BLUE: one level tone from nose to tip of tail, sound to the roots. Nose leather and paw pads: blue desirable.

RED: deep, rich, clear, brilliant red; without shading, markings, or ticking. Nose leather and paw pads: brick red desirable.

CREAM: one level shade of buff cream, without markings. Sound to the roots. Lighter shades preferred. Nose leather and paw pads: pink desirable.

CHINCHILLA SILVER: undercoat pure white. Coat on back, flanks, head, and tail sufficiently tipped with black to give the characteristic sparkling silver appearance. Legs may be slightly shaded with tipping. Chin, ear tufts, stomach, and chest, pure white. Rims of eyes, lips, and nose outlined with black. Nose leather: brick red desirable. Paw pads: black desirable.

SHADED SILVER: undercoat white with a mantle of black tipping shading down from sides, face, and tail from dark on the ridge to white on the chin, chest, stomach and under the tail. Legs to be the same tone as the face. The general effect to be much darker than a chinchilla. Rims of eyes, lips, and nose outlined with black. Nose leather: brick red desirable. Paw pads: black desirable.

CHINCHILLA GOLDEN: undercoat rich warm cream. Coat on back, flanks, head, and tail sufficiently tipped with black to give golden appearance. Legs may be slightly shaded with tipping. Chin, ear tufts, stomach, and chest, cream. Rims of eyes, lips, and nose outlined with black. Nose leather: deep rose desirable. Paw pads: black desirable.

SHADED GOLDEN: undercoat rich warm cream with a mantle of black tipping shading down from the sides, face, and tail from dark on the ridge to cream on the chest, stomach, and under the tail. Legs to be the same tone as the face. The general effect to be much darker than a chinchilla. Rims of eyes, lips, and nose outlined with black. Nose leather: deep rose desirable. Paw pads: black desirable.

SHELL CAMEO (Red Chinchilla): undercoat white, the coat on the back, flanks, head, and tail to be sufficiently tipped with red to give the characteristic sparkling appearance. Face and legs may be very slightly shaded with tipping. Chin, ear tufts, stomach, and chest, white. Nose leather and paw pads: rose desirable.

SHADED CAMEO (Red Shaded): undercoat white with a mantle of red tipping shading down the sides, face, and tail from dark on the ridge to white on the chin, chest, stomach, and under the tail. Legs to be the same tone as face. The general effect to be much redder than the shell cameo. Nose leather and paw pads: rose desirable.

SHELL TORTOISESHELL: undercoat white. Coat on the back, flanks, head, and tail to be delicately tipped in black with well-defined patches of red and cream tipped hairs as in the pattern of the tortoiseshell. Face and legs may be slightly shaded with tipping. Chin, ear tufts, stomach, and chest, white to

very slightly tipped. Blaze of red or cream tipping on face is desirable.

SHADED TORTOISESHELL: undercoat white. Mantle of black tipping and clearly defined patches of red and cream tipped hairs as in the pattern of the tortoiseshell. Shading down the sides, face, and tail from dark on the ridge to slightly tipped or white on the chin, chest, stomach, legs, and under the tail. The general effect is to be much darker than the shell tortoiseshell. Blaze of red or cream tipping on the face is desirable.

BLACK SMOKE: white undercoat, deeply tipped with black. Cat in repose appears black. In motion the white undercoat is clearly apparent. Points and mask (i.e., face, ears, paws and tip of tail) black with narrow band of white at base of hairs next to skin which may be seen only when fur is parted. Light silver frill and ear tufts. Nose leather and paw pads: black desirable.

BLUE SMOKE: white undercoat, deeply tipped with blue. Cat in repose appears blue. In motion the white undercoat is clearly apparent. Points and mask (i.e., face, ears, paws and tip of tail) blue with narrow band of white at base of hairs next to skin which may be seen only when fur is parted. White frill and ear tufts. Nose leather and paw pads: blue desirable.

CREAM SMOKE: white undercoat, deeply tipped with cream. Cat in repose appears cream. In motion the white undercoat is clearly apparent. Points and mask (i.e., face, ears, paws and tip of tail) cream with narrow band of white at base of hairs next to skin which may be seen only when fur is parted. White frill and ear tufts. Nose leather and paw pads: pink desirable.

CAMEO SMOKE (Red Smoke): white undercoat, deeply tipped with red. Cat in repose appears red. In motion the white undercoat is clearly apparent. Points and mask (i.e., face, ears, paws and tip of tail) red, with narrow band of white at base of hairs next to skin which may be seen only when fur is parted. White frill and ear tufts. Nose leather, rims of eyes and paw pads: rose desirable.

SMOKE TORTOISESHELL: white undercoat, deeply tipped with black with clearly defined unbrindled patches of red and cream tipped hairs as in the pattern of the tortoiseshell. Cat in repose appears tortoiseshell. In motion the white undercoat is clearly apparent. Points and mask (i.e., face, ears, paws, tip of tail) tortoiseshell pattern with narrow band of white at the base of the hairs next to the skin that may be seen only when fur is parted. White ruff and ear tufts. Blaze of red or cream tipping on face is desirable.

BLUE-CREAM SMOKE: white undercoat deeply tipped with blue, with clearly defined patches of cream as in the pattern of the blue-cream. Cat in repose appears blue-cream. In motion the white undercoat is clearly apparent. Points and mask (i.e., face, ears, paw, tip of tail) blue-cream pattern with narrow band of white at the base of the hair next to the skin that may be seen only when fur is parted. White ruff and ear tufts. Blaze of cream tipping on face is desirable.

CLASSIC TABBY PATTERN: markings dense, clearly defined, and broad. Legs evenly barred with bracelets coming up to meet the body markings. Tail evenly ringed. Several necklaces on neck and upper chest, with locket allowed. Frown marks on forehead form an intricate letter "M." Unbroken line runs back from outer corner of eye. Swirls on cheeks. Vertical lines over back of head extend to shoulder markings which are in the shape of a butterfly with both upper and lower wings distinctly outlined and marked with dots inside outline. Back markings consist of a vertical line down the spine from butterfly to tail with a vertical stripe paralleling it on each side, the three stripes separated by stripes of the ground color. Large solid blotch on each side to be encircled by one or more unbroken rings. Side markings should be the same on both sides. Double vertical rows of buttons on chest and stomach. White buttons and/or lockets allowed.

MACKEREL TABBY PATTERN: markings dense, clearly defined, and all narrow pencillings. Legs evenly barred with narrow bracelets coming up to meet the body markings. Tail barred. Necklaces on neck and chest distinct; white locket allowed. Head barred with an "M" on the forehead. Unbroken lines running back from the eyes. Lines running down the head to meet the shoulders. Spine lines run together to form a narrow saddle. Narrow pencillings run around body. White buttons and/or lockets allowed.

PATCHED TABBY PATTERN: a patched tabby (torbie) is an established silver, brown, or blue tabby with patches of red and/or cream. White buttons and/or lockets allowed.

SPOTTED TABBY PATTERN: markings on the body to be spotted. May vary in size and shape with preference given to round, evenly distributed spots. Spots should not run together in

a broken mackerel pattern. A dorsal stripe runs the length of the body to the tip of the tail. The stripe is ideally composed of spots. The markings on the face and forehead shall be typically tabby markings. Underside of the body to have "vest buttons." Legs and tail are barred. White buttons and/or lockets allowed.

TICKED TABBY PATTERN: body hairs to be ticked with various shades of marking color and ground color. Body when viewed from top to be free from noticeable spots, stripes or blotches, except for darker dorsal shading. Lighter underside may show tabby markings. Face, legs and tail must show distinct tabby striping. White buttons and/or lockets allowed.

BROWN PATCHED TABBY: ground color brilliant coppery brown with classic or mackerel tabby markings of dense black with patches of red and/or cream clearly defined on both body and extremities; a blaze of red and/or cream on the face is desirable. Lips and chin the same shade as the rings around the eyes.

BLUE PATCHED TABBY: ground color, including lips and chin, pale bluish ivory with classic or mackerel tabby markings of very deep blue affording a good contrast with ground color. Patches of cream clearly defined on both body and extremities; a blaze of cream on the face is desirable. Warm fawn overtones or patina over the whole.

SILVER PATCHED TABBY: ground color, including lips and chin, pale silver with classic or mackerel tabby markings of dense black with patches of red and/or cream clearly defined on both body and extremities. A blaze of red and/or cream on the face is desirable.

SILVER TABBY (classic, mackerel, spotted, ticked): ground color, including lips and chin, pale, clear silver. Markings dense black. Nose leather: brick red desirable. Paw pads: black desirable.

BLUE-SILVER TABBY (classic, mackerel, spotted, ticked): ground color pale, clear silver. Markings a deep blue affording a good contrast with ground color. White trim around chin and lip allowed. Nose leather: old rose desirable. Paw pads: rose desirable.

RED TABBY (classic, mackerel, spotted, ticked): ground color red. Markings deep, rich red. Lips and chin red. Nose leather and paw pads: brick red desirable.

BROWN TABBY (classic, mackerel, spotted, ticked): ground color brilliant

coppery brown. Markings dense black. Back of leg black from paw to heel. Nose leather and paw pads: black or brown desirable.

BLUE TABBY (classic, mackerel, spotted, ticked): ground color, including lips and chin, pale bluish ivory. Markings a very deep blue affording a good contrast with ground color. Warm fawn overtones or patina over the whole. Nose leather and paw pads: rose desirable.

CREAM TABBY (classic, mackerel, spotted, ticked): ground color, including lips and chin, very pale cream. Markings of buff or cream sufficiently darker than the ground color to afford good contrast, but remaining within the dilute color range. Nose leather and paw pads: pink desirable.

CAMEO TABBY (classic, mackerel, spotted, ticked): ground color off-white. Markings red. Nose leather and paw pads: rose desirable.

TORTOISESHELL: black with unbrindled patches of red and cream. Patches clearly defined and well broken on both body and extremities. Blaze of red or cream on face is desirable.

CALICO: white with unbrindled patches of black and red. As a preferred minimum, the cat should have white feet, legs, undersides, chest, and muzzle. Inverted "V" blaze on face desirable.

DILUTE CALICO: white with unbrindled patches of blue and cream. As a preferred minimum, the cat should have white feet, legs, undersides, chest, and muzzle. Inverted "V" blaze on face desirable.

BLUE-CREAM: blue with patches of solid cream. Patches clearly defined and well broken on both body and extremities.

BI–COLOR: black and white, blue and white, red and white, or cream and white.

VAN BI-COLOR: black and white, blue and white, red and white, or cream and white. White cat with color confined to the extremities; head, tail, and legs. One or two small colored patches on body allowable.

VAN CALICO: white cat with unbrindled patches of black and red confined to the extremities; head, tail, and legs. One or two small colored patches on body allowable.

VAN DILUTE CALICO: white cat with unbrindled patches of blue and

cream confined to the extremities; head, tail, and legs. One or two small colored patches on body allowable.

(NOTE: cats having more than two small body spots should be shown in the regular bi-color class.)

TABBY AND WHITE: white with colored portions, the colored portions of the cat to conform to the currently established tabby color standards.

SMOKE/SHADED/SHELL AND WHITE: white with colored portions, the colored portions of the cat to conform to the color standard.

TORTOISESHELL AND WHITE: white with colored portions, the colored portions of the cat to conform to the tortoiseshell standard.

BLUE-CREAM AND WHITE: white with colored portions, the colored portions of the cat to conform to the blue-cream standard.

ANY OTHER NFC COLORS: any other color or pattern with the exception of those showing hybridization resulting in the colors chocolate, lavender/lilac, the himalayan pattern, or these combinations with white.

Norwegian Forest Cat allowable outcross breeds: none.

OCICAT

■ POINT SCORE

HEAD (25)	
Skull	5
Muzzle	10
Ears	5
Eyes	5
BODY (25)	
Torso	15
Legs and Feet	5
Tail	5
COAT and COLOR (25)	
Texture	5
Coat Color	5
Contrast	10
Eye Color	5
PATTERN	25

GENERAL: the Ocicat is a medium to large, well-spotted agouti cat of moderate type. It displays the look of an athletic animal: well-muscled and solid, graceful and lithe, yet with a fullness of body and chest. It is alert to its surroundings and shows great vitality. The Ocicat is found in many colors with darker spots appearing on a lighter background. Each hair (except on the tip of tail) has several bands of color. It is where these bands fall together that a thumbprint shaped spot is formed. This powerful, athletic, yet graceful spotted cat is particularly noted for its "wild" appearance.

HEAD: the skull is a modified wedge showing a slight curve from muzzle to cheek, with a visible, but gentle, rise from the bridge of the nose to the brow. The muzzle is broad and well defined with a suggestion of square-ness and in profile shows good length. The chin is strong and the jaw firm with a proper bite. The moderate whisker pinch is not too severe. The head is carried gracefully on an arch-ing neck. An allowance is made for jowls on mature males.

EARS: alert, moderately large, and set so as to corner the upper, outside dimensions of the head. If an imagi-nary horizontal line is drawn across the brow, the ears should be set at a 45 degree angle, i.e., neither too high nor too low. When they occur, ear tufts extending vertically from the tips of the ears are a bonus.

EYES: large, almond shaped, and angling slightly upwards toward the ears with more than the length of an eye between the eyes.

TORSO: solid, hard, rather long-bod-ied with depth and fullness but never coarse. The Ocicat is a medium to large cat with substantial bone and muscle development, yet with an athletic appearance, and should have surprising weight for its size. There should be some depth of chest with ribs slightly sprung, the back is level to slightly high-er in the rear, and the flank reasonably level. Preference is given to the athletic, powerful, and lithe, and objection taken to the bulky or coarse. It should be noted that females are generally smaller than males. The overall structure and quality of this cat should be of greater consideration than mere size alone.

LEGS and FEET: legs should be of good substance and well-muscled, medium-long, powerful and in good proportion to the body. Feet should be oval and compact with five toes in front and four in back, with size in propor-tion to legs.

TAIL: fairly long, medium-slim with only a slight taper and with a dark tip.

COAT TEXTURE: short, smooth and satiny in texture with a lustrous sheen. Tight, close-lying and sleek, yet long enough to accommodate the necessary bands of color. There should be no suggestion of woolliness.

TICKING: all hairs except the tip of the tail are banded. Within the mark-ings, hairs are tipped with a darker color, while hairs in the ground color are tipped with a lighter color.

COAT COLOR: all colors should be clear and pleasing. The lightest color is usually found on the face around the eyes, and on the chin and lower jaw. The darkest color is found on the tip of the tail. Contrast is scored separately.

CONTRAST: distinctive markings should be clearly seen from any orien-tation. Those on the face, legs, and tail may be darker than those on the torso. Ground color may be darker on the saddle and lighter on the underside, chin, and lower jaw. Penalties should be given if spotting is faint or blurred, though it must be remembered that pale colors will show less contrast than darker ones.

EYE COLOR: all eye colors except blue are allowed. There is no corre-spondence between eye color and coat color. Depth of color is preferred.

PATTERN: there is an intricate tabby "M" on the forehead, with markings extending up over the head between the ears and breaking into small spots on the lower neck and shoulders. Mascara markings are found around the eyes and on cheeks. Rows of round spots run along the spine from shoul-der blades to tail. The tail has horizon-tal brush strokes down the top, ideally alternating with spots, and a dark tip. Spots are scattered across the shoul-ders and hindquarters, extending as far as possible down the legs. There are broken bracelets on the lower legs and broken necklaces at the throat – the more broken the better. Large well-scattered, thumbprint-shaped spots appear on the sides of the torso, with a subtle suggestion of a classic tabby pattern – a spot circled by spots in place of the bull's eye. The belly is also well spotted. The eyes are rimmed with the darkest coat color and sur-rounded by the lightest color. Penalties should be given for elongated spots following a mackerel pattern.

DISQUALIFY: white locket or spot-ting, or white anywhere other than around eyes, nostrils, chin, and upper throat (except white agouti ground in silvered colors). Kinked or otherwise deformed tail. Blue eyes. Incorrect number of toes. Due to the spotted patched tabby (torbie) cats resulting from the sex-linked O gene, no reds, creams, or torbies are allowed. Very rufous cinnamons and fawns may resemble red or cream, but never pro-duce female torbies.

OCICAT COLORS

TAWNY (brown spotted tabby): black or dark brown spotting on a ruddy or bronze agouti ground. Nose leather: brick red rimmed with black. Paw pads: black or seal.

CHOCOLATE: chocolate spotting on a warm ivory agouti ground. Nose leather: pink rimmed with chocolate. Paw pads: chocolate-pink.

CINNAMON: cinnamon spotting on

a warm ivory agouti ground. Nose leather: pink rimmed with cinnamon. Paw pads: pink or rose.

BLUE: blue spotting on a pale blue or buff agouti ground. Nose leather: blue rimmed with dark blue. Paw pads: blue.

LAVENDER: lavender spotting on a pale buff or ivory agouti ground. Nose leather: pink rimmed with dark laven-der. Paw pads: lavender-pink.

FAWN: fawn spotting on a pale ivory agouti ground. Nose leather: pink rimmed in fawn. Paw pads: pink.

SILVER: black spotting on a pale sil-ver/white agouti ground. Nose leather: brick red rimmed with black. Paw pads: black.

CHOCOLATE SILVER: chocolate spotting on a white agouti ground. Nose leather: pink rimmed with chocolate. Paw pads: chocolate-pink.

CINNAMON SILVER: cinnamon spotting on a white agouti ground. Nose leather: pink rimmed with cin-namon. paw pads: pink or rose.

BLUE SILVER: blue spotting on a white agouti ground. Nose leather: blue rimmed with dark blue. paw pads: blue.

LAVENDER SILVER: lavender spot-ting on a white agouti ground. Nose leather: pink rimmed with dark laven-der. paw pads: lavender-pink.

FAWN SILVER: fawn spotting on a white agouti ground. Nose leather: pink rimmed in fawn. paw pads: pink. Ocicat allowable outcross breeds: Abyssinian for litters born before 1/1/2005.

ORIENTAL LONGHAIR

(Provisional Breed Standard)
■ POINT SCORE
HEAD (20)

Long, flat profile	6
Wedge, fine muzzle, size	5
Ears	4
Chin	3
Width between eyes	2

EYES (10)

Shape, size, slant, and placement	10

BODY (30)

Structure and size, including neck	12
Muscle tone	10
Legs and Feet	5
Tail	3

COAT | 10
COLOR (30)

Coat color (color 10; pattern 10)	20
Eye color	10

GENERAL: the ideal Oriental Longhair is a svelte cat with long, tapering lines, very lithe but muscular. Excellent physical condition. Eyes clear. Strong and lithe, neither bony nor flabby. Not fat. Because of the longer coat the Oriental Longhair appears to have softer lines and less extreme type than other breeds of cats with similar type.

HEAD: long tapering wedge, in good proportion to body. The total wedge starts at the nose and flares out in straight lines to the tips of the ears forming a triangle, with no break at the whiskers. No less than the width of an eye between the eyes. When the whiskers and face hair are smoothed back, the underlying bone structure is apparent. Allowance must be made for jowls in the stud cat.

SKULL: flat. In proflle, a long straight line is seen from the top of the head to the tip of the nose. No bulge over eyes. No dip in nose.

NOSE: long and straight. A continua-tion of the forehead with no break. Muzzle: fine, wedge shaped.

CHIN and JAW: medium size. Tip of chin lines up with tip of nose in the same vertical plane. Neither receding nor excessively massive.

EARS: strikingly large, pointed, wide at the base, continuing the lines of the wedge.

EYES: almond shaped, medium size. Neither protruding nor recessed. Slanted towards the nose in harmony with lines of wedge and ears. Uncrossed.

BODY: long and svelte. A distinctive combination of fine bones and firrm muscles. Shoulders and hips continue the same sleek lines of tubular body. Hips never wider than shoulders. Abdomen tight. Males may be some-what larger than females.

NECK: long and slender.

LEGS: long and slim. Hind legs higher than front. In good proportion to body.

PAWS: dainty, small and oval. Toes: five in front and four behind.

TAIL: long, thin at the base, and tapered to a fine point. Tail hair spreads out like a plume.

COAT: medium length, fine, silky without downy undercoat, lying close to the body, the coat may appear shorter than it is. Hair is longest on the tail.

COAT COLOR: the Oriental Longhair's reason for being is the coat color whether it is solid or tabby pat-temed. In the solid color cat, the coat color should be of uniform density and color from the tip to the root of each hair and from the nose to the tail. The full coat color score (20) should be used to assess the quality and the correctness of the color. In the tabby patterned cat, the quality of the pattern is an essential part of the cat. The pattern should match the description for the particular pattern and be well defined. The pattern should be viewed while the cat is in a natural standing position. Ten points are allocated to the correctness of the color; it matches the color description. The division of points for coat color applies only to the Tabby Color Class.

PENALIZE: crossed eyes. Palpable and/or visible protrusion of the cartilage at the end of the sternum.

DISQUALIFY: any evidence of illness or poor health. Weak hind legs. Mouth breathing due to nasal obstruction or poor occlusion. Emaciation. Visible kink in tail. Miniaturization. Lockets and buttons. Incorrect number of toes. Definite double coat (i.e., downy undercoat).
EYE COLOR: green. White Oriental Longhairs may have blue, green or odd-eyed eye color.

ORIENTAL LONGHAIR COLORS

BLUE: blue, one level tone from nose to tip of tail. Sound to the roots. Nose leather and paw pads: blue.
CHESTNUT: rich chestnut brown, sound throughout. Whiskers and Nose leather same color as coat. Paw pads: cinnamon.
CINNAMON: a light reddish brown, distinctly warmer and lighter than chestnut, sound and even throughout. Whiskers same color as coat. Nose leather and paw pads: tan to pinkish beige.
CREAM: one level shade of buff cream, without markings. Sound to the roots. Lighter shades preferred. Nose leather and paw pads: pink.
EBONY: dense coal black, sound from roots to tip of fur. Free from any tinge of rust on tips or smoke undercoat. Nose leather: black. paw pads: black or brown.
FAWN: a light lavender with pale cocoa overtones, sound and even throughout. Nose leather and paw pads: a light shade of dusty rose pink (no blue or lavender tones). Whiskers same color as coat.
LAVENDER: frosty-grey with a pinkish tone, sound and even throughout. Nose leather and paw pads: lavender-pink.
RED: deep, rich, clear, brilliant red; without shading, markings, or ticking. Lips and chin the same color as coat. Nose leather and paw pads: flesh or coral pink.
WHITE: pure, glistening white. Nose leather and paw pads: pink.
BLUE SILVER: undercoat white with

a mantle of blue tipping shading down from sides, face and tail from dark on the ridge to white on the chin, chest, underside and under the tail. Legs to be the same tone as the face. Rims of eyes, lips and nose outlined with blue. Nose leather: old rose. Paw pads: blue.

CHESTNUT SILVER: undercoat white with a mantle of chestnut tipping shading down from sides, face and tail from dark on the ridge to white on the chin, chest, underside and under the tail. Legs to be the same tone as the face. Rims of eyes, lips and nose outlined with chestnut. Nose leather: pink. Paw pads: coral pink.

CINNAMON SILVER: undercoat white with a mantle of cinnamon tipping shading down from sides, face and tail from dark on the ridge to white on the chin, chest, underside and under the tail. Legs to be the same tone as the face. Rims of eyes, lips and nose outlined with cinnamon. Nose leather: pink. Paw pads: coral pink.

CREAM SILVER: (Dilute Cameo): undercoat white with a mantle of cream tipping shading down from sides, face and tail from dark on the ridge to white on the chin, chest, underside and under the tail. Legs to be the same tone as the face. Nose leather, rims of eyes and paw pads: pink.

EBONY SILVER: undercoat white with a mantle of black tipping shading down from sides, face and tail from dark on the ridge to white on the chin, chest, underside and under the tail. Legs to be the same tone as the face. Rims of eyes, lips and nose outlined with black. Nose leather: brick red. Paw pads: black.

FAWN SILVER: undercoat white with a mantle of fawn tipping shading down from sides, face and tail from dark on the ridge to white on the chin, chest, underside and under the tail. Legs to be the same tone as the face. Rims of eyes, lips and nose outlined with fawn. Nose leather: pink. Paw pads: pink.

LAVENDER SILVER: undercoat white with a mantle of lavender tipping shading down from sides, face and tail from dark on the ridge to white on the chin, chest, underside and under the tail. Legs to be the same tone as the face. Rims of eyes, lips and nose outlined with lavender. Nose leather: lavenderpink. Paw pads: lavenderpink.

PARTI–COLOR SILVER: undercoat white with a mantle of black, blue, chestnut, cinnamon, fawn or lavender

tipping mottled or patched with red and/or cream as in the pattern of the PartiColor, shading down from sides, face and tail from dark on the ridge to white on the chin, chest, underside and under the tail. Nose leather: may be mottled with pink. Paw pads: may be mottled with pink.

RED SILVER (Cameo): undercoat white with a mantle of red tipping shading down from sides, face and tail from dark on the ridge to white on the chin, chest, underside and under the tail. Legs to be the same tone as the face. Nose leather, rims of eyes and paw pads: rose.

BLUE SMOKE: white undercoat, deeply tipped with blue. Cat in repose appears blue. In motion the white undercoat is clearly apparent. Points and mask blue with narrow band of white at base of hairs next to skin which may be seen only when fur is parted. Nose leather and paw pads: blue.

CAMEO SMOKE (Red Smoke): white undercoat, deeply tipped with red. Cat in repose appears red. In motion the white undercoat is clearly apparent. Points and mask red with narrow band of white at base of hairs next to skin which may be seen only when fur is parted. Nose leather, rims of eyes and paw pads: rose.

CHESTNUT SMOKE: white undercoat, deeply tipped with chestnut brown. Cat in repose appears chestnut brown. In motion the white undercoat is clearly apparent. Points and mask chestnut brown with narrow band of white at base of hairs next to skin which may be seen only when fur is parted. Nose leather and paw pads: lavender-pink.

CINNAMON SMOKE: white undercoat, deeply tipped with cinnamon. Cat in repose appears cinnamon. In motion the white undercoat is clearly apparent. Points and mask cinnamon with narrow band of white at base of hairs which may be seen only when fur is parted. Nose leather: cinnamon. paw pads: coral.

DILUTE CAMEO SMOKE: (Cream Smoke): white undercoat deeply tipped with cream. Cat in repose appears cream. In motion the white undercoat is clearly apparent. Points and mask cream with narrow base of white at base of hairs next to skin which may be seen only when the fur is parted. Nose leather, rims of eyes, and paw pads: pink.

EBONY SMOKE: white undercoat, deeply tipped with black. Cat in repose

appears black. In motion the white undercoat is clearly apparent. Points and mask black with narrow band of white at base of hairs next to skin which may be seen only when fur is parted. Nose leather and paw pads: black.

FAWN SMOKE: white undercoat, deeply tipped with fawn. Cat in repose appears fawn. In motion the white undercoat is clearly apparent. Points and mask fawn with narrow band of white at base of hairs which may be seen only when fur is parted. Nose leather: fawn. paw pads: pink.

LAVENDER SMOKE: white undercoat, deeply tipped with lavender. Cat in repose appears lavender. In motion the white undercoat is clearly apparent. Points and mask lavender with narrow band of white at base of hairs next to skin which may be seen only when fur is parted. Nose leather and paw pads: lavender-pink.

PARTI-COLOR SMOKE: white undercoat deeply tipped with black, blue, chestnut, cinnamon, fawn or lavender, mottled or patched with red and/or cream tipped hairs as in the pattern of the Parti-Color. Cat in repose appears Parti-Color. In motion, the white undercoat is clearly apparent. Face and ears have Parti-Color pattern with a narrow band of white at the base of the hairs next to the skin, which may be seen only when the fur is parted. Nose leather and paw pads: may be mottled with pink.

CLASSIC TABBY PATTERN: markings dense, clearly defined, and broad. Legs evenly barred with bracelets coming up to meet the body markings. Tail evenly ringed. Several unbroken necklaces on neck and upper chest, the more the better. Frown marks on forehead form an intricate letter "M." Unbroken line runs back from outer corner of eye. Swirls on cheeks. Vertical lines over back of head extend to shoulder markings which are in the shape of a butterfly with both upper and lower wings distinctly outlined and marked with dots inside outline. Back markings consist of a vertical line down the spine from butterfly to tail with a vertical stripe paralleling it on each side, the three stripes well separated by stripes of the ground color. Large solid blotch on each side to be encircled by one or more unbroken rings. Side markings should be the same on both sides. Double vertical rows of buttons on chest and stomach.

MACKEREL TABBY PATTERN: markings dense, clearly defined, and all narrow pencillings. Legs evenly barred with narrow bracelets coming up to meet the body markings. Tail barred.

Necklaces on neck and chest distinct, like so many chains. Head barred with an "M" on the forehead. Unbroken lines running back from the eyes. Lines running down the head to meet the shoulders. Spine lines run together to form a narrow saddle. Narrow pencillings run around body.

SPOTTED TABBY PATTERN: markings on the body to be spotted. May vary in size and shape with preference given to round, evenly distributed spots. Spots should not run together in a broken Mackerel pattern. A dorsal stripe runs the length of the body to the tip of the tail. The stripe is ideally composed of spots. The markings on the face and forehead shall be typically tabby markings. Underside of the body to have "vest buttons." Legs and tail are barred.

TICKED TABBY PATTERN: body hairs to be ticked with various shades of marking color and ground color. Body when viewed from top to be free from noticeable spots, stripes, or blotches, except for darker dorsal shading. Lighter underside may show tabby markings. Face, legs, and tail must show distinct tabby striping. Cat must have at least one distinct necklace.

PATCHED TABBY PATTERN: a patched tabby is an established Classic, Mackerel, Spotted or Ticked Tabby in blue, chestnut, cinnamon, ebony, fawn or lavender, or any of these colors in silver, mottled or patched with red and/or cream. Nose leather and paw pads: same as non-patched tabbies, may be mottled with pink.

BLUE SILVER TABBY: ground color, including lips and chin, pale, clear bluish silver. Markings sound blue. Nose leather: blue or old rose trimmed with blue. paw pads: blue.

BLUE TABBY: ground color, including lips and chin, pale bluish ivory. Markings a very deep blue affording a good contrast with ground color. Warm fawn overtones or patina over the whole. Nose leather: blue, or old rose trimmed with blue. paw pads: bluish rose.

CAMEO TABBY: ground color off-white. Markings red. Nose leather and paw pads: rose.

DILUTE CAMEO TABBY: ground color off-white. Markings cream. Nose leather and paw pads: pink.

CINNAMON SILVER TABBY: ground color, including lips and chin, pale glistening silver. Markings dense cinnamon. Nose leather: cinnamon, or pink rimmed with cinnamon. paw pads: coral pink.

CINNAMON TABBY: ground color, including lips and chin, a pale warm honey, markings a dense cinnamon, affording a good contrast with ground color. Nose leather: cinnamon or coral rimmed with cinnamon. paw pads: cinnamon.

CHESTNUT SILVER TABBY: ground color, including lips and chin, a snowy silver. Markings rich chestnut. Nose leather: chestnut, or pink rimmed with chestnut. paw pads: coral pink.

CHESTNUT TABBY: ground color warm fawn. Markings are rich chestnut. Nose leather: chestnut, or pink rimmed with chestnut. Paw pads: cinnamon.

CREAM TABBY: ground color, including lips and chin, very pale cream. Markings of buff or cream sufficiently darker than the ground color to afford good contrast but remaining within the dilute color range. Nose leather and paw pads: pink.

EBONY TABBY: ground color brilliant coppery brown. Markings dense black. Lips and chin the same shade as the rings around the eyes. Back of leg black from paw to heel. Nose leather: black, or brick red rimmed with black. Paw pads: black or brown.

FAWN TABBY: ground color, including lips and chin, pale ivory. Markings dense fawn, affording good contrast with ground color. Nose leather and paw pads: pale fawn.

FAWN SILVER TABBY: ground color, including lips and chin, pale glistening silver. Markings dense fawn. Nose leather: fawn, or pink rimmed with fawn. Paw pads: pink.

LAVENDER SILVER TABBY: ground color, including lips and chin, a cold clear silver. Markings sound lavender. Nose leather: lavender, or pink rimmed with lavender.Paw pads: lavender-pink.

LAVENDER TABBY: ground color is pale lavender. Markings are rich lavender affording a good contrast with the ground color. Nose leather: lavender, or pink rimmed with lavender. Paw pads: lavender-pink.

RED TABBY: ground color red. Markings deep, rich red. Lips and chin red. Nose leather and paw pads: flesh or coral pink.

EBONY SILVER TABBY: ground color, including lips and chin, pale clear silver. Markings dense black. Nose leather: black, or brick red rimmed with black. Paw pads: black.

BLUE-CREAM: blue mottled or patched with cream.

CINNAMON TORTOISESHELL: cinnamon mottled or patched with red and/or cream.

CHESTNUT TORTOISESHELL: chestnut brown mottled or patched with red and/or cream.

FAWN-CREAM: fawn mottled or patched with cream.

LAVENDER-CREAM: lavender mottled or patched with cream.

EBONY TORTOISESHELL: black mottled or patched with red and/or cream

Oriental Longhair Allowable Outcross Breeds: Oriental Shorthair Balinese, Javanese, Colorpoint Shorthair or Siamese.

ORIENTAL SHORTHAIR

■ POINT SCORE

HEAD (20)
Long, flat profile	6
Wedge, fine muzzle, size	5
Ears	4
Chin	3
Width between eyes	2

EYES (10)
Shape, size, slant, placement	10

BODY (30)
Structure and size, including neck	12
Muscle tone	10
Legs and Feet	5
Tail	3

COAT 10

COLOR (30)
Coat color (color 10; pattern 10)	20
Eye color	10

GENERAL: the ideal Oriental Shorthair is a svelte cat with long, tapering lines, very lithe but muscular. Excellent physical condition. Eyes clear. Strong and lithe, neither bony nor flabby. Not fat.

HEAD: long tapering wedge, in good proportion to body. The total wedge starts at the nose and flares out in straight lines to the tips of the ears forming a triangle, with no break at the whiskers. No less than the width of an eye between the eyes. When the whiskers are smoothed back, the underlying bone structure is apparent. Allowance must be made for jowls in the stud cat.

SKULL: flat. In profile, a long straight line is seen from the top of the head to the tip of the nose. No bulge over eyes. No dip in nose.

NOSE: long and straight. A continuation of the forehead with no break.

MUZZLE: fine, wedge-shaped.

CHIN and JAW: medium size. Tip of chin lines up with tip of nose in the same vertical plane. Neither receding nor excessively massive.

EARS: strikingly large, pointed, wide at the base, continuing the lines of the wedge.

EYES: almond shaped, medium size. Neither protruding nor recessed. Slanted towards the nose in harmony with lines of wedge and ears. Uncrossed .

BODY: long and svelte. A distinctive combination of fine bones and firm muscles. Shoulders and hips continue the same sleek lines of tubular body. Hips never wider than shoulders. Abdomen tight. Males may be somewhat larger than females.

NECK: long and slender.

LEGS: long and slim. Hind legs higher than front. In good proportion to body.

PAWS: dainty, small, and oval. Toes: five in front and four behind.

TAIL: long, thin at the base, and tapered to a fine point.

COAT: short, fine textured, glossy, lying close to body.

COAT COLOR: the Oriental Shorthair's reason for being is the coat color whether it is solid or tabby patterned. In the solid color cat, the coat color should be of uniform density and color from the tip to the root of each hair and from the nose to the tail. The full coat color score (20) should be used to assess the quality and the correctness of the color. In the tabby patterned cat, the quality of the pattern is an essential part of the cat. The pattern should match the description for the particular pattern and be well defined. The pattern should be viewed while the cat is in a natural standing position. Ten points are allotted to the correctness of the color; it matches the color description. The division of points for coat color applies only to the Tabby Colors Class.

PENALIZE: crossed eyes. Palpable and/or visible protrusion of the cartilage at the end of the sternum.

DISQUALIFY: any evidence of illness or poor health. Weak hind legs. Mouth breathing due to nasal obstruction or poor occlusion. Emaciation. Visible kink. Miniaturization. Lockets and buttons. Incorrect number of toes.

EYE COLOR: green. White Orientals may have blue, green or odd-eyed eye color.

ORIENTAL SHORTHAIR COLORS
Solid Color Class

BLUE: blue, one level tone from nose

to tip of tail. Sound to the roots. Nose leather and paw pads: blue.

CHESTNUT: rich chestnut brown, sound throughout. Whiskers and Nose leather same color as coat. Paw pads: cinnamon.

CINNAMON: a light reddish brown, distinctly warmer and lighter than chestnut, sound and even throughout. Whiskers same color as coat. Nose leather and paw pads: tan to pinkish beige.

CREAM: one level shade of buff cream, without markings. Sound to the roots. Lighter shades preferred. Nose leather and paw pads: pink.

EBONY: dense coal black, sound from roots to tip of fur. Free from any tinge of rust on tips or smoke undercoat. Nose leather: black. paw pads: black or brown.

FAWN: a light lavender with pale cocoa overtones, sound and even throughout. Nose leather and paw pads: a light shade of dusty rose pink (no blue or lavender tones). Whiskers same color as coat.

LAVENDER: frosty-grey with a pinkish tone, sound and even throughout. Nose leather and paw pads: lavender-pink.

RED: deep, rich, clear, brilliant red; without shading, markings, or ticking. Lips and chin the same color as coat. Nose leather and paw pads: flesh or coral pink.

WHITE: pure, glistening white. Nose leather and paw pads: pink.
Shaded Color Class

BLUE SILVER: undercoat white with a mantle of blue tipping shading down from sides, face and tail from dark on the ridge to white on the chin, chest, underside and under the tail. Legs to be the same tone as the face. Rims of eyes, lips and nose outlined with blue. Nose leather: old rose. Paw pads: blue.

CHESTNUT SILVER: undercoat white with a mantle of chestnut tipping shading down from sides, face and tail from dark on the ridge to white on the chin, chest, underside and under the tail. Legs to be the same tone as the face. Rims of eyes, lips and nose outlined with chestnut. Nose leather: pink. Paw pads: coral pink.

CINNAMON SILVER: undercoat white with a mantle of cinnamon tipping shading down from sides, face and tail from dark on the ridge to white on the chin, chest, underside and under the tail. Legs to be the same tone as the face. Rims of eyes, lips and nose outlined with cinnamon. Nose leather: pink. Paw pads: coral pink.

CREAM SILVER: (Dilute Cameo): undercoat white with a mantle of cream tipping shading down from sides, face and tail from dark on the ridge to white on the chin, chest, underside and under the tail. Legs to be the same tone as the face. Nose leather, rims of eyes and paw pads: pink.

EBONY SILVER: undercoat white with a mantle of black tipping shading down from sides, face and tail from dark on the ridge to white on the chin, chest, underside and under the tail. Legs to be the same tone as the face. Rims of eyes, lips and nose outlined with black. Nose leather: brick red. Paw pads: black.

FAWN SILVER: undercoat white with a mantle of fawn tipping shading down from sides, face and tail from dark on the ridge to white on the chin, chest, underside and under the tail. Legs to be the same tone as the face. Rims of eyes, lips and nose outlined with fawn. Nose leather: pink. Paw pads: pink.

LAVENDER SILVER: undercoat white with a mantle of lavender tipping shading down from sides, face and tail from dark on the ridge to white on the chin, chest, underside and under the tail. Legs to be the same tone as the face. Rims of eyes, lips and nose outlined with lavender. Nose leather: lavenderpink. Paw pads: lavenderpink.

PARTI–COLOR SILVER: undercoat white with a mantle of black, blue, chestnut, cinnamon, fawn or lavender tipping mottled or patched with red and/or cream as in the pattern of the PartiColor, shading down from sides, face and tail from dark on the ridge to white on the chin, chest, underside and under the tail. Nose leather: may be mottled with pink. Paw pads: may be mottled with pink.

RED SILVER (Cameo): undercoat white with a mantle of red tipping shading down from sides, face and tail from dark on the ridge to white on the chin, chest, underside and under the tail. Legs to be the same tone as the face. Nose leather, rims of eyes and paw pads: rose.
Smoke Color Class

BLUE SMOKE: white undercoat, deeply tipped with blue. Cat in repose appears blue. In motion the white undercoat is clearly apparent. Points and mask blue with narrow band of white at base of hairs next to skin which may be seen only when fur is parted. Nose leather and paw pads: blue.

CAMEO SMOKE (Red Smoke): white undercoat, deeply tipped with red. Cat in repose appears red. In motion the white undercoat is clearly apparent. Points and mask red with narrow band of white at base of hairs next to skin which may be seen only when fur is parted. Nose leather, rims of eyes and paw pads: rose.

CHESTNUT SMOKE: white undercoat, deeply tipped with chestnut brown. Cat in repose appears chestnut brown. In motion the white undercoat is clearly apparent. Points and mask chestnut brown with narrow band of white at base of hairs next to skin which may be seen only when fur is parted. Nose leather and paw pads: lavender-pink.

CINNAMON SMOKE: white undercoat, deeply tipped with cinnamon. Cat in repose appears cinnamon. In motion the white undercoat is clearly apparent. Points and mask cinnamon with narrow band of white at base of hairs which may be seen only when fur is parted. Nose leather: cinnamon. paw pads: coral.

DILUTE CAMEO SMOKE: (Cream Smoke): white undercoat deeply tipped with cream. Cat in repose appears cream. In motion the white undercoat is clearly apparent. Points and mask cream with narrow base of white at base of hairs next to skin which may be seen only when the fur is parted. Nose leather, rims of eyes, and paw pads: pink.

EBONY SMOKE: white undercoat, deeply tipped with black. Cat in repose appears black. In motion the white undercoat is clearly apparent. Points and mask black with narrow band of white at base of hairs next to skin which may be seen only when fur is parted. Nose leather and paw pads: black.

FAWN SMOKE: white undercoat, deeply tipped with fawn. Cat in repose appears fawn. In motion the white undercoat is clearly apparent. Points and mask fawn with narrow band of white at base of hairs which may be seen only when fur is parted. Nose leather: fawn. paw pads: pink.

LAVENDER SMOKE: white undercoat, deeply tipped with lavender. Cat in repose appears lavender. In motion the white undercoat is clearly apparent. Points and mask lavender with narrow band of white at base of hairs next to skin which may be seen only when fur is parted. Nose leather and paw pads: lavender-pink.

PARTI-COLOR SMOKE: white undercoat deeply tipped with black, blue, chestnut, cinnamon, fawn or lavender, mottled or patched with red and/or cream tipped hairs as in the pattern of the Parti-Color. Cat in repose appears Parti-Color. In motion, the white undercoat is clearly apparent. Face and ears have Parti-Color pattern with a narrow band of white at the base of the hairs next to the skin, which may be seen only when the fur is parted. Nose leather and paw pads: may be mottled with pink.
Tabby Color Class

CLASSIC TABBY PATTERN: markings dense, clearly defined, and broad. Legs evenly barred with bracelets coming up to meet the body markings. Tail evenly ringed. Several unbroken necklaces on neck and upper chest, the more the better. Frown marks on forehead form an intricate letter "M." Unbroken line runs back from outer corner of eye. Swirls on cheeks. Vertical lines over back of head extend to shoulder markings which are in the shape of a butterfly with both upper and lower wings distinctly outlined and marked with dots inside outline. Back markings consist of a vertical line down the spine from butterfly to tail with a vertical stripe paralleling it on each side, the three stripes well separated by stripes of the ground color. Large solid blotch on each side to be encircled by one or more unbroken rings. Side markings should be the same on both sides. Double vertical rows of buttons on chest and stomach.

MACKEREL TABBY PATTERN: markings dense, clearly defined, and all narrow pencillings. Legs evenly barred with narrow bracelets coming up to meet the body markings. Tail barred. Necklaces on neck and chest distinct, like so many chains. Head barred with an "M" on the forehead. Unbroken lines running back from the eyes. Lines running down the head to meet the shoulders. Spine lines run together to form a narrow saddle. Narrow pencillings run around body.

SPOTTED TABBY PATTERN: markings on the body to be spotted. May vary in size and shape with preference given to round, evenly distributed spots. Spots should not run together in a broken Mackerel pattern. A dorsal stripe runs the length of the body to the tip of the tail. The stripe is ideally composed of spots. The markings on the face and forehead shall be typically tabby markings. Underside of the body to have "vest buttons." Legs and tail are barred.

TICKED TABBY PATTERN: body hairs to be ticked with various shades of marking color and ground color. Body when viewed from top to be free from noticeable spots, stripes, or blotches, except for darker dorsal shading. Lighter underside may show tabby markings. Face, legs, and tail must show distinct tabby striping. Cat must have at least one distinct necklace.

PATCHED TABBY PATTERN: a patched tabby is an established Classic, Mackerel, Spotted or Ticked Tabby in blue, chestnut, cinnamon, ebony, fawn or lavender, or any of these colors in silver, mottled or patched with red and/or cream. Nose leather and paw pads: same as non-patched tabbies, may be mottled with pink.

BLUE SILVER TABBY: ground color, including lips and chin, pale, clear bluish silver. Markings sound blue. Nose leather: blue or old rose trimmed with blue. paw pads: blue.

BLUE TABBY: ground color, including lips and chin, pale bluish ivory. Markings a very deep blue affording a good contrast with ground color. Warm fawn overtones or patina over the whole. Nose leather: blue, or old rose trimmed with blue. paw pads: bluish rose.

CAMEO TABBY: ground color off-white. Markings red. Nose leather and paw pads: rose.

DILUTE CAMEO TABBY: ground color off-white. Markings cream. Nose leather and paw pads: pink.

CINNAMON SILVER TABBY: ground color, including lips and chin, pale glistening silver. Markings dense cinnamon. Nose leather: cinnamon, or pink rimmed with cinnamon. paw pads: coral pink.

CINNAMON TABBY: ground color, including lips and chin, a pale warm honey, markings a dense cinnamon, affording a good contrast with ground color. Nose leather: cinnamon or coral rimmed with cinnamon. paw pads: cinnamon.

CHESTNUT SILVER TABBY: ground color, including lips and chin, a snowy silver. Markings rich chestnut. Nose leather: chestnut, or pink rimmed with chestnut. paw pads: coral pink.

CHESTNUT TABBY: ground color warm fawn. Markings are rich chestnut. Nose leather: chestnut, or pink rimmed with chestnut. Paw pads: cinnamon.

CREAM TABBY: ground color, including lips and chin, very pale cream. Markings of buff or cream sufficiently darker than the ground color to afford good contrast but remaining within the dilute color range. Nose leather and paw pads: pink.

EBONY TABBY: ground color brilliant coppery brown. Markings dense black. Lips and chin the same shade as the rings around the eyes. Back of leg black from paw to heel. Nose leather: black, or brick red rimmed with black. Paw pads: black or brown.

FAWN TABBY: ground color, including lips and chin, pale ivory. Markings dense fawn, affording good contrast with ground color. Nose leather and paw pads: pale fawn.

FAWN SILVER TABBY: ground color, including lips and chin, pale glistening silver. Markings dense fawn. Nose leather: fawn, or pink rimmed with fawn. Paw pads: pink.

LAVENDER SILVER TABBY: ground color, including lips and chin, a cold clear silver. Markings sound lavender. Nose leather: lavender, or pink rimmed with lavender.Paw pads: lavender-pink.

LAVENDER TABBY: ground color is pale lavender. Markings are rich lavender affording a good contrast with the ground color. Nose leather: lavender, or pink rimmed with lavender. Paw pads: lavender-pink.

RED TABBY: ground color red. Markings deep, rich red. Lips and chin red. Nose leather and paw pads: flesh or coral pink.

EBONY SILVER TABBY: ground color, including lips and chin, pale clear silver. Markings dense black. Nose leather: black, or brick red rimmed with black. Paw pads: black. Parti-Color Color Class

BLUE-CREAM: blue mottled or patched with cream.

CINNAMON TORTOISESHELL: cinnamon mottled or patched with red and/or cream.

CHESTNUT TORTOISESHELL: chestnut brown mottled or patched with red and/or cream.

FAWN-CREAM: fawn mottled or patched with cream.

LAVENDER-CREAM: lavender mottled or patched with cream.

EBONY TORTOISESHELL: black mottled or patched with red and/or cream.

Oriental Shorthair allowable outcross breeds: Siamese or Colorpoint.

PERSIAN

■ POINT SCORE

HEAD (including size and shape of eyes,ear shape and set) | 30
TYPE (including shape, size, bone, and length of tail) | 20
COAT | 10
BALANCE | 5
REFINEMENT | 5
COLOR | 20
EYE COLOR | 10

In all tabby varieties, the 20 points for color are to be divided 10 for markings and 10 for color. In all "with white" varieties (calico, dilute calico, bi-color, van bi-color, van calico, van dilute calico, and tabby and white), the 20 points for color are to be divided 10 for "with white" pattern and 10 for color.

GENERAL: the ideal Persian should present an impression of a heavily boned, well-balanced cat with a sweet expression and soft, round lines. The large round eyes set wide apart in a large round head contribute to the overall look and expression. The long thick coat softens the lines of the cat and accentuates the roundness in appearance.
HEAD: round and massive, with great breadth of skull. Round face with round underlying bone structure. Well set on a short, thick neck.
NOSE: short, snub, and broad, with "break" centered between the eyes.
CHEEKS: full.
JAWS: broad and powerful.
CHIN: full, well-developed, and firmly rounded, reflecting a proper bite.
EARS: small, round tipped, tilted forward, and not unduly open at the base. Set far apart, and low on the head, fitting into (without distorting) the rounded contour of the head.
EYES: brilliant in color, large, round, and full. Set level and far apart, giving a sweet expression to the face.
BODY: of cobby type, low on the legs, broad and deep through the chest, equally massive across the shoulders and rump, with a well-rounded midsection and level back. Good muscle tone with no evidence of obesity. Large or medium in size. Quality the determining consideration rather than size.
LEGS: short, thick, and strong. Forelegs straight.
PAWS: large, round, and firm. Toes carried close, five in front and four behind .
TAIL: short, but in proportion to body length. Carried without a curve and at an angle lower than the back.
COAT: long and thick, standing off from the body. Of fine texture, glossy and full of life. Long all over the body, including the shoulders. The ruff immense and continuing in a deep frill between the front legs. Ear and toe tufts long. Brush very full.

DISQUALIFY: locket or button. Kinked or abnormal tail. Incorrect number of toes. Any apparent weakness in the hind quarters. Any apparent deformity of the spine. Deformity of the skull resulting in an asymmetrical face and/or head. Crossed eyes. For pointed cats, also disqualify for white toes, eye color other than blue.*
*The above listed disqualifications apply to all Persian cats. Additional disqualifications are listed under "Colors."

PERSIAN COLORS

WHITE: pure glistening white. Nose leather and paw pads: pink. Eye color: deep blue or brilliant copper. Odd-eyed whites shall have one blue and one copper eye with equal color depth.

BLACK: dense coal black, sound from roots to tip of fur. Free from any tinge of rust on tips or smoke undercoat. Nose leather: black. Paw pads: black or brown. Eye color: brilliant copper.

BLUE: blue, lighter shade preferred, one level tone from nose to tip of tail. Sound to the roots. A sound darker shade is more acceptable than an unsound lighter shade. Nose leather and paw pads: blue. Eye color: brilliant copper.

RED: deep, rich, clear, brilliant red; without shading, markings, or ticking. Lips and chin the same color as coat. Nose leather and paw pads: brick red. Eye color: brilliant copper.

CREAM: one level shade of buff cream, without markings. Sound to the roots. Lighter shades preferred. Nose leather and paw pads: pink. Eye color: brilliant copper.

CHOCOLATE: rich, warm chocolate-brown, sound from roots to tip of fur. Nose leather and paw pads: brown. Eye color: brilliant copper.

LILAC: rich, warm lavender with a pinkish tone, sound and even throughout. Nose leather and paw pads: pink. Eye color: brilliant copper.

CHINCHILLA SILVER: undercoat pure white. Coat on back, flanks, head, and tail sufficiently tipped with black to give the characteristic sparkling silver appearance. Legs may be slightly shaded with tipping. Chin, ear tufts, stomach, and chest, pure white. Rims of eyes, lips, and nose outlined with black. Nose leather: brick red. Paw pads: black. Eye color: green or blue-green. Disqualify for incorrect eye color, incorrect eye color being copper, yellow, gold, amber, or any color other than green or blue-green.

SHADED SILVER: undercoat white with a mantle of black tipping shading down from sides, face, and tail from dark on the ridge to white on the chin, chest, stomach, and under the tail. Legs to be the same tone as the face. The general effect to be much darker than a chinchilla. Rims of eyes, lips, and nose outlined with black. Nose leather: brick red. Paw pads: black. Eye color: green or blue-green. Disqualify for incorrect eye color, incorrect eye color being copper, yellow, gold, amber, or any color other than green or blue-green.

CHINCHILLA GOLDEN: undercoat rich warm cream. Coat on back, flanks, head, and tail sufficiently tipped with black to give golden appearance. Legs may be slightly shaded with tipping. Chin, ear tufts, stomach, and chest, cream. Rims of eyes, lips, and nose outlined with black. Nose leather: deep rose. Paw pads: black. Eye color: green or blue-green. Disqualify for incorrect eye color, incorrect eye color being copper, yellow, gold, amber, or any color other than green or blue-green.

SHADED GOLDEN: undercoat rich warm cream with a mantle of black tipping shading down from the sides, face, and tail from dark on the ridge to cream on the chin, chest, stomach, and under the tail. Legs to be the same tone as the face. The general effect to be much darker than a chinchilla. Rims of eyes, lips, and nose outlined with black. Nose leather: deep rose. Paw pads: black. Eye color: green or blue-green. Disqualify for incorrect eye color, incorrect eye color being copper yellow, gold, amber, or any color other than green or blue-green.

SHELL CAMEO (Red Chinchilla): undercoat white, the coat on the back, flanks, head, and tail to be sufficiently tipped with red to give the characteristic sparkling appearance. Face and legs may be very slightly shaded with tipping. Chin, ear tufts, stomach, and chest, white. Nose leather, rims of eyes and paw pads: rose. Eye color: brilliant copper.

SHADED CAMEO (Red Shaded): undercoat white with a mantle of red tipping shading down the sides, face, and tail from dark on the ridge to white on the chin, chest, stomach, and under the tail. Legs to be the same tone as face. The general effect to be much redder than the shell cameo. Nose leather, rims of eyes and paw pads: rose. Eye color: brilliant copper.

SHELL TORTOISESHELL: undercoat white. Coat on the back, flanks, head, and tail to be delicately tipped in black with well-defined patches of red and cream tipped hairs as in the pattern of the tortoiseshell. Face and legs may be slightly shaded with tipping. Chin, ear tufts, stomach, and chest, white to very slightly tipped. Blaze of red or cream tipping on face is desirable. Eye color: brilliant copper.

SHADED TORTOISESHELL: undercoat white. Mantle of black tipping and clearly defined patches of red and cream tipped hairs as in the pattern of the tortoiseshell. Shading down the sides, face, and tail from dark on the ridge to slightly tipped or white on the chin, chest, stomach, and under the tail. The general effect is to be much darker than the shell tortoiseshell. Blaze of red or cream tipping on the face is desirable. Eye color: brilliant copper.

BLACK SMOKE: white undercoat, deeply tipped with black. Cat in repose appears black. In motion the white undercoat is clearly apparent. Points and mask black with narrow band of white at base of hairs next to skin which may be seen only when fur is parted. Light silver frill and ear tufts. Nose leather and paw pads: black. Eye color: brilliant copper.

BLUE SMOKE: white undercoat, deeply tipped with blue. Cat in repose appears blue. In motion the white undercoat is clearly apparent. Points and mask blue, with narrow band of white at base of hairs next to skin which may be seen only when fur is parted. White frill and ear tufts. Nose leather and paw pads: blue. Eye color: brilliant copper.

CREAM SMOKE: white undercoat, deeply tipped with cream. Cat in repose appears cream. In motion the white undercoat is clearly apparent. Points and mask cream, with narrow band of white at base of hairs next to skin which may be seen only when fur is parted. White frill and ear tufts. Nose leather and paw pads: pink. Eye color: brilliant copper.

CAMEO SMOKE (Red Smoke): white undercoat, deeply tipped with red. Cat in repose appears red. In motion the white undercoat is clearly apparent. Points and mask red, with narrow band of white at base of hairs next to skin which may be seen only when fur is parted. White frill and ear tufts. Nose leather, rims of eyes and paw pads: rose. Eye color: brilliant copper.

SMOKE TORTOISESHELL: white undercoat, deeply tipped with black with clearly defined unbrindled patches of red and cream tipped hairs as in the pattern of the tortoiseshell. Cat in repose appears tortoiseshell. In motion

the white undercoat is clearly apparent. Face and ears tortoiseshell pattern with narrow band of white at the base of the hairs next to the skin that may be seen only when fur is parted. White ruff and ear tufts. Blaze of red or cream tipping on face is desirable. Eye color: brilliant copper.

BLUE-CREAM SMOKE: white undercoat deeply tipped with blue, with clearly defined patches of cream as in the pattern of the blue-cream. Cat in repose appears blue-cream. In motion the white undercoat is clearly apparent. Face and ears blue-cream pattern with narrow band of white at the base of the hair next to the skin that may be seen only when fur is parted. White ruff and ear tufts. Blaze of cream tipping on face is desirable. Eye color: brilliant copper.

SMOKE AND WHITE: white with colored portions, the colored portions of the cat to conform to the currently established smoke color standards. As a preferred minimum, the cat should have white feet, legs, undersides, chest, and muzzle. Less white than this minimum should be penalized proportionately. Inverted "V" blaze on face desirable. Eye color: brilliant copper.

VAN SMOKE AND WHITE: white cat with colored portions confined to the extremities; head, tail, and legs. The colored portions conform to the currently established smoke color standards. One or two small colored patches on body allowable. Eye color: brilliant copper.

CLASSIC TABBY PATTERN: markings dense, clearly defined, and broad. Legs evenly barred with bracelets coming up to meet the body markings. Tail evenly ringed. Several unbroken necklaces on neck and upper chest, the more the better. Frown marks on forehead form an intricate letter "M." Unbroken line runs back from outer corner of eye. Swirls on cheeks. Vertical lines over back of head extend to shoulder markings which are in the shape of a butterfly with both upper and lower wings distinctly outlined and marked with dots inside outline. Back markings consist of a vertical line down the spine from butterfly to tail with a vertical stripe paralleling it on each side, the three stripes well separated by stripes of the ground color. Large solid blotch on each side to be encircled by one or more unbroken rings. Side markings should be the same on both sides. Double vertical rows of buttons on chest and stomach.

MACKEREL TABBY PATTERN: markings dense, clearly defined, and all narrow pencillings. Legs evenly barred

with narrow bracelets coming up to meet the body markings. Tail barred. Necklaces on neck and chest distinct, like so many chains. Head barred with an "M" on the forehead. Unbroken lines running back from the eyes. Lines running down the head to meet the shoulders. Spine lines run together to form a narrow saddle. Narrow pencillings run around body.

PATCHED TABBY PATTERN: a patched tabby (torbie) is an established silver, brown, or blue tabby with patches of red and/or cream.

BROWN PATCHED TABBY: ground color brilliant coppery brown with classic or mackerel tabby markings of dense black with patches of red and/or cream clearly defined on both body and extremities; a blaze of red and/or cream on the face is desirable. Lips and chin the same shade as the rings around the eyes. Eye color: brilliant copper.

BLUE PATCHED TABBY: ground color, including lips and chin, pale bluish ivory with classic or mackerel tabby markings of very deep blue affording a good contrast with ground color. Patches of cream clearly defined on both body and extremities; a blaze of cream on the face is desirable. Warm fawn overtones or patina over the whole. Eye color: brilliant copper.

SILVER PATCHED TABBY: ground color, including lips and chin, pale silver with classic or mackerel tabby markings of dense black with patches of red and/or cream clearly defined on both body and extremities. A blaze of red and/or cream on the face is desirable. Eye color: brilliant copper or hazel.

SILVER TABBY (classic, mackerel): ground color, including lips and chin, pale, clear silver. Markings dense black. Nose leather: brick red. Paw pads: black. Eye color: green, brilliant copper, or hazel.

BLUE SILVER TABBY (classic, mackerel): ground color pale bluish silver. Markings sound blue. Undercoat white. Lips and chin the same shade as the rings around the eyes. Nose leather: blue or old rose trimmed with blue. Paw pads: blue or old rose. Eye color: green, hazel, or brilliant copper.

BLUE SILVER PATCHED TABBY (classic, mackerel): ground color pale bluish silver with patches of cream on both body and extremities. Markings sound blue. Undercoat white. Lips and chin the same shade as the rings around the eyes. Nose leather: blue or old rose trimmed with blue and/or pink. Paw pads: blue or old rose and/or pink. Eye color: green, hazel, or brilliant copper.

RED TABBY (classic, mackerel): ground color red. Markings deep, rich red. Lips and chin the same shade as the rings around the eyes. Nose leather and paw pads: brick red. Eye color: brilliant copper.

RED TABBY (classic, mackerel): ground color red. Markings deep, rich red. Lips and chin the same shade as the rings around the eyes. Nose leather and paw pads: brick red. Eye color: brilliant copper.

BROWN TABBY (classic, mackerel): ground color brilliant coppery brown. Markings dense black. Lips and chin the same shade as the rings around the eyes. Back of leg black from paw to heel. Nose leather: brick red. Paw pads: black or brown. Eye color: brilliant copper.

BLUE TABBY (classic, mackerel): ground color, including lips and chin, pale bluish ivory. Markings a very deep blue affording a good contrast with ground color. Warm fawn overtones or patina over the whole. Nose leather: old rose. Paw pads: rose. Eye color: brilliant copper.

CREAM TABBY (classic, mackerel): ground color, including lips and chin, very pale cream. Markings of buff or cream sufficiently darker than the ground color to afford good contrast, but remaining within the dilute color range. Nose leather and paw pads: pink. Eye color: brilliant copper.

CAMEO TABBY (classic, mackerel): ground color off-white. Markings red. Nose leather and paw pads: rose. Eye color: brilliant copper.

VAN TABBY AND WHITE: white cat with colored portions confined to the extremities; head, tail, and legs. The colored portions conform to the currently established classic, mackerel and patched tabby color standards. One or two small colored patches on body allowable. Eye color: to conform to the established tabby pattern requirements.

TORTOISESHELL: black with unbrindled patches of red and cream. Patches clearly defined and well broken on both body and extremities. Blaze of red or cream on face is desirable. Eye color: brilliant copper.

CHOCOLATE TORTOISESHELL: rich, warm chocolate brown with patches of red. Patches clearly defined and well broken on both body and extremities. Nose leather and paw

pads: brown and/or brick red. Eye color: brilliant copper.

CALICO: white with unbrindled patches of black and red. As a preferred minimum, the cat should have white feet, legs, undersides, chest, and muzzle. Less white than this minimum should be penalized proportionately. Inverted "V" blaze on face desirable. Eye color: brilliant copper.

DILUTE CALICO: white with unbrindled patches of blue and cream. As a preferred minimum, the cat should have white feet, legs, undersides, chest, and muzzle. Less white than this minimum should be penalized proportionately. Inverted "V" blaze on face desirable. Eye color: brilliant copper.

BLUE-CREAM: blue with patches of solid cream. Patches clearly defined and well broken on both body and extremities. Eye color: brilliant copper.

LILAC-CREAM: rich, warm pinkish toned lavender with patches of cream. Patches clearly defined and well broken on both body and extremities. Nose leather and paw pads: pink. Eye color: brilliant copper.

BI-COLOR: black and white, blue and white, red and white, or cream and white. As a preferred minimum, the cat should have white feet, legs, undersides, chest, and muzzle. Less white than this minimum should be penalized proportionately. Inverted "V" blaze on face desirable. Eye color: brilliant copper.

VAN BI-COLOR: Black and white, red and white, blue and white, or cream and white. White cat with color confined to the extremities; head, tail, and legs. One or two small colored patches on body allowable. Eye color: brilliant copper.

VAN CALICO: white cat with unbrindled patches of black and red confined to the extremities; head, tail, and legs. One or two small colored patches on body allowable. Eye color: brilliant copper.

VAN DILUTE CALICO: white cat with unbrindled patches of blue and cream confined to the extremities; head, tail, and legs. One or two small colored patches on body allowable. Eye color: brilliant copper.

(NOTE: cats having more than two small body spots should be shown in the regular Bi-color class.)

TABBY AND WHITE: white with colored portions, the colored portions

of the cat to conform to the currently established classic, mackerel and patched tabby color standards. As a preferred minimum, the cat should have white feet, legs, undersides, chest, and muzzle. Less white than this minimum should be penalized proportionately. Inverted "V" blaze on face desirable. Eye color: to conform to the established tabby pattern requirements.

PEKE-FACE RED and PEKE-FACE RED TABBY: the peke-face cat should conform in color and general type to the standard set forth for the red and red tabby cat; however, allowance should be made for the slightly higher placement of the ears to conform with the underlying bone structure of the head which differs greatly from that of the standard Persian. The nose should be short, depressed and indented between the eyes. The muzzle should be wrinkled. Eyes should be large, round and set wide apart. The horizontal break, which is located between the usual nose break and the top dome of the head, runs straight across the front of the head creating half-moon boning above the eyes and an additional horizontal indentation located in the center of the forehead bone structure. This bone structure results in a very round head with a strong chin. Eye color: brilliant copper.

SEAL POINT: body even pale fawn to cream, warm in tone, shading gradually into lighter color on the stomach and chest. Points deep seal brown. Nose leather and paw pads: same color as points. Eye color: deep vivid blue.

CHOCOLATE POINT: body ivory with no shading. Points milk-chocolate color, warm in tone. Nose leather and paw pads: cinnamon pink. Eye color: deep vivid blue.

BLUE POINT: body bluish white, cold in tone, shading gradually to white on stomach and chest. Points blue. Nose leather and paw pads: slate blue. Eye color: deep vivid blue.

LILAC POINT: body glacial white with no shading. Points frosty grey with pinkish tone. Nose leather and paw pads: lavender pink. Eye color: deep vivid blue.

FLAME (RED) POINT: body creamy white. Points deep orange flame to deep red. Nose leather and paw pads: flesh or coral pink. Eye color: deep vivid blue.

CREAM POINT: body creamy white with no shading. Points buff cream with no apricot. Nose leather and paw pads: flesh pink or salmon coral. Eye

color: deep vivid blue.

TORTIE POINT: body creamy white or pale fawn. Points seal with unbrindled patches of red and/or cream. Blaze of red or cream on face is desirable. Nose leather and paw pads: seal brown with flesh and/or coral pink mottling to conform with colors of points. Eye color: deep vivid blue.

CHOCOLATE-TORTIE POINT: body ivory with no shading. Points chocolate with unbrindled patches of red and/or cream. Nose leather and paw pads: chocolate with flesh and/or coral pink mottling to conform with the point color. Eye color: deep vivid blue.

BLUE-CREAM POINT: body bluish white or creamy white, shading gradually to white on the stomach and chest. Points blue with patches of cream. Nose leather and paw pads: slate blue, pink, or a combination of slate blue and pink. Eye color: deep vivid blue.

LILAC-CREAM POINT: body glacial white with no shading. Points lilac with patches of cream. Nose leather and paw pads: lavender pink, pink or a combination of lavender pink and pink. Eye color: deep vivid blue.

SEAL LYNX POINT: points beige-brown ticked with darker brown tabby markings. Body color pale cream to fawn, warm in tone. Mask must be clearly lined with dark stripes vertical on forehead with classic "M" on forehead, horizontal on cheeks and dark spots on whisker pads clearly outlined in dark color edges. Inner ear light with thumbprint on outer ear. Markings dense, clearly defined and broad. Legs evenly barred with bracelets. Tail barred. No striping or mottling on body, but consideration to be given to shading in older cats. Nose leather: seal or brick red. Paw pads: seal. Eye color: deep vivid blue.

BLUE LYNX POINT: points light, silvery blue, ticked with darker blue tabby markings. Body color bluish white, cold in tone. Mask must be clearly lined with dark stripes vertical on forehead with classic "M" on forehead, horizontal on cheeks and dark spots on whisker pads clearly outlined in dark color edges. Inner ear light with thumbprint on outer ear. Markings dense, clearly defined and broad. Legs evenly barred with bracelets. Tail barred. No striping or mottling on body, but consideration to be given to shading in older cats. Nose leather: blue or brick red. Paw pads: blue. Eye color: deep vivid blue.

FLAME (RED) LYNX POINT: points deep orange flame ticked with deep red tabby markings. Body color creamy white. Mask must be clearly lined with dark stripes vertical on forehead with classics "M" on forehead, horizontal on cheeks and dark spots on whisker pads clearly outlined in dark color edges. Inner ear light with thumbprint on outer ear. Markings dense, clearly defined and broad. Legs evenly barred with bracelets. Tail barred. Nose leather and paw pads: flesh or coral pink. Eye color: deep vivid blue.

CREAM LYNX POINT: points pale cream ticked with dark cream tabby markings. Body color creamy white, significantly lighter in tone than the points. Mask must be clearly lined with dark stripes vertical on forehead with classics "M" on forehead, horizontal on cheeks and dark spots on whisker pads clearly outlined in dark color edges. Inner ear light with thumbprint on outer ear. Markings dense, clearly defined and broad. Legs evenly barred with bracelets. Tail barred. Nose leather and paw pads: flesh or coral pink. Eye color: deep vivid blue.

TORTIE LYNX POINT: points beige-brown with dark brown tabby markings and patches of red. Body color creamy white or pale fawn. Mask must be clearly lined with dark stripes vertical on forehead with classic "M" on forehead, horizontal on cheeks and dark spots on whisker pads clearly outlined in dark color edges. Inner ear light with thumbprint on outer ear. Markings dense, clearly defined and broad. Legs evenly barred with bracelets. Tail barred. Nose leather and paw pads: seal brown and/or flesh or coral pink. Eye color: deep vivid blue.

BLUE-CREAM LYNX POINT: points blue with darker blue tabby markings and patches of cream. Body color bluish white, cold in tone. mask must be clearly lined with dark stripes vertical on forehead with classic "M" on forehead, horizontal on cheeks and dark spots on whisker pads clearly outlined in dark color edges. Inner ear light with thumbprint on outer ear. Markings dense, clearly defined and broad. Legs evenly barred with bracelets. Tail barred. Nose leather and paw pads: slate blue and/or pink. Eye color: deep vivid blue.

CHOCOLATE LYNX POINT: points milk-chocolate ticked with darker chocolate tabby markings. Body color ivory. Mask must be clearly lined with dark stripes vertical on forehead with classic "M" on forehead, horizontal on cheeks and dark spots on whisker pads clearly outlined in dark color edges. Inner ear light with thumbprint on outer ear. Markings dense, clearly defined and broad. Legs evenly barred

with bracelets. Tail barred. Nose leather and paw pads: cinnamon pink. Eye color: deep vivid blue.

LILAC LYNX POINT: points pale frosty grey with pinkish tone ticked with darker lilac tabby markings. Body color glacial white. Mask must be clearly lined with dark stripes vertical on forehead with classic "M" on forehead, horizontal on cheeks and dark spots on whisker pads clearly outlined in dark color edges. Inner ear light with thumbprint on outer ear. Markings dense, clearly defined and broad. Legs evenly barred with bracelets. Tail barred. Nose leather and paw pads: lavender pink. Eye color: deep vivid blue.

CHOCOLATE-TORTIE LYNX POINT: points milk-chocolate ticked with darker chocolate tabby markings and patches of red. Body color ivory. Mask must be clearly lined with dark stripes vertical on forehead with classic "M" on forehead, horizontal on cheeks and dark spots on whisker pads clearly outlined in dark color edges. Inner ear light with thumbprint on outer ear. Markings dense, clearly defined and broad. Legs evenly barred with bracelets. Tail barred. Nose leather and paw pads: cinnamon pink and/or coral pink. Eye color: deep vivid blue.

LILAC-CREAM LYNX POINT: points pale frosty grey with pinkish tone ticked with darker lilac tabby markings and patches of cream. Body color glacial white. Mask must be clearly lined with dark stripes vertical on forehead with classic "M" on forehead, horizontal on cheeks and dark spots on whisker pads clearly outlined in dark color edges. Inner ear light with thumbprint on outer ear. Markings dense, clearly defined and broad. Legs evenly barred with bracelets. Tail barred. Nose leather and paw pads: lavender pink and/or coral pink. Eye color: deep vivid blue. Persian allowable outcross breeds: none.

RAGDOLL

There are currently no CFA standards for this breed.

REX (CORNISH REX)

■ POINT SCORE

HEAD (25)	
Size and shape	5
Muzzle and Nose.	5
Eyes	5
Ears	5
Profile	5
BODY (30)	
Size	3

Torso	10
Legs and Paws	5
Tail	5
Bone	5
Neck	2
COAT (40)	
Texture	10
Length	5
Wave, extent of wave	20
Close lying	5
COLOR	5

GENERAL: the Cornish Rex is distinguished from all other breeds by its extremely soft, wavy coat and racy type. It is surprisingly heavy and warm to the touch. All contours of the Cornish Rex are gently curved. By nature, the Cornish Rex is intelligent, alert, and generally likes to be handled.

PROFILE: a curve comprised of two convex arcs. The forehead is rounded, the nose break smooth and mild, and the Roman nose has a high prominent bridge.

HEAD: comparatively small and narrow; egg shaped. Length about one-third greater than the width. A definite whisker break, oval with gently curving outline in front and in profile.

MUZZLE: narrowing slightly to a rounded end.

EARS: large and full from the base, erect and alert; set high on the head.

EYES: medium to large in size, oval in shape, and slanting slightly upward. A full eye's width apart. Color should be clear, intense, and appropriate to coat color.

NOSE: Roman. Length is one-third length of head. In profile a straight line from end of nose to chin with considerable depth and squarish effect.

CHEEKS: cheek bones high and prominent, well chiseled.

CHIN: strong, well-developed.

BODY: small to medium, males proportionately larger. Torso long and slender, not tubular; hips, muscular and somewhat heavy in proportion to the rest of the body. Back is naturally arched with lower line of the body approaching the upward curve. The arch is evident when the cat is standing naturally.

SHOULDERS: well-knit.

RUMP: rounded, well-muscled.

LEGS: very long and slender. Hips well-muscled, somewhat heavy in proportion to the rest of the body. The Cornish Rex stands high on its legs.

PAWS: dainty, slightly oval. Toes: five in front and four behind.

TAIL: long and slender, tapering toward the end and extremely flexible.

NECK: long and slender.

BONE: fine and delicate.

COAT: short, extremely soft, silky, and completely free of guard hairs. Relatively dense. A tight, uniform marcel wave, lying close to the body

and extending from the top of the head across the back, sides, and hips continuing to the tip of the tail. Size and depth of wave may vary. The fur on the underside of the chin and on chest and abdomen is short and noticeably wavy.

CONDITION: firm and muscular.

PENALIZE: sparse coat or bare spots.

DISQUALIFY: kinked or abnormal tail. Incorrect number of toes. Any coarse or guard hairs. Any signs of lameness in the hindquarters. Signs of poor health.

CORNISH REX COLORS

WHITE: pure glistening white. Nose leather and paw pads: pink. Eye color: deep blue or brilliant gold. Odd-eyed whites shall have one blue and one gold eye with equal color depth.

BLACK: dense coal black, sound from roots to tip of fur. Free from any tinge of rust on the tips. Nose leather: black. Paw pads: black or brown. Eye color: gold.

BLUE: blue, lighter shade preferred, one level tone from nose to tip of tail. Sound to the roots. A sound darker shade is more acceptable than an unsound lighter shade. Nose leather and paw pads: blue. Eye color: gold.

RED: deep, rich, clear, brilliant red; without shading, markings, or ticking. Lips and chin the same color as the coat. Nose leather and paw pads: brick red. Eye color: gold.

CREAM: one level shade of buff cream, without markings. Sound to the roots. Lighter shades preferred. Nose leather and paw pads: pink. Eye color: gold.

CHINCHILLA SILVER: undercoat pure white. Coat on back, flanks, head, and tail sufficiently tipped with black to give the characteristic sparkling appearance. Legs may be slightly shaded with tipping. Chin, stomach and chest, pure white. Rims of eyes, lips, and nose outlined with black. Nose leather: brick red. Paw pads: black. Eye color: green or blue-green.

SHADED SILVER: undercoat white with a mantle of black tipping shading down from sides, face, and tail from dark on the ridge to white on the chin, chest, stomach, and under the tail. Legs to be the same tone as the face. The general effect to be much darker than a chinchilla. Rims of eyes, lips, and nose outlined with black. Nose leather: brick red. Paw pads: black. Eye color: green or blue-green.

BLACK SMOKE: white undercoat, deeply tipped with black. Cat in repose appears black. In motion the white undercoat is clearly apparent. Points and mask black with narrow band of white at base of hairs next to skin which may be seen only when fur is parted. Nose leather and paw pads: black. Eye color: gold.

BLUE SMOKE: white undercoat, deeply tipped with blue. Cat in repose appears blue. In motion the white undercoat is clearly apparent. Points and mask blue with narrow band of white at base of hairs next to skin which may be seen only when fur is parted. Nose leather and paw pads: blue. Eye color: gold.

CLASSIC TABBY PATTERN: markings dense, clearly defined, and broad. Legs evenly barred with bracelets coming up to meet the body markings. Tail evenly ringed. Several unbroken necklaces on neck and upper chest, the more the better. Frown marks on forehead form an intricate letter "M." Unbroken line runs back from outer corner of eye. Swirls on cheeks. Vertical lines over back of head extend to shoulder markings which are in the shape of a butterfly with both upper and lower wings distinctly outlined and marked with dots inside outline. Back markings consist of a vertical line down the spine from butterfly to tail with a vertical stripe paralleling it on each side, the three stripes well separated by stripes of the ground color. Large solid blotch on each side to be encircled by one or more unbroken rings. Side markings should be the same on both sides. Double vertical rows of buttons on chest and stomach.

MACKEREL TABBY PATTERN: markings dense, clearly defined, and all narrow pencillings. Legs evenly barred with narrow bracelets coming up to meet the body markings. Tail barred. Necklaces on neck and chest distinct, like so many chains. Head barred with an "M" on the forehead. Unbroken lines running back from the eyes. Lines running down the head to meet the shoulders. Spine lines run together to form a narrow saddle. Narrow pencillings run around body.

PATCHED TABBY PATTERN: a patched tabby (torbie) is an established silver, brown, or blue tabby with patches of red and/or cream.

BROWN PATCHED TABBY: ground color brilliant coppery brown with classic or mackerel tabby markings of dense black with patches of red and/or cream clearly defined on both the body and extremities; a blaze of red and/or cream on the face is desirable. Lips and

chin the same shade as the rings around the eyes. Eye color: brilliant gold.

BLUE PATCHED TABBY: ground color, including lips and chin, pale bluish ivory with classic or mackerel tabby markings of very deep blue affording a good contrast with ground color. Patches of cream clearly defined on both body and extremities; a blaze of cream on the face is desirable. Warm fawn overtones or patina over the whole. Eye color: brilliant gold.

SILVER PATCHED TABBY: ground color, including lips and chin, pale silver with classic or mackerel tabby markings of dense black with patches of red and/or cream clearly defined on both body and extremities. A blaze of red and/or cream on the face is desirable. Eye color: brilliant gold or hazel.

SILVER TABBY (classic, mackerel): ground color, including lips and chin, pale clear silver. Markings dense black. Nose leather: brick red. Paw pads: black. Eye color: green or hazel.

RED TABBY (classic, mackerel): ground color red. Markings deep, rich red. Lips and chin red. Nose leather and paw pads: brick red. Eye color: gold.

BROWN TABBY (classic, mackerel): ground color brilliant coppery brown. Markings dense black. Lips and chin the same shade as the rings around the eyes. Back of leg black from paw to heel. Nose leather: brick red. Paw pads: black or brown. Eye color: gold.

BLUE TABBY (classic, mackerel): ground color, including lips and chin, pale bluish ivory. Markings a very deep blue affording a good contrast with ground color. Warm fawn overtones or patina over the whole. Nose leather: old rose. Paw pads: rose. Eye color: gold.

CREAM TABBY (classic, mackerel): ground color, including lips and chin, very pale cream. Markings buff or cream sufficiently darker than the ground color to afford good contrast but remaining within the dilute color range. Nose leather and paw pads: pink. Eye color: gold.

TORTOISESHELL: black with unbrindled patches of red and cream. Patches clearly defined and well broken on both body and extremities. Blaze of red or cream on face is desirable. Eye color: gold.

CALICO: white with unbrindled patches of black and red. White predominant on underparts. Eye color: gold, odd-eyed or blue.

VAN CALICO: white cat with unbrindled patches of black and red confined to the extremities; head, tail and legs. One or two small colored patches on body allowable.

DILUTE CALICO: white with unbrindled patches of blue and cream. White predominant on underparts. Eye color: gold.

BLUE-CREAM: blue with patches of solid cream. Patches clearly defined and well broken on both body and extremities. Eye color: gold.

VAN BLUE-CREAM AND WHITE: white cat with unbrindled patches of blue and cream confined to the extremities; head, tail, and legs. One or two small colored patches on body allowable.

BI-COLOR: solid color and white, smoke and white, tabby and white, etc. Cats with no more white than a locket and/or button do not qualify for this color class. Such cats shall be judged in the color class of their basic color with no penalty for such locket and/or button. Eye color: gold, odd-eyed or blue.

VAN BI-COLOR: black and white, red and white, blue and white, cream and white. White cat with color confined to the extremities; head, tail, and legs. One or two small colored patches on body allowable.

ORC: (Other Rex Colors): any other color or pattern. Eye Color: appropriate to the predominant color of the cat. Cornish Rex allowable outcross breeds: none.

REX (DEVON REX)

■ POINT SCORE

HEAD (35)	
Size and shape	10
Muzzle and Chin	5
Profile	5
Eyes	5
Ears	10
BODY (30)	
Torso	10
Legs and Paws	10
Tail	5
Neck	5
COAT (30)	
Density	10
Texture and length	10
Waviness	10
COLOR	5

GENERAL: the Devon Rex is a breed of unique appearance. Its large eyes, short muzzle, prominent cheekbones, and huge, low-set ears create a characteristic elfin look. A cat of medium

fine frame, the Devon is well covered with soft, wavy fur; the fur is of a distinctive texture, as the mutation which causes its wavy coat is cultivated in no other breed. The Devon is alert and active and shows a lively interest in its surroundings.

HEAD: modified wedge. In the front view, the wedge is delineated by a narrowing series of three (3) distinct convex curves: outer edge of ear lobes, cheekbones, and whisker pads. Head to be broad but slightly longer than it is broad. Face to be full-cheeked with pronounced cheekbones and a whisker break. In profile, nose with a strongly marked stop; forehead curving back to a flat skull.

MUZZLE: short, well-developed. Prominent whisker pads.

CHIN: strong, well-developed.

EYES: large and wide set, oval in shape, and sloping towards outer edges of ears. Color should be clear, intense, and appropriate to coat color.

EARS: strikingly large and set very low, very wide at the base, so that the outside base of ear extends beyond the line of the wedge. Tapering to rounded tops and well covered with fine fur. With or without earmuffs and/or ear-tip tufts.

BODY: hard and muscular, slender, and of medium length. Broad in chest and medium fine in boning, with medium fine but sturdy legs. Carried high on the legs with the hind legs somewhat longer than the front. Allowance to be made for larger size in males, as long as good proportions are maintained.

LEGS and PAWS: legs long and slim. Paws small and oval, with five toes in front and four behind.

TAIL: long, fine, and tapering, well covered with short fur.

NECK: medium long and slender.

COAT: Density: the cat is well covered with fur, with the greatest density occurring on the back, sides, tail, legs, face, and ears. Slightly less density is permitted on the top of head, neck, chest, and abdomen. Bare patches are a fault in kittens and a serious fault in adults; however the existence of down on the underparts of the body should not be misinterpreted as bareness. Sparse hair on the temples (forehead in front of the ears) is not a fault. Texture: the coat is soft, fine, full-bodied, and rexed (i.e., appearing to be without guard hairs). Length: the coat is short on the back, sides, upper legs, and tail. It is very short on the head, ears, neck, paws, chest, and abdomen. Kittens may have very short fur all over; even if not long enough to wave, it must cover the kitten evenly, so that no bare patches are evident. Waviness: a rippled wave effect should be apparent when the coat is smoothed with one's hand. The wave is most evident where the coat is the longest, on the body and tail.

PENALIZE: narrow, long, round or domestic-type head; extremely short muzzle; small or high set ears; short, bare, or bushy tail; straight or shaggy coat; bare patches.

DISQUALIFY: extensive baldness, kinked or abnormal tail, incorrect number of toes, crossed eyes, weak hind legs. Any evidence of illness or poor health.

DEVON REX COLORS
WHITE: pure glistening white. Nose leather and paw pads: pink. Eye color: deep blue or brilliant gold. Odd-eyed whites shall have one blue and one gold eye with equal color depth.

BLACK: dense coal black, sound from roots to tip of fur. Free from any tinge of rust on the tips. Nose leather: black. Paw pads: black or brown. Eye color: gold.

BLUE: blue, lighter shade preferred, one level tone from nose to tip of tail. Sound to the roots. A sound darker shade is more acceptable than an unsound lighter shade. Nose leather and paw pads: blue. Eye color: gold.

RED: deep, rich, clear, brilliant red; without shading, markings or ticking. Lips and chin the same color as the coat. Nose leather and paw pads: brick red. Eye color: gold.

CREAM: one level shade of buff cream, without markings. Sound to the roots. Lighter shades preferred. Nose leather and paw pads: pink. Eye color: gold.

CHOCOLATE: rich chestnut brown, sound throughout. Nose leather: brown. Paw pads: brown or cinnamon. Eye color: gold.

LAVENDER: frosty-grey with a pinkish tone, sound throughout. Nose leather and paw pads: lavender-pink. Eye color: gold.

CINNAMON: cinnamon, sound throughout. Nose leather and paw pads: cinnamon. Eye color: gold.

FAWN: pale pinkish fawn, sound throughout; lighter shades preferred. Nose leather and paw pads: pale fawn. Eye color: gold.

SHADED PATTERN: undercoat white with a mantle of specified marking color tipping shading down from sides, face and tail from dark on the ridge to white on the chin, chest, stomach and under the tail. Legs to be the same tone as the face. Rims of eyes, lips and nose outlined with marking color. Nose leather, Paw pads, and Eye color as defined below.

SHADED SILVER: Nose leather: brick red. Paw pads: black. Eye color: green or blue-green.

BLUE SHADED: Nose leather: blue or blue with pink tone. Paw pads: blue or blue with pink tone. Eye color: gold.

CHOCOLATE SHADED: Nose leather: pink. Paw pads: cinnamon. Eye color: gold.

LAVENDER SHADED: Nose leather: lavender-pink. Paw pads: lavender-pink. Eye color: gold.

CAMEO SHADED: Nose leather: rose. Paw pads: rose. Eye color: gold.

CINNAMON SHADED: Nose leather: pink. Paw pads: coral. Eye color: gold.

FAWN SHADED: Nose leather: fawn. Paw pads: pink. Eye color: gold.
TORTOISESHELL SHADED: Nose leather and paw pads: as in the solids; may be mottled with pink. Eye color: gold.

BLUE-CREAM SHADED: Nose leather and paw pads: as in the solids; may be mottled with pink. Eye color: gold.

CHOCOLATE TORTOISESHELL SHADED: Nose leather and paw pads: as in the solids; may be mottled with pink. Eye color: gold.

CINNAMON TORTOISESHELL SHADED: Nose leather and paw pads: as in the solids; may be mottled with pink. Eye color: gold.

LAVENDER-CREAM SHADED: Nose leather and paw pads: as in the solids; may be mottled with pink. Eye color: gold.
FAWN-CREAM SHADED: Nose leather and paw pads: as in the solids; may be mottled with pink. Eye color: gold.

CHINCHILLA: undercoat pure white. Coat on back, flanks, head, and tail sufficiently tipped with specified marking color (i.e., black, blue, red, cream, tortoiseshell, etc.) to give the characteristic sparkling appearance. Legs may be slightly shaded with tipping. Chin, stomach and chest, pure white. Rims of eyes, lips and nose outlined with marking color. Nose leather: appropriate to pattern and marking color (black/brick red; blue/old rose; red and cream/rose, etc.). Paw pads: appropriate to pattern and marking color (black/black; blue/rose; red and cream/rose, etc.). Eye color: green or blue-green.

SMOKE PATTERN: white undercoat more deeply tipped with specified marking color. Cat in repose appears to be of marking color. In motion the white undercoat is apparent. Points and mask of marking color with narrow band of white at base of hairs next to skin which may be seen only when fur is parted. Nose leather and paw pads: appropriate to pattern and marking color (see below). Eye color: gold.

BLACK SMOKE: Nose leather and paw pads: black.

BLUE SMOKE: Nose leather and paw pads: blue.
RED SMOKE CAMEO (Cameo): Nose leather and paw pads: rose.

CHOCOLATE SMOKE: Nose leather and paw pads: brown or brick.
LAVENDER SMOKE: Nose leather and paw pads: lavender-pink.
CINNAMON SMOKE: Nose leather and paw pads: cinnamon.

CREAM SMOKE: Nose leather and paw pads: pink.

FAWN SMOKE: Nose leather and paw pads: pale fawn.

TORTOISESHELL SMOKE: Nose leather and paw pads: mottled with pink on nose and paws.

BLUE-CREAM SMOKE: Nose leather and paw pads: mottled with pink on nose and paws.

CHOCOLATE TORTOISESHELL SMOKE: Nose leather and paw pads: mottled with pink on nose and paws.
LAVENDER-CREAM SMOKE: Nose leather and paw pads: mottled with pink on nose and paws.

CINNAMON TORTOISESHELL SMOKE: Nose leather and paw pads: mottled with pink on nose and paws.
FAWN-CREAM SMOKE: Nose leather and paw pads: pink.

CLASSIC TABBY PATTERN: markings dense, clearly defined, and broad. Legs evenly barred with bracelets coming up to meet the body markings. Tail evenly ringed. Several unbroken necklaces on neck and upper chest, the more the better. Frown marks on forehead form an intricate letter "M." Unbroken line runs back from outer corner of eye. Swirls on cheeks. Vertical lines over back of head extend to shoulder markings which are in the shape of a butterfly with both upper and lower wings distinctly outlined and marked with dots inside outline. Back markings consist of a vertical line down the spine from butterfly to tail with a vertical stripe paralleling it on each side, the three stripes well separated by stripes of the ground color. Large solid blotch on each side to be encircled by one or more unbroken rings. Side markings should be the same on both sides. Double vertical rows of buttons on chest and stomach.

MACKEREL TABBY PATTERN: markings dense, clearly defined, and all narrow pencillings. Legs evenly barred with narrow bracelets coming up to meet the body markings. Tail barred. Necklaces on neck and chest distinct, like so many chains. Head barred with an "M" on the forehead. Unbroken lines running back from the eyes. Lines running down the head to meet the shoulders. Spine lines run together to form a narrow saddle. Narrow pencillings run around body.

SPOTTED TABBY PATTERN: markings on the body to be spotted. The spots can be round, oblong, or rosette-shaped. Any of these are of equal merit but the spots, however shaped or placed, shall be distinct. Spots should not run together in a broken Mackerel pattern. A dorsal stripe runs the length of the body to the tip of the tail. The stripe is ideally composed of spots. The markings on the face and forehead shall be typically tabby markings. Underside of the body to have "vest buttons." Legs and tail are barred.

PATCHED TABBY PATTERN: a patched tabby (torbie) is an established silver, brown, blue, red, cream etc. tabby with patches of red, cream, lavender, fawn, etc. clearly defined on both the body and extremities; a blaze on the face is desirable.

SILVER TABBY: ground color, including lips and chin, pale clear silver. Markings dense black. Nose leather: brick red. Paw pads: black. Eye color: green or hazel.

BROWN TABBY: ground color brilliant coppery brown. Markings dense black. Lips and chin the same shade as the rings around the eyes. Back of leg black from paw to heel. Nose leather: brick red. Paw pads: black or brown. Eye color: gold.

BLUE TABBY: ground color, including lips and chin, pale bluish ivory. Markings a very deep blue affording a good contrast with ground color. Warm fawn overtones or patina over the whole. Nose leather: old rose. Paw pads: rose. Eye color: gold.

RED TABBY: ground color red. Markings deep, rich red. Lips and chin red. Nose leather and paw pads: brick red. Eye color: gold.

CREAM TABBY: ground color, including lips and chin, very pale cream. Markings buff or cream sufficiently darker than the ground color to afford good contrast but remaining within the dilute color range. Nose leather and paw pads: pink. Eye color: gold.

CHOCOLATE (Chestnut) TABBY: ground color is warm fawn, markings are rich chestnut brown. Nose leather: chestnut, or pink rimmed with chestnut. Paw pads: cinnamon. Eye color: gold.

CHOCOLATE SILVER TABBY: ground color, including lips and chin, is silver. Markings rich chestnut. Nose leather: chestnut or pink rimmed with chestnut. Paw pads: cinnamon. Eye color: gold.

CINNAMON TABBY: ground color, including lips and chin, a pale, warm honey, markings a dense cinnamon, affording a good contrast with ground color. Nose leather: cinnamon or coral rimmed with cinnamon. Paw pads: cinnamon. Eye color: gold.

CINNAMON SILVER TABBY: ground color, including lips and chin, a pale glistening silver. Markings dense cinnamon. Nose leather: cinnamon. Paw pads: coral.

LAVENDER TABBY: ground color is pale lavender. Markings are a rich lavender, affording a good contrast with ground color. Nose leather: lavender, or pink rimmed with lavender. Paw pads: lavender-pink.

LAVENDER SILVER TABBY: ground color, including lips and chin, a cold clear silver. Markings sound lavender. Nose leather: lavender or pink rimmed with lavender. Paw pads: lavender-pink.

FAWN TABBY: ground color, including lips and chin, pale ivory, markings dense fawn, affording good contrast with ground color. Nose leather and paw pads: pale fawn. Eye color: gold.

CAMEO TABBY: ground color off-white. Markings red. Nose leather and paw pads: rose. Eye color: gold.

BLUE SILVER, CREAM SILVER, and FAWN SILVER TABBIES: tabby pattern with colors and leathers same as for corresponding shaded colors. Eye

color: gold.

TORTOISESHELL: black mottled or patched with red and/or cream. Blaze on face is desirable. Eye color: gold.

BLUE-CREAM: blue mottled or patched with cream. Blaze on face is desirable. Eye color: gold.

CHOCOLATE (Chestnut) TORTOISESHELL: rich chestnut brown mottled or patched with red and/or cream. Blaze on face desirable. Eye color: gold.

CINNAMON TORTOISESHELL: cinnamon mottled or patched with red and/or cream. Blaze on face desirable. Eye color: gold.

LAVENDER-CREAM: lavender mottled or patched with cream. Blaze on face desirable. Eye color: gold.

FAWN-CREAM: fawn mottled or patched with cream. Blaze on face desirable. Eye color: gold.

CALICO: white with unbrindled patches of black and red. White predominant on underparts. Eye color: gold.

VAN CALICO: white cat with unbrindled patches of black and red confined to the extremities; head, tail, legs. One or two small patches of color on body allowable. Eye color: gold.

DILUTE CALICO: white with unbrindled patches of blue and cream. White predominant on underparts. Eye color: gold.

DILUTE VAN CALICO: white cat with unbrindled patches of blue and cream confined to the extremities; head, tail, legs. One or two small patches of color on body allowable. Eye color: gold.

BI-COLOR: solid color and white, tabby and white, tortoiseshell and white, etc. Eye color: as appropriate.

VAN BI-COLOR: solid color and white, tabby and white, tortoiseshell and white, etc., with color confined to the extremities; head, tail, and legs. One or two small patches on body allowable. Eye color: as appropriate.

FAWN-CREAM CALICO, LAVENDER-CREAM CALICO, and CINNAMONCREAM CALICO: as for CALICO above, with appropriate marking color. Eye color: gold.

FAWN-CREAM VAN CALICO, LAVENDER-CREAM VAN CALICO, and CINNAMON-CREAM

VAN CALICO: as for VAN CALICO above, with appropriate marking color. Eye color: gold.

ODRC (Other Devon Rex Colors): any other color or pattern. Cats with no more than a locket and/or button do not qualify for this class, such cats shall be judged in the color class of their basic color with no penalty for such locket and/or button. Examples: any color with one, two, three, or four white feet. Ticked tabbies. All point restricted colors such as seal point, chocolate point, blue point, lilac point, cream point, lynx points, cinnamon point, etc.
Devon Rex allowable outcross breeds: American Shorthair or British Shorthair for litters born before 5/1/98.

REX (GERMAN REX)

There are currently no CFA standards for this breed.

RUSSIAN BLUE

■ POINT SCORE

HEAD and NECK	20
BODY TYPE	20
EYE SHAPE	5
EARS	5
COAT	20
COLOR	20
EYE COLOR	10

GENERAL: the good show specimen has good physical condition, is firm in muscle tone, and alert.
HEAD: smooth, medium wedge, neither long and tapering nor short and massive. Muzzle is blunt, and part of the total wedge, without exaggerated pinch or whisker break. Top of skull long and flat in profile, gently descending to slightly above the eyes, and continuing at a slight downward angle in a straight line to the tip of the nose. No nose break or stop. Length of top-head should be greater than length of nose. The face is broad across the eyes due to wide eye-set and thick fur.
MUZZLE: smooth, flowing wedge without prominent whisker pads or whisker pinches.
EARS: rather large and wide at the base. Tips more pointed than rounded. The skin of the ears is thin and translucent, with little inside furnishing. The outside of the ear is scantily covered with short, very fine hair, with leather showing through. Set far apart, as much on the side as on the top of the head.
EYES: set wide apart. Aperture rounded in shape.
NECK: long and slender, but appear-

ing short due to thick fur and high placement of shoulder blades.
NOSE: medium in length.
CHIN: perpendicular with the end of the nose and with level under-chin. Neither receding nor excessively massive.
BODY: fine boned, long, firm, and muscular; lithe and graceful in outline and carriage without being tubular in appearance.
LEGS: long and fine boned.
PAWS: small, slightly rounded. Toes: five in front and four behind.
TAIL: long, but in proportion to the body. Tapering from a moderately thick base.
COAT: short, dense, fine, and plush. Double coat stands out from body due to density. It has a distinct soft and silky feel.

DISQUALIFY: kinked or abnormal tail. Locket or button. Incorrect number of toes. Any color other than blue.

RUSSIAN BLUE COLOR

COLOR: even bright blue throughout. Lighter shades of blue preferred. Guard hairs distinctly silver-tipped giving the cat a silvery sheen or lustrous appearance. A definite contrast should be noted between ground color and tipping. Free from tabby markings. Nose leather: slate grey. Paw pads: lavender pink or mauve. Eye color: vivid green.
Russian Blue allowable outcross breeds: none.

SCOTTISH FOLD

■ POINT SCORE

HEAD (55)		
	Ears	25
	Head shape, muzzle, neck, chin, profile	15
	Eyes	15
BODY (40)		
	Body structure of torso, legs and paws	10
	Tail	20
	Coat	10
COLOR (5)		
	Color of coat and eyes	5

GENERAL: the Scottish Fold cat occurred as a spontaneous mutation in farm cats in Scotland. The breed has been established by crosses to British Shorthair and domestic cats in Scotland and England. In America, the outcross is the American and British Shorthair. All bona fide Scottish Fold cats trace their pedigree to Susie, the first fold-ear cat discovered by the founders of the breed, William and Mary Ross.
HEAD: well rounded with a firm chin and jaw. Muzzle to have well rounded

whisker pads. Head should blend into a short neck. Prominent cheeks with a jowly appearance in males.

EYES: wide open with a sweet expression. Large, well rounded, and separated by a broad nose. Eye color to correspond with coat color. Blue-eyed and odd-eyed are allowed for white and white dominated coat patterns, i.e., all van patterns.

NOSE: nose to be short with a gentle curve. A brief stop is permitted but a definite nose break considered a fault. Profile is moderate in appearance.

EARS: fold forward and downward. Small, the smaller, tightly folded ear preferred over a loose fold and large ear. The ears should be set in a caplike fashion to expose a rounded cranium. Ear tips to be rounded.

BODY: medium, rounded, and even from shoulder to pelvic girdle. The cat should stand firm on a well padded body. There must be no hint of thickness or lack of mobility in the cat due to short, coarse legs. Toes to be neat and well rounded with five in front and four behind. Overall appearance is that of a well founded cat with medium bone; fault cats obviously lacking in type. Females may be slightly smaller.

TAIL: tail should be medium to long but in proportion to the body. Tail should be flexible and tapering. Longer, tapering tail preferred.

COAT (SHORTHAIR): dense, plush, medium-short, soft in texture, full of life. Standing out from body due to density; not flat or close-lying. Coat texture may vary due to color and/or region or seasonal changes.

COAT (LONGHAIR): medium to long hair length. Full coat on face and body desirable but short hair permissible on face and legs. Britches, tail plume, toe tufts, and ear furnishings should be clearly visible with a ruff being desirable. Seriously

PENALIZE: cottony coat, except in kittens.

DISQUALIFY: kinked tail. Tail that is foreshortened. Tail that is lacking in flexibility due to abnormally thick vertebrae. Splayed toes, incorrect number of toes. Any evidence of illness or poor health.

SCOTTISH FOLD COLORS

WHITE: pure glistening white. Nose leather and paw pads: pink. Eye color: deep blue or brilliant gold. Odd-eyed whites shall have one blue and one gold eye with equal color depth.

BLACK: dense, coal black, sound from roots to tip of fur. Free from any tinge of rust on tips or smoke undercoat. Nose leather: black. Paw pads: black or brown. Eye color: brilliant gold.

BLUE: blue, lighter shade preferred, one level tone from nose to tip of tail. Sound to roots. A sound darker shade is more acceptable than an unsound lighter shade. Nose leather and paw pads: blue. Eye color: brilliant gold.

RED: deep, rich, clear, brilliant red; without shading, markings, or ticking. Lips and chin the same color as coat. Nose leather and paw pads: brick red. Eye color: brilliant gold.

CREAM: one level shade of buff cream, without markings. Sound to the roots. Lighter shades preferred. Nose leather and paw pads: pink. Eye color: brilliant gold.

CHINCHILLA SILVER: undercoat pure white. Coat on back, flanks, head and tail sufficiently tipped with black to give the characteristic sparkling silver appearance. Legs may be slightly shaded with tipping. Chin, ear tufts, stomach, and chest, pure white. Rims of eyes, lips, and nose outlined with black. Nose leather: brick red. Paw pads: black. Eye color: green or blue-green.

SHADED SILVER: undercoat white with a mantle of black tipping shading down from sides, face, and tail from dark on the ridge to white on the chin, chest, stomach, and under the tail. Legs to be the same tone as the face. The general effect to be much darker than a chinchilla. Rims of eyes, lips, and nose outlined with black. Nose leather: brick red. Paw pads: black. Eye color: green or blue-green.

SHELL CAMEO (Red Chinchilla): undercoat white, the coat on the back, flanks, head, and tail to be sufficiently tipped with red to give the characteristic sparkling appearance. Face and legs may be very slightly shaded with tipping. Chin, ear tufts, stomach, and chest white. Nose leather and paw pads: rose. Eye color: brilliant gold.

SHADED CAMEO (Red Shaded): undercoat white with a mantle of red tipping shading down the sides, face, and tail from dark on the ridge to white on the chin, chest, stomach, and under the tail. Legs to be the same tone as face. The general effect to be much redder than the shell cameo. Nose leather, rims of eyes and paw pads: rose. Eye color: brilliant gold.

BLACK SMOKE: white undercoat, deeply tipped with black. Cat in repose appears black. In motion the white undercoat is clearly apparent. Points and mask black with narrow band of white at base of hairs next to skin which may be seen only when fur is parted. Nose leather and paw pads:

black. Eye color: brilliant gold.

BLUE SMOKE: white undercoat, deeply tipped with blue. Cat in repose appears blue. In motion the white undercoat is clearly apparent. Points and mask blue with narrow band of white at base of hairs which may be seen only when fur is parted. Nose leather and paw pads: blue. Eye color: brilliant gold.

CAMEO SMOKE (Red Smoke): white undercoat, deeply tipped with red. Cat in repose appears red. In motion the white undercoat is clearly apparent. Points and mask red with narrow band of white at base of hairs next to skin which may be seen only when fur is parted. Nose leather, rims of eyes and paw pads: rose. Eye color: brilliant gold.

CLASSIC TABBY PATTERN: markings dense, clearly defined, and broad. Legs evenly barred with bracelets coming up to meet the body markings. Tail evenly ringed. Several unbroken necklaces on neck and upper chest, the more the better. Frown marks on forehead form an intricate letter "M." Unbroken line runs back from outer corner of eye. Swirls on cheeks. Vertical lines over back of head extend to shoulder markings which are in the shape of a butterfly with both upper and lower wings distinctly outlined and marked with dots inside outline. Back markings consist of a vertical line down the spine from butterfly to tail with a vertical stripe paralleling it on each side, the three stripes well separated by stripes of the ground color. Large solid blotch on each side to be encircled by one or more unbroken rings. Side markings should be the same on both sides. Double vertical rows of buttons on chest and stomach.

MACKEREL TABBY PATTERN: markings dense, clearly defined, and all narrow pencillings. Legs evenly barred with narrow bracelets coming up to meet the body markings. Tail barred. Necklaces on neck and chest distinct, like so many chains. Head barred with an "M" on the forehead. Unbroken lines running back from the eyes. Lines running down the head to meet the shoulders. Spine lines run together to form a narrow saddle. Narrow pencillings run around body.

PATCHED TABBY PATTERN: a patched tabby (torbie) is an established silver, brown, or blue tabby with patches of red and/or cream.

SPOTTED TABBY PATTERN: markings on the body to be spotted. The spots can be round, oblong or rosette

shaped. Any of these are of equal merit but the spots, however shaped or placed, shall be distinct. Spots should not run together in a broken Mackerel pattern. A dorsal stripe runs the length of the body to the tip of the tail. The stripe is ideally composed of spots. The markings on the face and forehead shall be typically tabby markings. Underside of the body to have "vest buttons." Legs and tail are barred.

SILVER TABBY: ground color, including lips and chin, pale clear silver. Markings dense black. Nose leather: brick red. paw pads: black. Eye color: green or hazel.

BLUE SILVER TABBY (Pewter Tabby): ground color, including lips and chin, pale, clear, bluish silver. Markings sound blue. Nose leather: blue or old rose trimmed with blue. Paw pads: blue.

BLUE SILVER (Pewter): undercoat white with a mantle of blue tipping shading down from sides, face and tail from dark on the ridge to white on the chin, chest, underside and under the tail. Legs to be the same tone as the face. Rims of eyes, lips and nose: outlined with blue. Nose leather: blue or old rose trimmed with blue. Paw pads: blue.

RED TABBY: ground color red. Markings deep, rich red. Lips and chin red. Nose leather and paw pads: brick red. Eye color: brilliant gold.

BROWN TABBY: ground color brilliant coppery brown. Markings dense black. Lips and chin the same shade as the rings around the eyes. Back of leg black from paw to heel. Nose leather: brick red. paw pads: black or brown. Eye color: brilliant gold.

BLUE TABBY: ground color. including lips and chin, pale bluish ivory. Markings a very deep blue affording a good contrast with ground color. Warm fawn overtones or patina over the whole. Nose leather: old rose. paw pads: rose. Eye color: brilliant gold.

CREAM TABBY: ground color, including lips and chin, very pale cream. Marking of buff or cream sufficiently darker than the ground color to afford good contrast but remaining within the dilute color range. Nose leather and paw pads: pink. Eye color: brilliant gold.

CAMEO TABBY: ground color off-white. Markings red. Nose leather and paw pads: rose. Eye color: brilliant gold.

TORTOISESHELL: black with unbrindled patches of red and cream.

Patches clearly defined and well broken on both body and extremities. Blaze of red or cream on face is desirable. Eye color: brilliant copper.

CALICO: white with unbrindled patches of black and red. White predominant on underparts. Eye color: brilliant gold.

DILUTE CALICO: white with unbrindled patches of blue and cream. White predominant on underparts. Eye color: brilliant gold.

BLUE-CREAM: blue with patches of solid cream. Patches clearly defined and well broken on both body and extremities. Eye color: brilliant gold.

BI-COLOR: white with unbrindled patches of black, white with unbrindled patches of blue, white with unbrindled patches of red, or white with unbrindled patches of cream. Eye color: brilliant gold.

OSFC (Other Scottish Fold Colors): any other color or pattern with the exception of those showing evidence of hybridization resulting in the colors chocolate, lavender, the Himalayan pattern, or these combinations with white. Eye color: appropriate to the dominant color of the cat.
Scottish Fold allowable outcross Breeds: British Shorthair, American Shorthair.

SIAMESE

■ POINT SCORE
HEAD (20)

Long, flat profile	6
Wedge, fine muzzle, size	5
Ears	4
Chin	3
Width between eyes	2

EYES (10)

Shape, size, slant, placement	10

BODY (30)

Structure and size, including neck	12
Muscle tone	10
Legs and feet	5
Tail	3

COAT 10
COLOR (30)

Body color	10
Point color (matching points of dense color,	10
proper foot pads and nose leather)	
Eye color	10

GENERAL: the ideal Siamese is a medium sized, svelte, refined cat with long tapering lines, very lithe but muscular. Males may be proportionately larger.
HEAD: long tapering wedge. Medium in size in good proportion to body. The total wedge starts at the nose and flares out in straight lines to the tips of the ears forming a triangle, with no break at the whiskers. No less than the width of an eye between the eyes. When the whiskers are smoothed back, the underlying bone structure is apparent. Allowance must be made for jowls in the stud cat.
SKULL: flat. In profile, a long straight line is seen from the top of the head to the tip of the nose. No bulge over eyes. No dip in nose.
EARS: strikingly large, pointed, wide at base; continuing the lines of the wedge.
EYES: almond shaped. Medium size. Neither protruding nor recessed. Slanted towards the nose in harmony with lines of wedge and ears. Uncrossed.
NOSE: long and straight. A continuation of the forehead with no break.
MUZZLE: fine, wedge-shaped.
CHIN and JAW: medium size. Tip of chin lines up with tip of nose in the same vertical plane. Neither receding nor excessively massive.
BODY: medium size. Graceful, long, and svelte. A distinctive combination of fine bones and firm muscles. Shoulders and hips continue same sleek lines of tubular body. Hips never wider than shoulders. Abdomen tight.
NECK: long and slender.
LEGS: long and slim. Hind legs higher than front. In good proportion to body.
PAWS: dainty, small, and oval. Toes: five in front and four behind.
TAIL: long, thin, tapering to a fine point.
COAT: short, fine textured, glossy. Lying close to body.
CONDITION: excellent physical condition. Eyes clear. Muscular, strong, and lithe. Neither flabby nor boney. Not fat.

COLOR: Body: even, with subtle shading when allowed. Allowance should be made for darker color in older cats as Siamese generally darken with age, but there must be definite contrast between body color and points. Points: mask, ears, legs, feet, tail dense and clearly defined. All of the same shade. Mask covers entire face including whisker pads and is connected to ears by tracings. Mask should not extend over the top of the head. No ticking or white hairs in points.

PENALIZE: improper (i.e., off-color or spotted) nose leather or paw pads. Soft or mushy body.

DISQUALIFY: any evidence of illness or poor health. Weak hind legs. Mouth breathing due to nasal obstruction or poor occlusion. Emaciation. Visible kink. Eyes other than blue. White toes and/or feet. Incorrect number of toes. Malocclusion resulting in either undershot or overshot chin.

SIAMESE COLORS

SEAL POINT: body even pale fawn to cream, warm in tone, shading gradually into lighter color on the stomach and chest. Points deep seal brown. Nose leather and paw pads: same color as points. Eye color: deep vivid blue.

CHOCOLATE POINT: body ivory with no shading. Points milk-chocolate color, warm in tone. Nose leather and paw pads: cinnamon-pink. Eye color: deep vivid blue.

BLUE POINT: body bluish white, cold in tone, shading gradually to white on stomach and chest. Points deep blue. Nose leather and paw pads: slate colored. Eye color: deep vivid blue.

LILAC POINT: body glacial white with no shading. Points frosty grey with pinkish tone. Nose leather and paw pads: lavender-pink. Eye color: deep vivid blue.
Siamese allowable outcross breeds: none.

SINGAPURA

■ POINT SCORE
HEAD (25)

Ears	10
Head shape	4
Width at eye	4
Muzzle shape	4
Profile	3

EYES (10)

Size and placement	6
Shape	3
Color	1

BODY, LEGS and TAIL (20)

Neck	3
Proportion	10
Legs and feet	5
Tail	2

COAT 15
COLOR 15
MARKINGS 15

GENERAL: the appearance of an alert healthy small to medium sized muscular bodied cat with noticeably large eyes and ears. Cat to have the illusion of refined delicate coloring.

HEAD: skull rounded with rounded width at the outer eye narrowing to a definite whisker break and a medium-short, broad muzzle with a blunt nose. In profile, a rounded skull with a very slight stop well below eye level. Straight line nose to chin. Chin well developed.
EARS: large, slightly pointed, wide open at the base, and possessing a deep cup. Medium set. Outer lines of the ear to extend upward at an angle slightly wide of parallel. Small ears a serious fault.
EYES: large, almond shaped, held wide open but showing slant. Neither protruding nor recessed. Eyes set not less than an eye width apart. Color hazel, green or yellow with no other color permitted. Brilliance preferred. Small eyes a serious fault.
BODY: small to medium overall size cat. Moderately stocky and muscular body, legs and floor to form a square. Mid-section not tucked but firm.
NECK: short and thick.
LEGS and FEET: legs heavy and muscled at the body tapering to small short oval feet.
TAIL: length to be short of the shoulder when laid along the torso. Tending towards slender but not whippy. Blunt tip.
COAT: fine, very short, lying very close to the body. Allowance for longer coat in kittens. Springy coat a fault.
MARKINGS: each hair to have at least two bands of dark ticking separated by light bands. Light next to skin and a dark tip. Dark tail tip with color extending back toward the body on the upper side. Cat to show some barring on inner front legs and back knee only. Allowance to be made for undeveloped ticking in kittens. Spine line NOT a fault.

PENALIZE: dark coat coloring next to skin, definite grey tones, barring on outer front legs, necklaces, non-visible tail faults.

DISQUALIFY: white spotting, barring on tail, top of the head unticked, unbroken necklaces or leg bracelets. Very small eyes or ears. Visible tail faults. Blue eyes.

SINGAPURA COLOR
COLOR: Sepia agouti only, color to be dark brown ticking on a warm old ivory ground color. Muzzle, chin, chest and stomach to be the color of unbleached muslin. Nose leather: pale to dark salmon. Eyeliner, lips, whisker apertures, hair between the toes, and nose outline to be dark brown. Foot pads a rosy brown. Salmon tones to the ears and nose bridge NOT a fault. Warm light shades preferred.
Singapura allowable outcross breeds: none.

SNOWSHOE

There are currently no CFA standards for this breed.

SOMALI

■ POINT SCORE

HEAD (25)

Skull	6
Muzzle	6
Ears	7
Eye shape	6

BODY (25)

Torso	10
Legs and feet	10
Tail	5

COAT (20)

Texture	10
Length	10

COLOR (30)

Color	15
Ticking	10
Eye color	5

GENERAL: the overall impression of the Somali is that of a well proportioned medium to large cat, firm muscular development, lithe, showing an alert, lively interest in all surroundings, with an even disposition and easy to handle. The cat is to give the appearance of activity, sound health, and general vigor.

HEAD: a modified, slightly rounded wedge without flat planes; the brow, cheek, and profile lines all showing a gentle contour. A slight rise from the bridge of the nose to the forehead, which should be of good size with width between the ears flowing into the arched neck without a break.

MUZZLE: shall follow gentle contours in conformity with the skull, as viewed from the front profile. Chin shall be full, neither undershot nor overshot, having a rounded appearance. The muzzle shall not be sharply pointed and there shall be no evidence of snippiness, foxiness, or whisker pinch. Allowance to be made for jowls in older males.

EARS: large, alert, moderately pointed, broad, and cupped at the base. Ear set on a line towards the rear of the skull. The inner ear shall have horizontal tufts that reach nearly to the other side of the ear; tufts desirable.

EYES: almond shaped, large, brilliant, and expressive. Skull aperture neither round nor oriental. Eyes accented by dark lidskin encircled by light colored area. Above each a short dark vertical pencil stroke with a dark pencil line continuing from the upper lid towards the ear.

BODY: torso medium long, lithe, and graceful, showing well-developed muscular strength. Rib cage is rounded; back is slightly arched giving the appearance of a cat about to spring; flank level with no tuck up. Conformation strikes a medium between the extremes of cobby and svelte lengthy types.

LEGS and FEET: legs in proportion to torso; feet oval and compact. When standing, the Somali gives the impression of being nimble and quick. Toes: five in front and four in back.

TAIL: having a full brush, thick at the base, and slightly tapering. Length in balance with torso.

COAT: texture very soft to the touch, extremely fine and double coated. The more dense the coat, the better. Length: a medium length coat, except over shoulders, where a slightly shorter length is permitted. Preference is to be given to a cat with ruff and breeches, giving a full-coated appearance to the cat.

PENALIZE: color faults – cold grey or sandy tone to coat color; mottling or speckling on unticked areas. Pattern faults – necklaces, leg bars, tabby stripes, or bars on body; lack of desired markings on head and tail. Black roots on body.

DISQUALIFY: white locket or groin spot or white anywhere on body other than on the upper throat, chin, or nostrils. Any skeletal abnormality. Wrong color paw pads or nose leather. Unbroken necklace. Incorrect number of toes. Kinks in tail.

SOMALI COLORS

Coat Color: warm and glowing. Ticking: distinct and even, with dark colored bands contrasting with lighter colored bands on the hair shafts. Undercoat color clear and bright to the skin. Deeper color shades desired, however, intensity of ticking not to be sacrificed for depth of color. Darker shading along spine continuing through tip of tail. Darker shading up the hocks, also shading allowed at the point of the elbow. Preference given to cats UNMARKED on the undersides, chest, and legs; tail without rings. Facial Markings: dark lines extending from eyes and brows, cheekbone shading, dots and shading on whisker pads are all desirable enhancements. Eyes accentuated by fine dark line, encircled by light colored area. Eye color: gold or green, the more richness and depth of color the better.

RUDDY: ground color burnt-sienna, ticked with various shades of darker brown or black; the extreme outer tip to be the darkest. Tail tipped with black. The underside and inside of legs to be a tint to harmonize with the ground color. Nose leather: tile red. Paw pads: black or dark brown, with black between toes, extending slightly beyond the paws.

RED: ground color rich, warm glowing red, ticked with chocolate-brown, the extreme outer tip to be darkest. Tail tipped with chocolate-brown. The underside and inside of legs to be a tint to harmonize with the ground color. Nose leather: rosy pink. Paw pads: pink, with chocolate-brown between toes, extending slightly beyond the paws.

BLUE: ground color ivory-oatmeal, ticked with various shades of slate blue, the extreme outer tip to be the darkest. Tail tipped with slate blue. The underside and inside of legs to be a warm blush-beige/apricot to harmonize with the ground color. Nose leather: old rose. Paw pads: mauve, with slate blue between toes, extending slightly beyond the paws.

FAWN: ground color warm rose-beige, ticked with light cocoa-brown, the extreme outer tip to be the darkest. Tail tipped with light cocoa-brown. The underside and inside of legs to be a tint to harmonize with the ground color. Nose leather: salmon. Paw Pads: pink with light cocoa-brown between the toes, extending slightly beyond the paws.

(PLEASE NOTE: the Somali is extremely slow in showing mature ticking and allowances should be made for kittens and young cats.)

Somali allowable outcross breeds: Abyssinian.

SPHYNX

There are currently no CFA standards for this breed.

TIFFANY

There are currently no CFA standards for this breed.

TONKINESE

■ POINT SCORE

HEAD (25)

Profile	8
Muzzle	6
Ears	6
Eye shape and set	5

BODY (30)

Torso	15
Legs and feet	5
Tail	5
Muscle tone	5

COAT | 10

COLOR (35)

Body color	15
Point color	10
Eye color	10

GENERAL: the Tonkinese cat was originally the result of a Siamese to Burmese breeding. The ideal Tonkinese is intermediate in type, being neither cobby nor svelte. The Tonkinese should give the overall impression of an alert, active cat with good muscular development. The cat should be surprisingly heavy. While the breed is to be considered medium in size, balance and proportion are of greater importance.

HEAD AND MUZZLE: the head is a modified wedge somewhat longer than it is wide, with high gently planed cheekbones. The muzzle is blunt, as long as it is wide. There is a slight whisker break, gently curved, following the lines of the wedge. There is a slight stop at eye level. In profile the tip of the chin lines with the tip of the nose in the same vertical plane. There is a gentle rise from the tip of the nose to the stop. There is a gentle contour with a slight rise from the nose stop to the forehead. There is a slight convex curve to the forehead.

EARS: alert, medium in size. Oval tips, broad at the base. Ears set as much on the sides of the head as on the top. Hair on the ears very short and close-lying. Leather may show through.

EYES: open almond shape. Slanted along the cheekbones toward the outer edge of the ear. Eyes are proportionate in size to the face.

EYE COLOR: aqua. A definitive characteristic of the Tonkinese breed, best seen in natural light. Depth, clarity, and brilliance of color preferred.

BODY: torso medium in length, demonstrating well-developed muscular strength without coarseness. The Tonkinese conformation strikes a midpoint between the extremes of long, svelte body types and cobby, compact body types. Balance and proportion are more important than size alone. The abdomen should be taut, well-muscled, and firm.

LEGS and FEET: fairly slim, proportionate in length and bone to the body. Hind legs slightly longer than front. Paws more oval than round. Trim. Toes: five in front and four behind.

TAIL: proportionate in length to body. Tapering.

COAT: medium short in length, close-lying, fine, soft and silky, with a lustrous sheen.

BODY COLOR: the mature specimen should be a rich, even, unmarked color, shading almost imperceptibly to a slightly lighter hue on the underparts. Allowance to be made for lighter body color in young cats. With the dilute colors in particular, development of full body color may take up to 16 months. Cats do darken with age, but there must be a distinct contrast between body color and points.

POINT COLOR: mask, ears, feet, and tail all densely marked, but merging gently into body color. Except in kittens, mask and ears should be connected by tracings. Allowance to be made for slight barring in young cats.

PENALIZE: palpable tail fault. Extreme ranginess or cobbiness. Definite nose break. Round eyes.

DISQUALIFY: yellow eyes. White locket or button. Visible tail kink. Crossed eyes.

TONKINESE COLORS

NATURAL MINK: Body: medium brown. Ruddy highlights acceptable. Points: dark brown. Nose leather: dark brown (corresponding to the intensity of the point color). Paw pads: medium to dark brown (may have a rosy undertone).

CHAMPAGNE MINK: Body: buff-cream. Points: medium brown. Nose leather: cinnamon-brown (corresponding to the intensity of the point color). Paw pads: cinnamon-pink to cinnamon-brown.

BLUE MINK: Body: soft, blue-gray with warm overtones. Points: slate blue, distinctly darker than the body color. Nose leather: blue-gray (corresponding to the intensity of the point color). Paw pads: blue-gray (may have a rosy undertone).

PLATINUM MINK: Body: pale, silvery gray with warm overtones. Not white or cream. Points: frosty gray, distinctly darker than the body color. Nose leather: lavender-pink to lavender-gray. Paw pads: lavender-pink.

AOV COLOR STANDARDS

General description - Solid Colors (AOV): body color in solid AOVs may be a slightly lighter shade of the point color, with very little contrast with points. There will be more contrast between points and body color for the Champagne and Platinum solid than for the Natural and Blue solids. Eye color: green to gold.
Natural Solid (AOV) Body: sable brown. Points: dark brown. Nose leather: dark brown (corresponding to the intensity of the point color). Paw pads: medium to dark brown (may have a rosy undertone).
Champagne Solid (AOV): Body: golden tan to light coffeebrown. Points: medium brown. Nose leather: cinnamon brown (corresponding to the intensity of the point color). Paw pads: cinnamon-pink to cinnamon-brown.
Blue Solid (AOV): Body: slate blue with warm overtones. Points: slate blue. Nose leather: blue-gray (corresponding to the intensity of the point color). Paw pads: blue-gray (may have a rosy undertone).

Platinum Solid (AOV): Body: dove gray. Points: frosty gray. Nose leather: lavender-pink to lavender-gray. Paw pads: lavender-pink.
General description - Pointed Colors (AOV): Body color in pointed AOVs should be off-white, any shading relative to the point color; overall body color should be in marked contrast to the points. Eye color: blue.
Natural Point (AOV): Body: fawn to cream. Points: dark brown. Nose leather: dark brown (corresponding to the intensity of the point color). Paw pads: medium to dark brown (may have a rosy undertone).
Champagne Point (AOV): Body: ivory with buff-tan shading. Points: medium brown. Nose leather: cinnamon-brown (corresponding to the intensity of the point color). Paw pads: cinnamon-pink to cinnamon-brown.
Blue Point (AOV): Body: off-white with warm gray shading. Points: slate blue. Nose leather: blue-gray (corresponding to the intensity of the point color). Paw pads: blue-gray (may have a rosy undertone).
Platinum Point (AOV): Body: pearly white. Points: frosty-gray. Nose leather: lavender-pink to lavender-gray (corresponding to the intensity of the point color). Paw pads: lavender-pink.
Tonkinese allowable outcross breeds: none.

TURKISH ANGORA

■ POINT SCORE
HEAD (55)

Head shape & profile	15
Ears	15
Size	5
Shape & placement	10
Eye size, shape and placement	10
BODY (35)	
Size and Boning	10
Torso, including neck	15
Legs and Tail	5
Muscle Tone	5
BALANCE	10
COAT	10
COLOR	5

GENERAL: the ideal Turkish Angora is a balanced, graceful cat with a fine, silky coat that shimmers with every movement, in contrast to the firm, long muscular body beneath it.
HEAD: Size: small to medium, in balance with the length of the body and extremities. Shape: a medium long, smooth wedge. Allowance is to be made for jowls. Profile: two planes formed by a flat top head and the line of the nose meeting at an angle slightly above the eyes. NO BREAK.
Muzzle: a continuation of the smooth lines of the wedge with neither pronounced whisker pad nor pinch.

EARS: large, wide at base, pointed and tuffed. Set closely together, high on the head, vertical and erect.
EYES: large, almond-shaped, slanting slightly upward with open expression.
EYE COLOR: eye color can be any shade of green, gold, green-gold, copper, blue, or odd eyed. There is no relationship between eye color and coat color. Uniformity and depth of eye-color should be taken into consideration as a part of the overall head score, with deeper, richer color preferred.
NOSE: medium in length.
NECK: slim, graceful and rather long.
CHIN: firm, gently rounded. Tip in profile to form perpendicular line with nose.
BODY: medium size, however, overall balance, grace and fineness of bone are more important than actual size. Males may be slightly larger than females. Torso long and slender. Shoulders the same width as hips. Rump slightly higher than shoulders. Finely boned with firm muscularity.
LEGS: long. Hind legs longer than front.
PAWS: small, round and dainty. Tufts between toes preferable.
TAIL: long and tapering from a wide base to a narrow end, with a full brush.
COAT: single coated. Length of body coat varies, but tail and ruff should be long, full, finely textured and have a silk-like sheen. "Britches" should be apparent on the hind legs.
BALANCE: proportionate in all physical aspects with a graceful, lithe appearance.

PENALIZE: obviously oversized, coarse appearance.

DISQUALIFY: cobby body type. Kinked or abnormal tail. Crossed eyes.

TURKISH ANGORA COLORS
WHITE: pure white, no other coloring. Nose leather and paw pads: pink.

BLACK: dense coal black, sound from roots to tip of fur. Free from any tinge of rust on tips or smoke undercoat. Nose leather: black. Paw pads: black or brown.

BLUE: blue, lighter shade preferred. One level tone from nose to tip of tail. Sound to the roots. A sound darker shade is more acceptable than an unsound lighter shade. Nose leather and paw pads: blue.

CREAM: one level shade of buff cream without markings. Sound to the roots. Lighter shades preferred. Nose leather and paw pads: pink.

RED: deep, rich, clear, brilliant red; without shading, markings, or ticking. Lips and chin the same color as coat. Nose leather and paw pads: brick red.

BLACK SMOKE: white undercoat, deeply tipped with black. Cat in repose appears black. In motion, the white undercoat is clearly apparent. Points and mask black with narrow band of white at base of hairs next to skin which may be seen only when fur is parted. Nose leather and paw pads: black.

BLUE SMOKE: white undercoat, deeply tipped with blue. Cat in repose appears blue. In motion the white undercoat is clearly apparent. Points and mask blue with narrow band of white at base of hairs next to skin which may be seen only when fur is parted. Nose leather and paw pads: blue.

CLASSIC TABBY PATTERN: markings dense, clearly defined, and broad. Legs evenly barred with bracelets coming up to meet the body markings. Tail evenly ringed. Several unbroken necklaces on neck and upper chest, the more the better. Frown marks on forehead form an intricate letter "M." Unbroken line runs back from outer corner of eye. Swirls on cheeks. Vertical lines over back of head extend to shoulder markings which are in the shape of a butterfly with both upper and lower wings distinctly outlined and marked with dots inside outline. Back markings consist of a vertical line down the spine from butterfly to tail with a vertical stripe paralleling it on each side, the three stripes well separated by stripes of the ground color. Large solid blotch on each side to be encircled by one or more unbroken rings. Side markings should be the same on both sides. Double vertical rows of buttons on chest and stomach.

MACKEREL TABBY PATTERN: markings dense, clearly defined, and all narrow pencillings. Legs evenly barred with narrow bracelets coming up to meet the body markings. Tail barred. Necklaces on neck and chest distinct, like so many chains. Head barred with an "M". Unbroken lines running back from the eyes. Lines running down the head to meet the shoulders. Spine lines run together to form a narrow saddle. Narrow pencillings run around body. Patched Tabby Pattern: a patched tabby (torbie) is an established silver, brown or blue tabby with patches of red and/or cream.

SILVER TABBY (classic, mackerel): ground color, including lips and chin, pale clear silver. Markings dense black. Nose leather: brick red. Paw pads: black.

RED TABBY (classic, mackerel): ground color red. Markings deep rich red. Lips and chin red. Nose leather and paw pads: brick red.

BROWN TABBY (classic, mackerel): ground color brilliant coppery brown. Markings dense black. Lips and chin the same shade as the rings around the eyes. Back of leg black from paw to heel. Nose leather: brick red. Paw pads: black or brown.

BLUE TABBY (classic, mackerel): ground color, including lips and chin, pale bluish ivory. Markings a very deep blue affording a good contrast with ground color. Warm fawn overtones or patina over the whole. Nose leather: old rose. Paw pads: rose.

CREAM TABBY (classic, mackerel): ground color, including lips and chin, very pale cream. Markings of buff or cream sufficiently darker than the ground color to afford good contrast but remaining within the dilute color range. Nose leather and paw pads: pink.

TORTOISESHELL: black with unbrindled patches of red and cream. Patches clearly defined and well broken on both body and extremities. Blaze of red or cream on face is desirable.

CALICO: white with unbrindled patches of black and red. White predominant on underparts.

DILUTE CALICO: white with unbrindled patches of blue and cream. White predominant on underparts.

BLUE-CREAM: blue with patches of solid cream. Patches clearly defined and well broken on both body and extremities.

BI-COLOR: black and white, blue and white, red and white, or cream and white. White feet, legs, undersides, chest, and muzzle. Inverted "V" blaze on face desirable. White under tail and white collar allowable.

OTAC (Other Turkish Angora Colors): any other color or pattern with the exception of those showing hybridization resulting in the colors chocolate, lavender, the Himalayan pattern, or these combinations with white.
Turkish Angora allowable outcross breeds: none.

TURKISH VAN

■ POINT SCORE

HEAD (30)

Shape (boning, chin, nose, cheekbones, profile)	18
Ears (shape, placement and size)	7
Eyes (shape, placement and size)	5

BODY (35)

Type (boning, muscle, length, size)	20
Legs and feet	5
Tail	10
COAT	15
COLOR and PATTERN	20

GENERAL: The Turkish Van is a natural breed from the rugged, remote and climatically varied region of the Middle East. The breed is known for its unique, distinctive pattern...the term "van" has been adopted by a variety of breeds to describe white cats with colored head and tail markings. The Turkish Van is a solidly-built, semi-longhaired cat with great breadth to the chest. The strength and power of the cat is evidenced in its substantial body and legs. This breed takes a full 3 to 5 years to reach full maturity and development, therefore allowances must be made for age and sex. Despite age and sex, as adults, individuals should convey an overall impression of a well-balanced and well-proportioned appearance in which no feature is exaggerated to foster weakness or extremes. Turkish Vans are very intelligent and alert cats, and as such feel more secure, and handle better with all four feet on a solid surface.
HEAD: Substantially broad wedge, with gentle contours and a medium length nose to harmonize with the large muscular body, ears are not to be included in the wedge. Prominent cheekbones. In profile, the nose has a slight dip below eye level marked by a change in the direction the hair lays. Allowances must be made for jowling in the males. Firm chin in a straight line with the nose and upper lip; rounded muzzle.
EARS: Moderately large to large, set fairly high and well apart; the inside edge of the ear is slightly angled to the outside with the outside edge fairly straight but not necessarily in line with the side of the face; wide at the base. Tips are slightly rounded. Insides should be well feathered.
EYES: Moderately large, a rounded aperture slightly drawn out at the corners, set at a slant, equidistant from the outside base of the ear to the tip of the nose. Eyes should be clear, alert and expressive.
BODY: moderately long, sturdy, broad, muscular and deep-chested. Mature males should exhibit marked muscular development in the neck

and shoulders. The shoulders should be at least as broad as the head, and flow into the well-rounded ribcage and then into a muscular hip and pelvic area. Turkish Van males are substantially larger than females and exhibit much greater development.
LEGS AND FEET: Moderately long, muscular legs. They are set wide apart and taper to rounded moderately large feet. Legs and feet should be in proportion to the body. Toes, five in front, four behind.
TAIL: Long, but in proportion to the body, with a brush appearance. Tail hair length is keeping with the semi-long coat length.
COAT: Semi-long with a cashmere-like texture; soft to the roots with no trace of undercoat. Due to the extremes in climate of their native region, the breed carries two distinctive coat lengths and allowances must be made for the seasonal coat. The summer coat is short, conveying the appearance of a shorthair; the winter coat is substantially longer and thicker. There is feathering on the ears, legs, feet and belly. Facial fur is short. A frontal neck ruff and full brush tail become more pronounced with age. The above description is that of an adult, allowances must be made for short coats and tail hair on kittens and young adults.

COLOR and PATTERN: Van-pattern only on glistening chalk-white body with colored markings confined to the head and tail desirable. One or more random markings, up to color on 20% of the entire body, are permissible. Random markings should not be of a size or number to detract from the van pattern, making a specimen appear bi-color. A blaze (a white streak up the nose) to at least between the front edge of the ears is desirable.

PENALIZE: any evidence toward extremes (i.e. short cobbiness or svelte, fine-boning); flat profile.

DISQUALIFY: total absence of color on the head or tail; definite nose break; genetic/skeletal defects such as flattened ribcage, kinked or abnormal tail, incorrect number of toes, crossed eyes.

TURKISH VAN COLORS

Eye color on all coat colors: amber, blue and odd-eyed. Eye color may fade with age.
Nose leather on all coat colors: pink. Paw pads on all coat colors: pink is preferable but color spot(s) on paw pads acceptable due to the two colors in the pattern.
Solid and White Colors

RED: ranging from warm red to deep auburn, but should be one level shade, sound to the roots.
Cream: One level shade of buff cream, sound to the roots.
BLACK: dense coal black, sound to the roots. Free of any tinge of rust on tips or smoke undercoat.
BLUE: one level tone of blue, sound to the roots.

TABBY AND WHITE COLORS
Tabby markings are dense and clearly defined. How much of the tabby marking is seen is highly dependent on the size and placement of the head and body spots. A spot may be of a size that only ground color or only the tabby stripe is seen, thus there may not be enough color to determine whether the markings are classic or mackerel.
RED TABBY: ground color creamy red. Tabby markings range from warm red to deep auburn.
CREAM TABBY: ground color very pale cream. Tabby markings of buff cream sufficiently darker than the ground color to afford good contrast but remaining within the dilute range.
Brown tabby: ground color creamy beige. Tabby markings dense black.
Blue tabby: ground color pale bluish ivory. Tabby markings a deep blue affording a good contrast with ground color. Warm fawn or patina over the colored portions.

PARTI-COLOR AND WHITE COLORS
Tortoiseshell: black and red patches with tabby markings allowed in the red portion.
Dilute Tortoiseshell: blue and cream patches with tabby markings allowed in the cream portion.
BROWN PATCHED TABBY (torbie): brown tabby description with patches of red or red tabby.
BLUE PATCHED TABBY (dilute torbie): blue tabby description with patches of cream or cream tabby.

*Note: It is characteristic of the Turkish Van breed to carry tabby markings in the red/cream portions of the tortoiseshell colors.

OTVC (Other Turkish Van Colors): van pattern only – any other color and white (silver tabby, smokes, etc.) with the exception of those showing evidence of hybridization resulting from the Himalayan pattern (point restricted) and colors (chocolate, lilac, etc.). Turkish Van allowable outcross breeds: none.

EUROPEAN BURMESE

See Burmese

LIVING WITH A CAT

ANANTOMY

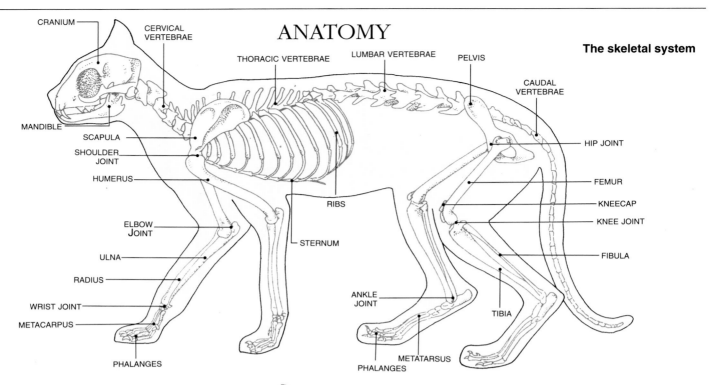

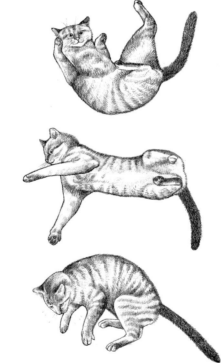

The skeletal system

CRANIUM
CERVICAL VERTEBRAE
THORACIC VERTEBRAE
LUMBAR VERTEBRAE
PELVIS
CAUDAL VERTEBRAE
MANDIBLE
SCAPULA
SHOULDER JOINT
HUMERUS
HIP JOINT
ELBOW JOINT
FEMUR
KNEECAP
KNEE JOINT
RIBS
ULNA
STERNUM
RADIUS
FIBULA
WRIST JOINT
METACARPUS
ANKLE JOINT
TIBIA
PHALANGES
METATARSUS
PHALANGES

Graceful and lithe, thoughtful and enigmatic, harmonious in movement and elegant in demeanor, the cat has always been considered one of nature's masterpieces. And yet, it is a common enough animal and not particularly impressive in size. On the average, adult domestic cats rarely reach more than 16 to 20 inches in body length with a tail extending another 12 to 14 inches and a total weight of 5½ to 15 pounds. Its physical structure is that of a perfect 'living machine' capable of the incredible gymnastics that have always amazed, enchanted and, at times, even frightened some and aroused suspicion among others of its human companions. Man admires the cat as a prodigy of nature but, at times, has seen it as a suspect and quasi-demonic creature. Probably originating in North Africa and becoming part of man's everyday life during early times in Ancient Egypt, the cat is now found throughout the world. There are many breeds with substantial differences in their overall build and head shape between two broad categories of domestic and wild cats; the smallest wild cat is the Dark Spotted Cat, originally from India, weighing only 3 pounds. There are the 'cobby' breeds with their solid physiques, broad shoulders and flanks, rounded heads and short, thick legs; the 'muscular' breeds with legs of medium length, somewhat rounded heads and their shoulders and flanks of medium width; and, finally, the elegant 'slender' breeds with their long thin legs, tubular bodies, triangular shaped heads, and narrow shoulders and flanks.

An extraordinary coordination of movements & great muscular vigor allow the cat to change its position in mid-air. This spectacular ability, which it possesses

almost alone in the animal kingdom, permits it always to fall on its feet. By arching its back, as only the cat can do, it cushions the force of impact with the ground.

■ The skeletal system

The skeleton of the cat is designed for suppleness and agility rather than strength and consists of 245 light and fairly delicate bones. The long, highly flexible vertebral column has 30 vertebrae (7 cervical, 13 thoracic, 7 lumbar and 3 sacral), with a variable number in the long tail (from 14 to 28 caudal vertebrae, except for the tailless Manx Cat and Japanese Bobtail with its curved, shortened bobtail. The cat's inter vertebral joints are less rigid than in other mammals and it is this, together with their rudimentary clavicle, which allows the cat to pass through very narrow openings and to arch its back in the characteristic manner for which it is well known. The thoracic cavity is composed of 13 pairs of ribs; the pelvis is narrow and elongated. The head is relatively small; the neck, is either generally long and supple allowing the head to turn backwards through 180 degrees, or it is short, and set close on powerful, well knit shoulders which compliment a cobby, muscular body.

■ The muscular system

The slender, simple, but strong muscular system allows the cat to run at remarkable speeds, to display tremendous agility in jumping, and utilize lightning reflexes when pouncing on its prey. This exceptional agility, allied to a sure sense of balance, allows the cat to twist in mid-air and always land on its feet. This ability and its overall lightness insure that it generally emerges unscathed even when it falls from a considerable height (as much as 65 feet and more) which, for other animals, would be fatal; during any fall, the paws extend to the front to help absorb the shock of landing. Paradoxically, it is more dangerous for a cat to fall short distances since this does not give it time to prepare for the impact with the ground. Its weak point, which is often struck, is the nose, since when falling, the cat cannot resist the temptation to look forward, and even when descending from a tree, it always does so head (and nose) first. The musculature of the jaws and neck is also strong allowing the cat to seize and tear apart prey of considerable size and strength.

■ The limbs

A cat's step is sure and silent; the paws are compact which gives elegance to its gait. The longer back legs provide the major thrust for *running* and for making great leaping bounds while allowing the forepaws to seize its prey. The cat is digitigrade; that is, it runs on its toes with light, delicate, steps. Our fingertips are the human equivalent of the cat's paws; they conceal the most deadly weapons...the sharp, cutting, retractile claws that the cat (unsheathed only when while hunting or fighting) uses to strike or intimidate its adversary or for self protection. The claws are also necessary for climbing trees or other objects at which the cat is expert, especially going up. It is not, however, as skillful in the descent which it always tackles head first. To keep its claws in perfect condition, the cat sharpens them by scratching on rough surfaces such tree bark.

■ The respiratory system

The habits of great hunters are still recognizable in the cat. Even its breathing is quiet, and almost imperceptible. The normal number of respirations per minute for the cat is 30, com-

pared to 11 to 12 per minute in man. Even when domesticated and well provided with food, the cat retains those characteristics that insure successful hunt-

Respiratory system

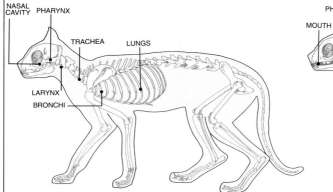

ing. In quiet moments of repose, the breathing is sometimes accompanied by the familiar noise of purring. This usually expresses contentment but sometimes occurs when a cat is frightened, in pain, or as an effort at propitiation. Zoologists cannot fully explain how cats produce this sound. One theory is that cats, which have both true and false vocal chords, use the true chords for vocalization while possibly using the false chords for purring.

■ The digestive system

The cat feeds by digesting and assimilating nutritional substances from food through a series of organs. Digestion begins in the mouth where the teeth and the rough tongue quickly tear up the food before passing it on to the esophagus and into the stomach. Here, the food is dissolved by gastric juices (hydrochloric acid and digestive enzymes) before entering the small intestine where it is broken down by the actions of the liver, pancreatic and enteric juices, and is slowly absorbed. Water is re absorbed by the body during the digested food's passage through the large intestine. Residue is expelled with the feces. The cat's intestine is relatively short...only a little over two yards long (versus man's 8 2/3 yards). The entire digestive process is consequently rather slow; therefore, the best diet consists almost exclusively of easily digestible foods with a high caloric content...especially meat and fish. This is more noticeable in the wild cat than in the domestic which is already

used to a more varied diet. In all, it takes about four hours for food to be digested by the cat.

■ The teeth

In the course of evolution, the dentition of the feline has reached a refined functionalism. Adult cats have 30 teeth: 16 in the upper jaw and 14 in the lower. The 4 molars are used for mastication, the 4 canines, pointed and curved inwards to prevent prey from escaping, are the principle weapons for fighting and hunting; and the 12 small incisors have lost any truly usable function. In effect, the cat neither chews nor has any grinding power; rather, the cat rips and tears meat into pieces small enough to swallow. While feeding, it is characteristic for the cat's head to shake from side to side as the jaw does not have the articulation to carry out necessary sideways movements. As with many mammals, the cat is born without teeth; after two or three weeks the milk teeth begin to appear. After about six months these are replaced by permanent teeth.

■ The skin and coat

The cat's skin and fur protect it from both excessive heat and cold. The skin forms a fibrous, elastic covering for the muscles. The fur, which forms the cat's coat, is rooted in this loose, flexible skin. A normal coat has four types of hair: the evenly tapered long, straight, thick guard hairs which are part of the topcoat, the awn hairs which are also part of the topcoat, the proximally thin, crimped awned down-hairs, and the evenly thin and

Digestive system

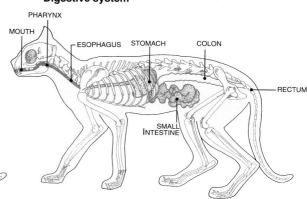

Dentition (front view)

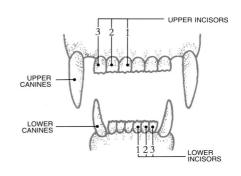

Dentition (side view)

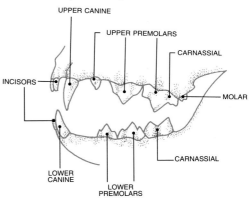

crimped down-hair. Each type is present in different quantities depending upon whether the cat has long hair or short hair and whether the coat is smooth or coarse. The wild cat's coat blends into its surroundings, but selective breeding of the domestic varieties has produced a wide range of coats

Action of the legs in running

(differing in color, pattern, texture, and length) which no longer serve as a natural camouflage. The coat has become an important part of the classification of breeds as well as contributing to the overall elegance and beauty of the cat.

■ The visual function
From a strictly anatomical viewpoint, the cat's eye is not too unlike man's, but its uses are markedly different. The cat's cornea, pupil, and lens are more highly developed and can utilize the weakest rays of light. In addition, unlike other mammals, the eye of the cat has a specific feature, the *tapetum lucidum*, located behind the retina. This acts as a mirror which increases the intensity of any light falling on the retina causing the cat's eyes to shine in the dark; more importantly, it increases the cat's ability to see in nearly complete darkness. Degeneration of the *tapetum lucidum* causes blindness.

The pupil of the eye is shaped like a narrow vertical slit; but, when dilated in the dark, the pupil becomes fully round in shape. The cat's visual field is far greater than that of man with the maximum angle for both eyes being nearly 285 degrees. However, the overlapping of visual fields produced by the frontal positioning of the cat's eyes is 130 degrees which produces a slightly less precise perception of distance than that of man (but far greater than that of the dog). The retina, compared with that of man, is made up of a large number of rods (the light-sensitive surface that allows the cat see in almost total darkness) and a smaller number of cones (these provide the ability to recognize different colors even though the cat does not appear to have any special color preference). Recent studies have shown that cats can distinguish colors, but the tests are complicated and, although

they have proved that cats are not color-blind, it is difficult to determine if this ability benefits the animal. The cat's eye is protected both by movable eyelids edged with eyelashes and by a third eyelid or nictitating membrane, the haw.

■ The olfactory function
As with most carnivorous animals, the cat has a highly developed sense of smell (four times more sensitive than that of man); however, it does not have the dog's great specialization of this sense (which exceeds man's by at least six times). The cat's sense of smell is important in its daily life for locating food or prey on which it does not pounce voraciously, but inspects so attentively that it almost seems distrustful of it. The sense of smell also plays an important part in choosing a mate and is, therefore, a vital adjunct to the reproductive cycle.

■ The tactile function
The cat always keeps its coat scrupulously clean as the fur plays an important part in its sense of touch. The skin contains minute sense organs that react to tactile stimuli. The cat and especially the kitten recognize objects through touching them with their paws; the paw pads are particularly sensitive. The vibrissae, or whiskers, are not just part of the animal's appearance. These long, stiff, delicate filaments growing on

The ear and its section

the cheeks and forehead constitute sensory elements that, even in the most complete darkness, inform the cat of any obstacle in its immediate path; there are about 12 whiskers on either slide of the cat's face.

■ The auditory function
The cat's hearing, which is one of its most highly developed senses, far exceeds that of man (and also the dog) both in range and location. This acute sense of hearing, allied to a great flexibility of the neck, allows it to detect and analyze nearly inaudible sounds and to know exactly from which direction they come. Cats can differentiate very similar sounds from as far away as 60 feet and a mere 1½ feet apart. Moreover, as it can hear its prey on an ultrasonic level, that is to say, on a frequency too high for man to detect, the cat

can single it out and pounce upon it even in darkness. It is the anatomical structure of the auditory system that permits such sensitivity to noise due both to its wide, pointed ears and to two special resonance chambers in the cranium, the *bullae*.

■ The tongue
The tongue is long, flexible and muscular; it curls up to form a 'ladle' when the cat laps up water. The surface is rough and is covered with numerous hard, raised papillae, (backward hooks particularly adapted to washing the fur) which help the cat to hold prey and food in its mouth.

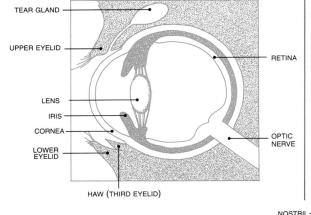

The eye and its section

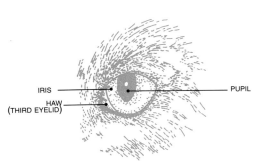

Extent of the field of vision

A) Human eyes
B) Cats eyes

On the left, the profile of the cat and its whiskers; on the right, its main toilet accessory: the tongue.

CHOOSING A CAT

The cat is probably the least demanding of all domestic animals. It does not require a lot of room and can adapt to living in the restricted space of a small apartment or the many rooms of a mansion. It is not noisy and creates few, if any, problems with neighbors; it seldom causes any damage and controls its bodily functions so that the house stays clean. The cat is a fascinating creature because of its intelligence and capricious behavior, and is a gentle and sensitive playmate for small children. But its accommodating disposition must not mislead anyone into thinking that the cat has no needs of its own. It should be remembered that a cat's life span can vary from 14 to 20 years. A cat is a lifetime commitment for those who would enjoy its company.

■ How to choose a cat

A male or a female? One cat or two? A kitten or a grown cat? A cat with long or short hair? A pedigreed cat or a more modest specimen? These are the major questions to consider when choosing a cat. If altered, the differences between a male and a female cat are minor. Altered cats pose few problems and become quieter, more companionable animals. The operation (in males, removal of the testicles, or *orchidectomy*) is performed by a veterinary surgeon, usually at between four to five months, but never before the cat is three months old. The removal of the ovaries and uterus in the female is called spaying (*ovarohysterectomy*) and is a more delicate operation involving major surgery. Ideally, this should be done before the cat comes in estrous, when it is about five months old, although the operation can be done at any age. (If parturition has been difficult, it is best to spay.)

There are, of course, those who do not believe in submitting an animal to an operation which, in their opinion, will suppress its natural instincts. For them, a few words of warning: If the cat is under any stress such as another cat's being introduced into the house or perhaps the arrival of a new baby, it is liable to spray. This is different from normal urination. The tom will deliberately choose an object (the curtains, for example) and emit a jet of strong smelling liquid at it. It is very difficult to get rid of the accompanying pungent smell. Also, a whole (not neutered) cat will sometimes disappear, either through wanderlust or to seek a mate, and

then unexpectedly return after several days oblivious to the anguish it has caused its owner. Generally, it will also be in bad physical shape after fighting with other males over territory or females, and be in need of medical care, a good meal, and a bath. Those who prefer a whole (not spayed) female must be prepared to make adequate arrangements to provide suitable homes for its kittens. To abandon newly born kittens is extremely cruel. For those who have chosen a pedigree cat, the birth of kittens will be a happy event given that the newborn will be considered valuable if the mother has been mated with an equally pure bred partner also endowed with an impressive pedigree. But the choice of a mating pedigree cat also presents some challenges: the cost of stud fees, a genetically sound mating programming, added care during the gestation period, immunization, veterinary fees, and the registration of the kittens at about six weeks of age. The kittens must be registered as an litter; subsequently, individual registrations are then obtained from C.F.A.. If the kittens are to be shared, the owner of the stud male and the owner of the queen (female) must also have made a prior written contractual agreement.

In spite of its reputation as the animal 'that walks by itself', the cat too, especially when young, appreciates companionship. The town dweller who is often away from home should have

two cats; the two cats, living together, will be spared long hours of boredom. The life style of today's families who live in cities poses a problem that should be realized from the start: what to do with the family cat during holidays and vacations? If the family moves to a house in the country or at the beach, the cat can easily go too; however, it must not be allowed out of the new house for the first few days in case it gets lost or trapped. If the holiday entails a lot of traveling about, the cat should be left at home in the care of a responsible cat sitter. Being moved around causes stress in many cats; this should be considered before taking it from its home. The cat should NEVER be left out-of-doors to fend for itself while the owner is away.

A kitten needs special care, especially if it has just been weaned from its mother. Usually, for the kitten's sake, it is best to refrain from giving it to a small child until the child has been taught how to accept the responsibility for a somewhat fragile living creature. The kitten is not an object; rather, it is a living creature with its own feelings. Therefore, whoever makes a present of a cat must first be absolutely sure that it is really wanted, and that it will be given a warm and lasting welcome. If a kitten is given to a child, it must be remembered that both the child and the cat grow with the passing of time, but at different rhythms, as shown in the table on this page.

■ Breeds, standards and pedigrees

Throughout the world there are national and international feline associations. The largest and most important in the United States is the Cat Fanciers' Association Inc., which was

HOW A CAT AGES	
Cat's Age	Human Equiv.
1 month	6-8 months
2 months	1 year
3 months	4 years
4 months	6 years
5 months	8 years
6 months	10 years
7 months	14 years
8 months	16 years
12 months	18 years
2 years	25 years
3 years	30 years
4 years	35 years
5 years	40 years
6 years	42 years
7 years	45 years
8 years	50 years
9 years	55 years
10 years	60 years
11 years	65 years
12 years	70 years
13 years	75 years
14 years	80 years
15 years	82 years
16 years	85 years

founded in 1906; however, there are other American associations including ACA, CFF ACFA, TICA, and AACE. In Great Britain, the Governing Council of the Cat Fancy (GCCF) was chartered in 1910. Most responsible American breeders choose to register their kittens with C.F.A. (as do British breeders with GCCF), so that C.F.A. and GCCF pedigrees are well authenticated. Owners of stud males will accept only properly registered queens. The C.F.A. Year Book is an annual celebration of the best show cats containing hundreds of pictures (most in color) and important articles regarding the Cat Fancy around the world. There are also Breed Councils for each breed recognized by C.F.A. The desired physical characteristics of any breed are defined by its corresponding Breed Council which produces, along with the approval of the C.F.A. Executive Board, the official C.F.A. Show Standards which describe the perfect specimen of each breed and color. The equivalent registering body in Europe is the Fédération Internationale Féline de l'Europe, FIFe. Regularly, usually in late fall and early winter when cats look at their best, many exhibitions are held for pedigreed cats. These shows give enormous pleasure to cat lovers; a Best Cat in Show or a Supreme Exhibit is selected, and Championships, Grand Championships as well as other important titles are achieved through these competitions. Also, these exhibitions are of great importance to breeders not only as a competition, but also to facilitate meetings and exchanges to promote the most favorable pairings and, consequently, the improvement of their cats so they more closely approximate the perfect cat of each breed and color.

■ **Where to find a kitten**
There are several choices:
• **Qualified breeders.** This is the best solution for the prospective owner who wants a purebred cat with an authenticated pedigree. This is also a possibility for those who want a prestigious breed of cat even if it lacks all of the perfect qualities required for showing.
• **Humane societies.** A good cat is guaranteed, and its state of health is checked. These cats are to be altered.
• **Local veterinarians.** They are often aware of any kittens needing a good home.
• **Private owners of kittens.** In this case it is necessary to know that the kitten has been vaccinated against enteritis, cat 'flu', FeLV, etc., at least one week previously.
• **At a C.F.A. cat show.** Each weekend, cat shows are licensed by C.F.A. throughout the United States, Canada, Japan, South America and Europe. Gathered in one hall will be examples of most of the more popular breeds and colors. Prospective owners can meet and talk with responsible breeders as well as see beautiful examples of pedigreed kittens, adult cats and altered cats.
• **If a purebred is involved**, it should have been registered with C.F.A.; the registration papers gcontain the names of its parents, sex, color, eye color, breeder and, ultimately the owner. This is required if the kitten is to bred and/or exhibited.

■ **When you have chosen a cat**
A kitten, with its charming ways, is more often chosen than is an adult cat. It is vital that either should immediately be taken to the vet for a thorough check up. It is necessary to know from the very beginning if the new cat is suffering from any problem. However, you should also examine the cat or kitten to determine its age, sex, and general state of health. Before starting an examination, your hands should be carefully washed. Next, you should play with the animal to gain its confidence and calm it down and make it feel safe. Then, gently hold the animal while you carefully and thoroughly examine it.

■ **Determination of sex**
In adult cats, the determination of sex is quite easy, but in very young kittens it can be difficult as the external sex organs are not well developed. Carefully lift the cat's tail and look at the external sex organs which you will find are closer to the anus than, for example, those of the dog.
• During the first months, the male kitten's testicles and scrotum are not yet well formed, are scarcely visible, and are easily confused with the vulvar labia of a female. The male's genital

orifice is merely a round spot and is quite different from the female's. (fig. 1).
• In the female, the vulvar orifice appears as a small vertical slit below the anus and is closer to the anus than are the genitalia of the male (fig. 2).

ASSESSING THE STATUS OF A CAT'S HEALTH
• **Vigor and appetite:** even the cat, more self-composed than other animals and hardly introspective, is sometimes frightened; however, even in a new home it must have a vigilant, alert look. If it is in good health it should soon settle down and, after a few exploratory sniffs and some prudent taps with its paw at some food, it will eat. If it refuses food, especially for more than a day or two, it may be showing early symptoms of illness.
• **Body temperature:** this should be101.5°F (38.6°C). Two people are needed to take a cat's temperature using a rectal thermometer. First, put the cat at its ease by fondling it, then one person holds the front feet (without squeezing), while the other supports the abdomen and gently inserts the greased thermometer, gently rotating it. A rectal thermometer should never be forced or pushed in hard.
• **Eyes:** the eyes must be very clean with no encrustation of matter or pus. Any inflammation of the delicate membrane protecting the eye (the conjunctiva) can be seen by observing the third eyelid, which may be made to raise by pressing gently on the eyeball through the upper lid (fig. 3). If there are signs of redness, the vet should be consulted. If proper treatment is not immediately available, the irritation may be relieved by bathing the eye with mild, warm salt water. Boil one pint of water with one teaspoonful of salt; cool completely before using.
• **Dehydration:** the cat's skin should have good elasticity verifiable by the fact that, if a fold of skin is squeezed between thumb and index finger, it readily flattens out again after being released. When an animal is dehydrated, the fold disappears slowly.

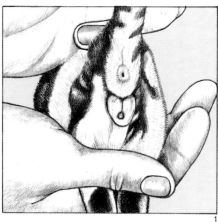

1 2 3

DETERMINATION OF AGE

An exact estimate of any cat's age requires experience and is best left to the vet. However, it is easy to tell the approximate difference between a mature and a very young cat. The points listed here make it possible to be more precise in the determination of the age group in a given subject:

• From birth to 10 days: the eyes and ears are closed (fig. A)

• At 2 weeks: the eyes and ears begin to open; there are still no teeth, but the kitten begins to crawl.

• At 3 weeks: the kitten starts walking; the teeth begin to show.

• At 1 month: it is able to run and begins washing itself (see fig. B).

• At 6 weeks: the front milk teeth appear.

• At 3 months: the eyes take on their definitive color.

• From 4 to 6 months: the permanent incisors appear.

• From 7 to 8 months: the permanent canines appear.

• From 9 to 12 months: the cat is now grown; the external sex organs are clearly visible.

• After the 3rd or 4th year: the first deposits of dental tartar may begin to collect.

• The 10th year: senescence begins to set in; the cat's

A

B

liveliness and combative spirit decline. It sleeps for longer periods; the coat becomes thinner although it does not turn gray, and it loses flesh around the eyes and along the spine.

• After the 12th year: the teeth may begin falling out and should be allowed to do so naturally (unless the gums show signs of soreness or bleeding, in which case a visit to the vet will be required.)

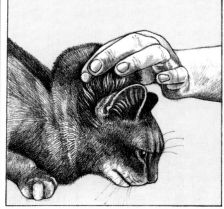
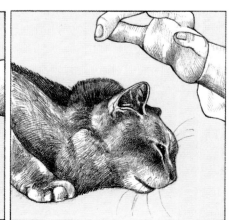

4 5

• **Ears:** the inside of the ear should be clean and should not emit a bad odor.

• **Nose:** there should be no discharge from the nostrils nor any dry crusts. This is a very sensitive organ vulnerable to severe and lasting damage if struck.

• **Anus:** the fur around the anus should show no residue from diarrhea or dried feces. If this occurs in orphaned kittens or older cats, it can be gently washed and the area carefully dried.

• **Skin and fur:** the appearance of badly soiled fur can be misleading; health may be suspect when all that is needed is a good bath (see p. 207). It is more important to look for areas in which the fur is thin or completely missing. The fur should be parted in several places, starting at the tail and methodically moving forward to the head, while carefully examining the skin for irregularities.

• **Parasites:** Examination of the fur and skin may reveal the presence of parasites. The care with which a cat washes itself is generally protection enough, but strays are often affected.

Fleas (Fig. A): These are the most common parasites to infect cats and can be transmitted to humans. They are usually located on the back, near the tail, and around the neck. They are hard to see and their presence is often discovered through their feces: black *(Fig. B)* specks which appear in the combings during grooming or which can be felt as a tiny, gritty substance in the coat. When in doubt and when even an examination through a magnifying glass has revealed nothing, a few of the suspected gritty flecks can be put on a large piece of white paper and wet with a drop of water. If a red patch forms, the cat has fleas.

Ticks: These turn up quite rarely except in rural areas and are easily recognized by their size (sometimes as large as a small pea) and shaped similar to a watermelon seed (fig. C male; fig. D female). They attach themselves to the head, especially near the eyes, the limbs, and between the toes. When engorged after about 10 days, they fall off. They should not be roughly pulled off the cat as the head often remains in the flesh and results in a festering sore.

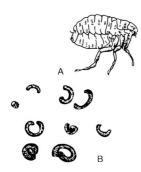

A

B

Lice (Fig. E): These are rare and because they are only 1 to 2 centimeters wide, are hard to find; it is easier to see their eggs (called nits) which stick to the fur. If the cat is badly infected, it should be taken to its vet rather than treated by its owner.

Mites: If the cat scratches itself restlessly, especially about the head and neck, it could be

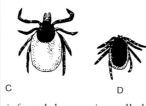

infected by a mite called *Trombicula autumnalis* which

usually attacks in rural areas in the summer and autumn. If the affected part is carefully examined through a magnifying glass, small red, orange or yellow 'pin-points' may be seen. Raw, wet patches of skin around the cat's lips and ears, armpits, groin, abdomen and between the toes will also be evident.

• **Intestinal worms:** There are two types of worms: tapeworm and roundworm. The tapeworm or flatworm lives part of its life on a flea, and the infected cat must be treated for fleas as well as worms, otherwise it will continue to develop tapeworms. A feral cat could drink polluted water or come in contact with the contaminated feces of another animal. The worms enter the stomach or intestinal tract causing digestive disturbances and affect physical condition. The roundworm lives in the small intestine where it lays its eggs; it causes vomiting, diarrhea, scruffy skin and a swollen or "pot belly." A sample of the cat's feces, which may be blood-stained, should be taken to the vet.

• **Alterations to the skin:** Sometimes the cat's body will have:

• reddened areas of skin, often accompanied by swelling;

• inflamed areas exuding sticky, foul-smelling mucus;

• scabs;

• nodules of varying size and shape under the skin;

• wounds, minor or serious.

Other more serious symptoms may indicate ill health; the vet should be consulted without delay. These signs may include:

• sneezing fits, coughing, alterations in the breathing accompanied by hissing or whistling sounds, wheezing and gasping;

• diarrhea, vomiting, difficulty in having a bowel movement, irregular, painful, or excessive urination–sometimes in dribbles and accompanied by excessive thirst;

• paralysis, loss of equilibrium.

Choosing Among the Breeds

	1. Tranquil	2. Adapts to leash	3. Needs extra grooming	4. Good Mouser	5. Needs vital space	6. Long–lived
7. Playful	Korat (8,12)	Colorpoint Shorthair (6,9,11) Ocicat (5) Oriental Shorthair (6,9,11,12) Siamese (6,9,11,12)	Somali (4,5)	Balinese (11) Cymric (8,12) Havana (8) Javanese (11) Manx (8,12) Norwegian Forest Cat(5) Somali (3,5)	Abyssinian Norwegian Forest Cat (4) Ocicat (2) Somali (3,4)	Colorpoint Shorthair (2,9,11) Oriental (2,9,11,12) Siamese (2,9,11,12) Tonkinese (9,11)
8. Home–loving	Birman (3,12) Bombay Egyptian Mau (4) Exotic (4,12) Korat (7,12) Persian (3,4) Ragdoll (3,12) Rex Russian Blue Snowshoe Sphynx Turkish Angora (3,12) Turkish Van (3,12)		Birman (1,12) Colorpoint Shorthair (4,7,12) Maine Coon (4,5) Persian (1,4) Ragdoll (1,12) Turkish Angora (1,12) Turkish Van (1,12)	Burmese (6,11,12) Chartreux Cymric (7,12) Egyptian Mau (1) Exotic (1,12) Havana Brown (7) Japanese Bobtail Maine Coon (3,5) Manx (7,12) Persian (1,3) Scottish Fold	Maine Coon (3,4)	
9. Likes to travel		Colorpint Shorthair (6,7,11) Oriental Shorthair (6,7,11,12) Siamese (6,7,11,12)	Tiffany (4)	Burmese (6,11,12) Tiffany (3)		Burmese (4,11,12) Colorpoint Shorthair (2,7,11) Oriental (2,7,11,12) Siamese (2,7,11,12) Tonkinese (7,11)
10. Plays with children	Singapura			American Shorthair (5) British Shorthair	American Shorthair (4)	
11. Vocal		Colorpoint Shorthair (6,7,9) Oriental Shorthair (6,7,9,12) Siamese (6,7,9,12)		Balinese (7) Burmese (6,9,12) Javanese (7)		Burmese (4,9,12) Colorpoint Shorthair (2,7,9) Oriental Shorthair (2,7,9,12) Siamese (2,7,9,12) Tonkinese (7,9)
12. Intelligent	Birman (3,8) Exotic (4,8) Korat (7,8) Ragdoll (3,8) Turkish Angora (3,8) Turkish Van (3,8)	Oriental Shorthair (6,7,9,12) Siamese (6,7,9,12)	Birman (1,8) Ragdoll (1,8) Turkish Angora (1,8) Turkish Van (1,8)	American Wirehair (5) Burmese (6,9,11) Cymric (7,8) European Shorthair (6) Exotic (1,8) Manx (7,8)	American Wirehair (4) Bengal	Burmese (4,9,11) European Shorthair (4) Oriental Shorthair (2,7,9,11) Siamese (2,7,9,11)

The wide variety of characteristics and temperaments generally found in the different breeds allow all cat lovers to select the breed most suited to their needs and tastes. However, the choice is often difficult. How best to choose just one from among the many beautiful breeds and colors? This table may assist you in making your selection.

When two desirable characteristics are found, one on a horizontal line, the other in a vertical column, the square in the table at which the two intersect contains the names of the breeds that generally possess both qualities. The numbers following the breed names (which refer to the headings of columns and horizontal lines) indicate additional breed characteristics which give you more information on which to base your decision. Ultimately, of course, you must judge each animal with your own eyes.

FEEDING

The cat's intestine is shorter than that of other animals; this makes digestion difficult. Hence, the cat requires food with a high caloric value such as meat or fish and does not like experimentation with many different flavors. To get the food to which it is accustomed, a cat can often become very stubborn obstinately refusing other food and seeming to seek to exploit to the limit its remarkable capacity to survive without eating. (In exceptional cases, a cat may lose up to 40% of its weight before dying of hunger.) Cat owners are often heard to complain about their pet's being spoiled and pigheaded since the cat refuses everything that is offered to it, demanding its favorite delicacy. Even a cat, however, needs the basic substances contained in foods other than meat and fish and must have the balanced and varied diet to which it should have been trained from kitten hood and even before weaning. But the cat can certainly not be turned into a vegetarian. It is a very definite carnivore and cannot survive without meat.

• THE CORRECT DIET

Many wild, carnivore relatives of the domestic cat which live in forests or grasslands (such as the tiger and the lion) prefer to eat the vegetable contents of its stomach first when they have caught their prey. This is the natural form of their dietary supplementation; for the same reason, wild cats will usually devour smaller prey completely. Carbohydrates can be fed to the domestic cat in the form of cereals, pasta, or bread…foods which it accepts in small quantities only, but which are useful for their vegetable fiber content. About a quarter of the domestic cat's diet should consist of protein. A good, healthy diet for an adult cat leading a moderately active life could be designed following these percentage guidelines:
• protein 15%, but up to 25 per cent for newly-weaned kittens
• fats 12%
• carbohydrates 20 per cent
• minerals 3%
• water 50%
The diet should be planned according to the cat's age. Requirements differ among the nursing kitten, the adult cat, and the old cat. During pregnancy, a diet richer in meat (protein) mixed with foods containing calcium (milk or cottage cheese) to compensate for the loss of minerals and support bone development in the fetus is required,.

Proteins.
Proteins are manufactured from amino acids and are vital for building the tissue which the animal must constantly renew. They are of special importance for young animals which are still growing. The cat is a carnivore and therefore should be given more meat and fish protein than a dog. Foods containing protein: meat (beef, lamb), poultry, rabbit, fish, eggs, cheeses, milk.

Fats.
Most of the cat's energy comes from fats, the lack of which will overload the kidneys. Because fats are easily digested, the amount can be increased as the cat gets older. This helps to avoid renal disease. A lack of fat will make the cat apathetic or nervous and can cause unpleasant

alterations to the skin. Foods containing fat: animal or vegetable oils, meat, milk, eggs cheeses.

Carbohydrates.
Complex carbohydrates furnish energy, are easily digested, and contain the fiber useful in maintaining health and making the intestines work efficiently. For a carnivorous animal such as the cat, carbohydrates are not strictly necessary from a dietary aspect, but are needed for the special functions from the fiber they provide. Foods containing complex carbohydrates: cereals, bread.

Minerals.
Calcium and phosphorous are indispensable for strengthening the bones; sodium, potassium and magnesium are also very important. During pregnancy queens need these in large quantities. Normally, a well-balanced diet contains a sufficient amount; added minerals should be given only on the advice of a vet, and in pre-determined and controlled quantities.Food containing minerals: milk (calcium, phosphorous, other trace minerals), fish (iodine, magnesium), cheese (calcium, phosphorous, potassium), meat (phosphorous, potassium, copper, iron, zinc, sodium, chlorine), bread (calcium, iron), eggs and green vegetables (iron, magnesium, iodine).

Water.
An adult cat is approximately 73% water (fat-free body weight). It is a vital part of the cat's diet at all times. Although water is present in all nutrients (especially milk, tripe, cooked fish), it is absolutely necessary that it be drunk on its own as a separate liquid. It is essential for the cat to have access to clean water at all times even if it has never been seen actually drinking it.

Vitamins.
Supplies of fresh meat and frequent exposure to sunlight are sufficient to allow a cat the vitamins necessary for proper growth and development. Vitamin D is spontaneously formed in the skin through exposure to the sun. Only in rare cases would a vet need to prescribe vitamin supplements for a cat's normal diet. Liver, once a week, provides added vitamins.

Vitamin A helps bone development; is found in milk, eggs, liver, carrots, cod liver oil (no more than a teaspoonful a week), cod.
Vitamin B is necessary for the transfer of carbon; is found in meat, liver, yeast, greens. Cats fed entirely on canned food are may suffer from Vitamin B deficiency.
Vitamin D: necessary for strengthening the bones (a deficiency in kittens causes rickets), and for the fixing of calcium; is produced naturally in the organism; is found in milk, eggs, oily fish, cod, cod liver oil.
Vitamin E: helps form cell walls; is found in cereals, some meat.

Administered in excess, vitamins can do as much harm as from a deficiency. It is NOT a case wherein "if little is good, then lots will be even better." The specific requirements vary among individual cats and at different times within the cat's life; no more and certainly no less should be given than is necessary. While a daily yeast tablet can do no harm (most cats love these as a special treat), a veterinarian should be consulted if you suspect that your cat may be suffering any vitamin deficiency.

When should food be given
A new-born kitten, an adult cat, and an aged feline have different food needs. First, the amount of food must be given in relation to individual age, but must also be proportionate to the amount of exercise the animal gets during the day (and night). Particularly during the early stages of its life, a cat requires special care.

The early months: The best possible food is obviously the mother's milk which contains a special substance called colostrum, and is quite different from cow's milk. When this is unavailable, a substitute can be given made from powdered or concentrated milk, rich and double strength, which is sold commercially. If this is unobtainable, it may be possible to find a surrogate mother, i.e. a queen who has had a litter at around the time the orphaned kittens' mother died (but care must be taken that she does not attack the orphan kittens), or even a lactating bitch. Failing all these, following these instructions:
• heat a glassful of whole cow's milk in a double boiler to a temperature of about104°F (test with a fingertip; it should be neither too hot, nor too cool);
• add a teaspoon of thick cream, a teaspoon of egg yolk, and a drop of lemon juice;
• mix until all the ingredients are well blended;
• feed the kittens every two to three hours around the clock and until they can be given solid food such as canned baby food and cereals.(Small nippled bottles are available in which to put the warm milk mixture for feeding.)

How many meals?
Kittens whose eyes have not yet opened must be fed every 2 to 3 hours. When the eyes have opened, give the above mixture every 5 to 6 hours. The required amounts vary according to age and size, but within these limits :
• if the kitten is newborn, i.e. with the umbilical cord still showing, one teaspoon;
• while the kitten continues to develop but the eyes are still closed, two teaspoons;
• when the eyes have opened, three teaspoons;
• if the milk teeth have begun to show, six teaspoons.

How to feed
The nursing queen feeds her kittens with such care that the little ones must not be taken from her until they are completely weaned (eight weeks). Sometimes, especially if the mother has died, an artificial method of feeding them must be found. Feeding bottles adapted for kittens can be obtained from the vet or pet stores. Otherwise, a large plastic syringe (with the needle removed) or a plastic medicine dropper with many small holes can be used. The kitten should be held in one hand in the easiest possible position for feeding. The first few times, so that it will understand that it is for feeding, allow a drop of milk to fall on its mouth until it begins to suck. Wait for the kitten to swallow between each drop. After feeding, it is a good idea to rub its tummy very gently to help the digestion and then, with the corner of a cloth, or a chamois slightly dampened in tepid water, give it a light rub down, following the direction the fur grows, so that it will not miss its mother's licking and grooming. Very gentle pressure on the sex organs will bring about elimination which the mother cat handles through the licking and grooming of her babies.

How to wean: When the milk

teeth appear and the kitten seems more sure of its movements, the time has come to introduce it to a mixed diet adding a little solid food. To start with, this can be a some finely shredded meat added to a generous amount of the enriched milk prepared according to the instructions given earlier. Even kittens suckled by their mother must now learn to feed themselves from a saucer of milk which is gradually enriched with meat or tinned baby foods. Perhaps in the early stages, its face should be gently moved towards the saucer and its mouth moistened with a finger dipped in the milk. It will soon learn how to feed itself. In the second month of life, the diet must become progressively more similar to that of an adult cat, with differences of quantity relative to its weight.

to keep, they are not always rich in protein and fats, and lack water. They should not be given to the cat unless there is always plenty of fresh water available. Too much of some types of dry food in the diet has been suspect in causing renal difficulty, especially in neutered males.

Wet or soft foods

Dry foods

Young cats and adults

The cat would always prefer a diet consisting of only fresh meat, but to keep healthy it must become accustomed to a more varied, balanced, and controlled diet.
The following proportions of different types of food are recommended:
• 50% of red or white meat, cooked and cut into small pieces, raw, or scalded;
• 25% of rice or pasta, cooked until very soft, rinsed, and well drained;
• 25% of finely chopped vegetables (carrots, zucchini, lettuce, spinach);
the total amount of food must relate to the cat's body weight.

• The presentation of food

While a starving cat will seek food in trash bins, one that lives in a home often becomes fussy; it expects fresh food...not leftovers from the day before. Further, it will refuse to eat if served on unwashed dishes. Food, therefore, must be served on clean dishes and on a separate dish for each cat. It may even be worthwhile to purchase the special type of server that keeps the food free from insects

by opening only when the cat steps on a pedestal. If possible, dishes should always be placed in the same area of the house where the cat is always fed and not in the open where they might attract insects and mice.

• Forbidden food

The cat has difficulty in eliminating any and all poisonous substances including certain food additives used in preservation of human tinned foods. Also to be avoided are chocolate (which many cats love), sweets in general, legumes, overripe or fermented cheeses, and spicy or over-salted food.

• Canned or packaged food: To vary the diet, or to have food available during journeys, prepared food can be useful. There are healthy, well-balanced foods available which are hygienically prepared and easily kept. It is not advisable, however, for a cat to be fed exclusively on these commercial products; they should be alternated with fresh food which is, among other things, usually more economical. There are three types of packaged food:

• Canned food: contains meat, fish, chicken or rabbit and

Feeding bowls

For solid foods

One dish for solid foods,

one for water

For water and milk

gelatin, and are agreeably flavored. The high water content makes them suitable for journeys, but also, in nutritive value, proportionately expensive. They often contain other items such as vegetables and grains.

• Wet or soft foods: these are chunks consisting of soy, meat and animal fats, and are about one-third water. They are moderately priced and fairly nutritious, but are less easy to preserve than some other commercial products.

• Dry food: generally comes in the form of biscuits of various sizes, shapes, and flavors; easy

ADVICE ON FEEDING

• The cat is unlikely to eat everything in its dish at one time; it prefers snacking and having a taste now and then. If it does not eat everything at once, there is no cause for anxiety.
• Food should not be given cold, directly from the refrigerator, nor should it be boiling hot.
• Fish must only be lightly cooked, not boiled, or will then lose its nutritive value. Place it in a little water, bring it quickly to the boil, turn off the heat, cover the pan and leave to cool.
• Prepared foods must be those produced specifically for cats. Dog foods do not contain sufficient nutrients. Food for human consumption contains too many preservatives for the cat's delicate stomach.
• Organ meats, and especially liver, are a good source of nutrition and should be given once a week as a change from meat and fish. Lungs (called lights), however, do not have a high calorific value, and should only be given to an obese cat that needs to lose weight.
• Be very careful of chicken bones! They are small and splin-

ter easily with the accompanying risk of cutting the inside of the mouth, getting stuck in the throat, and causing death. Cooked chicken should be carefully inspected until every scrap of bone is found.
• Milk is rich in minerals and vitamins, but difficult to digest, and often causes diarrhea. Never give milk to nursing kittens. If necessary, they should be given whole milk mixed as already explained.
• Eggs, if cooked, are acceptable, but never more than twice a week.
• Cleanliness and freshness of food are extremely important to the cat; its dish must be washed before every meal. Water must be fresh, clean, and constantly renewed.
• If the cat is used to eating meat and fish, mix in a small amount of cooked vegetables to give the vitamins, mineral salts and vegetable fiber necessary for a healthy diet.
• If the cat likes them, give it a slice of fresh apple or a segment of orange from time to time; some even like grapes.

DAILY AMOUNTS OF FOOD FOR YOUNG CATS

Body Weight	Food	Water
1 pound	2 1/2 oz.	⅛ cup
2 - 2 1/2 pounds	3 1/2 oz.	¼ cup
3 1/2 - 4 pounds	4 1/4 oz.	½ cup

DAILY AMOUNTS OF FOOD FOR ADULTS

Body weight	Food	Water
5 - 6 1/2 pounds	4 1/4 oz.	¾ cup
8 - 9 pounds	7 oz.	1 cup

Even when free and homeless, the cat is never a great wanderer. It is a territorial animal tending to live within clearly defined limits. Following its solitary lifestyle it prefers to venture forth on explorations in a more or less wide radius, but always returns to its original surroundings: a little-frequented, small square, an abandoned or neglected garden, deserted buildings, anywhere it can find companionship with other homeless cats. The opportunity to mate and the food provided by nearby cat lovers who admire their dignified independence are all that is necessary. Other cats, who lead a semi-independent life around a friendly house without actually living there (as often happens in the vicinity of a factory or a farm), know when it is time to eat. They gather together to share the food without fighting…though they often react violently against an intruder cat. After eating, off they go again, each in a different direction, each to explore its own hunting ground, each jealous of its independence.

■ The cat in the home

Not even when it lives permanently in an apartment or house does a cat regard itself as being dependent; it always preserves the independence that gives it complete freedom to choose how to regulate its own life, unfettered by its owner's arrangements, and behaving as if it were the only one entitled to decide the 'rules of the game'. However, it is not difficult to teach a cat to live in a new home. Their natural instincts prompt them to think of the apartment in which they live as their own territory which they will never dirty, and where, if they are female, they will seek the safest place in which to have their kittens. Its reliance on the house has often made people think that it is fond only of the place, and that it has no feeling for the people there. On the contrary, the cat establishes amicable relationships with members of the family with which it lives, following them about, knowing their ways, and rubbing against their legs to leave the scent by which it will recognize a friend. When it feels the absence of a person of whom it is fond, the cat will often lie on something belonging to that person and which has their special odor. Generally, cats are not jealous; as soon as they are certain that there is plenty to eat for all, most cats can live peacefully together.

■ The bed, the litter tray and the eating place

When a cat comes into a home, be it a kitten or an adult, it needs to familiarize itself with its new surroundings and, **above all,** to learn where to sleep. It is better not to let it choose for itself but to show it the exact location of its bed. Left to its own devices, a new cat is likely to prefer somewhere unsuitable or even dangerous, such as a cupboard in which it could be trapped or, worse, a basket of laundry on its way to the washing machine. The bed must be roomy enough for it to sleep stretched out or curled up,

but not too big. It does not need a roof, but its sides should be at least 8-10 inches high to give the cat a feeling of security and to protect it from draughts. The box can be lined with a warm material, but the bottom should be covered with something that can be easily washed or periodically replaced: folded newspapers, a woolen cloth, or a small cushion. Wicker baskets or plastic containers that can be used as beds are commercially available; however, an old work-box, a small wooden chest (without the lid), or even a strong cardboard box will serve just as well. It is most important that the bed be clean and replaceable if necessary since cats are very particular about clean sleeping quarters. The bed should be placed in a quiet corner, be easily accessible, and not be moved about; cats are creatures of habit. The cat must learn to use its litter

tray. As it is fastidious animal, it will probably know the tray's purpose instinctively; otherwise, if it is taken gently to the tray after some mishap, it will soon understand. It should never be punished in these cases. The tray should be placed somewhere easily reached but secluded such as on a sheltered balcony or in a corner (but not where a door is likely to be accidentally left shut so that the cat has no access.) The sides of the tray should not be too high for the cat to get into it easily, nor too low so that, while digging in the litter, it throws litter all over the floor. The bottom of the tray should be covered with a 2 to 3 inch-deep layer of commercial cat litter, white wood shavings, or sand. Sawdust must not be used as it can be ingested causing great intestinal trouble and mats in the coats of longhairs. In the United States, heat-dried clay is generally used in the litter tray. Ideally, used cat litter should be removed after each visit to the tray; but, failing that, it should be certainly be changed every day. Even if the cat has the use of a garden, a litter tray should

be provided for cold nights or during illness. Should the cat ever have to stay in a cattery, it is well that it should know how to use a litter tray. Another place in the house with which the cat should become familiar is where it eats; its water bowl will be left here (with the water changed at least once each day) as well as its food dish. From the start, it is advisable to provide a cat with a piece of cardboard, a strip of soft wood, or a bit of carpet on which it can 'knead dough'; that is, sharpen its claws without ruining the furniture or the carpets. Scratching posts for this purpose are available in pet shops or large department stores. Also, a rubber ball or toy

with which it can play without too much noise (especially if the cat is more energetic at night than in the day) should also be provided. Sometimes a simple, open paper sack placed on the floor will provide hours of entertainment for your cat as well as for you while watching.

■ Cat doors

If the litter tray is outside on a balcony, or if the cat is used to leaving the house to roam about without having to wait for some-

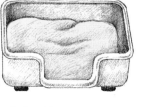

Left, wicker; above, plastic

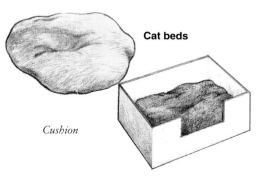

Cat beds

Cushion

Cardboard box

WHEN TRAVELING BY TRAIN

In each country, the railway system has its own regulations; the following are the most usual:

• A cat is usually permitted to travel in the compartment with the passengers.

• Because most cats are not leash trained, it is advisable for the animal to be shut inside its own traveling carrier or basket. This should be large enough to allow the cat to lie down, but it should not be too bulky.

• For every eventuality, the carrier should have a card firmly attached giving the destination, the name, the address and the telephone number of the cat's owner, plus the words, "LIVE ANIMAL."

• Only one animal should be inside a carrier unless they are small kittens who are used to each other.

• Because it is never easy to take a cat on a crowded train, it is wise to choose a timetable and route that will avoid peak travel times. If this is impossible, it would be better for the cat to travel in the luggage compartment. In this case, the cat in it's carrier should be taken to the station a couple of hours before the train's departure and arrangements made for someone to stay with it.

• The cost is economical, about half the price of an ordinary ticket when the cat travels with its owner; the cost is a little extra when the cat travels in the luggage compartment.

RULES FOR AIR TRAVEL

Since each country has its own laws for the entry of animals, cat owners should obtain all the necessary information regarding both their destination as well as any stopover countries. It is vital to know all the quarantine regulations of the country of destination and of any stops en route.

• Airlines have their own rules regarding animal transport, and carriers have various required specifications. On some airlines, the animal may not travel with the luggage because this area is subject to variations in temperature; on others, cats are not permitted to travel in the passenger cabins. When booking a flight these details should clarified, taken into consideration, and fully understood.

• In all cases, the cat must be in a suitable carrier or strong, comfortable fiberglass box (cardboard is not strong enough for air travel) as stipulated by the IATA (International Air Transport Association). No airline company will permit embarkation of animals without adequate containers.

• In general, cats may travel with their owners; but, sometimes no more than one animal at a time is allowed in the cabin. The captain or flight attendant may decide to move a cat to the baggage hold if this is considered necessary.

• It is essential in every case for a label with the name, destination and telephone number of the cat's owner to be firmly attached to the carrier as well as the notation in large letters, "LIVE ANIMAL".

• If the cat has to travel in the baggage hold, it is possible at most in transit airports during long journeys for the owner to gain access to their cat to care for it personally.

• Before embarking, it is generally not wise to feed; in the event the cat becomes airsick, you don't want to endanger its safety. If the cat is nervous, sedation may be given shortly before departure, but only under the veterinarian's strict instructions.

RULES FOR CAR TRANSPORT

Even if a cat causes no disturbance in the car and is a good traveling companion, it is essential that it should be safely shut inside its carrier. The slightest accident could cause it to panic if it were free, and do considerable harm to the passengers. There have also been dreadful cases of cats getting out of the windows of moving cars. If the journey is long, it is advisable to stop periodically to let the cat have a drink and use its litter tray.

• Some cars have a closed-off division at the back where animals may travel; however, it is unwise to have more than one animal in the same area. Usually it is better for a dog to stay in this special space, and for the cat to be in its carrier. The cat (or any other animal) must never be left confined in a car during a halt, especially in the sun. The consequences, for the animal, could be fatal. Even if the car is left parked in the shade, after a time it can be in full sunlight. The windows must open just enough to allow for ventilation during a short stop but not so much that the cat will suffer from draughts or escape in order to investigate the strange surroundings.

one to open the door, it is a good idea to install its own doorway. This is a cat flap fixed to a hole near the bottom of an outside door. It is just big enough to let the cat pass through and swings from a hinge at the top. However, this arrangement also allows other cats entry which is a disadvantage, particularly if your female cat is in heat, ready to breed, and lives in the house…all the neighborhood toms will come calling. There are magnetic cat flaps which open only through interaction to a small magnet attached to the resident cat's collar which act as keys; these assure that only your cat enters. Of course, free access to the out-of-doors is not generally recommended in a busy, urban environment for obvious reasons of the questionable safety for your cat.

■ **Journeys**

It is not very difficult to take the cat along when the whole family is going away, for example, on vacation. A cat is not too big to carry, and it takes calmly to traveling with its owners. Unfortunately this docility might cause necessary precautions to be ignored. When journeying by car, the cat must be safely shut in its traveling basket or cat carrier. Even if it appears placid, never forget that, should there be even a minor accident, a placid cat could take fright and quickly become a crazed fury causing harm to itself and the passengers. Also, if it is allowed to move around in the car, the cat could get under the driver's feet and, should the brakes need to be suddenly applied, could grievously hurt itself or cause the brakes to malfunction as the pedal cannot, due to the cat, be sufficiently depressed to engage them. Strict rules apply to train and airplane journeys which vary from country to country and from one airline to another. Before setting out on vacation, inquiries should be made about these rules to avoid any later inconvenience. In any case, it is wise to get the cat accustomed to wearing a collar, while under your supervision, with the name, address and telephone number of its owners inscribed on a metal plate or tag. Care must be taken to assure that the cat can, in an emergency, get out of collar to avoid a fatal accident to the cat brought on by the collar's getting caught on some hindrance.

■ **Playing**

By playing, the cat learns to put its abilities to full use, develops its senses, and burns up excess energy that a house-bound life leaves unexpended. Play is therefore essential to it.

The cat will get its exercise from very little: a ball of yarn, a rag mouse, a ball (but not a soft rubber one, from which it might chew and swallow small pieces that could cause choking or intestinal problems).

This passion for play has its risks; the cat gets into dangerous places, tries bite into electric wires, or gets too close to the fire and may scorch itself. The owner must keep an eye open to forestall possible accidents.

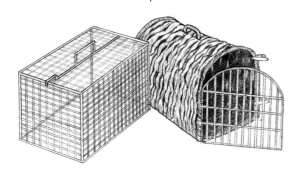

GROOMING

Of all animals, both domestic and wild, the cat enjoys the well-merited reputation of being the cleanest; the animal that takes the greatest care of its personal hygiene as well as its surrounding environment.

■ When the cat washes itself

A domestic cat spends a large part of its time washing itself. Using its long, rough tongue, which is particularly well-designed for the purpose, it carefully licks every accessible part of its body; then it licks its paws using them to reach other body parts. Washing is quite often a social activity as when two cats wash one another, or when a mother looks after her young. This spontaneous activity has many functions. First, it removes dead hair and cells from the skin as well as any foreign objects sticking to the fur, and can eliminate parasites that have reached the skin or that are buried in the fur. Second, it stimulates special subcutaneous glands to produce substances which, when evenly spread over the fur, render it shiny and impermeable. But there is another purpose. While it is licking itself, the moisture distributed produces a lowering in body temperature. The cat does not perspire, and when the skin overheats, it needs to bathe its body in saliva to obtain the cooling that is a byproduct of the evaporation of moisture. The cat tidies up its fur and licks its whiskers with its tongue, even when there seems no urgent necessity to do so; clearly, it is looking after its appearance, making itself smart, like a dandy setting off for the city.

• CATMINT

The assiduous care of its body, however, creates some problems. The main one is, especially for longhairs, the formation of troublesome balls of ingested fur in the intestines which can block the digestion. In these cases, the cat knows what to do and searches for certain kinds of grass which, when eaten, (due to their fiber and their emetic or purgative properties) facilitate the clearing out of the stomach by making the cat regurgitate. This generally solves a "hair ball" problem. There is a particular kind of grass, *Nepeta mussinii*, commonly called catmint or catnip, which contains a chemical so attractive to cats that it can induce temporary euphoria. For indoor cats, a small pot of this grass can be grown (or purchased from pet shops) specifically for the use of your cat and to avoid the cat's eating your house plants which, among other things, may be poisonous.

• THE BATH

Only Turkish Van cats will spontaneously take to water; all others will obstinately resist any prospect of bathing. Sometimes, however, when it has gotten very dirty, the cat must be bathed; then, great patience on the part of the owner is needed. At first the cat will be terrified and will try to escape from the bathing ordeal. Precautions are necessary. Before getting the cat near the water, it needs to be petted and given proof of affection to demonstrate that there are no evil intentions towards it. Then its bath can proceed. If a short-hair cat does not accept a bath in water, there is another method: dry-cleaning with bran.

The method is to warm a pound of bran in the oven to 160°C for about 20 minutes, then cover the cat's fur with it, massaging gently, and finally brushing it all off. For convenience, and to avoid dirtying the house, the cat should be placed on a table covered with a newspaper to catch the brushed out bran. Better yet, there are commercial dry shampoos available which do an excellent job.

■ Short hair cats

The washing that short-hair cats perform on their own is generally enough to keep them in perfect condition. Only on special occasions is intervention by the owner required such as when the animal has been soiled with sticky substances, engine oil for example, which requires a suitable solvent. However, care must be taken to assure that the cure is not worse than the condition or that substances used are not be poisonous if ingested or absorbed through the skin. In any event, a periodic, weekly brushing and combing with a fine-toothed comb is helpful, especially if there is any question of entering the cat in a cat show. Combing should always follow the lie of the hair from the head back to the tail (fig.1). Only in a few cases and for certain breeds is a preliminary back-combing needed to eliminate dead skin. In general, brushing should be done using a brush with soft natural bristles; only for those cats with a particularly delicate skin, for example, the Rex, is it best to use a rubber brush that will not irritate. In this case, too, brushing should be with the lie of the hair. A light rub

with a tonic lotion using a chamois leather or a silk or velvet cloth will provide an ideal finish to pre-show grooming.

■ Long hair cats

The long hair cat requires more frequent grooming, daily at a minimum, and especially during the shedding period. The animal will benefit in health and well-being, and the house will be less littered with cat hair. If brushing is neglected for long, mats and tangles of hair will form which will be difficult to unravel. To get rid of mats and tangles, it is sometimes necessary to trim away a little fur which can be a troublesome and is often painful operation for the cat (fig. 2). For this reason, long-haired cats should be regularly groomed .

Once a week, a more thorough grooming is necessary during which the fur may be lightly dusted with unscented talcum powder or fuller's earth. (Take care to keep the powder out of the cat's eyes and nose.) The powder is then gently massaged into the coat so as to penetrate it fully and evenly. Cats do not mind this massage.

The cat should be combed daily from head to tail, first with a wide-toothed comb taking care

1

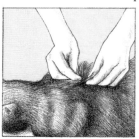

2

3

to untangle all knots, and then with a finer-toothed one. A metal-bristled brush may be carefully used to remove loose hair...especially along the back where most of it occurs. The coat of the long hair is somewhat fragile and vigorous combing or brushing has been known to remove too much of the live coat...particularly on the tail. If this happens, it may be several months before your long hair cat returns to its usual long coated, beautiful appearance. Finally, combing with a fine-toothed comb, this time using an upward, movement, fluffs up the fur around the neck into a fine collar known as the ruff (fig. 3). A soft toothbrush can be used on the fur of the muzzle with care taken to avoid the eyes.

■ Cleaning the ears, eyes and teeth

Before brushing and combing, the eyes and ears should be carefully cleaned; this is also a good time to check the general health of the animal. During this process, the cat must be held in your arms and calmed down so that it does not fidget during the cleaning operations. This will become an activity that is enjoyed by both you and your cat.

Ears. Normally, a cat keeps itself very clean and rarely needs help. If, in exceptional cases, it is necessary to clean the ears, cotton buds such as Q-tips should be used dipped in slightly warm olive oil, not water, taking care not to damage the ear canals. Movement should be upwards only along the wall of the canal, keeping the stick of the bud vertical, moving it down only as far as you can easily see into the ear and never beyond the curve that separates the horizontal and vertical branches of the auricular canal. Be extremely careful. Good quality cotton buds should be used that will not leave any cotton residue. This process is, however, best left to the vet as the ears are very fragile.

Eyes. Especially with long-haired breeds, crusts may form around the eyes which need to be removed. To do this, it is preferable to use pads of sterile gauze soaked in an eye-wash solution (for example, a mild boric acid solution or an emollient infusion of chamomile); avoid the use of cotton pads which may leave filaments or scratch the eye itself. The pad should be passed delicately over the upper and lower eyelids, from the nose outwards.

Mouth and teeth. Cats are

prone, though less so than dogs, to the formation of tartar along the base of their teeth and their gums. They are, however, reluctant to put up with any cleaning operation; it is therefore often necessary to go to the vet. A meal of tough meat or of crunchy cat food once a fortnight may help to counteract the formation of tartar.

There are two methods of cleaning teeth: with a child's toothbrush or with a piece of sterile gauze wrapped around a finger. The brush or gauze, soaked in a weak disinfectant solution recommended by the vet should be gently rubbed, using a rotary motion, on the part of the teeth nearest the gums.

■ Clipping the claws

If the cat is young and leads a normal life with plenty of activity, the length of its claws will be self-regulating through their daily use; if, however, the cat is older or relatively inactive, the claws may grow longer than they should be and will press against the fleshy pads of the paw (in which case the vet should be consulted). Before that stage is reached, it is advisable to reduce their length by clipping. To do this, the cat should be held firmly on your knees while you press the pads of the paw one at a time to extend each claw. Using a nail clipper, preferably of the guillotine type, cut off only the tips of the dead, white-colored part of the claw. The pink part, the quick containing the nerve endings, should never be touched. This operation may present some difficulties; the cat generally will react against this practice

the first few times. It is essential, at first, to obtain instructions and a demonstration of the correct technique from a veterinarian. It is likely that the cat will be less nervous if the operation were to be done by its vet.

■ Specialized grooming

Whoever decides to own a cat often does so, if living in the country, for the benefits of its hunting ability which keeps away undesirable animals; if in the city , the cat provides the enjoyment of its company. Often from this first impulse there arises a passion for the aesthetic qualities of a purebred cat, and the desire to possess a pedigreed animal for showing. In such cases and to be presented in all its beauty, the cat must be prepared with care.

First, it is essential that all the required vaccinations are effected at the proper time, and that the certificates relating to them are in order; otherwise, the animal will not be accepted. It must be gradually accustomed to being in the show ring without becoming restless or impatient with the curious public. In grooming for the show, particular care must be taken so that the fur is spotlessly clean, properly combed, and shows no signs of powders or talc. The coat tail of the long hair must be full carefully prepared. The short hair cat mist be scrupulously clean and sparkling in appearance. The cat's claws must be carefully clipped; ears, eyes and mouth must be carefully cleaned. For short-hair cats, a good polishing with a velvet cloth or chamois leather may be given.

GROOMING INSTRUMENTS

It is best to buy good quality instruments which will give better results and will remain in good condition provided that, after each grooming session, they are carefully cleansed of any residue and hair and are properly dried. Instruments should be kept in their own tin, or cloth, or plastic bag, and in a dry place.

Nail clippers

<u>Clipping tools:</u> used for trimming particular parts of the fur, and for cutting the claws.

<u>Scissors:</u> those with rounded points are best; they are essential for trimming the fur round the eyes, and for removing stubborn knots.

<u>Nail-clippers:</u> used for trimming the claws, especially of domestic cats living indoors. To avoid harming the cat, it is best to use the guillotine type.

<u>Combs and brushes:</u> the basic tools for care of the coat.

<u>Fine-toothed combs:</u> for both short and long-haired cats.

<u>Wide-toothed combs:</u> for initial combing of long-haired cats.

<u>Rubber brushes:</u> for use on short-hair cats, especially those whose skin is very delicate and easily irritated.

<u>Bristle and metal brushes:</u> these are double-sided, bristle on one side and metal on the other for use especially with long hair cats.

<u>Soft-bristled brushes:</u> an ordinary brush with natural bristles, useful for short-hair cats.

<u>Slicker brush:</u> used to give good appearance to the coat, especially in preparation for showing.

<u>Soft toothbrush:</u> for cleaning the teeth and brushing the muzzle.

OTHER MATERIALS

<u>Chamois leather or velvet or silk cloth:</u> to give shine to the coat of short hair cats.

<u>Sponges:</u> it is well not mix to these up with those used by the family.

<u>Q-tips:</u> Cotton buds for cleaning ears and other delicate parts; must be of good quality.

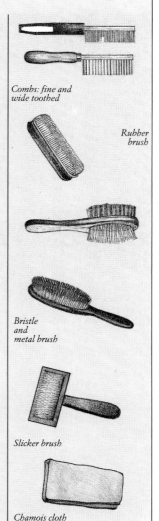

Combs: fine and wide toothed

Rubber brush

Bristle and metal brush

Slicker brush

Chamois cloth

HOW TO GIVE A BATH

For a cat, being given a bath is always traumatic, and great care should be taken. The animal should always be calmed first by a few caresses and soft, vocal reassurances. Before beginning, everything needed should be at hand to avoid any interruption in the entire operation. It is wise, as well, to have an efficient and sympathetic (to the cat) helper and to wear an apron if you wish to protect against splashing.

• To avoid the cat's being too alarmed by the water, it should be placed in a small container such as a basin or a baby's bath while it is still empty. At the same time, pet the cat to

soothe it. Only then should water be gently poured over the cat's body (fig. A) checking to assure that the water is neither too hot nor too cold and that it doesn't get into the cat's eyes or ears.

• The cat must be held firmly with one hand while a small amount of baby shampoo (no tears type) is poured over the coat (fig. B) and gently rubbed into the fur taking care that no water gets into the eyes or ears. When finished with the shampoo, rinse with care pouring small quantities of warm water through the coat. It is better not to use running water; use an unbreakable dipper. pitcher, or a container

with a handle. At this point the cat generally stops protesting and has accepted the inevitable (fig. C). The cat usually will shake and quiver so that you believe that it is freezing.

• Wrap the cat in a warm towel, preferably a terry towel. (fig. D) A hair dryer should not be used unless the cat is familiar with it; the noise may frighten the animal if it is unaccustomed to this device.

• Remember to wash the nose using a cotton cloth dampened with warm water, but not dripping wet. Water should never get up into the nostrils.

• It is desirable, especially in winter, to place the cat in a warm place for final drying and combing. Keep the cat out of

A

C

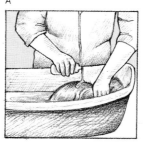

B

D

REPRODUCTION

The evolutionary success of cats as a species owes something to the 'promiscuous' nature of their sexual relationships. During a single period of heat, a queen, given the opportunity, will mate with various tom cats who are notorious for widely spreading their favors. This contributes to the natural selection of the superior individuals because it is the most virile spermatozoa that wins the contest to fertilize the ova. In the same parturition the female may give birth to kittens from different sires with accordingly different characteristics through a phenomenon known as superfecundation. In the wild state, competition among males often finds expression in ferocious fights; these insure that the strongest males mate with the best females. Even males accustomed to a quiet domestic life periodically leave home for long, roaming adventures from which they almost always return weary, starving, and often with scratches and bites suffered in mating combats.

ESTRUS

Mating behavior begins in females at about six months of age…in some cases earlier and in others at about one year. This depends on individual growth rate, and on the breed (long-haired breeds may only come in heat once a year during the period of the year in which they were born) The most favorable moment for a cat's estrus has a precise relationship with the seasons by virtue of a mechanism which, to date, remains far from clear. It appears to depend on the length of daylight hours; in Europe and North America, this period lasts from February to as late as October being shorter in northern areas than in the southern. A female can give birth to one, two, or more litters per annum for many years with her sexual cycles remaining active until late in life. Her cycles do tend to become less frequent towards the end of her fecundity.

MATING

As the mating season approaches and the female enters her pro-estrus phase, her owner must face the problem of arranging a suitable mate, especially if she is purebred, or if she is not free to find her own companion. The problem is complex since females with pedigrees require a pedigreed partner of equal quality to avoid inferior offspring. For other, less aristocratic females, the problems are simpler; it is enough to seek out a young, good-looking, healthy male and start thinking about the responsibility of placing the kittens in good homes. It would be cruel, indeed, to allow the birth of kittens which end being put down; far better not to permit a mating, and better yet to have the female spayed. During the mating season, the tom cat is attracted by the olfactory stimuli emitted by the queen through the production of special substances called pheromones. The intense and characteristic calling of the female at these times also reinforces her sex-appeal.

As the male approaches, the female intensifies her calling, rubs her head on the ground, and assumes a characteristic posture, known as lordosis, with her haunches raised and her tail inclined sideways to uncover the vulva. The male holds her with his mouth, grabs her by the scruff of her neck, and introduces his penis with thrusting movements. Mating is brief; immediately afterwards, the female adopts a hostile attitude, turning on her partner, showing her fangs, and driving him away. She rolls and rubs on the floor attending to her personal grooming before again calling and assuming the characteristic position for further mating which can continue throughout the period of her being in heat and which can continue to produce kittens.

PREGNANCY

The average duration of pregnancy for cats is from 64 to 65 days, but can be as short as 52, or as long as 71 days. Within these limits, gestation may still be considered normal though the survival of kittens born at 56 days or less may be doubtful and, at the other end of the scale, difficulties may arise from the size of the kittens; sometimes cesarean intervention is required.

During this period, the cat needs peace and quiet and a diet richer in calcium (added milk, cheese or bone meal), with a more generous ration of meat (up to 6 oz.), but lighter in starches (so less bread, pasta and rice). To determine the date of parturition knowing the date of the first mating, reference should be made to the table below, remembering to subtract a day, where appropriate, during a leap year.

In the first half of pregnancy, no somatic changes are evident, and it is only after the 40th day that a progressive enlargement of the abdomen is noticeable with a swelling and "pinking -up" of the teats which take on a decided pink or rosy tone when the cat is pregnant.

In the last week, the cat becomes more quiet and begins a methodical search for a suitable place for the birth of its litter exploring the entire house or territory in which it lives. Boxes lined with layers of paper placed in darkened cupboards or other secluded spots, will help her by providing a suitable "nest."

BIRTH

Unlike dogs, cats do not invariably exhibit a lowering of their temperature in the hours immediately preceding parturition; that this symptom cannot be safely relied upon for advance warning. Behavior may vary among individuals: some cats, in the last days, show a loss of appetite or become more aggressive, a behavior recalling the need for self-defense, natural when the animal was living in the wild. Others, to the contrary, seek the company of their owners following them continually, rubbing themselves against their legs, and crouching on the bed as if to convey the need for assistance. Almost all, however, show signs of restlessness, and meow frequently. When the time for the birth arrives, the cat withdraws to the nesting place it has preselected. Often, meowing insistently, it invites the owner to follow and to help. A litter may consist of from one to four kittens, though five or six are not infrequent. As soon as the kittens are born, the mother licks them carefully and checks that they are well formed. If one is seriously deformed, she herself may decide to eliminate it.

Gestation Periods

JANUARY		FEBRUARY		MARCH		APRIL		MAY		JUNE	
1	5 MAR	1	5 APR	1	3 MAY	1	3 JUN	1	3 JULY	1	3 AUG
2	6 MAR	2	6 APR	2	4 MAY	2	4 JUN	2	4 JULY	2	4 AUG
3	7 MAR	3	7 APR	3	5 MAY	3	5 JUN	3	5 JULY	3	5 AUG
4	8 MAR	4	8 APR	4	6 MAY	4	6 JUN	4	6 JULY	4	6 AUG
5	9 MAR	5	9 APR	5	7 MAY	5	7 JUN	5	7 JULY	5	7 AUG
6	10 MAR	6	10 APR	6	8 MAY	6	8 JUN	6	8 JULY	6	8 AUG
7	11 MAR	7	11 APR	7	9 MAY	7	9 JUN	7	9 JULY	7	9 AUG
8	12 MAR	8	12 APR	8	10 MAY	8	10 JUN	8	10 JULY	8	10 AUG
9	13 MAR	9	13 APR	9	11 MAY	9	11 JUN	9	11 JULY	9	11 AUG
10	14 MAR	10	14 APR	10	12 MAY	10	12 JUN	10	12 JULY	10	12 AUG
11	15 MAR	11	15 APR	11	13 MAY	11	13 JUN	11	13 JULY	11	13 AUG
12	16 MAR	12	16 APR	12	14 MAY	12	14 JUN	12	14 JULY	12	14 AUG
13	17 MAR	13	17 APR	13	15 MAY	13	15 JUN	13	15 JULY	13	15 AUG
14	18 MAR	14	18 APR	14	16 MAY	14	16 JUN	14	16 JULY	14	16 AUG
15	19 MAR	15	19 APR	15	17 MAY	15	17 JUN	15	17 JULY	15	17 AUG
16	20 MAR	16	20 APR	16	18 MAY	16	18 JUN	16	18 JULY	16	18 AUG
17	21 MAR	17	21 APR	17	19 MAY	17	19 JUN	17	19 JULY	17	19 AUG
18	22 MAR	18	22 APR	18	20 MAY	18	20 JUN	18	20 JULY	18	20 AUG
19	23 MAR	19	23 APR	19	21 MAY	19	21 JUN	19	21 JULY	19	21 AUG
20	24 MAR	20	24 APR	20	22 MAY	20	22 JUN	20	22 JULY	20	22 AUG
21	25 MAR	21	25 APR	21	23 MAY	21	23 JUN	21	23 JULY	21	23 AUG
22	26 MAR	22	26 APR	22	24 MAY	22	24 JUN	22	24 JULY	22	24 AUG
23	27 MAR	23	27 APR	23	25 MAY	23	25 JUN	23	25 JULY	23	25 AUG
24	28 MAR	24	28 APR	24	26 MAY	24	26 JUN	24	26 JULY	24	26 AUG
25	29 MAR	25	29 APR	25	27 MAY	25	27 JUN	25	27 JULY	25	27 AUG
26	30 MAR	26	30 APR	26	28 MAY	26	28 JUN	26	28 JULY	26	28 AUG
27	31 MAR	27	1 MAY	27	29 MAY	27	29 JUN	27	29 JULY	27	29 AUG
28	1 APR	28	2 MAY	28	30 MAY	28	30 JUN	28	30 JULY	28	30 AUG
29	2 APR	29		29	31 MAY	29	1 JULY	29	31 JULY	2931 AUG	
30	3 APR			30	1 JUNE	30	2 JULY	30	1 AUG	30 1 SEPT	
31	4 APR			31	2 JUNE			31	2 AUG		

JULY		AUGUST		SEPTEMBER		OCTOBER		NOVEMBER		DECEMBER	
1	2 SEPT	1	3 OCT	1	3 NOV	1	3 DEC	1	3 JAN	1	2 FEB
2	3 SEPT	2	4 OCT	2	4 NOV	2	4 DEC	2	4 JAN	2	3 FEB
3	4 SEPT	3	5 OCT	3	5 NOV	3	5 DEC	3	5 JAN	3	4 FEB
4	5 SEPT	4	6 OCT	4	6 NOV	4	6 DEC	4	6 JAN	4	5 FEB
5	6 SEPT	5	7 OCT	5	7 NOV	5	7 DEC	5	7 JAN	5	6 FEB
6	7 SEPT	6	8 OCT	6	8 NOV	6	8 DEC	6	8 JAN	6	7 FEB
7	8 SEPT	7	9 OCT	7	9 NOV	7	9 DEC	7	9 JAN	7	8 FEB
8	9 SEPT	8	10 OCT	8	10 NOV	8	10 DEC	8	10 JAN	8	9 FEB
9	10 SEPT	9	11 OCT	9	11 NOV	9	11 DEC	9	11 JAN	9	10 FEB
10	11 SEPT	10	12 OCT	10	12 NOV	10	12 DEC	10	12 JAN	10	11 FEB
11	12 SEPT	11	13 OCT	11	13 NOV	11	13 DEC	11	13 JAN	11	12 FEB
12	13 SEPT	12	14 OCT	12	14 NOV	12	14 DEC	12	14 JAN	12	13 FEB
13	14 SEPT	13	15 OCT	13	15 NOV	13	15 DEC	13	15 JAN	13	14 FEB
14	15 SEPT	14	16 OCT	14	16 NOV	14	16 DEC	14	16 JAN	14	15 FEB
15	16 SEPT	15	17 OCT	15	17 NOV	15	17 DEC	15	17 JAN	15	16 FEB
16	17 SEPT	16	18 OCT	16	18 NOV	16	18 DEC	16	18 JAN	16	17 FEB
17	18 SEPT	17	19 OCT	17	19 NOV	17	19 DEC	17	19 JAN	17	18 FEB
18	19 SEPT	18	20 OCT	18	20 NOV	18	20 DEC	18	20 JAN	18	19 FEB
19	20 SEPT	19	21 OCT	19	21 NOV	19	21 DEC	19	21 JAN	19	20 FEB
20	21 SEPT	20	22 OCT	20	22 NOV	20	22 DEC	20	22 JAN	20	21 FEB
21	22 SEPT	21	23 OCT	21	23 NOV	21	23 DEC	21	23 JAN	21	22 FEB
22	23 SEPT	22	24 OCT	22	24 NOV	22	24 DEC	22	24 JAN	22	23 FEB
23	24 SEPT	23	25 OCT	23	25 NOV	23	25 DEC	23	25 JAN	23	24 FEB
24	25 SEPT	24	26 OCT	24	26 NOV	24	26 DEC	24	26 JAN	24	25 FEB
25	26 SEPT	25	27 OCT	25	27 NOV	25	27 DEC	25	27 JAN	25	26 FEB
26	27 SEPT	26	28 OCT	26	28 NOV	26	28 DEC	26	28 JAN	26	27 FEB
27	28 SEPT	27	29 OCT	27	29 NOV	27	29 DEC	27	29 JAN	27	28 FEB
28	29 SEPT	28	30 OCT	28	30 NOV	28	30 DEC	28	30 JAN	28	1 MAR
29	30 SEPT	29	31 OCT	29	1 DEC	29	31 DEC	29	31 JAN	29	2 MAR
30	1 OCT	30	1 NOV	30	2 DEC	30 1 JAN		30	1 FEB	30	3 MAR
31	2 OCT	31	2 NOV			31 2 JAN.				31	4 MAR

208

CAT HEALTH

SEXUAL CYCLE OF THE FEMALE

Female cats manifest the sexual cycle (estrous or heat) several times a year during the period (common to all) of the reproductive season. The cycle is composed of four phases:

• Proestrus: not marked by any physical signs, no vaginal discharges, nor swelling of the vulva. The animal may show itself particularly affectionate and docile.

• Estrus: during this phase, the female's behavior pattern is quite distinctive. She emits characteristic calls, assumes a posture with the back arched and the tail to one side, rubs herself along the floor, and rolls over. Often there is some loss of appetite. The duration of this phase is brief if mating takes place quickly; but, if not, it can last a fortnight since ovulation occurs only during the male's penetration. Characteristic estrous behavior generally ceases a few days after mating.

• Metoestrus: if mating has not occurred, the period of time between the end of one heat and the start of the next is generally from two to four weeks; if mating has taken place, but the resulting ovulation has not led to successful fertilization, the time between two periods of heat may last for up to two months giving rise to a state called pseudo or false pregnancy.

• Anestrus: this is the period of rest for the ovaries between one cycle of reproduction and the next and varies in length. If a mating has been successful, the female enters a phase of infertility from the moment of weaning the kittens. Sometimes a heat can even occur during the early stages of pregnancy; In rare cases, the female may be fertilized again. The signs of heat may even appear a week after parturition, especially if the kittens have been separated too quickly from their mother.

THE STAGES OF PARTURITION

• Primary stage: the preparatory one in which the cervix of the uterus swells. This phase can last several hours until contractions begin. The animal may be calm or may be particularly agitated. It refuses food, and turns constantly to inspect its own flanks.

• Secondary stage: begins with the discharge of a dark liquid arising from the breaking of the first fetal envelope. This may be followed by the amniotic sac, which either breaks, or is torn open by the mother.
Finally, the fetus appears, generally emerging completely with just a few pushes. Presentation may be head first or hindquarters first (breech presentation); both are considered normal though problems are more likely to arise with breech presentations.

• Tertiary stage: the elimination of the fetal membranes (afterbirth). These may emerge one at a time after the birth of each fetus or following several or all of the fetuses. Sometimes, after the birth of a few kittens, it seems that parturition is ended, and only after one or two hours, during which the mother looks after the new-born kittens by licking and cleaning them, contractions re-commence and more kittens are born. The maximum duration of parturition is generally 24 hours.

CAT HEALTH

The extraordinary ability to fall from considerable heights and come to little or no harm, and the independence that make it one of the least troublesome animals known, have given rise to a legend of the cat's near-immunity from all physical ills: its famous 'nine lives'. In reality, the cat, as with other animals, is a prey to accidents and illnesses, to the vulnerability of youth, and to the infirmities of old age.

OBSERVATION OF SYMPTOMS

The cat spends much of its day dozing in a state of apparent drowsiness. After a reconnaissance of its territory to assure that no unpleasant surprises are in the offing, it curls up in a quiet corner and goes to sleep. This is, however, a light sleep from which the cat awakes at the slightest disturbance. This 'idleness' is not a sign of laziness and still less of illness, but is part of the ancestral habits of cats which are equipped to save all possible strength when not hunting, their method, in the wild state, of obtaining food which requires enormous, but necessarily short, bursts of energy. But if, when it opens its eyes it does not seem wide awake, remains drowsy, and moves uncertainly, its breathing becomes labored, its eyes reddened, and its coat dull or "spiky", then the cat is certainly sick.
Refusal of food, especially if continuing for more than a day, is one of the first symptoms of a state of poor health. It is not enough to just to feel the cat's nose; its temperature needs to be taken, its behavior watched more closely, and the vet consulted. This will be even more necessary and urgent if more serious symptoms appear: bleeding, vomiting, trembling, rashes, loss of balance, coughing, or difficult breathing.
Even if nothing serious seems to be wrong at first glance, a good owner should automatically carefully watch their cat, especially when it is washing itself. The state of its fur should be checked, as should the eyes and ears for signs of any purulent discharge, and the gums for signs of bleeding. Care should be taken to make sure there are no wounds or parasitic infestations (fleas, for example).
In any event, regular, periodic visits to the vet are necessary…perhaps at the time of its regular booster vaccinations, are all it needs to forestall avoidable risks. In addition, the cat owner must know, at least in general terms, which illnesses the cat is most likely to catch.

THE PRINCIPAL INFECTIOUS DISEASES

There are some rather dangerous diseases, especially for young animals.

Feline calicivirus infection (FCV): This is a feline respiratory virus to which young cats are the most vulnerable. Both this and rhinotracheitis (FVR), the other most common respiratory disease, are often labeled as 'cat flu'. The manifestations of the disease vary considerably, from slight forms characterized by ulceration of the tongue and hard palate, to symptoms of pneumonia. Rhinitis, conjunctivitis and tracheitis are not uncommon.

Feline leukemia virus (FeLV): This disease is very complex and is characterized by a great variety of manifestations arising from the primary and secondary effects of the virus attacking the animal's organism. Those linked directly to viral leukemia include anemia, reproductive disorders in the female, neurological disturbances, and pathological manifestations in bone, kidneys and the coat. There may also be a number of disorders, often of the tumoral type, linked indirectly to the action of the leukemia virus. Diagnosis is therefore possible by specific laboratory testing.

Feline viral immunodeficiency: This disease is characterized by immunosupression and by chronic, recurrent, secondary infections. It is, in many ways, similar to human AIDS, and, as with AIDS, the feline virus, by interfering with the body's defense mechanisms, opens the way for a wide spectrum of secondary diseases whose symptoms are therefore extremely variable. The most common manifestations are: fever, loss of appetite, emaciation, stomatitis, gingivitis, respiratory infections, dermatitis, vomiting, and diarrhea.

Panleucopaenia, or feline infectious enteritis (FIE): This is a viral disease that attacks all felines; transmission occurs through the feces, vomit, and urine. Young cats are particularly vulnerable to contagion. The symptoms are: loss of appetite, fever, abdominal pain, and diarrhea. The disease can be fatal.

Feline infectious peritonitis (FIP): This is currently one of the most important and complex diseases in cats. There are two phases in its progression: the first is, in most cases, asymptomatic; the second, invariably fatal, may appear from a few weeks to many years after the first and is characterized by chronic emaciation, depression, fever, progressive enlargement of the abdomen and sometimes breathing difficulties. Other tell-tale signs may be reproductive disorders, such as miscarriages, still-births, and infant mortality. The virus does not survive long in the environment and is most easily spread where a number of animals are kept in close quarters; for this reason, reputable catteries require proof of vaccination before acceptance of a cat.

Rabies: This disease is particularly dangerous because, unlike the preceding ones, it can also infect humans. Transmission is via the saliva, and occurs usually through a bite.

In very rare cases, if she is too disturbed or sees the kittens handled too much by the owner, she may destroy them even if they were born healthy. Usually, however, she looks after them lovingly, defends them fiercely against any perceived danger, and carries them off to another refuge if the first one is not deemed to be safe enough or is disturbed by too many visitors. Sometimes the kittens born in a litter present characteristics different from those expected, based on the attributes of the sire; this phenomenon, which is not well understood, is called 'superfeta-tion'. Adoption is not infrequent among stray animals, females often accept the feeding and raising of kittens which are not their own.

GESTATION PERIODS

The average gestation period is 65 days subject to the variations previously mentioned. The table on page 208 sets out most likely birth dates from the start of pregnancies.

Feline viral rhinotracheitis: This disease is widespread in stray cats. In its early stages, in addition to fever, there are often fits of sneezing and coughing; in subsequent stages, there appears a nasal discharge, clear at first, then yellowish and purulent, tending to block thenose, forcing the cat to breathe though its mouth. This is accompanied by a heavy inflammation of the eyes with purulent mucus which causes the eyelids to close.

■ **Vaccinations**
The diseases described above are extremely serious since they can cause the animal great suffering and even death. Rather than relying on cure, the only effective protection is through prevention; i.e., by vaccination. Various types of vaccines are available (multipurpose or single-purpose, with attenuated virus or inactive virus); all require regular boosters to maintain their protection. The use of suitable vaccines and a vaccination program should be established by the vet who will take into account the prevailing epidemiological situation. It should, however, be borne in mind that vaccination with live viruses should not be practiced on pregnant cats for whom only dead virus vaccines should be used. When traveling with their cat, owners should remember that some countries do not consider vaccinations sufficient, and impose a period of quarantine to prevent re-introduction of viruses considered to have been eradicated in the country or area in question.

■ **Health records**
All cats should be provided with their own health records, in which must be recorded:
• the name of the animal
• breed, sex, distinctive markings
• name and address of the owner and the vet
• date of all vaccinations administered and of boosters effected

■ **Protozoan diseases**
The cat is sometimes subject to parasitic infections due to the ingestion of, or contact with sources of infestation present in soil, rotten meat, pools and puddles, or which enter the body through cuts and scratches.

Coccidiosis: A contagious infection by coccidae. This is an intestinal illness which strikes animals of all ages. It can cause hemorrhagic diarrhea, dehydration, loss of appetite, and, eventually death.

Toxoplasmosis: Can arise from eating raw, contaminated meat. It may produce widely varying symptoms depending on the part of the body affected, and may provoke myositis, neuritis, lymphangitis, and neurological and ocular disorders. The cat is often suspected of being the principal transmitter of the disease in so far as it is the only species in which the protozoan parasite is able to complete its reproductive cycle. Because of this, the cat is often unjustly driven from houses in which there are small children. In fact, there is no great danger if normal hygienic precautions are taken, and if contact with feces is avoided.

HOW TO KEEP A CAT IN GOOD HEALTH
• During the early part of its life, any kitten should be carefully watched as this is its most vulnerable stage. It should not be taken from its mother too soon...not before being weaned or at eight weeks, whichever is later.
• A kitten is not a toy nor plaything to be given as a birthday present to please a child. It is important to make sure that it will be welcome and that its new owners are willing to look after it properly.
• Whether dealing with a stray or a pedigreed cat, it is essential to have them vaccinated. An immunization program must be devised by a veterinarian and scrupulously followed.

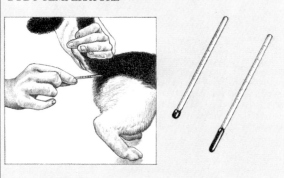

BODY TEMPERATURE

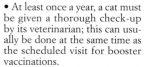

Cats have a temperature of 101.5°F, or a bit more or less. It is advisable to measure rectal temperature which is much more meaningful than any externally taken temperature; choose a moment when the animal is quiet. For accuracy, it is best to measure three times over the course of a day.

The thermometer: the prismatic type is most practical; these are available with either long or short, squat bulbs; the first are easier to insert, but the second are stronger and safer.

Measurement: when insertion is difficult, lubricate the thermometer with Vaseline or ordinary cooking oil. Push gently until the bulb has entered no more than a about ½ inch into the anus and wait about a minute before removing it for reading.

Assessment: a temperature between 100°F and 102°F is considered changed, but not a matter for concern. A reading above 102°F is feverish; between 104°F and 106°F is a high fever. Below 100°F indicates hypothermia, that is, lowering of the body temperature; this occurs in certain pathological conditions, such as serious states of shock, or exposure to extreme cold.

• At least once a year, a cat must be given a thorough check-up by its veterinarian; this can usually be done at the same time as the scheduled visit for booster vaccinations.
• To keep a cat in good condition, a healthy and plentiful diet is necessary and regularly scheduled meals given in scrupulously clean dishes.
• The cat's surroundings must always be kept hygienically clean. Watch carefully when the cat is grooming itself; at these moments, symptoms of illness might be evident and should be referred to the cat's regular veterinarian.
• The cat should always be protected from cold, dampness, and draughts.
• The cat reaches its full size between its first and fifth year; during this period it is at its most vigorous and at its peak for breeding.
• Before mating a female, carefully consider what to do with any kittens. If circumstances are unfavorable and good homes cannot be found for them, it would be better to avoid mating and to have the cat spayed.
• If a cat is well cared for, it should have few ailments, even in old age which will inevitably be a time of decline. An old cat becomes lazy; sometimes becomes deaf or blind, or may develop cataracts. In each case, it needs the best possible care. If its old age becomes too painful, its owner should decide to end needless suffering; the veterinarian can put it to sleep with a painless injection.

IMMUNIZATION PROGRAM				
Disease	Type of vaccine	How administered	Age at 1st vaccination	Boosters
Rhinotracheitis	attenuated	subcutaneous	6-12 weeks	annual
Panleuco paenia	inactive	subcutaneous	6-12 weeks	annual
Calici virus	attenuated	subcutaneous	6-12 weeks	annual
Leukemia	inactive	subcutaneous	6-12 weeks	annual
Rabies	inactive	intramuscular	3 months	annual in risk areas

HANDLING CATS AND ADMINISTERING MEDICINES

As with all domestic animals, cats require periodic vaccinations, specific medicines when ill, and special treatment during different phases of their lives such as when they are very young, very old, or pregnant. In each case, the owner should consult a veterinarian for advice on the best therapy.

Establishing a relationship of trust and collaboration with a veterinarian is a key concept for any pet owner, and to facilitate the relationship, pet owners should learn to take advantage of their constant closeness with their cats to recognize any indications of possible health problems so that they can answer questions from the veterinarian. The veterinarian will build a case history for your cat which will be critical in the event of a major trauma or illness.

Because of the affection for their pets, cat owners learn to note all the minute details of their cat's behavior, particularly details that might be indications of any dysfunction. To perform this function well, owners should follow the precise guidelines for observing cats given on page 201 (Assessing a cat's state of health).

Regular grooming offers an excellent opportunity to give your cat a simple, yet thorough examination.

An owner may sometimes be called on to administer medicines prescribed by the veterinarian and will develop a basic sense of the best way to handle a cat when giving any necessary medication.

HANDLING CATS

In order to observe an animal, administer medicine, or provide first aid, one must hold the cat firmly without upsetting it, so as to keep it from making any sudden movements. Holding a cat against its will is very difficult, and no one can do it successfully without first earning the animal's trust and willingness to collaborate.

Before doing anything to the cat, even before looking into its mouth or ears, you must convince the animal that you are not going to harm it. For this reason, you should hold the cat carefully in your arms; caress it, and make affectionate sounds.

Avoid making any sudden, jerky movements or strange sounds; do not speak in a loud voice. To avoid frightening the cat, you should act in a calm and controlled manner; the environment should be free of disturbances (bright lights, noise, loud music, moving people or objects.) When immobilizing the cat, make sure that you do not hold it in an unnatural position; try to hold the cat in as comfortable a position for the cat as possible.

1

3

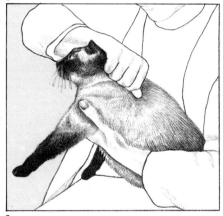

2

4

IMMOBILIZATION AND HOLDING BODY PARTS

…if you need to work on a leg, with one hand, firmly grasp a fold of skin on the scruff of the neck, as near as possible to the head (fig. 1); with the other hand, grasp the body of the cat so you can hold it as firmly as possible against your body leaving the area of the body that needs attention exposed such as the forelegs (fig. 2) or the hind quarters and hind legs (fig. 3);

…if you need to work on the cat's back, it is best to grasp the cat by the scruff of the neck and hold it solidly against a table, pushing firmly down on its back with the other hand;

…if the work is more complex, perhaps painful, or at least such that might frighten the animal, it is best to wrap the cat in a blanket or towel to keep it from trying to escape by clawing and scratching while leaving the part exposed that needs care (fig. 4);

If you need to work on the muzzle, while solidly holding the cat by the scruff of the neck with one hand, use the thumb and last three fingers of the other hand to hold the muzzle firmly while the index finger performs any necessary operation such as opening the mouth or giving the cat a pill.

Only after mastering and practicing these primary precautions in handing on your own cat can you administer the necessary medications or perform needed first aid.

INJECTIONS

It is always best to have your veterinarian or his trained assistant perform injections. However, it is also important that you understand the method in the event that an emergency arises.

SUBCUTANEOUS INJECTIONS

These involve injecting medication under the skin without penetrating muscle. The area where it is easiest to perform this type of injection is that on the upper part of the neck (fig. 1 following page), avoiding the trunk and the central part of the back.

To administer a subcutaneous injection in an emergency:

…disinfect the area with alcohol, which, evaporating, will chill the skin making it less sensitive;

…grasp the skin between thumb and index finger, lift it to form a clearly visible fold (fig. 2 following page);

…hold the syringe, keeping your index finger on the needle to make your hold more secure;

…insert the needle in the fold of skin, move from below and upward for about half inch (fig. 3);

…slowly push the plunger to inject the liquid;

…extract the needle and massage the area well.

PREPARING INJECTIONS:

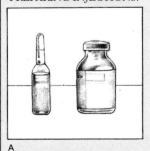

A

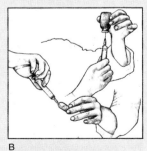

B

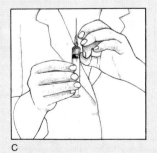

C

D

• Injectable medications are usually packaged in glass vials or in bottles with tops to be scored and broken off (A). To open vials: three small incisions must be made on the glass where the neck narrows using the small tool that accompanies the package. In some cases, the vial is already scored to ease your breaking it open. Grasp the body of the vial with two fingers of one hand and the neck of the vial with two fingers of the other hand; snap off the neck. Avoid the risk of cuts by protecting your fingers with sterile gloves or cloth.

• Bottles with rubber tops are not made to be opened but only freed from their protective cover and then disinfected. The needle of the hypodermic is inserted through the rubber seal on the container and medication drawn into the syringe by pulling back on the plunger.

• Check that the needle is well set in the syringe, then draw the necessary amount of the contents of the vial into the syringe; in the case of bottles with rubber tops, remember that the medicine can be drawn up more easily by making another hole in the top with another sterile needle so as to permit air to enter the bottle to replace the liquid removed. (B).

• To eliminate air from the syringe, hold it with the needle pointing up, draw the plunger back a little (C), then, after tapping the syringe with a fingernail to make any bubbles in the liquid rise, slowly push in the plunger until a drop of liquid appears on the point of the needle (D)

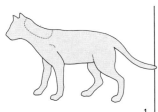

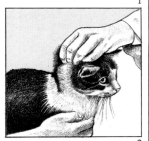

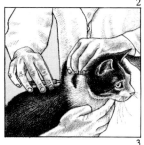

INTRAMUSCULAR INJECTIONS

Intramuscular injections are given when the most rapid absorption of a medication is necessary in order to achieve an immediate effect. The execution is simple; however, care must be taken to avoid damaging nerves or injecting the medicine directly into a vein or artery. Again, it is best to have your veterinarian perform all necessary injections.

Intramuscular injections are made into the rear area of the thigh (fig. 4). Injections in the thigh should be done carefully to avoid hitting the sciatic nerve. In the case of irritating medicines that might lame the animal if improperly administered, take extra precautions.

To administer an intramuscular injection in an emergency when your veterinarian is not available:

…the animal must be held

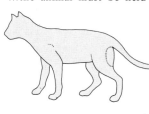

absolutely still; the presence of another person is required. In the case of docile cats, it is best to leave them in the standing position with their head and body held by the assistant (fig. 5);

…with one hand, hold the hind leg into which the injection is to be made; firmly grasp the leg immediately above the hock;

…with the other hand carefully disinfect the selected area;

…holding the syringe pointed slightly toward the back edge of the thigh, carefully push the needle into the muscle for approximately one quarter inch;

…before pressing the plunger, pull it back on it; if blood flows into the syringe, remove the needle and begin again in another place. Only when the withdrawal of the plunger does not draw blood is it safe to push the plunger in slowly to give the medication;

…withdraw the needle, and delicately massage the area.

PILLS, SYRUPS, OR DROPS

In many instances, medications are given in the form of pills, syrups, or drops which may be mixed into the cat's food. This method of administering a medication is less difficult; however, it sometimes is not easy to get your cat to eat the medicated food. When the veterinarian so directs or when the cat itself refuses to eat the medicated food because as it doesn't like the flavor of the medicine, you must administer the medicine directly.

PILLS

To avoid tiresome battles, avoid signaling your cat by letting him see you open the medicine container. Otherwise, the cat will take notice and may try to run and hide. While capsules and various confections can be easily swallowed, some tablets have dry surfaces that can create problems. In such cases, the tablets can be spread with little white Vaseline or some butter or cooking oil to make them slippery. Ask your veterinarian first, of course, as in certain cases oils, etc. might be contraindicated.

TO GIVE PILLS:

…hold the pill between the thumb and middle finger of one hand;

…with the other hand, make the cat open its mouth by pressing the upper lip against the teeth just behind the canine teeth, using the thumb on one side and the index and middle finger on other; as soon as an opening is formed, lower the jaw using the index finger of the hand holding the pill (fig. 6);

…when the animal opens its mouth, quickly push the pill into the back of the mouth toward the base of the tongue (fig. 7);

…close the cat's mouth; hold

its head slightly raised, and gently massage its throat, moving up and down, to help it swallow (fig. 8);

…if necessary, have the cat drink a little water to keep it from spitting out the pill.

TO GIVE SYRUPS AND DROPS:

The easiest way to administer syrups and drops is to put the necessary dosage in a clean, syringe (without a needle) or a plastic eye dropper. To administer the medication:

…insert the blunt tip of the syringe or eye dropper between the canines and the rear premolars while holding the head of the animal slightly raised (fig. 9);

…push the plunger or squeeze

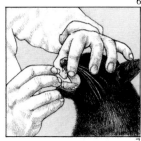

the bulb of the eye dropper to allow the liquid to trickle into the mouth cavity. As soon as the liquid leaves the syringe or dropper, the animal will begin to swallow.

…the medication should be administered relatively quickly, while, at the same time giving the cat enough time to swallow to avoid some of the medication's reaching the trachea making the cat cough.

…Be prepared to have the cat

shake its head or drool… particularly if the medication is unpalatable to the cat. Occasionally, the cat will drool and shake its head which means that you will probably be showered with saliva and medication.

EYE MEDICATIONS

Medications for eye disorders are usually in the form of eye drops or salves.

EYE DROPS:

Carefully clean the eye with cotton dipped in boric acid. Take care not to scratch the eye as cotton can be abrasive; to apply the drops:

…with one hand, raise the animal's head holding the muzzle between thumb and index finger; at the same time, gently pull down the lower eyelid with your middle finger;

…hold the eye dropper above the eye resting while your hand on the cat's forehead; carefully deposit the required number of drops into the eye. (fig. 10).

It is best to keep the eye dropper at a distance of at least one inch from the eye to avoid accidental contact if the cat sudden-

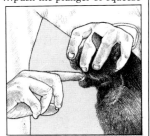

ly moves its head.

TO ADMINISTER SALVES TO THE EYE:

In the case of salves, extra attention must be paid so as not to touch the eyeball with the tube. To apply salves:

…apply the required amount of salve to the index finger of one hand;

…with the other hand grasp the

cat by the scruff of the neck;

…hold the muzzle with the first hand and use the middle finger to lower the eyelid;

…place the salve inside the lower eyelid (fig. 11);

…close the eyelid and lightly massage by opening and closing the eyelid.

EAR MEDICATIONS:

These are usually prepared in the form of drops, salves, or creams.

First the ear must be very carefully cleaned; remember, the blood vessels in a cat's ear are very fragile.

…hold the head firmly with one hand; with the other hand, drop the prescribed dosage into the ear canal (fig. 12);

…carefully massage the base of the ear pavilion to assure that the medicine penetrates and is dispersed within the ear canal.

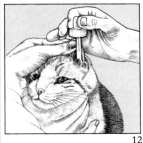

GUM RINSES:

Using mouth washes or gargles on cats is difficult. It is far simpler to apply these solutions directly to the gums.

…wrap some cotton around your index finger forming a cap which you can firmly hold with the thumb of the same hand (fig. 13).

…dip the wrapped finger in the solution to be applied and let the cotton absorb the product (fig. 14);

…rub the cotton covered finger across the gums delicately massaging while working from bottom of the gum in an upwards direction (fig. 15).

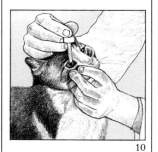

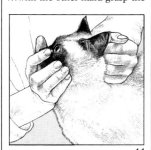

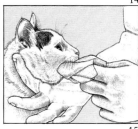

At times, particularly during the mating season, cats, and especially males, if allowed to roam, will spend days far from home. The owner worries, fearing the cat may be lost, stolen, or worse. In the end the cat usually returns, not only dirty and thinner, but also often in bad physical shape...scratched and cut from territorial battles with other cats. The cat must be given immediate proper treatment.

Other health problems and wounds can be caused by a wide variety of accidents. Many are caused because of domestic oversights such as burns caused by hot stoves or boiling water, poisonings caused by unguarded or improperly stored toxic products, or from the ingestion of poison which have been placed to eliminate rodents, insects or other household pests. Automobile accidents are also a common cause of fractures.

Because they are able to change their body position in midair landing squarely on all four feet, cats are rarely hurt by falls; however, falls from great heights can cause bone fractures.

In every case, owners must be able to apply first aid, both to avoid aggravating the injury during transportation to the nearest veterinarian and also to alleviate the cat's suffering. Properly applied, first aid can and often does save an animal's life.

SKIN CUTS
Skin cuts are the most common type of wound requiring first aid treatment. The wounds may be caused by sharp metal, bites, scratches, firearms, or can be external wounds which are a byproduct from grave traumas such as being hit by a car or falling from a great height. The first step is to determine the extent and depth of the wound. The wound may be only a slight graze or superficial cut that injures only the skin, or it may be deeper in which case damage may have been done beneath the skin...a vein or an artery may be cut or nerves and tendons may have suffered damage.

DANGEROUS WOUND AREAS
Some wounds present particular dangers because they are located in areas where vital organs may easily have suffered trauma (fig. 1).
NECK (a)
The trachea is located in the lower part of the neck; cuts to the trachea can cause breathing

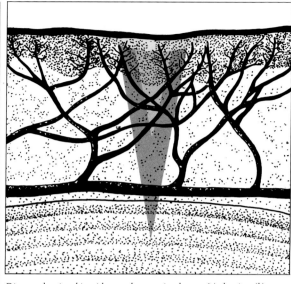

Diagram showing skin with wounds or varying degrees: (a) abrasions (b) superficial cuts (c) deep cuts.

difficulties.
Nicks or cuts to the jugular vein or carotid artery can cause life-threatening hemorrhages.

THORAX (b)
A deep wound to the thorax may penetrate the rib cage, causing dangerous wounds to the lungs often resulting in the entry of air into the pleural cavity (pneumothorax).

ABDOMEN (c)
Deep wounds in this area, particularly on the sides where the muscle layer is thin, may damage important internal organs; particularly large wounds may cause exposure of the viscera, a highly dangerous situation.

FORELEGS (d)
Large surface veins run down the upper part of the foreleg; if cut, this can lead to serious hemorrhages that may cause quickly death through the loss of blood.

HIND LEGS (e)
Just beneath the hock is the Achilles tendon which, if severed, may render he cat lame.

CONTROLLING HEMORRHAGES:
If the loss of blood is limited, it may be enough apply pressure on the wound using a pad of sterile cotton, a clean handkerchief, or a strip of clean cloth.
If the blood does not stop flowing, the wound must be chilled using ice that has been wrapped in a sterile cloth or, as a last resort, by using a clean cloth frequently wet in cold water and wrung out (keep the wound as clean and sterile as possible.)
If the wound is severe, the first step is to control the hemorrhaging by applying a tourniquet.

CLEANING AND DISINFECTING:
If the wound is located where it can be treated, the first thing to do is clean and disinfect it.
The hair around the wound must first be cut away, beginning with the hair nearest the border of the wound and without let-

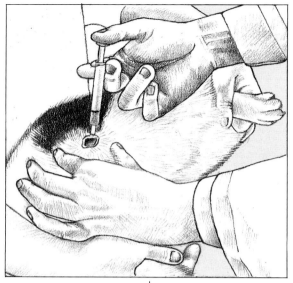

ting any hair fall into the wound itself. For this reason, it is a good idea to cover the wound first with sterile cotton or cloth before using sterile, blunt tipped scissors to cut away the hair.
Washing. If the wound is a graze or superficial cut, use a sterile cotton swab or cloth dipped in warm water mixed with disinfectant. If the wound is deep, it is best to use a syringe (without a needle) to inject water mixed

with a little disinfectant into the wound (fig. 2).
Disinfecting. Carefully disinfect the wound using water-based solutions of iodine, organic forms of mercury, chlorine, or hydrogen peroxide. Avoid using running water which is never sterile and may contain harmful chemical residues.
Protecting the wound. The wound must be protected with a bandage to avoid any further

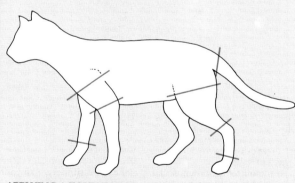

APPLYING A TOURNIQUET:

If the loss of blood is abundant and can't be stopped by a pressure bandage, a tourniquet must be applied until the animal arrives at the veterinary hospital. Tourniquets can be used only for wounds to the legs and the tail where they can be applied just above the wound at the points indicated in the above figure.
Applying the tourniquet:
...wrap the tourniquet at the chosen point and tie a simple knot;
...tighten the tourniquet until it slows the bleeding;
...finish by tying the two ends of the tourniquet. To make it easier

to remove, it is best to make a simple knot, but one that won't become loose (figure below).
...if a long time will pass before seeing the veterinarian, loosen the tourniquet for a few seconds every few minutes to permit some blood circulation.

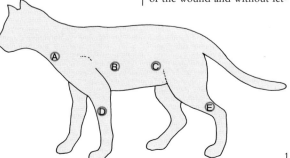

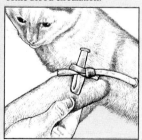

A FIRST AID KIT FOR YOUR CAT

Keep a cat first aid kit in your home and take one with you during trips. Doing so will assure that you are able to take immediate action, using the correct materials, in many emergency situations. Fully equipped kits are available for sale.

…Container. The container for the kit should be small and light but strong and preferably waterproof; a large toilet case or a plastic refrigerator bag with a hermetic seal are two practical and inexpensive possibilities.

…Instruments. All instruments

should be of good quality, carefully disinfected, cleaned and wrapped to avoid any contamination.

…Tweezers. Useful for removing thorns, foreign objects in the eye, nose, ears, and fragments of skin or other material contaminating wounds. The best shape are tweezers which have a narrow, blunt end.

…Scissors. These are used to cut gauze and bandages and to remove hair from around wounds; the easiest to use and least dangerous have rounded, slightly curved tips.

…Syringes. Used to inject medicines and, without the needle, to wash out deep wounds with disinfectant solutions.

… A flashlight and extra batteries. Used to look into ears, the mouth, and wounds. This should be small, easily handled, and have a well focused beam.

…Hemostatic materials. These are used to reduce the loss of blood from hemorrhages and must include sterile, gauze bandages.

…Tourniquet. Used to reduce or arrest localized hemorrhages on the legs and tail.

…Ice bag. Used to stop small hemorrhages and also for

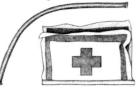

contusions, sprains, or heatstroke.

…Disinfectants. These should be highly antiseptic without, however, causing any burning, which would cause adverse reactions from the cat.

…Hydrogen peroxide. Good for disinfecting scrapes and superficial cuts, particularly those containing dirt, rust, or plant parts, since it reduces the danger from invasive tetanus bacteria.

…Iodiform disinfectant, non-alcoholic. Will not burn and is a good disinfectant. It can be diluted with sterile water to wash out dirty or deep wounds; may be applied undiluted on clean wounds.

…Sterile water. For cleansing wounds or washing out dust or foreign materials from the eyes.
Materials for dressings to be used as protective dressings or splints:

…Bandages. One to two inches wide, best if bordered.
…Gauze pads. Sterile, in single or multiple packages.
…Spools of adhesive tape-one to two inches wide.
…Sterile cotton batting.

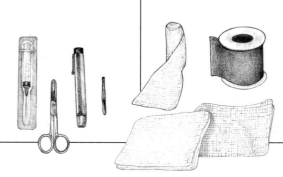

contamination and to keep movements of the animal from re-opening it causing a further loss of blood.

BANDAGING:
PAWS OR THE ENDS OF THE LEGS:
Place wads of cotton between the toes avoiding if possible, any direct contact between the cotton and the wound; apply a gauze pad over the wound;

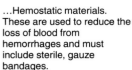
1

2

wrap a gauze bandage around the leg up to the foot pads;
to make the dressing more secure, twist the bandage every two turns (fig. 1);
apply strips of adhesive tape wrapping the dressing laterally as well as above and below (fig. 2);
finally, apply another strip of adhesive tape on the edge of the dressing making it partially adhere to the fur.

FRONT OR BACK LEGS:
Apply a gauze pad above the wound or, if not possible, a piece of cotton or linen cloth; do not use synthetic fabric (fig. 3);
fix the gauze with a strip of adhesive plaster to keep it from moving (fig. 4);
carefully wrap the dressing around the leg until you have at least three layers of gauze (fig. 5);
fix the dressing at the two ends with adhesive tape, making it adhere to the fur (fig. 6);
if the wound is located near a joint, it is best to include the joint in the dressing (fig. 7).

NECK AND SHOULDERS:
Place a gauze pad above the wound and hold it in place with a strip of bandage;
wrap the dressing several times around the neck and thorax (fig. 1 on page 215);
cross the dressing around the back and also between the fore limbs;
complete the dressing with

GRAVE TRAUMA

When a cat suffers grave trauma that puts its life in danger, the help giver must first ascertain if the animal is still alive and rush the animal immediately to the nearest veterinary hospital. If the cat is immobile and lifeless, check for vital life signs:
…closely observe the thorax and abdomen for breathing movement.
…check for a heartbeat by placing a hand on the lower part of the left side of the thorax (fig. A).
…check for arterial pulse at the level of the femoral artery by placing the index, middle, and ring finger of one hand inside the thigh (fig. B).
…check the vision by passing a hand in front of the eyes to see if they follow the movement.
…check consciousness by rapidly nearing a hand to an eye. If the animal still has conscious vision, it will shut its eyes.
…check photoreceptive reflexes by directing a flash-light at a pupil to see if it contracts. The absence of this reflex indicates a grave state of cerebral depression.

A

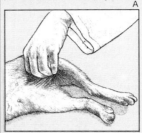
B

…make sure there are no wounds to the limbs before moving the animal.
…To move the animal, use a rigid flat-bottomed container with sides at least six to ten inches high that is large enough for the animal to lie down in a natural position.

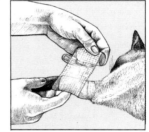
3

5

4

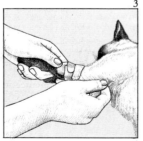
6

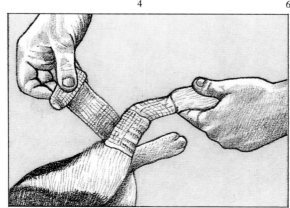
7

three or four passes over the area of the wound;

fix the dressing in front by wrapping the edge with adhesive tape that adheres partially to the fur (fig. 2);

fix the dressing with adhesive tape in the same way below the wound.

THORAX AND ABDOMEN:

Apply a gauze pad over the wound;

fix the pad in place with a ban-

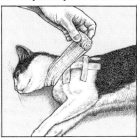

1

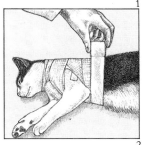

2

dage, making it adhere partially to the fur (fig. 3);

wrap the dressing with several turns (fig. 4);

fix the ends of the dressing with adhesive bandages and wrap the two ends along the edges of the dressing, taping them to adhere partially to the fur.

THIGHS AND GLUTEUS:

Apply a gauze pad to the wound;

fix the pad in place by wrapping a bandage around the part to be dressed (fig. 5);

to avoid movement of the bandage, wrap the thigh, flanks, and abdomen (fig. 6);

fix the dressing with two strips

3

4

of adhesive tape applied to the edges partially adhered to the fur.

Cats will not tolerate bandages on their muzzle, but sometimes they are necessary.

EYES:

Carefully apply a gauze pad over the eye;

wrap a gauze bandage or elastic bandage, beginning at the pad and wrapping the bandage around the neck and behind

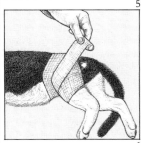

5

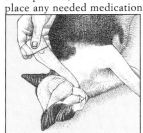

6

the ear on the opposite side (fig. 7);

after making several turns in the direction indicated, wrap the bandage around the healthy eye and ear on the same side, crossing the bandage and making a pair of turns (fix. 8) ; then fix the dressing with tape.

EARS:

The following is the easiest way to protect a cut on the inside of the ear:

Attach a strip of bandage to the edge of the ear pavilion that is wide enough so that part extends to the sides and long enough to run the entire length of the pavilion;

place any needed medication

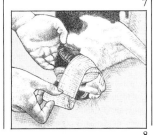

7

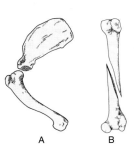

8

on the wound and cover it with a bandage;

apply a second strip of bandage over the first so that the edges of it adhere along the entire length of the first bandage.

DISLOCATIONS, FRACTURES, AND SPRAINS

Animals are sometimes involved in accidents that cause trauma to the bones, such as dislocations, fractures, and sprains. The most frequent cause is being hit by an automobile or other vehicle; however, such wounds can also be caused by a fall or from physical kicks and blows. These can be simple sprains (when the articular ligaments are wrenched but not broken); luxations (A) (when the two bony ends of an articulation are dislocated due to serious damage to the ligaments); or actual fractures. These can be complete fractures (B)—the bone is divided into two parts; multiple, fractures (C)—the bone is broken into several fractures that break into fragments of varying size, or may even be comminuted;; incomplete fractures (D)—the break does not affect the entire bone, which partially maintains its integrity.

Since the bones of kittens are more elastic because they have not yet calcified, and fractures to their bones are called green

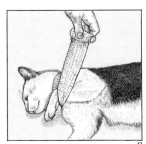

A   B

C   D   E

stick fractures (E) and are similar to what happens when a young branch cracks from being bent too far.

In the case of compound fractures, part of the broken bone cuts through the muscles and skin and is exposed and visible. Such wounds require immediate cleaning, disinfecting, and bandaging to prevent infection. All these events require the

immediate attention of veterinarian. When it is not possible to take the animal to a veterinarian immediately, the injured limb should be immobilized using a temporary splint.

IMMOBILIZING AND SPLINTING A LIMB: FORELIMB: ELBOW, ARM, AND SHOULDER

Wrap two sufficiently wide gauze bandages or long strips of canvas around the neck and injured limb, from the bottom up. The limb should be bent and held against the thorax (fig. 9);

to prevent the animal from straightening the limb, after several turns, change the direction of the wrapping and wrap the dressing around the front of the leg (fig. 10).

The dressing should then be held in place with bandages or adhesive tape.

HIND LIMB: LEG AND HOCK:

Wrap the limb with a gauze bandage or long strip of canvas. To keep it from slipping off, wrap it around the thigh and abdomen (fig. 11);

wrap a strip of cotton batting around the dressing. To keep it in place, wrap another dressing over the cotton batting (fig. 12); apply three splints of an adequate length to the limbone in front and the others at the sides (fig. 13);

9

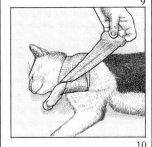

10

fix the splints with two or more strips of bandage or adhesive tape (fig. 14).

Ends of the leg and forearms

Wrap the limb with a gauze bandage or with long strips of canvas (fig. 15);

wrap a strip of cotton batting around the dressing. To hold it in place, a further dressing can be put over the cotton (fig. 1 on page 216);

apply three splints of an adequate length around the limb, two at the sides and one inside;

fix the splints with two or more strips of bandage or adhesive tape.

11

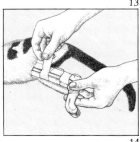

12

13

14

HIND LIMB: KNEE AND FEMUR:

—To immobilize the knee and also the hock, a crutch formed of strong wire such as from a bent coat hanger (as indicated in figure 2A,page 216) can be used, connected with bandages or adhesive tape; the area that will rest against the animal should be lined with a soft

15

material such as cotton batting attached with gauze bandages. Extend the limb within the crutch and hold it in place with strips of bandage. To increase

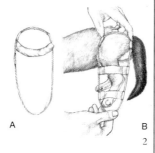

1

the adhesion, wrap strips of bandage around the crutch at the points where the strips are fixed, near the limb (fig. 2B).

FOREIGN OBJECTS

Cats are bothered greatly by foreign objects in the eyes, ears, or nose. In such cases, the animal will appear restless, will blink frequently, will keep one eye half-closed, will violently shake its head, scratch at its ear, or sneeze continuously. Such behavior indicates the presence of foreign objects and also will usually indicate its location.

IN THE EYE:

If the foreign object is lodged in the cornea, the cat must be taken to a veterinarian (fig. 3).

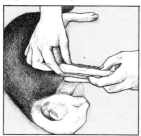

A   B
2

Only if the foreign object is on the surface and clearly visible: hold the cat's head still, or have the head immobilized so as to prevent the cat from making any sudden movements; pull back the area of skin above or beneath the eye to open the eyelid and ascertain the exact position of the body; using round tipped tweezers, carefully grab the foreign body and remove it quickly, but not

3

abruptly (fig. 4); clean the eye with a gauze pad and rinse it with a wash (such as boric acid).

IN THE EAR:

To extract a foreign object from the opening of the ear canal: look carefully inside the ear with a flashlight to find the foreign object; have someone else hold the cat's head still, and remove the body with round tipped tweezers (fig. 5);

4

if you cannot see a foreign object but the symptoms remain, take the cat to a veterinarian.

IN THE NOSE:

To remove a foreign object from the nose (something that rarely happens to cats): carefully clean any mucous from the nostril; look carefully to identify the foreign object; if possible, remove it with round tipped tweezers;

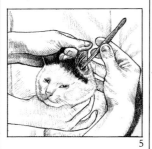

5

if you cannot find a foreign object and the symptoms remain, take the cat to a veterinarian.

IN THE MOUTH:

Things, even quite large things, can get into a cat's mouth that it can neither spit out nor swallow. To extract a foreign object from the mouth: raise the lips and check the teeth for pieces of wood or bone that have become stuck in the teeth and are cutting the tongue (fig. 6); if the body is located deeper within the cat's mouth, take it to a veterinarian.

BREATHING DIFFICULTIES:

If the cat is having difficulty breathing, it requires immediate care. To locate and extract the foreign object:

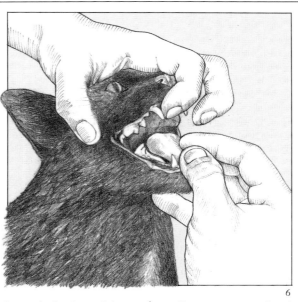

6

foreign bodies located deep in the pharynx can be located by looking down the cat's throat using good light after opening its jaws and pressing down its tongue; having found the foreign object, try to grab it either with your fingers or with round tipped tweezers, and remove it. If this is not successful, the animal should be suspended with its head down, holding it by the hind legs and tail; give the thorax a reasonably strong hit with one hand to try to expel the foreign object (fig. 7); this is similar to the Heimlich maneuver used on choking humans; if this method fails to obtain the desired result, have someone else hold the cat upside down and repeat the procedure; however, instead of striking the thorax, use both hands to apply quick compression to the sides of the thorax. If all else fails, take the cat immediately to the veterinarian.

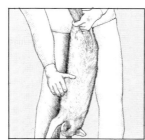

7

BURNS

To determine the seriousness of a burn, consider the source of heat. Burns from liquids (scalds), in particular those from boiling oil, are the most serious; those caused by contact with hot, solid objects are less dangerous because they are

usually more confined. Remember that burns can have serious systemic effects that can involve the entire organism resulting in lowered blood pressure, shock, or kidney failure. Such effects are related to amount of the body burned. Burns that involve more than half of the body can easily result in death.

FIRST AID FOR BURNS:

immediately chill the injured area with ice or cold water; apply a source of cold, such as a piece of ice wrapped in a sterile cloth, for 10-15 minutes (fig. 8); dry the area; do not rub it merely lightly pat the area dry using sterile cotton batting; cover the affected area with pieces of sterile canvas or gauze without using creams, salves, or oils; do not break any blisters.

DEGREES OF BURNS:

1st degree: Skin become red, often swollen; heals in a few days.

8

2nd degree: Reddening of skin and appearance of small blisters full of serous liquid; healing is slower but does not leave scars and the skin does not fall off.
3rd degree. Skin falls off and affected tissue is destroyed; a crust forms, and scars remain after healing.

ELECTRICAL BURNS:

In the case of electrical burns, make certain that contact with

the source of electricity has been broken before performing any first aid procedures. This operation should be done with all necessary caution to avoid coming in contact with the electric current yourself. Remember that the cat itself will conduct electricity and must not be touched while still in contact with the electrical source.

Electric shock can make the animal lose consciousness and appear lifeless. You must check to see if it is still alive and then perform artificial respiration.

In cases in which an electrical burn has caused cardiac arrest, cardiac massage must immediately be performed .

Burns caused by current at the specific point of contact should be treated as any other burns.

DROWNING

Because they are good swimmers, cats rarely drown.

ARTIFICIAL RESPIRATION:

…Keep the animal lying on its side with the neck and head extended and the muzzle raised.
…blow directly into the nostrils while holding the mouth shut with one hand, or blow directly into the mouth while holding the nostrils closed with the thumb and middle finger, using one hand to hold the cat's lips shut at the sides to prevent loss of air (fig. below). Use relatively strong, regular breaths; apply them rapidly (two to three per second) until the thorax is moving sufficiently on its own.
…Leaving the muzzle free, press on the thorax to facilitate the exhalation of air (fig. at bottom).
…Perform the artificial respiration procedures seven to ten times per minute until the cat is breathing on its own.

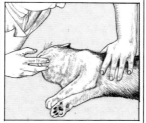

CARDIAC MASSAGE:

…Hold the cat on its side with the neck and head extended to facilitate breathing.

…Place one hand under the thorax and rest the other on the top the thorax and at the same relative place as the first hand. Since cats are small animals, two or three fingers are enough to use as opposed to using the entire palm of the hand.

…Rapidly press against the thorax and repeat the movements rhythmically with a frequency of 60-100 movements per minute.

…Continue until a heartbeat is felt; check the heartbeat's regularity for several minutes.

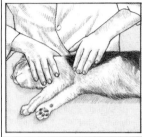

Drowning is more probable with kittens or old, debilitated animals or, even more often, with animals that have experienced an injury prior falling into the water.

If the animal seems lifeless when taken out of the water, check for its vital signs (see "Grave Trauma" on page 214).

FIRST AID FOR DROWNING:
free the air passages and stomach of any ingested water by hold the cat head-down by its hind legs (fig. below);
if necessary, help it expel the water by pressing on and then releasing the thorax while holding the cat by its feet:
if the cat does not regain consciousness, perform artificial respiration.

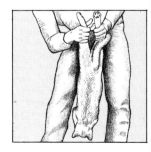

POISONING
Most incidents of accidental poisonings among cats are caused by a cat's contacting or ingesting a substance carelessly or accidentally left exposed in the wrong place by humans. Cats are also sometimes poi-

soned as the result of eating products set out to poison unwanted animals such as rats or mice. There are also many plants or parts of plants that can have toxic effects if ingested.

HOW TO ACT IN THE CASE OF A POISONING:
Poisonings are dangerous emergencies primarily because they cannot be correctly diagnosed, even by a veterinarian, unless the necessary information is provided.

If you observe apparent symptoms of poisoning in a cat (violent muscular contractions, acute vomiting, weakness, hemorrhaging, tremors, convulsions, collapse), immediately call the veterinarian; at the same time you should also try to identify any items that might help identify the cause of the poisoning.
Check to determine if there are any toxic plants nearby or any poisonous substances left within cat's reach;
check to determine if pesticides have been applied to nearby areas such as fields, plants, or refuse dumps;
check for the possible presence of poisonous bait or powders put out for mice or rats in area.
If possible, try to establish how much of the toxic substance was consumed, and how much time has passed since it was consumed.

While waiting for the veterinarian, if the poison was ingested less than a half hour ago, try to make the cat vomit by giving it the following substances as an emetic:
a teaspoon of a warm, concentrated solution of water and soap or water and salt; or
a teaspoon of hydrogen peroxide;
Whatever the cat vomits should be saved and shown to the veterinarian to help in the analysis to determine the poisoning agent.
If a chemical has caused external or internal burns, after washing the area with running water, apply compresses or have the cat swallow one of the following solutions, depending on the chemical involved:
water and vinegar or water and lemon juice to neutralize the action of alkalis such as caustic soda, potassium soda, or quicklime;
water and bicarbonate of soda or water and soap, but only if the burns are external, to neutralize the action of acids such as sulfuric, hydrochloric, or nitric.
Milk should be used only in poisonings involving heavy metals such as lead or mercury; however, since the milk's fat content favors the intestinal

COMMON POISONOUS PLANTS

PLANT	POISONOUS PARTS	TOXIC POWER	SYMPTOMS
Aquilegia vulgaris Columbine	the entire plant	•••	Vomiting, diarrhea, convulsions. Death from cardiovascular failure
Buxus sempervirens Box	leaves	••	Gastrointestinal irritation
Colchicum autumnalis Colchicum	the entire plant	•••	Gastrointestinal irritation. Muscular and respiratory paralysis
Conium maculatum Coniine	the entire plant	•••	Tremors, convulsions, progressive paralysis. Respiratory and cardiac failure, death
Dieffenbachia Dieffenbachia*	stems, apical meristems	••	Strong irritation of mouth, esophagus, stomach, intestines (latex irritant)
Euphorbia* Euphorbia	the entire plant	•	gastrointestinal irritation
Euphorbia pulcherrima Poinsettia	leaves, flowers	••	gastrointestinal irritation
Hedera helix Ivy	berries, leaves, stems	••	Gastrointestinal irritation. Elevated doses cause depression of the nervous and cardiac systems
Hydrangea macrophylla Hydrangea	leaves, flowers	••	Gastric pain, vomiting, diarrhea
Ilex aquifolium Holly	berries	••	Vomit and heavy diarrhea
Ipomoea purpurea Morning Glory	seeds	••	Hallucinogenic
Nerium oleander Oleander	the entire plant	•••	Gastrointestinal irritation. Depression of the nervous system and the heart
Philodendron* Philodendron	leaves, stems	•	Gastrointestinal irritation
Ranunculus acer Buttercup	stems, sap	••	Strong irritation on contact (mouth, esophagus, stomach, intestines)
Rhododendron* Rhododendron	leaves, flowers	••	Vomit. Nervous symptoms
Wisteria* Wisteria	seeds, fruit	•	Gastrointestinal irritation

• moderate; •• medium, mortal at high doses; ••• high, often mortal; * all species

COMMON POISONS

POISON	SOURCE	SYMPTOMS
Acetone	solvents	Inhalation: bronchopulmonary irritation Ingestion: vomiting, diarrhea, depression of breathing and heart rate
Acids, strong (sulfuric, hydrochloric, nitric)	Cleaning products, Metal detergents, Defoliants	Serious burns on contact or ingestion
Alkalies, strong (caustic and potassium soda, quicklime)	Cleaners for metal, pots, glassware	Serious burns on contact or ingestion
Ammonium chloride	detergents; antiseptics	Vomiting and gastric pains Cardiovascular collapse
Aniline	aniline dyes colored pencils, pastels, paints	Breathing difficulty, vomiting, convulsions

absorption of soluble toxins in fats, its use must be avoided in all other cases since this would only serve to aggravate the situation.

EXPOSURE AND FROSTBITE

Exposure is defined as an injury caused by the exposure to intense cold and is limited to the less-protected parts of the body: the ears, tail, legs, and paws. First aid in such cases is limited to wrapping the animal in a blanket and gently warming the injured areas with warm water (not above 104°F); the legs should be immersed in a basin; the ears and tail can be daubed with warm compresses. After ten minutes, gently pat the area dry to avoid damaging the skin. Then spread the affected areas with white Vaseline jelly.

Frostbite is a far more serious problem and is caused by extended exposure to cold. Adult cats are usually capable of protecting themselves from this danger, and frostbite more often strikes kittens, very old or ill cats. If a cat's internal rectal temperature drops below 98.6 degrees F. and its heartbeat slows, the degree of frostbite is dangerous; the cat requires immediate attention from a veterinarian.

Bring the cat to a dry, well heated area, delicately pat it dry if it is wet (do not use a blow-dryer for this causes rapid evaporation and could aggravate the situation), and wrap the cat in a warm blanket.

If the frostbite is serious, the cat should immediately be immersed in warm water (104-122°F) and massaged vigorously to reactivate circulation.

HEATSTROKE

Cats lack a built in cooling system such as that provided by perspiration and are therefore in danger of suffering from heatstroke if exposed to high temperatures for extended periods of time. The most common cause is cats left closed in cars exposed to a hot sun (even on a cloudy day, the hidden sun can cause the temperature in a closed car to rise to an intolerable degree). The increase in body temperature, which can go past 104°F, causes panting and a state of agitation followed by profound torpor and the loss of consciousness.

The cat should immediately be taken to a shaded, airy place and bathed with cold water or sprayed with alcohol. Both are systems of evaporation which result in lowering the body temperature of the cat.

When the cat regains consciousness, continue to apply cold wraps to its head.

Before continuing any trip by car, make sure that the car is cool. During any trip, leave a window partially open for air circulation and, in the case of treatment for heat stroke, continue to bathe the body and back of the cat at periodic intervals.

CONVULSIONS

Loss of consciousness and convulsions can be the result of different causes and only a veterinarian can diagnose the cause and suggest a treatment. Even so, it is best to take certain measures in the event of convulsions:

 do not move the animal during the attack unless it is in a dangerous position;

do not try to block its movements or to open its mouth;

dim lights and lower any sound;

 remove any objects it might strike against and injure itself.

If the convulsions are a result of heatstroke or of a disease the cat is known to have, take any further necessary steps.

INSECT OR SPIDER/ SCORPION (ARACHNID) BITES AND STINGS

Some insects (caterpillars A, bees B, wasps C., hornets D) and some arachnids (spiders E, scorpions F) secrete irritating substances, and sting or bite and inject venom causing local wounds and, in some cases, far more serious health problems.

If your cat's behavior makes you suspect it may have been bitten (restlessness or licking or appearing to bite itself frequently in one spot), examine the skin to locate the irritated area.

As a first aid precaution:

apply a cotton pad soaked in pure diluted ammonia to the site using care if it is near the eyes or mouth.

Take the cat to the veterinarian:

if it has been stung by a scorpion,

if there are many stings from bees or wasps,

if swelling seems excessive,

if there are signs of fever or any loss of consciousness.

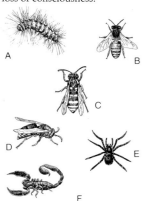

COMMON POISONS		
POISON	**SOURCE**	**SYMPTOMS**
Arsenic	rat poisons, herbicides, wood preservatives, dyes	Vomiting, diarrhea, and abdominal cramps, tremors, cyanosis, & cardiovascular collapse
Barbiturates	sleeping pills	Cerebral depression, coma, respiratory depression
Benzene	combustibles, solvents, detergents	Inhalation: coughs, breathing difficulty, depression of the nervous system. Ingestion: vomiting, diarrhea, nervous symptoms
Camphor	insect repellents, liniments	Gastrointestinal irritation, nervous excitement
Carbamates	insecticides, antiparasitics	Tremors, uncoordinated movements, muscular spasms, vomiting
Carbon monoxide	combustion of organic substances in a closed space	Uncoordinated movements, weakness, breathing difficulties.
Carbon tetrachloride	fire-retardant foams, solvents	Serious liver and kidney damage
Cyanide	rat poisons, herbicides	Asphyxia, coma, rapid death
Formalin	Domestic and industrial disinfectants	Serious gastrointestinal irritation, cardiovascular collapse
Hexachlorophene	soaps and antiseptic solutions	Vomiting, diarrhea, abdominal cramps, hepatic and nervous disturbances
Hypochloric acid	bleaches and disinfectants	Irritates and burns skin and mucous membranes
Mercury	fungicides, herbicides, insecticides	In the acute form: serious gastrointestinal irritation, stomatitis, convulsions and coma
Naphthalene	moth repellent, moth balls	Gastrointestinal irritation, anemia, and jaundice
Nitrobenzene	shoe polishes, dyes	Loss of coordination, convulsions, breathing difficulties, vomiting
Organophosphates	insecticides, antiparasitics	Vomiting, diarrhea, myosis, slavering, tremors, spasms, convulsions
Oxalic acid	bleaches, stain removers, detergents	oral irritation, vomiting and serious diarrhea
Perborates	bleaches	Irritation and burns of skin and mucous membranes
Phenol	disinfectants	Vomiting, diarrhea, abdominal cramps; hepatic disturbances
Soaps	detergents	Gastrointestinal irritation
Trichloro-ethylene	dry-cleaning solvent	Nervous-system depression, cardiovascular collapse, liver and kidney damage
Turpentine	solvents	Gastrointestinal irritation, kidney damage, blood in urine, respiratory failure

GLOSSARY

Agouti: coat composed of hairs each of which, from the root to the tip, has 2 or 3 bands of a color different from that of the hair (see Ticking). The name is derived from that of the rodent.

Albino: cat with white fur and pink eyes due to the total absence of pigment.

Allele: one of the two or more possible alternative forms of a gene, similar but not identical, that can occupy the same position on two chromosomes belonging to the same pair.

Anurous: having no tail (as in the rumpy variety of the Manx).

Bicolor: cats with white coats and black or other colored patches. The white must be from 1/3 to 1/2 (33 to 50 percent) and the color from 2/3 to 1/2 (66 to 50 percent).

Blotched (blotched tabby): See Classic Tabby.

Blue: color of coat that is pale gray to slate gray. It is obtained by dilution of the color black.

Break: an indentation in the skull formation, roughly at eye level or below, between the nose and the forehead.

Brindling: presence of de-pigmented hairs in the colored part of the coat.

Cameo: coat with white at the base and red on the tips. Cameo coats are divided into Smoke, Shaded, and Shell varieties according to the extent and amount of tipping.

C.F.A. (Cat Fanciers' Association): the world's largest pedigree cat registry, and the principal cat association in the United States; Canada, Japan Germany, Italy, France, Switzerland, Brazil, Argentina, also have member clubs.

Champagne: a buff-cream color variety.

Chinchilla: cats with a transluscent white coat with colored tips (tipping). Overall, the coat gives the impression of a silvery sparkle. The tipping varies. Green or blue-green eyes and the nose leather are outlined in black.

Chromosomes: structures in the cell nucleus consisting primarily of DNA and organized in a linear sequence of genes, and proteins. Chromosomes are responsible for the transmission of inherited characteristics.

Cinnamon: a reddish-brown coat color.

Classic Tabby: (Blotched Tabby) striking tabby pattern composed of wide stripes with clear, well-defined borders. Legs have bands of color (bracelets), the tail has regular rings; the chest has one or continuous stripes (necklaces). "M" design on the forehead and 1 or 2 spirals on the cheeks. The eyes are outlined by continuous lines. Vertical lines descend the neck toward the shoulders and form a butterfly design with clear wings. Three parallel lines (spinals) run along the back, the central of which runs from the neck to the end of the tail. On the flanks, symmetrical on each side, are the cahracteristic bullseyes (blotches) of color against a contrasting ground. On the chest and upper stomach is a double row of spots (vest buttons).

Colorpoint: cats with points (mask, tail, ears, and legs) that are of a darker color than the rest of the body. The difference in coloration is a result of the lower body temperature in those areas. The varieties of Persian, Siamese, and Tonkinese are divided according to the intensity of contrast between the points and the body.

Cream: the genetic dilution of red.

Dilute: color in which pigment is not uniformly distributed on the hairs but in gathered in granules, making it appear pale (see Dilution.)

Dilution: color in which pigment, rather than being uniformly distributed along the entire surface of the hair, is gathered in scattered granules. The overall effect is an attenuation of the color.

Distal: in anatomy, the extremity or part of an organ located at the greatest distance from its point of attachment or origin.

Dominance: the capacity of an allele to affect a phenotypic effect, thus suppressing the effects of a different allele in the same locus.

Fawn: light, pinkish-cream shade of color.

F.I.Fe. (Fédération Internationale Féline): principal cat association in Europe with members from other continents.

Fumé: French term for "smoke."

G.C.C.F. (Governing Council of the Cat Fancy): primary British cat association.

Gene: the fundamental unit of genetic heredity. Each gene occupies a certain locus on a pair of chromosomes. Genes can possess one or more variant forms (alleles) and contribute to determining one or more particular hereditary characteristics.

"Ghost" pattern: evanescent stripes of a tabby pattern; sometimes seen in solid color adults or young kittens.

Gloves: areas of depigmented (and thus white) fur on the distal ends of the legs of the Birman and Snowshoe.

Golden: tippped coats in which the undercoat and lighter areas of the coat are a rich,warm apricot color.

Harlequin: bicolor coat; white on 1/2 to 3/4 (50-75 percent) of the surface and colored or patterned spots on 1/2 to 1/4 (50 to 25 percent).

Heterozygote: individual in which pairs of homologous chromosomes bear different alleles at the same genetic locus.

Homologous chromosomes: two chromosomes that form a chromosomal pair. Each comes from one of the two parents and is morphologically the same. The sex chromosomes (X and Y) are an exception, being morphologically different.

Homozygote: individual in which the pairs of homologous chromosomes carry genetically equal alleles at the same genetic locus.

Inbreeding: pairing between blood-related individuals. Used to maintain rare hereditary characteristics. Excessive inbreeding can cause maladaptive phenotypical characteristics.

Kink: a structural abnormality of the bones in the tail.

Lavender: a pinkish-grey coat color; the dilute of chocolate brown.

Lilac: warm gray-pink color.

Locus: segment or position on a chromosome occupied by a given gene or one of its alleles.

Longie: Manx cat with a tail longer than one inch according to the F.I.Fe.; up to four inches according to other cat associations.

Lynx Point: a tabby point.

Mackerel tabby: tabby pattern with thin stripes, with sharp contrast. There is an intricate "M" design on the forehead, and two or three spirals on the cheeks. The chest is decorated with two or more continuous lines forming necklaces. Numerous thin stripes, clearly separated from one another, run perpendicular along the back and down to the chest; legs have regular bands; the tail is ringed. A double row of spots run down the chest to the stomach; a continuous line runs along the upper part of the back from the head to the tail.

Maculate: a tabby pattern marked with spots uniformly distributed on the body (as in the Egyptian Mau and the European Shorthair).

Manila: tawny color typical of the Ceylon. Includes a great number of different shadings, from sand to cinnamon, and form ginger to coffee.

Marbled: tabby design with broad stripes (see Classic).

Mask: front of the muzzle, including the nose and eyes. In pointed cats it has a darker coloration.

Melanin: pigment that causes the color in hair and skin. It is divided in two variants: eumelanin, which causes brown and black colors, and feomelanin, which causes variants from brown-orange to red.

Mi-Ke: the Japanese Bobtail of three colors (black, white, red).

Non-agouti: coat formed of a uniformly sold color without bands of other colors.

Odd-eyed: eyes of different color on the same animal. A trait that can occur in white cats.

Patched Tabby: a Torbie; a tabby patterned coat with areas of red and/or cream patches.

Pewter: a Blue-Silver Tabby coat color; lacks the rich, warm, fawn patina overall of the Blue Tabby

Phenotype: the group of anatomical and behavioral characteristics of a given individual; the expression of an organism's hereditary constitution.

Pigment: coloring substance that determines the color of the hair, skin, and iris.

Points: the extremities of the body—muzzle, ears, tail, legs, feet—that in some breeds (psuch as the Siamese) are more darkly colored than the body.

Recessive: phenomenon in which the phenotypical effects of an allele are masked by that of a different allele located on the same genetic locus and dominant (see Dominance).

Rumpy: Completely tailless Manx.

Seal: dark sable brown color.

Shading: coloration of hair in which pigment is present only on the distal tip or is more concentrated on the distal end than on the rest of the hair.

Shell: coat coloration in which pigment is present only on the distal ends of the hairs, covering up to about 1/8 of each hair's total length. The overall effect is that of a "white" coat with slight spraying of red or cream color.

Silver: Variety that includes cats in which the hair is colored on the tips and light at the roots through the lack of the yellowish pigmentation characteristic of the agouti coat. The variety is divided into Smoke, Shaded, Chinchilla or Shell, and Silver Tabby.

Smoke: coat with hairs that are more or less light gray (rarely white) at the base and darker colorationon the tips. The ruff and ear tufts are silvery white. The coat is characterized by contrasts; when the cat is at rest, the coat appears uniformly black,for example, but when it moves, the white, silvery undercoat becomes clearly visible.

Sorrel: brownish orange to light brown.

Spots: patches of color with well defined borders, characteristic of the tabby spotted coat.

Spotted (tabby spotted): see Maculate.

Stop: an indentation of the skull between the nose and forehead.

Striped (striped tabby): see Mackerel.

Stumpy: Manx with a partial tail .

Tabby: coat pattern in stripes or patches (see Botched, Mackerel, Spotted, Ticked). The name is derived from a kind of silk material, once woven in Baghdad that was based on the coat patterns of cats.

Taily: (Longy) a Manx with a normal-length tail.

Ticked: an agouti or ticked coat. (see: ticking).

Ticking: originally the distribution of pigmentation on hair characterized by alternating horizontal bands of black and yellow. The resulting effect is a grayish yellow. The fundamental characteristic of the agouti coloration.

Tipped: distribution of pigment in which only the tip of each hair is colored. The resulting coats can be chinchilla, cameo, shaded, and smoke.

Tortie: abbreviated name of tortoiseshell.

Tortoiseshell: a Black coat color with a pattern of irregular markings of red and/or cream reminiscent of a turtle's shell. The two colors must be distributed on the entire body, including the points. A blaze on the muzzle is highly valued. The tortoiseshell coat is a genetic characteristic that can appear only in females.

Tricolor: coat with three colors.

Uniform: said of a solid-color coat.

Van: bicolor cat in which the color appears only on the extremities with one or two small body spots o color permissable; more spots of color than this is defined as a harlequin

Wildcat mark: thumb print mark on the ears (typical of lynx points).

EDITOR'S NOTE

There are always new colors, patterns and even new breeds of cats being introduced to the cat-loving public. For example, the indigenous cat of Russia, the **Siberian**, is now gaining attention as cat shows increase in number in many areas of the former Soviet Union. A new mutation in the Rex spectrum is atracting notice gaining attention in the United States: the **Selkirk Rex**. There is another mutation from the Dales area of Oregon which has been dubbed the **Alpaca** due to a distinctive coat that falls in loose ringlets, reminiscent of the Komondor or Puli dog. Still other breeds are on the horizon, such as the **California Spangle** and the **Palomino**. The final arbiter is always the cat loving public, which now numbers in the millions.

It is impossible to predict what the cat of tomorrow may be. Tomorrow may produce another attractive mutation, and chance or a genetically planned program may produce a cat of extreme beauty, intelligence, and fabulous companionship qualitiies. As the mysteries of genetics continue to be unlocked, breeders learn how to improve our cat companions. Not only do dedicated, ethical cat breeders seek to perfect each breed to achieve a written standard for each breed and color, they concern themselves with increasing the health factors and the companionability in the cats they produce. (The Companion Index, an important measure added to the feline world by Will Thompson, is defined as the measurable level of compatibility between the human and feline; the higher the Campanion Index, the more amenable to human companionship the cat, and breeders strive to bring the Companion Index to a maximum level of 100%.)

One absolute, however, is that there will always be cats to share the homes and firesides of those who desire a companion animal with whom they must cooperate in order to earn mutual respect and to gain love and companionship. A cat returns only that which its human companion gives, thereby forming a partnership equation dependent upon both sides. The cat is truly the companion animal for the crowded world of today.

— Will Thompson

PHOTOGRAPHY CREDITS
Jacket
Chanan Photography: Front top
Isabelle Francais: Front jacket flap, back jacket flap, back bottom left, back bottom center, back bottom right
Lia Stein: Front bottom left, front bottom center, front bottom right

Breed Section
Chanan Photography: 16.4, 16.5, 18.1, 18.2, 20.1, 21.3, 22.5, 24.1-3, 25.4, 27.4, 29.9, 30.1-2, 31.3-4, 35.1, 36.3, 43.11, 47.7, 54.1, 55.3, 56.1-2, 57.3-4, 58.2, 60.5, 71.12, 74.2, 78.1-2, 79.3-5, 85.6, 90.1-2, 91.3, 93.3, 93.4, 94.6, 95.7, 96.9, 98.3, 99.6, 102.10, 104.14, 106.17, 109.24, 110.25, 111.26-28, 114.1, 117.10, 120.8, 122.2, 125.6, 126.1-2, 127.3-5, 129.2, 130.3, 133.8, 137.1-2, 139.1-2, 146.1-3, 147.4, 149.3.

Bruce Coleman Limited: 121.1-2.

Donna J. Coss: 14.2, 34.8, 35.2, 46.5, 54.2, 71.11, 77.4, 86.7, 98.4, 101.9, 108.21, 112.29, 132.7.

Isabelle Francais: 15.3, 17.6, 19.3, 23.6, 29.8, 32.2, 33.3, 43.10, 44.1, 50.1, 50.2, 51.3, 57.5, 58.1, 75.3, 76.1-2, 77.3, 80.2, 81.3, 89.6, 103.11, 103.12, 105.16, 106.18, 113.2, 122.1, 123.3, 124.4-5, 125.7, 125.8-9, 128.1, 130.4, 131.5, 132.6, 134.9, 134.10, 135.11-13, 138.3, 140.1, 141.4, 148.2.

Marc Henrie Asc.: 48.1-2, 49.3, 144.1-2, 145.3-4.

Vickie Jackson: 27.3.

Larry Johnson: 26.2, 44.2.

Tammy L. Morford: 20.2, 21.4, 36.4, 80.1, 100.7, 101.8, 108.22, 113.1.

Lia Stein: 14.1, 17.7, 26.1, 28.5-28.7, 32.1, 33.4-6, 34.7, 37.1-2, 38.3-4, 39.5, 40.6, 41.7-8, 42.9, 45.3, 46.4, 47.6, 51.4, 52.1-3, 53.4-5, 59.3, 60.4, 60.6, 61.1-3, 62.4-6, 63.7-8, 64.9-11, 65.12-14, 66.15-17, 67.18-19, 68.1-2, 69.3-5, 70.6-10, 72.1-2, 73.3, 74.1, 81.4-5, 82.6-8, 83.1-3, 84.4-5, 86.8, 87.1-2, 88.3-5, 92.1-2, 93.5, 95.8, 97.1-2, 98.5, 104.13, 105.15, 106.19, 107.20, 108.23, 114.2-3, 115.4-5, 116.6, 117.7-9, 118.1-2, 119.3-5, 120.6-7, 140.2-3, 141.5, 142.1-2, 143.3-4, 148.1, 150.4-5, 151.1-2, 152.3-4, 153.5-7.

Special Thanks: Chris Hart, Sy Howard, Jay Hyams, Ann Levy, Kristine Lubrano, Donald Williams, Leta Williams.